ARE YOU ALI

AI NINOMIYA

Translation and Lettering: Alexis Eckerman

This book is a work of fiction. Names, characters, places, and incidents are the product of the author's imagination or are used fictitiously. Any resemblance to actual events, locales, or persons, living or dead, is coincidental.

Are you Alice? © 2011 by Ai Ninomiya / Ikumi Katagiri. All rights reserved. First published in Japan in 2011 by ICHIJINSHA. English translation rights arranged with ICHIJINSHA through Tuttle-Mori Agency, Inc., Tokyo.

Translation © 2013 by Hachette Book Group, Inc.

All rights reserved. In accordance with the U.S. Copyright Act of 1976, the scanning, uploading, and electronic sharing of any part of this book without the permission of the publisher is unlawful piracy and theft of the author's intellectual property. If you would like to use material from the book (other than for review purposes), prior written permission must be obtained by contacting the publisher at permissions@hbgusa.com. Thank you for your support of the author's rights.

Yen Press
Hachette Book Group
1290 Avenue of the Americas, New York, NY 10104

www.HachetteBookGroup.com
www.YenPress.com

Yen Press is an imprint of Hachette Book Group, Inc. The Yen Press name and logo are trademarks of Hachette Book Group, Inc.

First Yen Press Edition: December 2013

ISBN: 978-0-316-25279-9

10 9 8 7 6 5 4 3

BVG

Printed in the United States of America

Are You Alice?

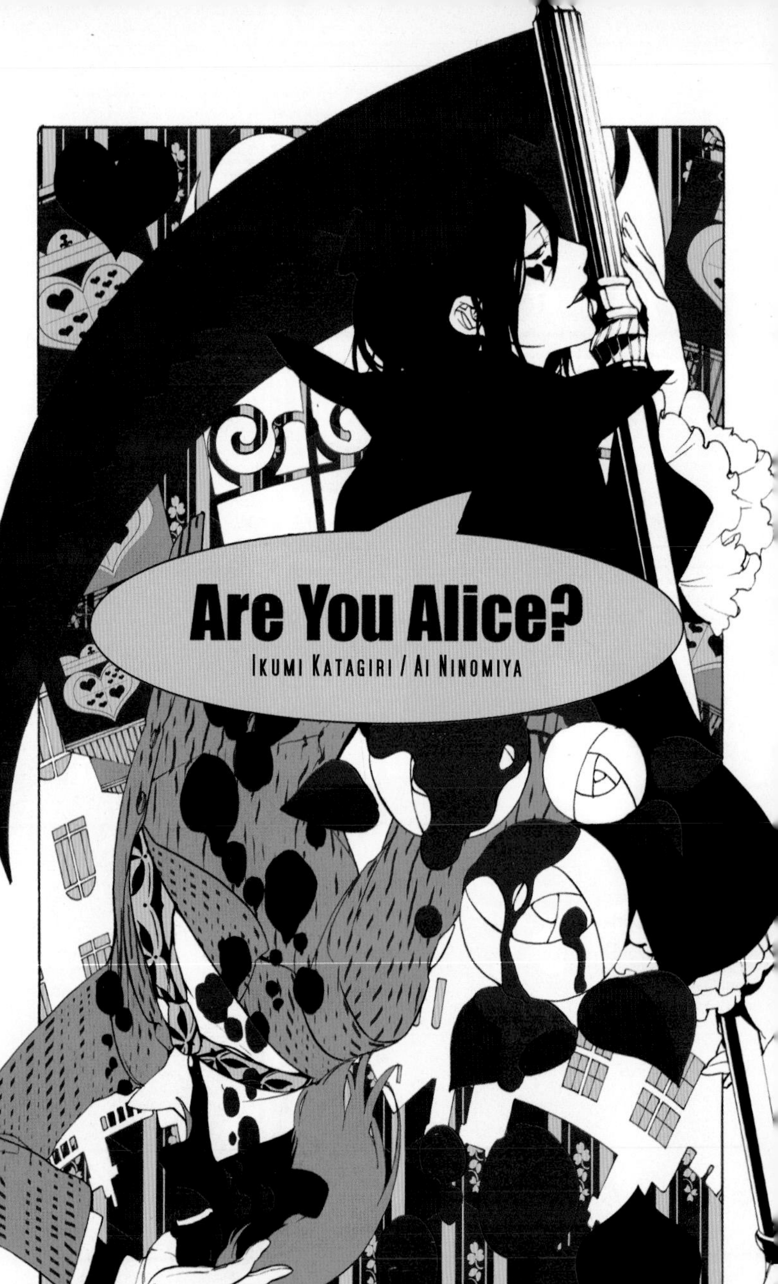

Are You Alice?
Ikumi Katagiri / Ai Ninomiya

Are You Alice?
3
CONTENTS!

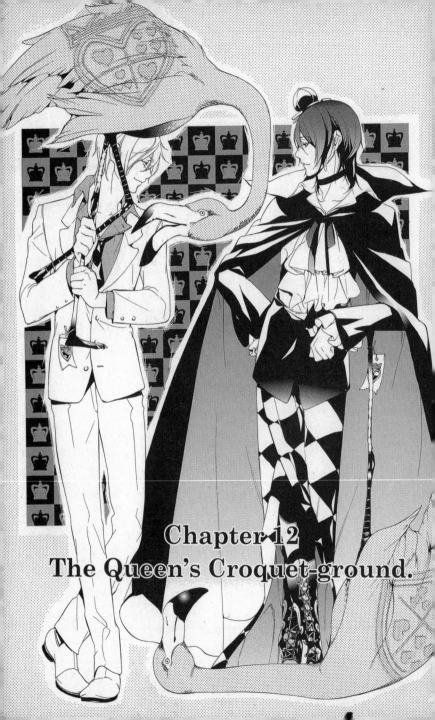

Chapter 12
The Queen's Croquet-ground.

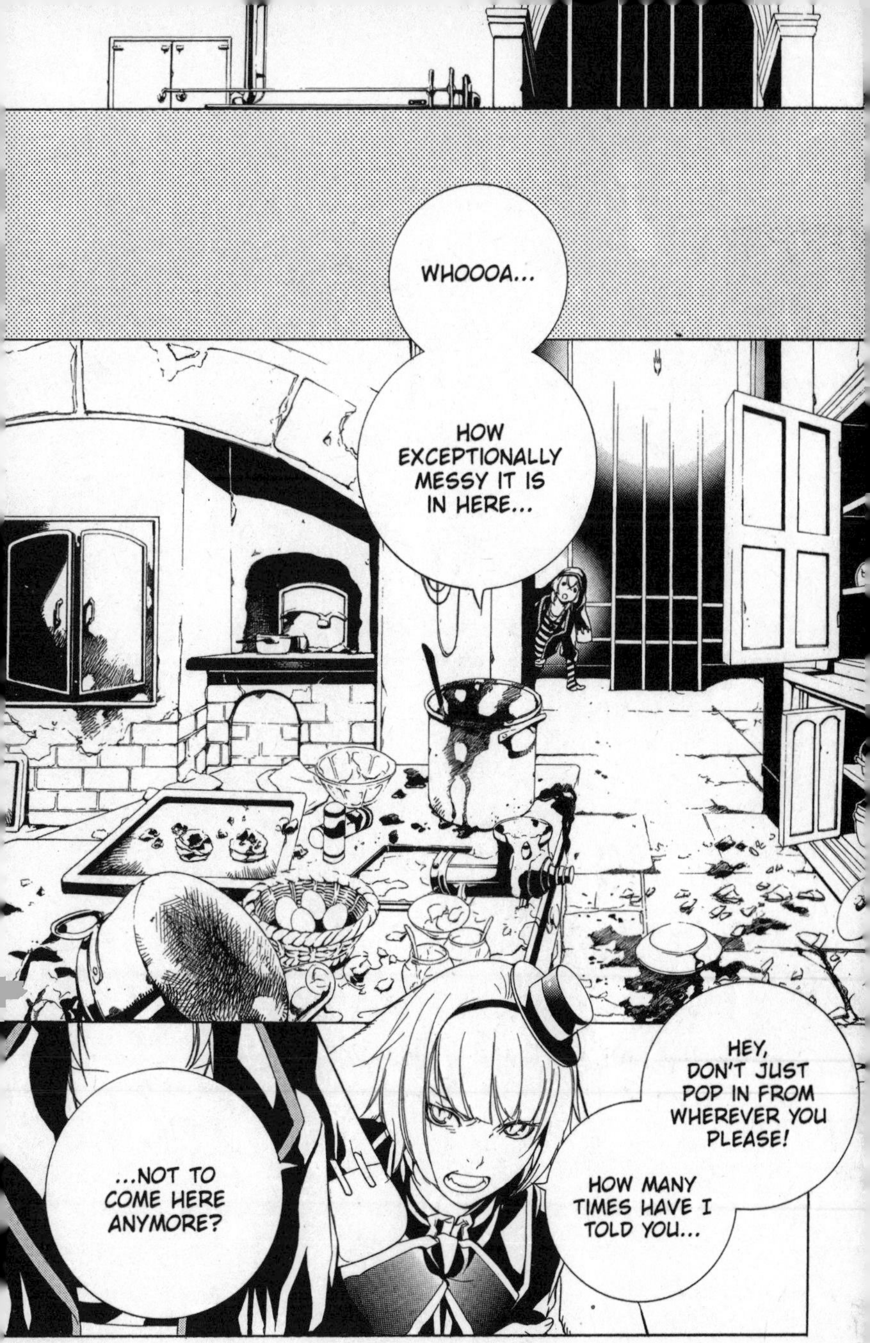
WHOOOA...
HOW EXCEPTIONALLY MESSY IT IS IN HERE...
HEY, DON'T JUST POP IN FROM WHEREVER YOU PLEASE!
HOW MANY TIMES HAVE I TOLD YOU...
...NOT TO COME HERE ANYMORE?

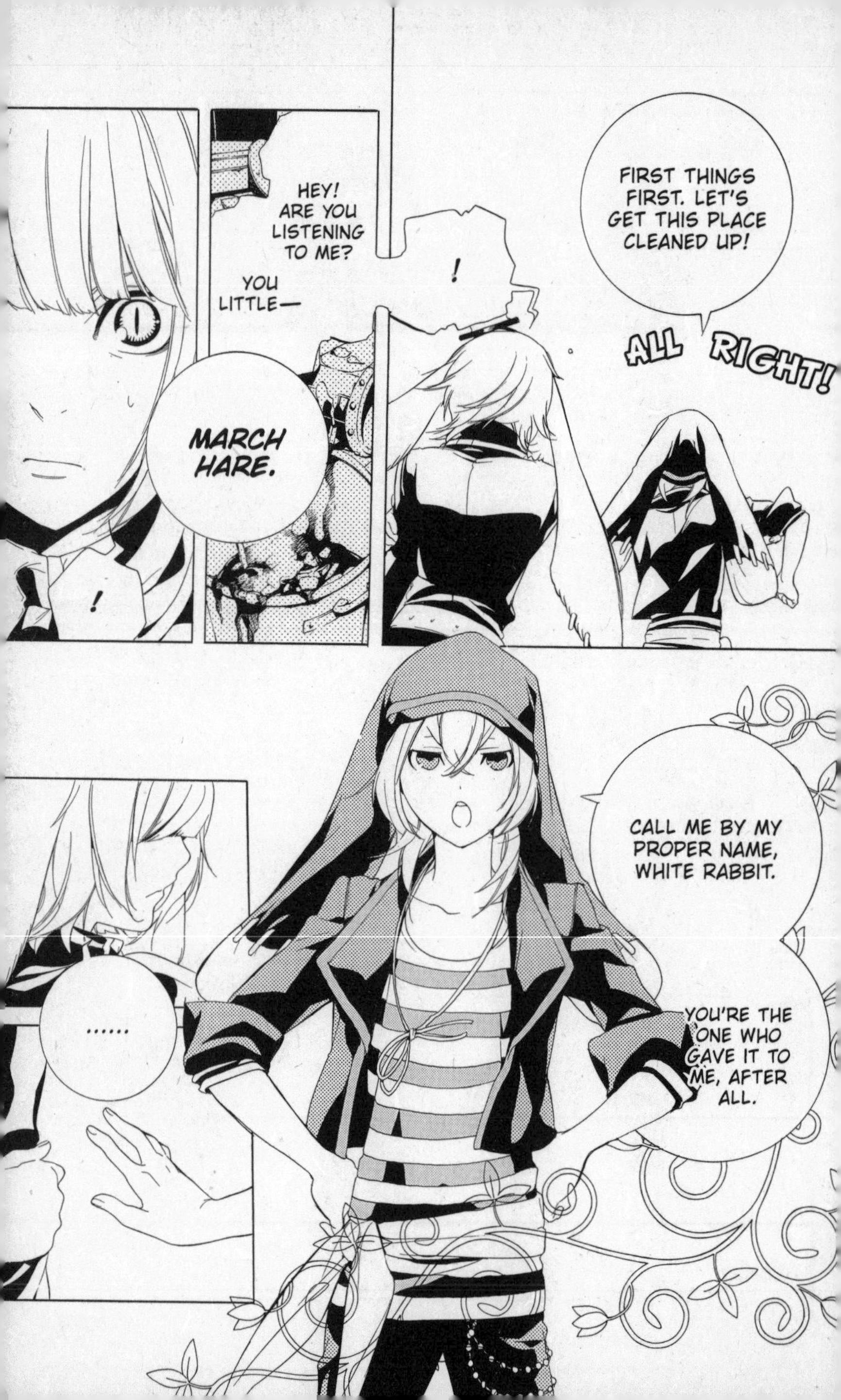
FIRST THINGS FIRST. LET'S GET THIS PLACE CLEANED UP!
ALL RIGHT!
!
HEY! ARE YOU LISTENING TO ME?
YOU LITTLE—
MARCH HARE.
!
CALL ME BY MY PROPER NAME, WHITE RABBIT.
YOU'RE THE ONE WHO GAVE IT TO ME, AFTER ALL.
......

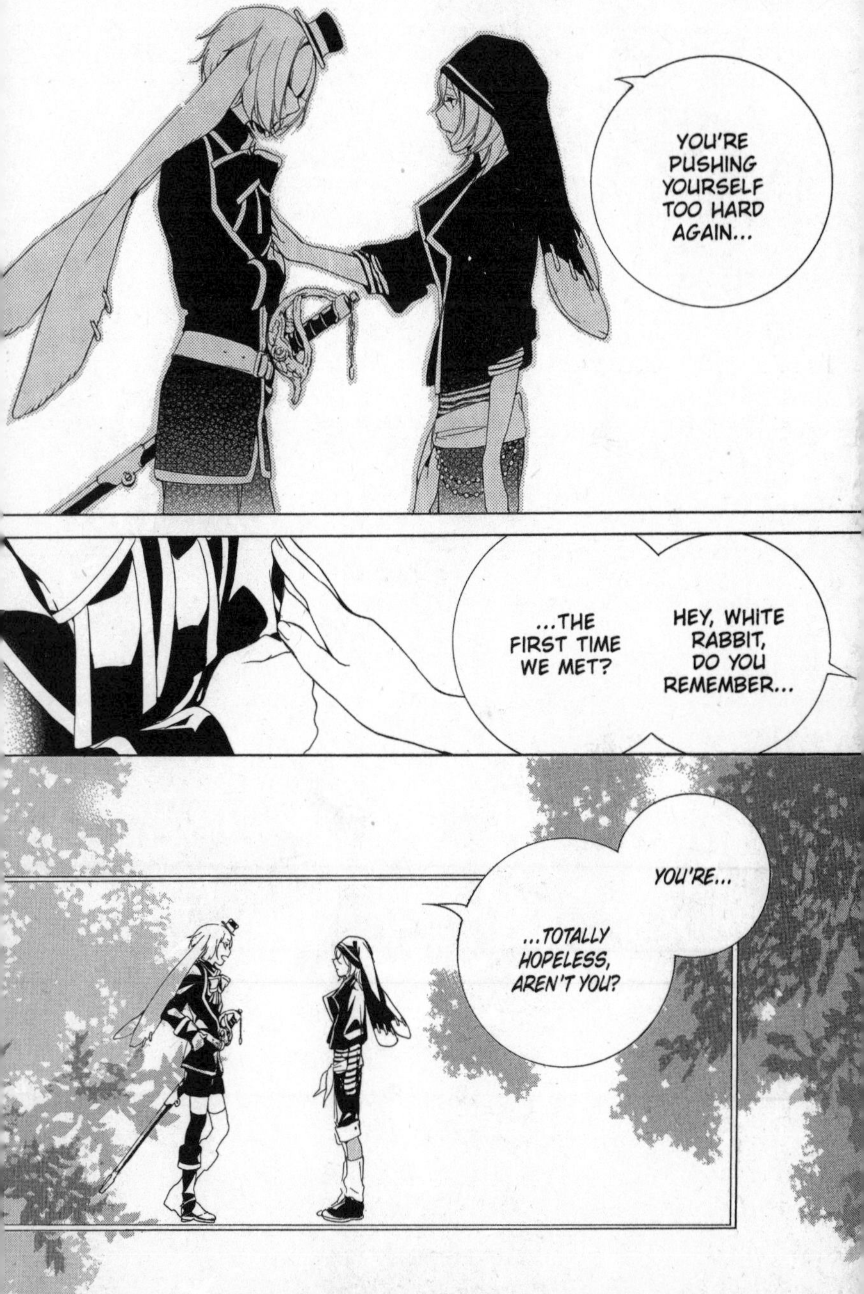
YOU'RE PUSHING YOURSELF TOO HARD AGAIN...
HEY, WHITE RABBIT, DO YOU REMEMBER...
...THE FIRST TIME WE MET?
YOU'RE...
...TOTALLY HOPELESS, AREN'T YOU?

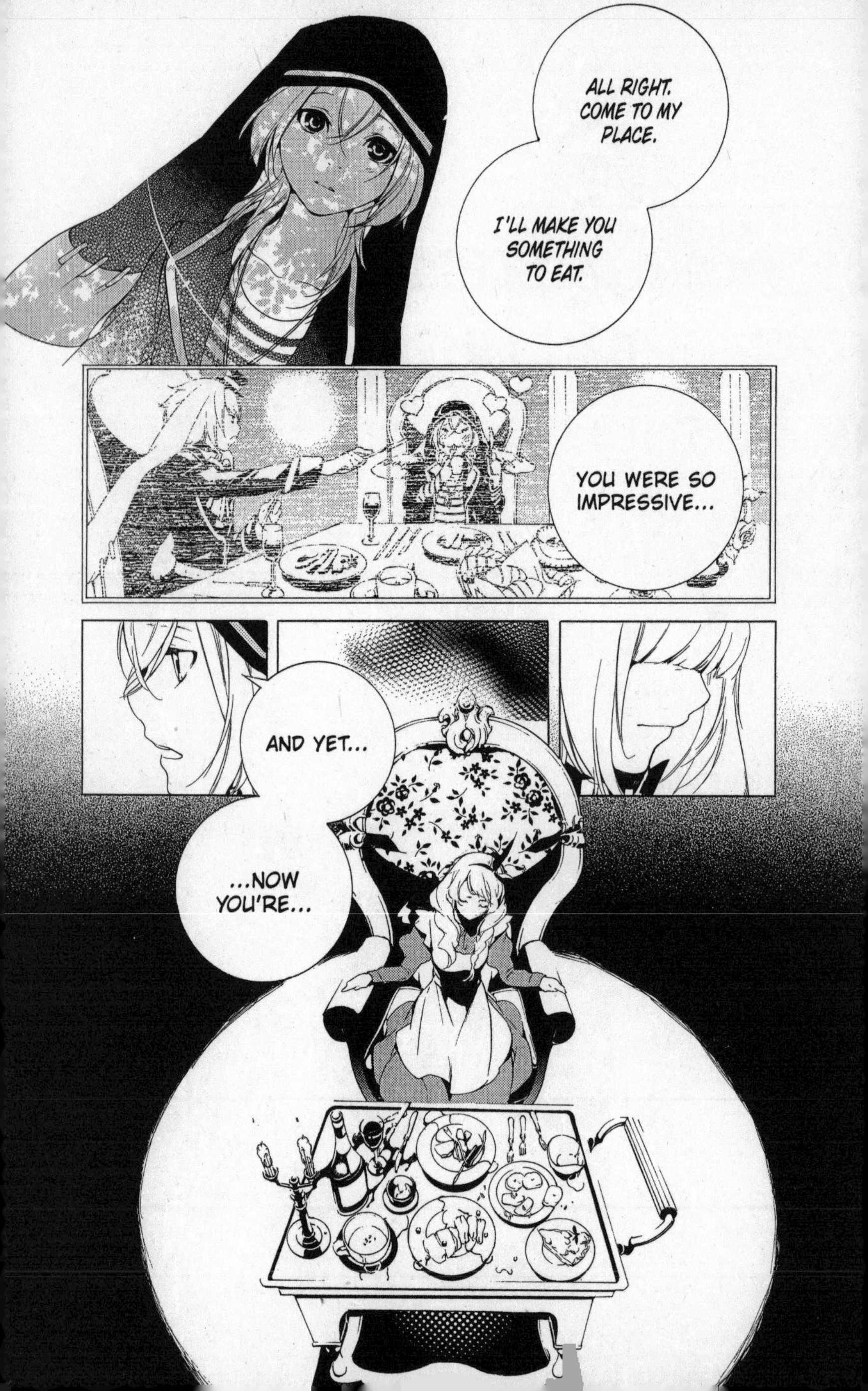
ALL RIGHT. COME TO MY PLACE.
I'LL MAKE YOU SOMETHING TO EAT.
YOU WERE SO IMPRESSIVE...
AND YET...
...NOW YOU'RE...

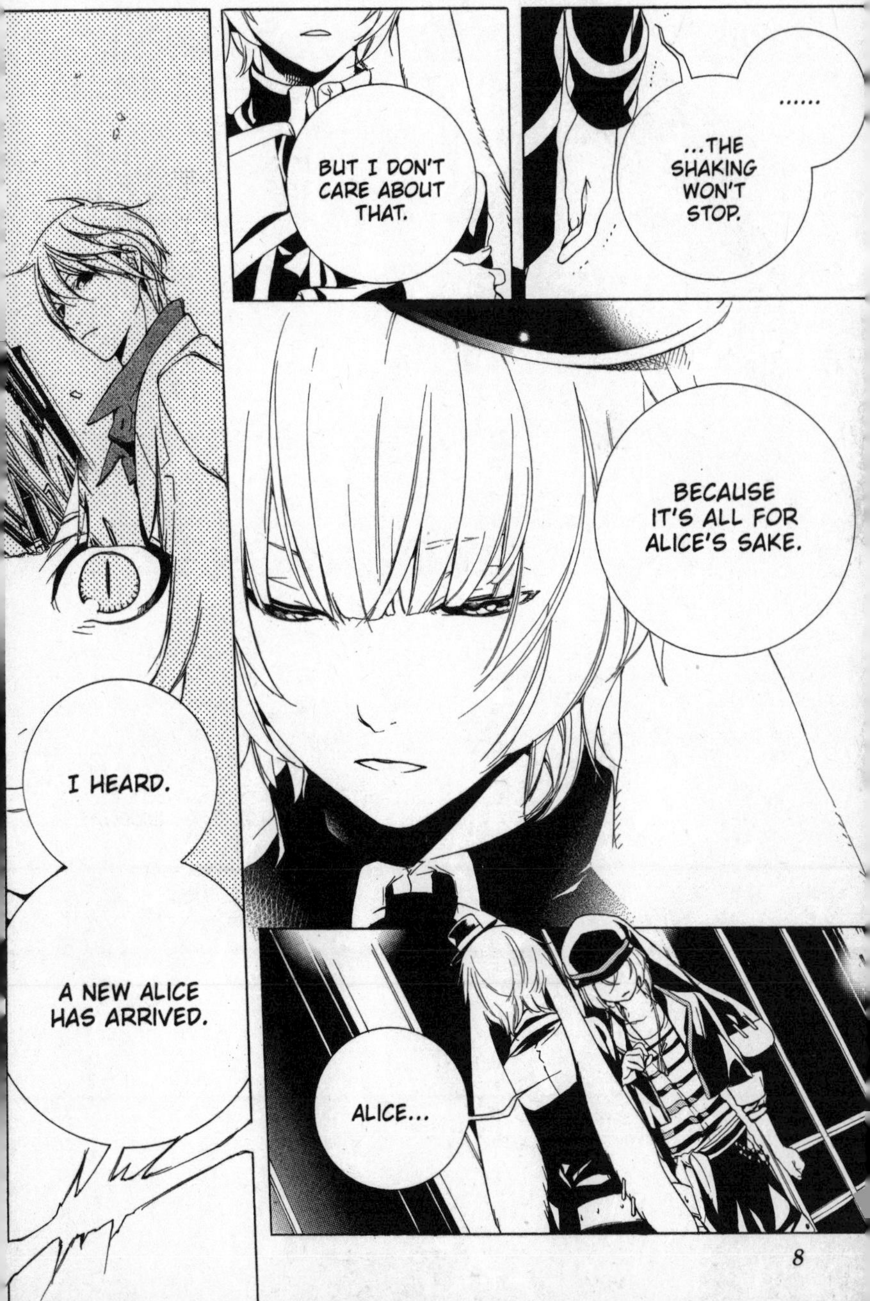
......
...THE SHAKING WON'T STOP.
BUT I DON'T CARE ABOUT THAT.
BECAUSE IT'S ALL FOR ALICE'S SAKE.
ALICE...
I HEARD.
A NEW ALICE HAS ARRIVED.

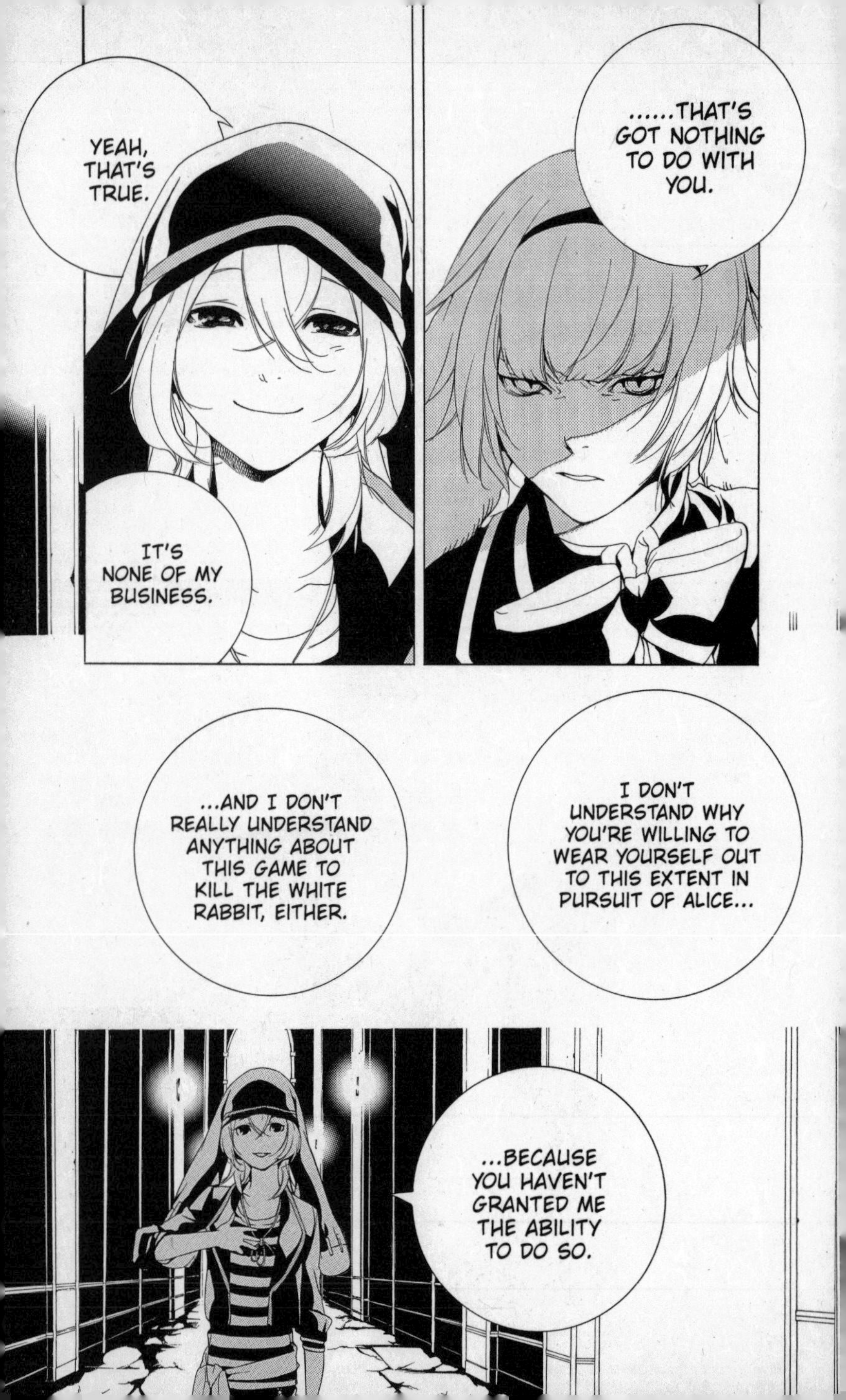
......THAT'S GOT NOTHING TO DO WITH YOU.
YEAH, THAT'S TRUE.
IT'S NONE OF MY BUSINESS.
I DON'T UNDERSTAND WHY YOU'RE WILLING TO WEAR YOURSELF OUT TO THIS EXTENT IN PURSUIT OF ALICE...
...AND I DON'T REALLY UNDERSTAND ANYTHING ABOUT THIS GAME TO KILL THE WHITE RABBIT, EITHER.
...BECAUSE YOU HAVEN'T GRANTED ME THE ABILITY TO DO SO.

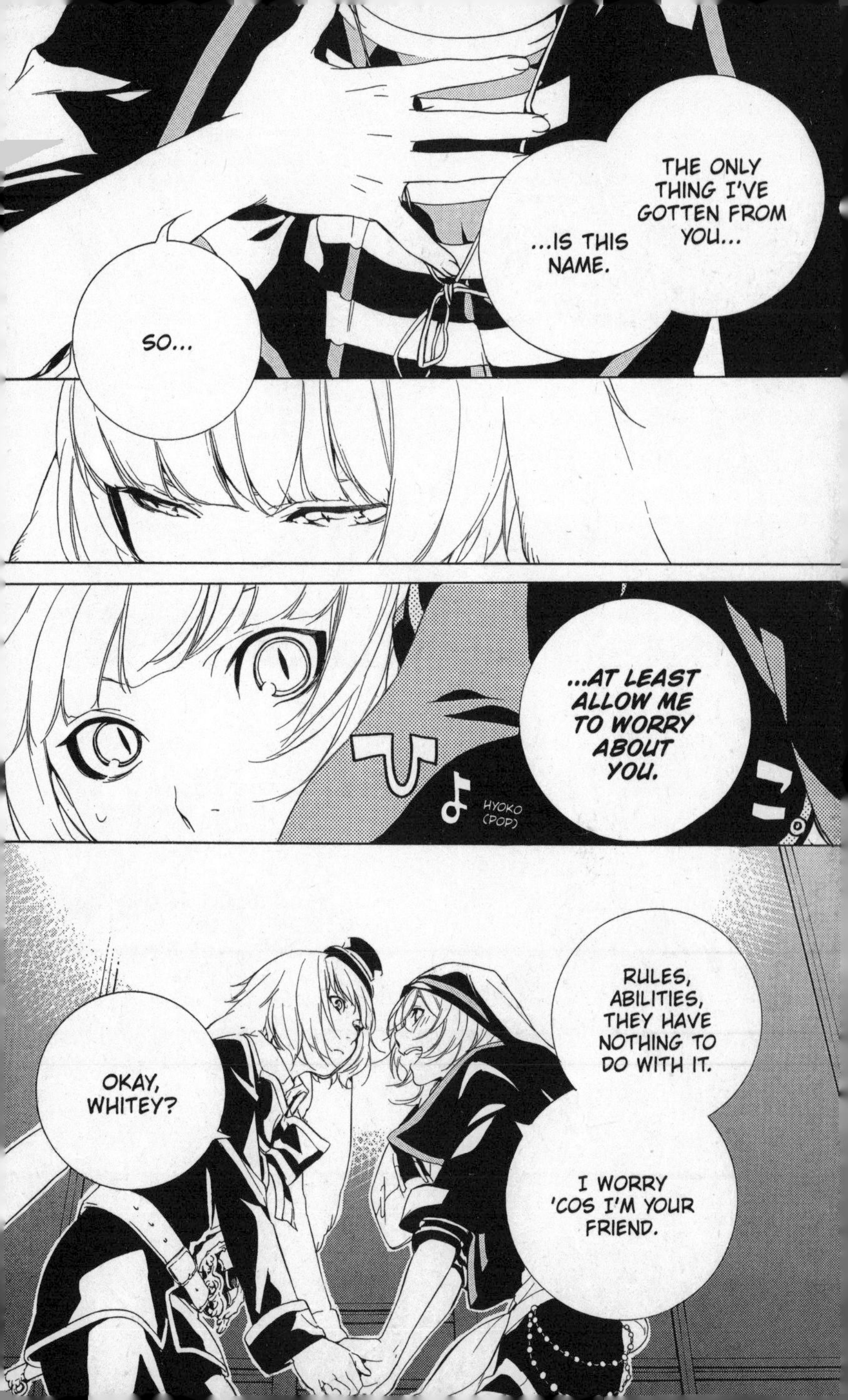
THE ONLY THING I'VE GOTTEN FROM YOU...
...IS THIS NAME.
SO...
...AT LEAST ALLOW ME TO WORRY ABOUT YOU.
HYOKO (POP)
RULES, ABILITIES, THEY HAVE NOTHING TO DO WITH IT.
I WORRY 'COS I'M YOUR FRIEND.
OKAY, WHITEY?

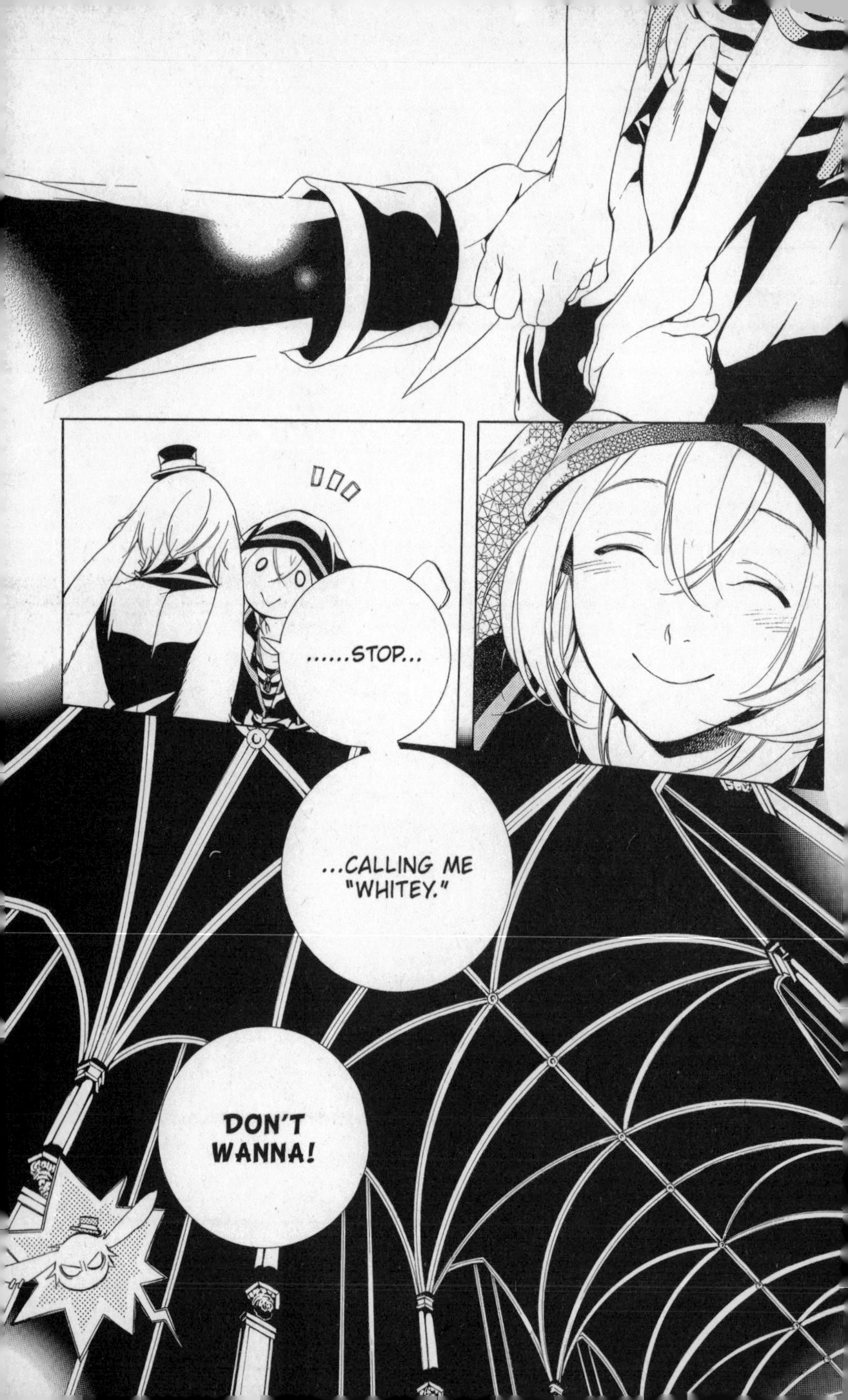
......STOP...
...CALLING ME "WHITEY."
DON'T WANNA!

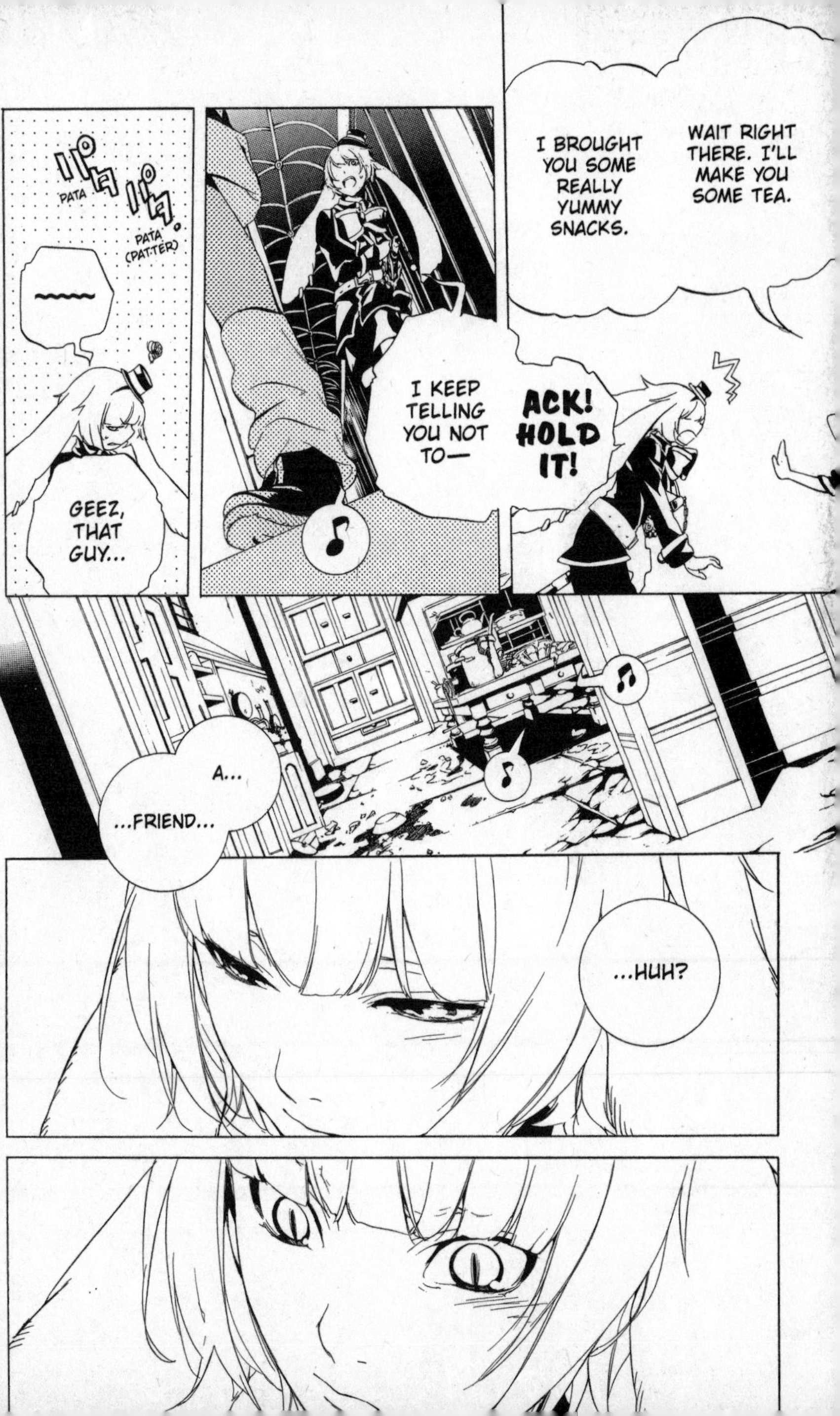
WAIT RIGHT THERE. I'LL MAKE YOU SOME TEA.
I BROUGHT YOU SOME REALLY YUMMY SNACKS.
ACK! HOLD IT!
I KEEP TELLING YOU NOT TO—
♪
PATA
PATA (PAT-TER)
~~~~
GEEZ, THAT GUY...
♪
♪
A...
...FRIEND...
...HUH?
~~~~

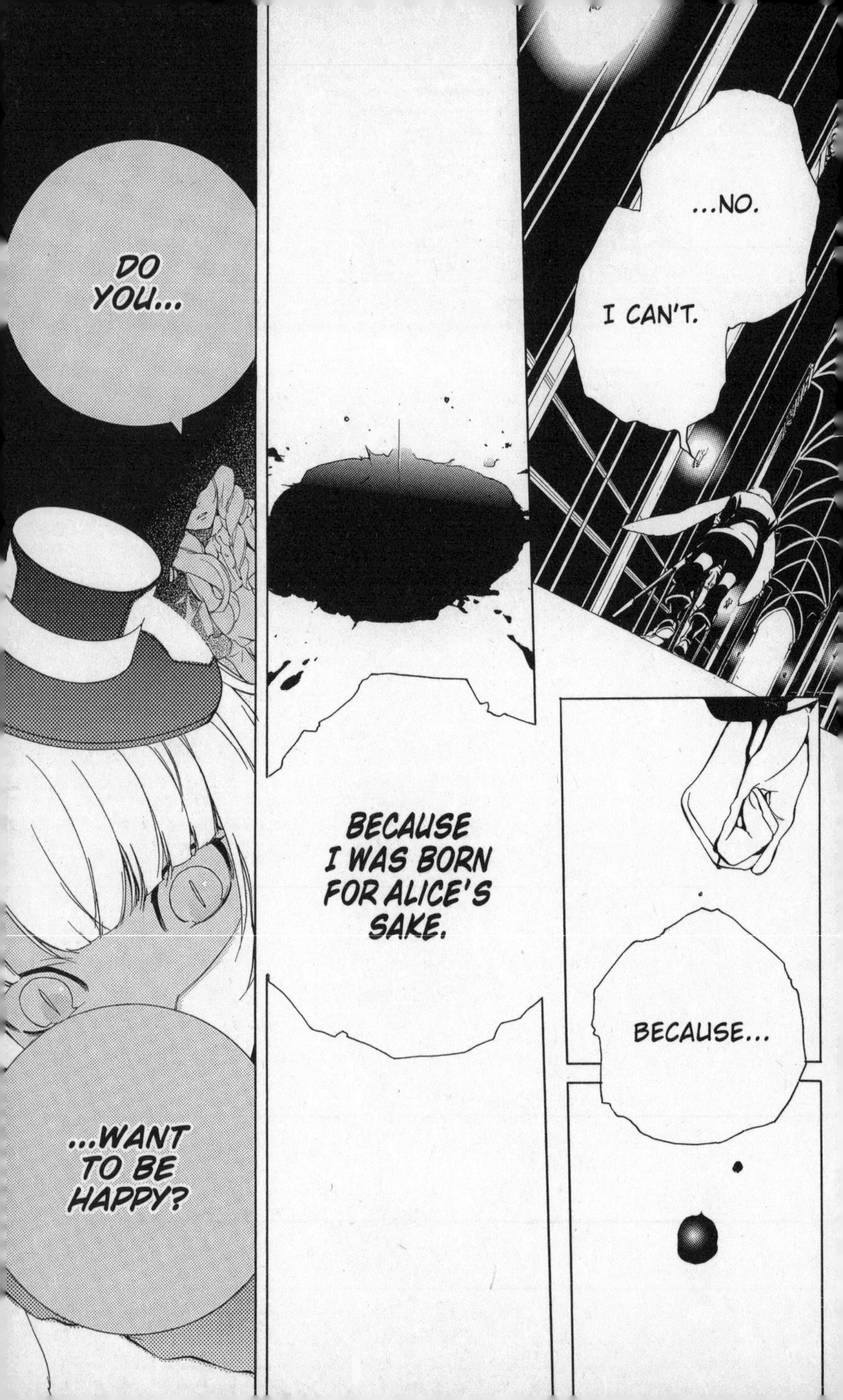
...NO.
I CAN'T.
BECAUSE...
BECAUSE I WAS BORN FOR ALICE'S SAKE.
DO YOU...
...WANT TO BE HAPPY?

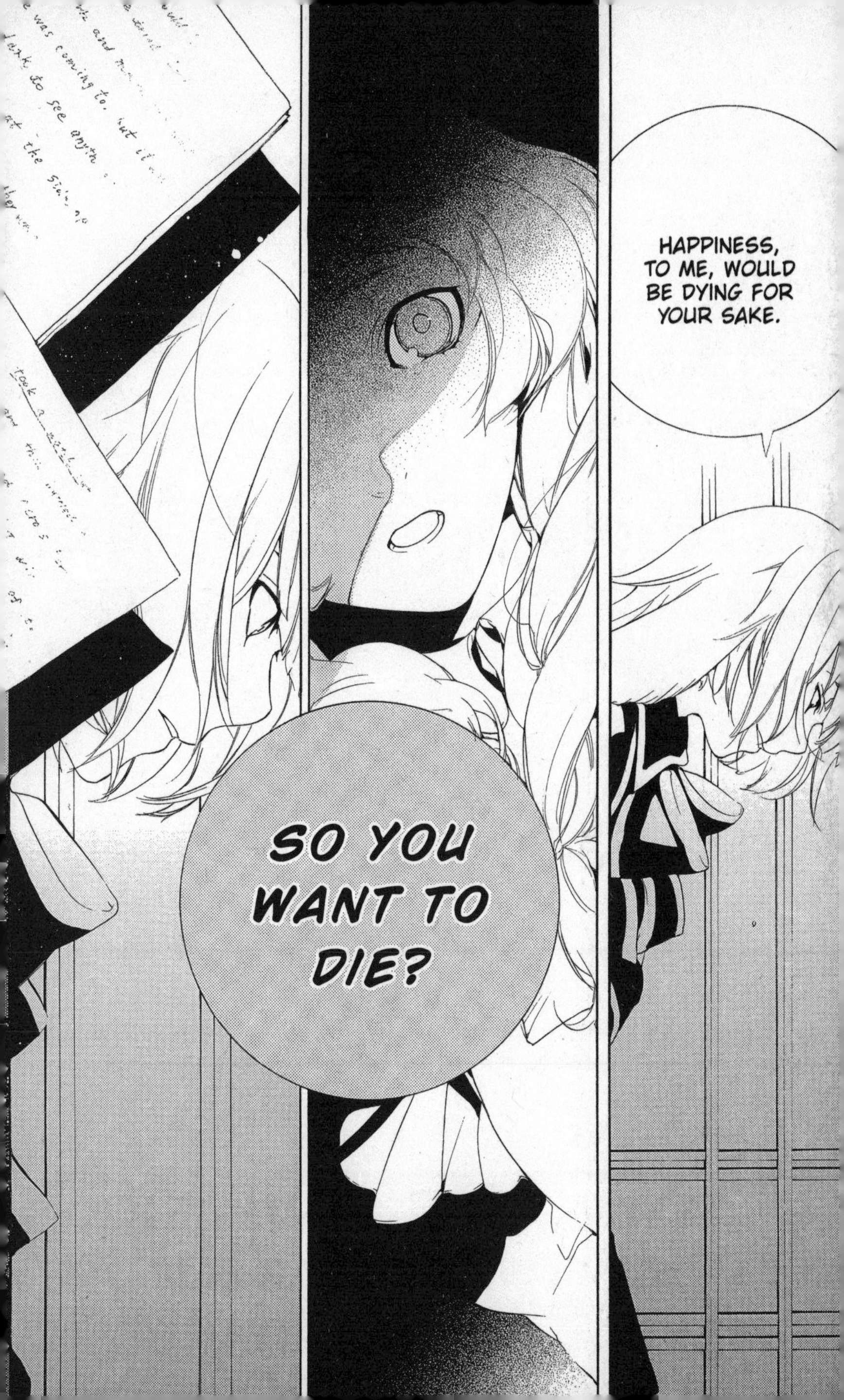
HAPPINESS, TO ME, WOULD BE DYING FOR YOUR SAKE.
SO YOU WANT TO DIE?

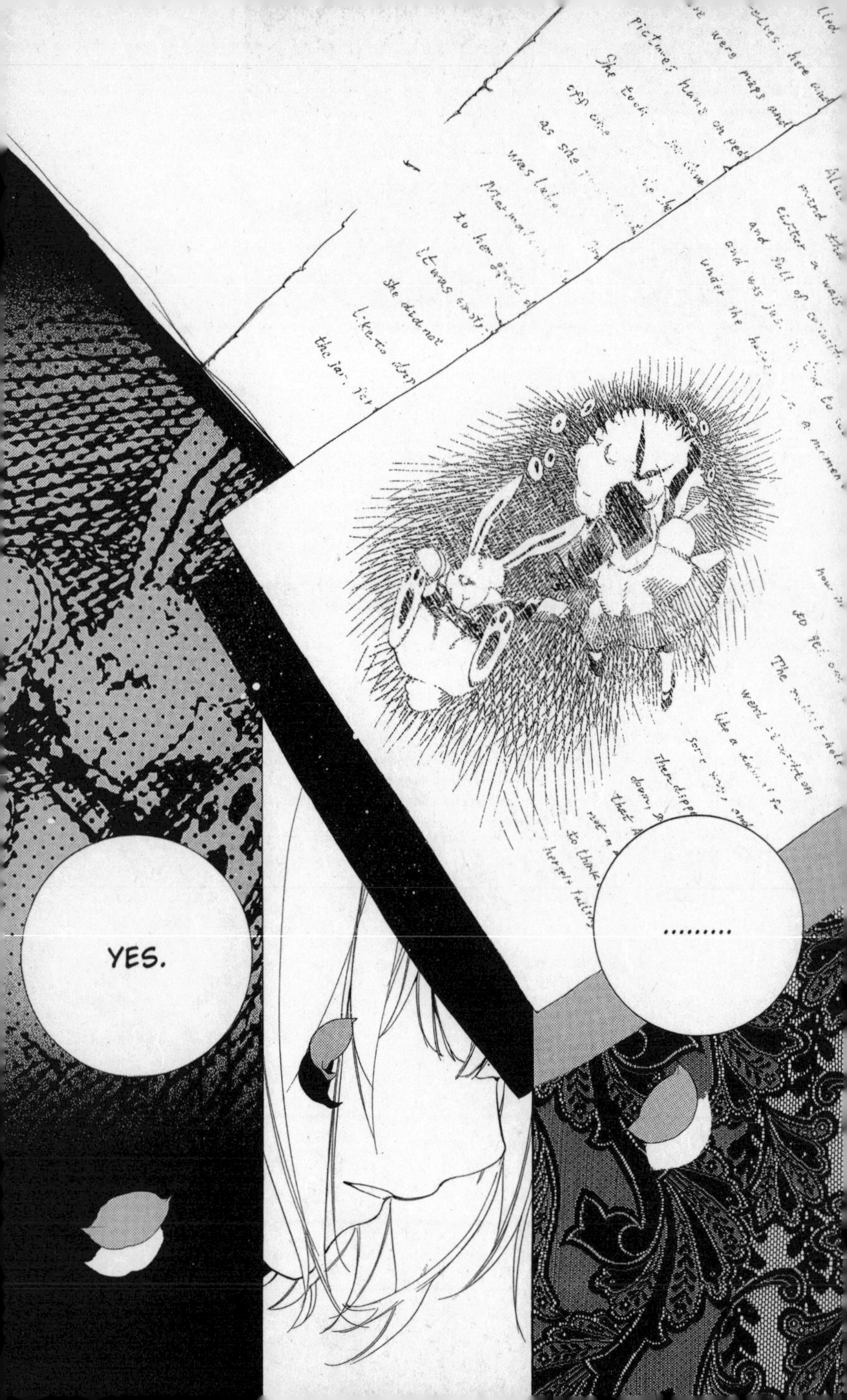
....
YES.

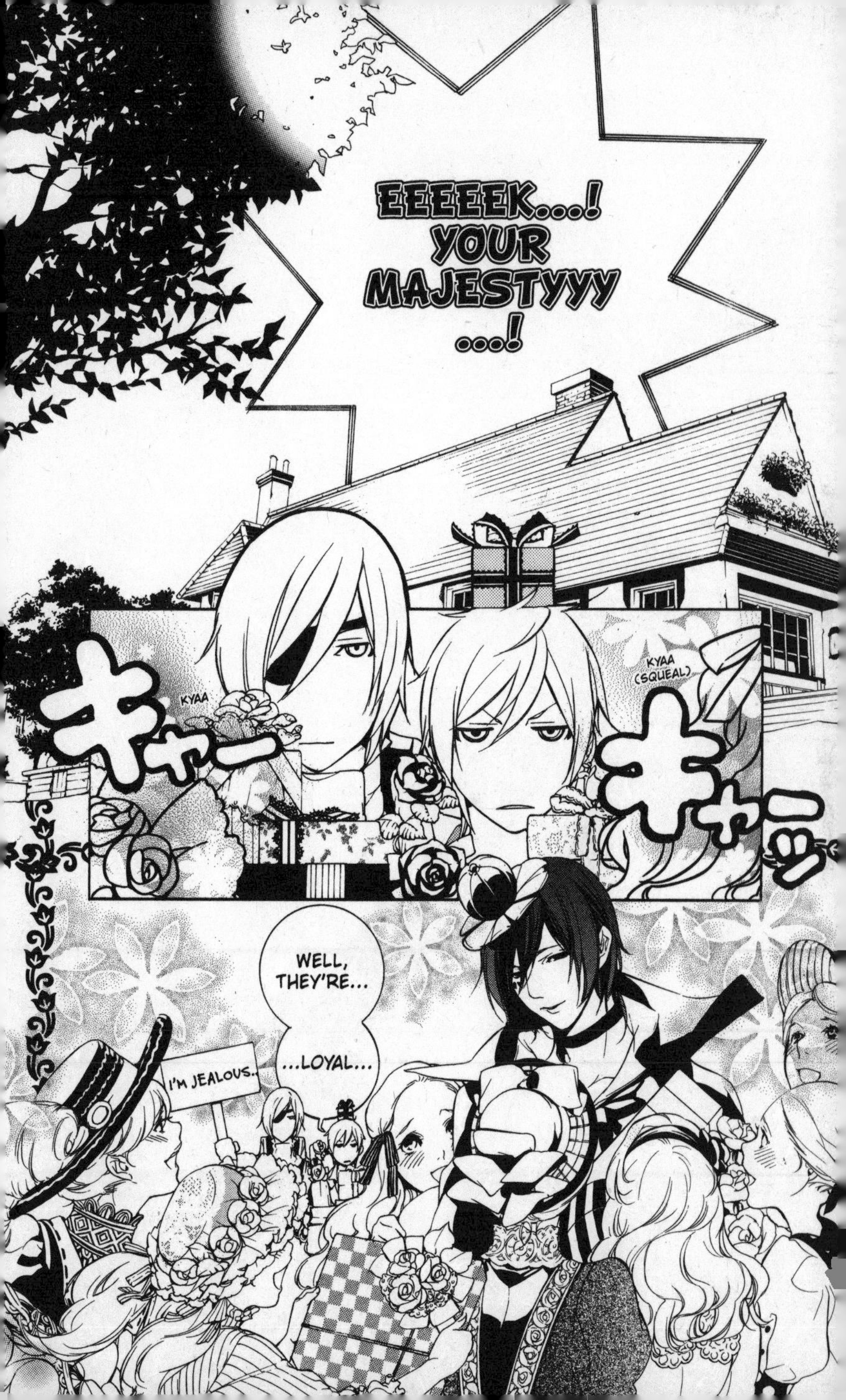
EEEEEK...!
YOUR
MAJESTYYY
...!
KYAA
(SQUEAL)
キャーッ
KYAA
キャー
WELL, THEY'RE...
...LOYAL...
I'M JEALOUS..

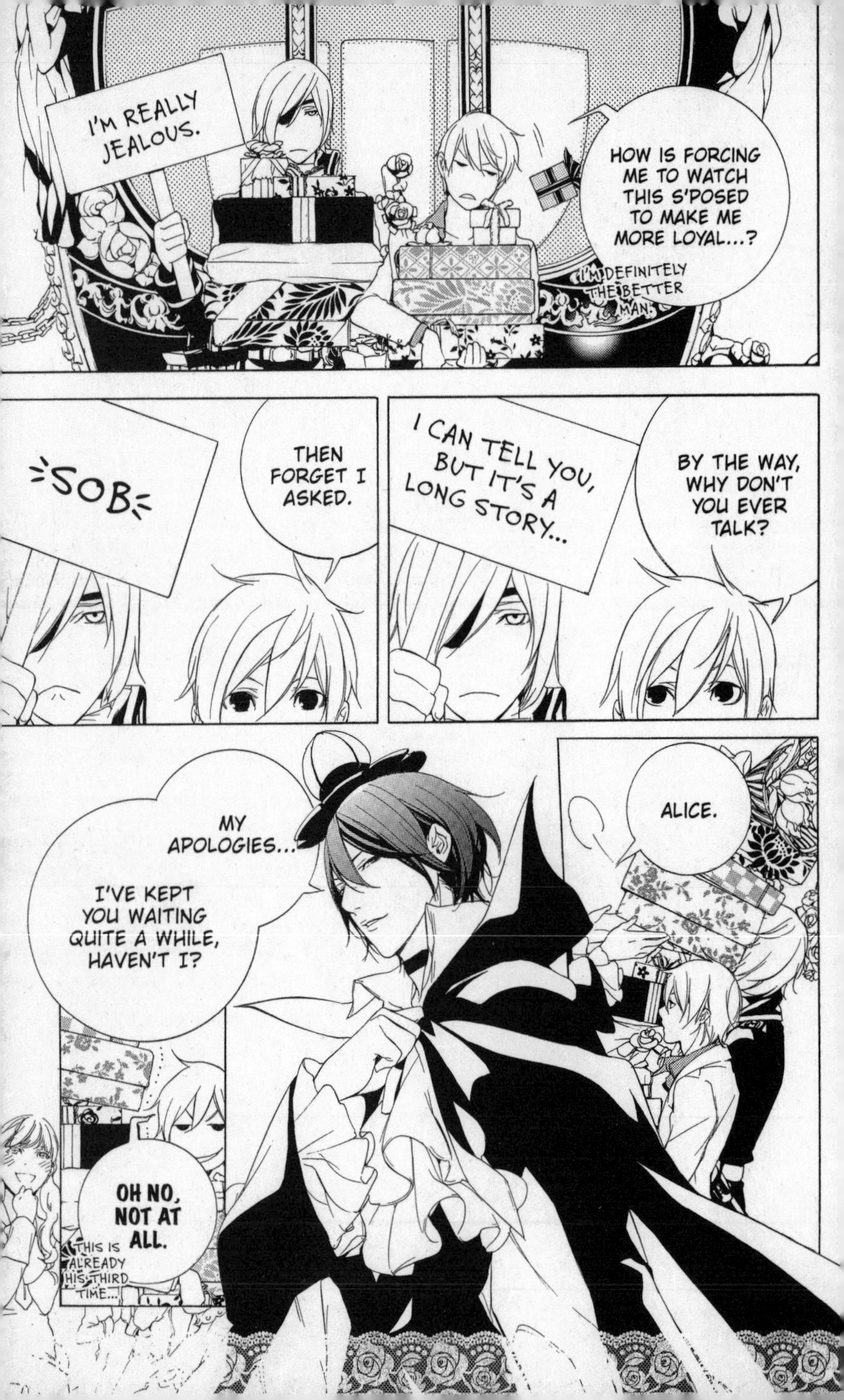
HOW IS FORCING ME TO WATCH THIS S'POSED TO MAKE ME MORE LOYAL...?
I'M DEFINITELY THE BETTER MAN.
I'M REALLY JEALOUS.
BY THE WAY, WHY DON'T YOU EVER TALK?
I CAN TELL YOU, BUT IT'S A LONG STORY...
THEN FORGET I ASKED.
SOB
ALICE.
MY APOLOGIES...
I'VE KEPT YOU WAITING QUITE A WHILE, HAVEN'T I?
OH NO, NOT AT ALL.
THIS IS ALREADY HIS THIRD TIME...

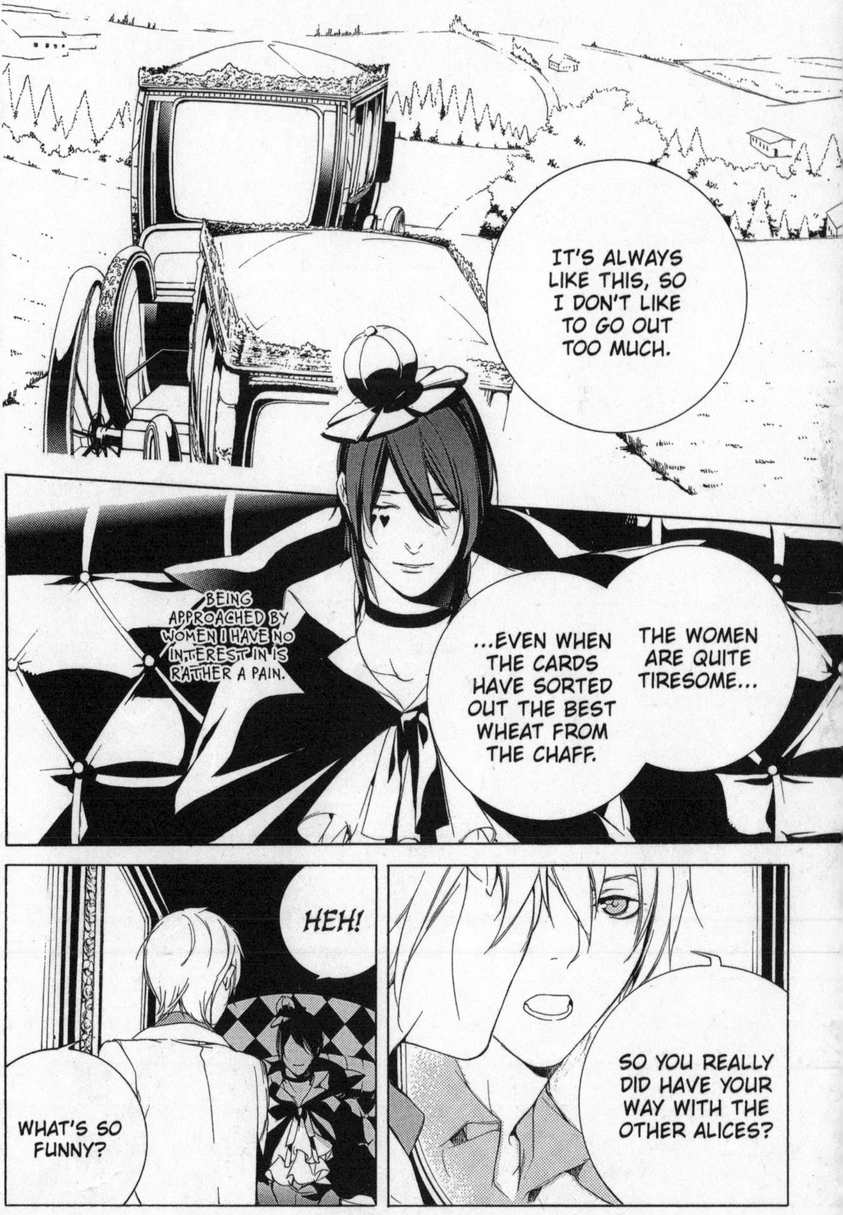
IT'S ALWAYS LIKE THIS, SO I DON'T LIKE TO GO OUT TOO MUCH.
THE WOMEN ARE QUITE TIRESOME...
...EVEN WHEN THE CARDS HAVE SORTED OUT THE BEST WHEAT FROM THE CHAFF.
BEING APPROACHED BY WOMEN I HAVE NO INTEREST IN IS RATHER A PAIN.
SO YOU REALLY DID HAVE YOUR WAY WITH THE OTHER ALICES?
HEH!
WHAT'S SO FUNNY?

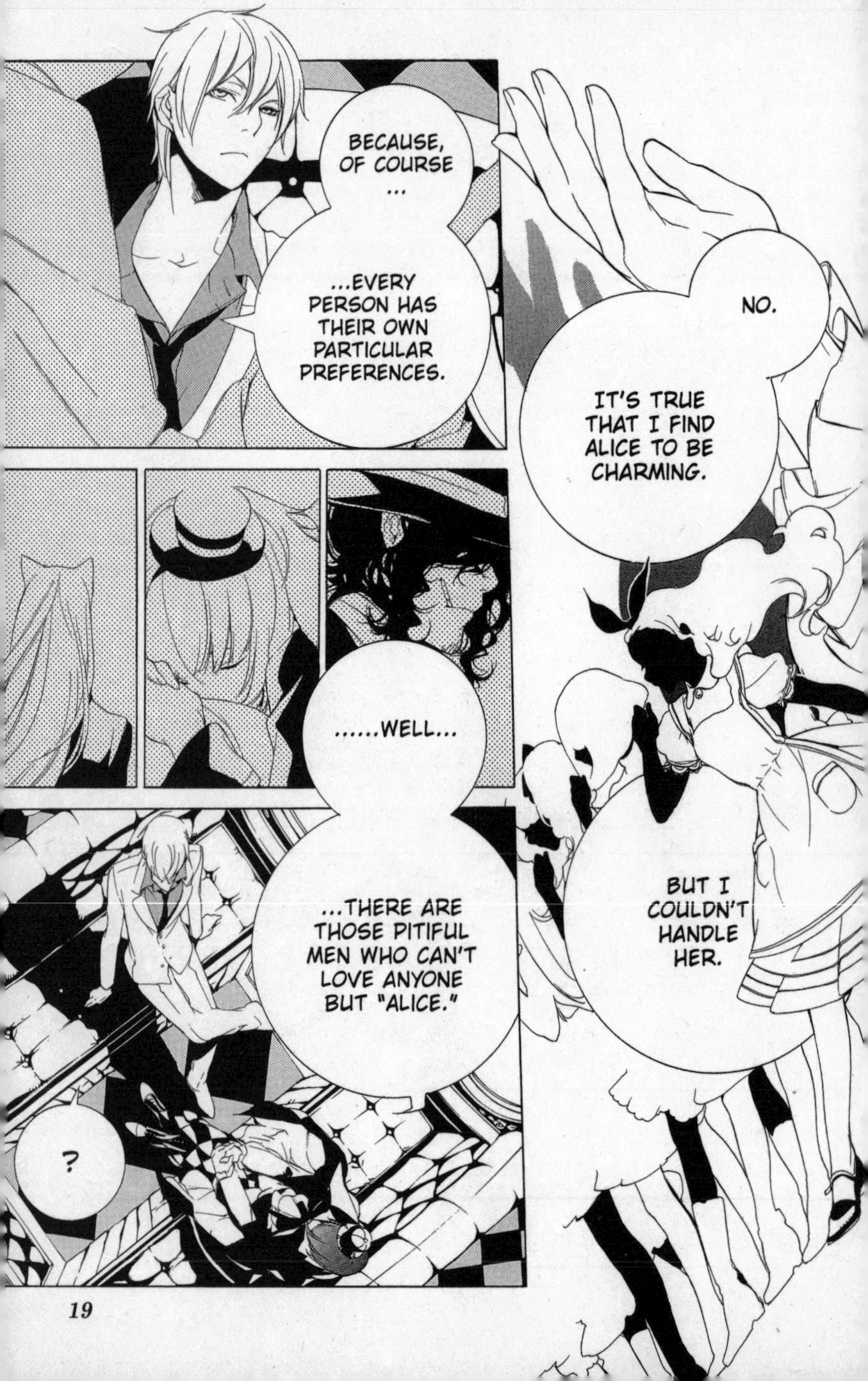
NO.
IT'S TRUE THAT I FIND ALICE TO BE CHARMING.
BUT I COULDN'T HANDLE HER.
BECAUSE, OF COURSE ...
...EVERY PERSON HAS THEIR OWN PARTICULAR PREFERENCES.
......WELL...
...THERE ARE THOSE PITIFUL MEN WHO CAN'T LOVE ANYONE BUT "ALICE."
?

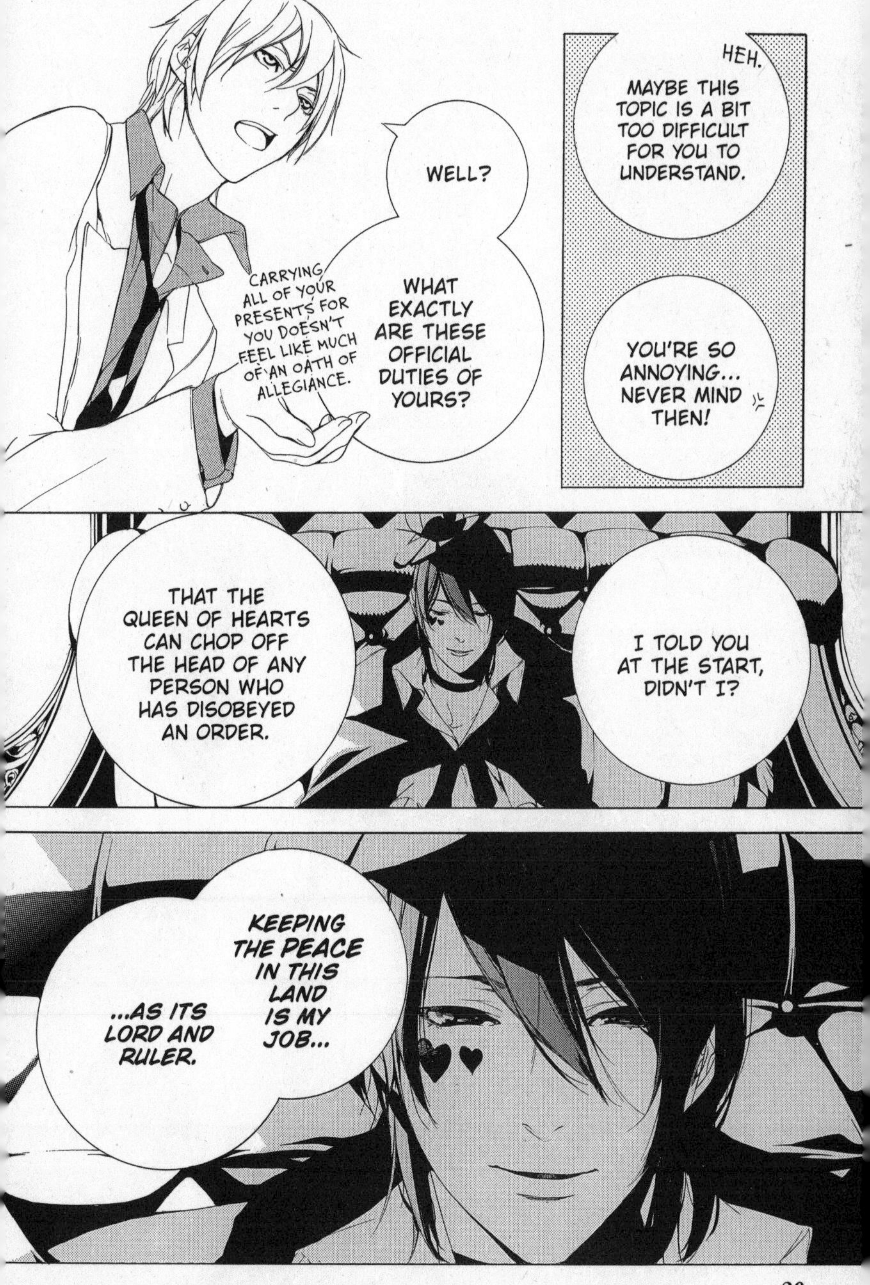
HEH.
MAYBE THIS TOPIC IS A BIT TOO DIFFICULT FOR YOU TO UNDERSTAND.
YOU'RE SO ANNOYING... NEVER MIND THEN!
WELL?
WHAT EXACTLY ARE THESE OFFICIAL DUTIES OF YOURS?
CARRYING ALL OF YOUR PRESENTS FOR YOU DOESN'T FEEL LIKE MUCH OF AN OATH OF ALLEGIANCE.
I TOLD YOU AT THE START, DIDN'T I?
THAT THE QUEEN OF HEARTS CAN CHOP OFF THE HEAD OF ANY PERSON WHO HAS DISOBEYED AN ORDER.
KEEPING THE PEACE IN THIS LAND IS MY JOB...
...AS ITS LORD AND RULER.

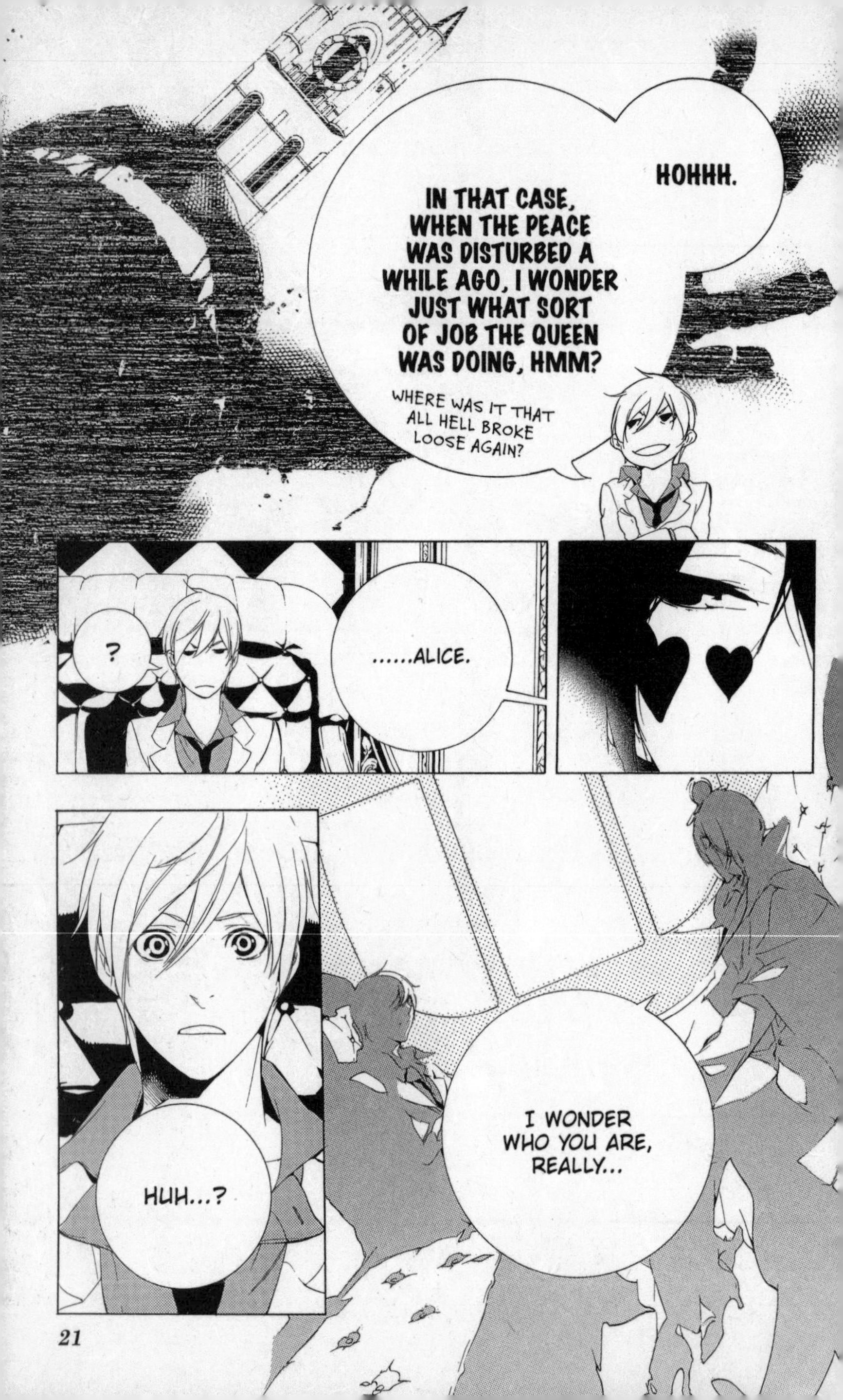
HOHHH.
IN THAT CASE, WHEN THE PEACE WAS DISTURBED A WHILE AGO, I WONDER JUST WHAT SORT OF JOB THE QUEEN WAS DOING, HMM?
WHERE WAS IT THAT ALL HELL BROKE LOOSE AGAIN?
......ALICE.
?
I WONDER WHO YOU ARE, REALLY...
HUH...?

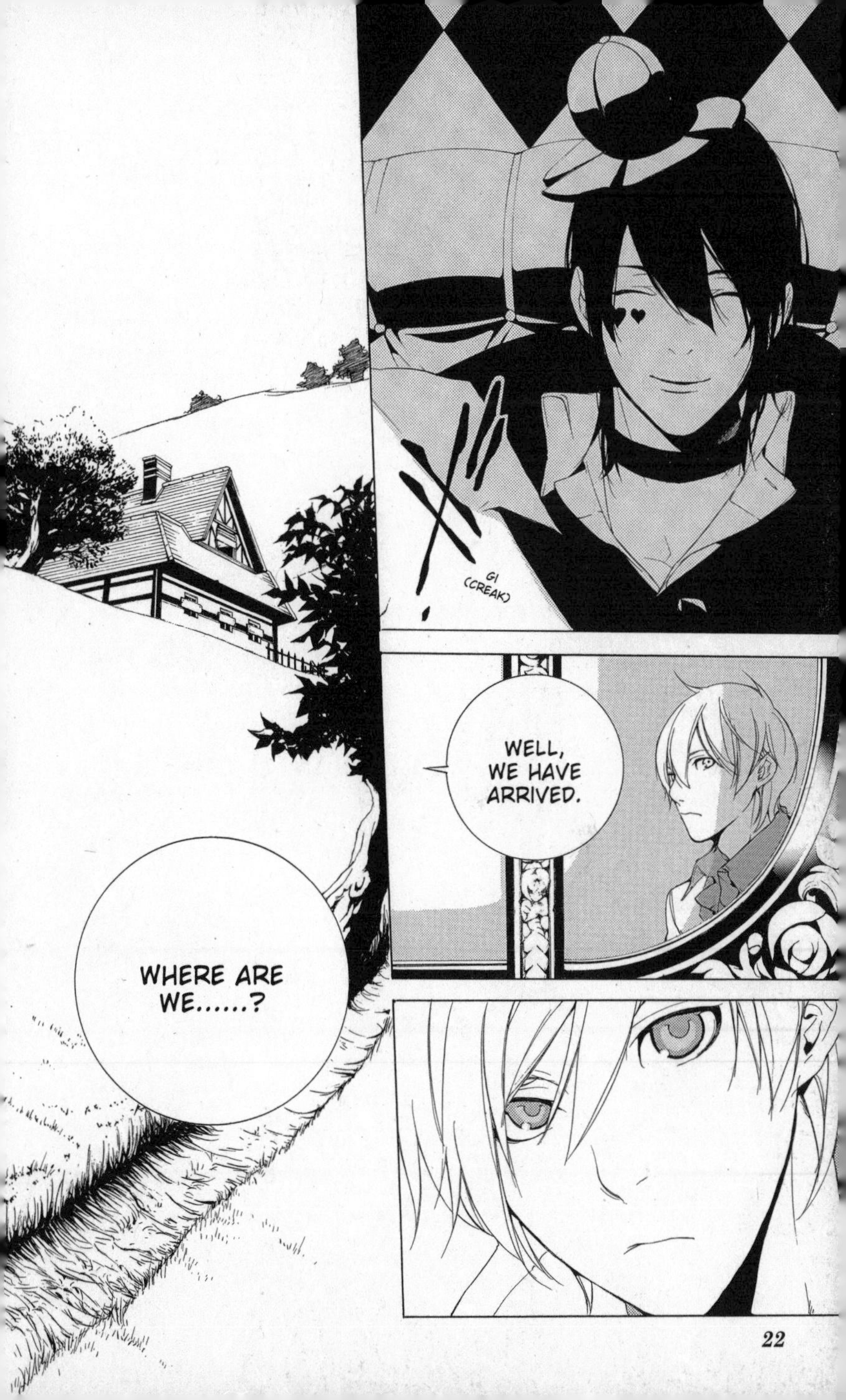
GI (CREAK)
WELL, WE HAVE ARRIVED.
WHERE ARE WE......?

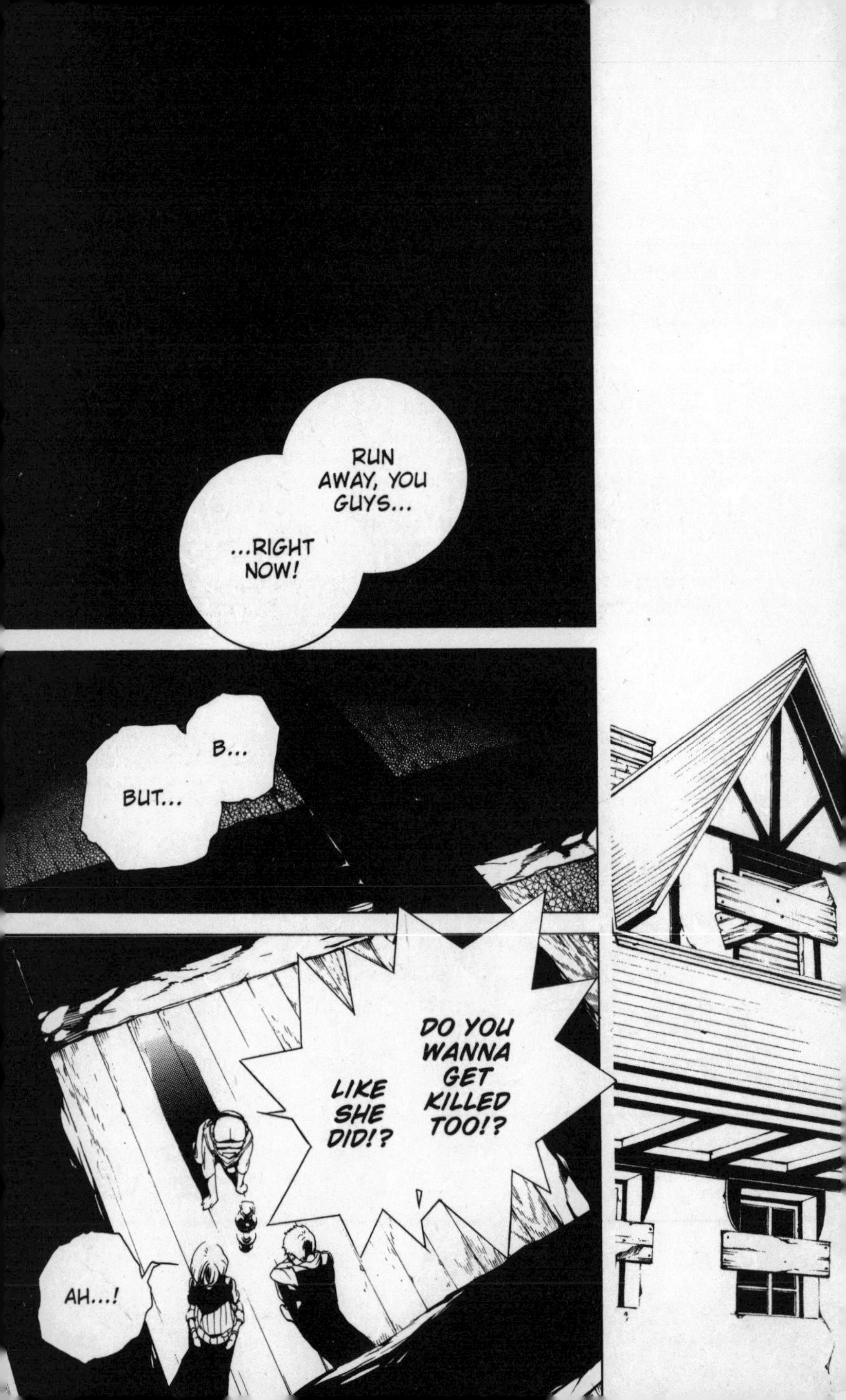
RUN AWAY, YOU GUYS...
...RIGHT NOW!
B...
BUT...
DO YOU WANNA GET KILLED TOO!?
LIKE SHE DID!?
AH...!

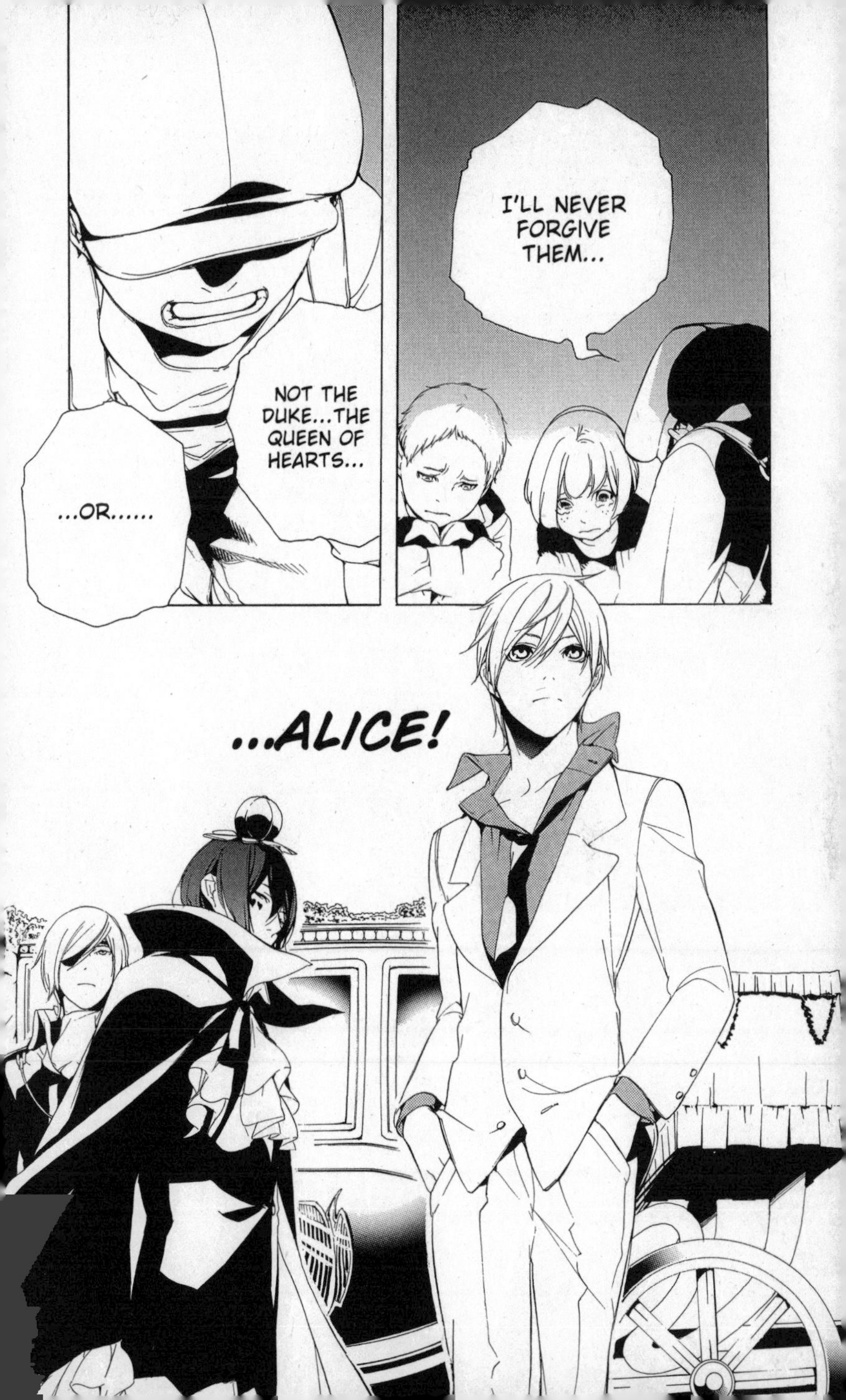
I'LL NEVER FORGIVE THEM...
NOT THE DUKE...THE QUEEN OF HEARTS...
...OR......
...ALICE!

Chapter 13 Hands Up! Children.

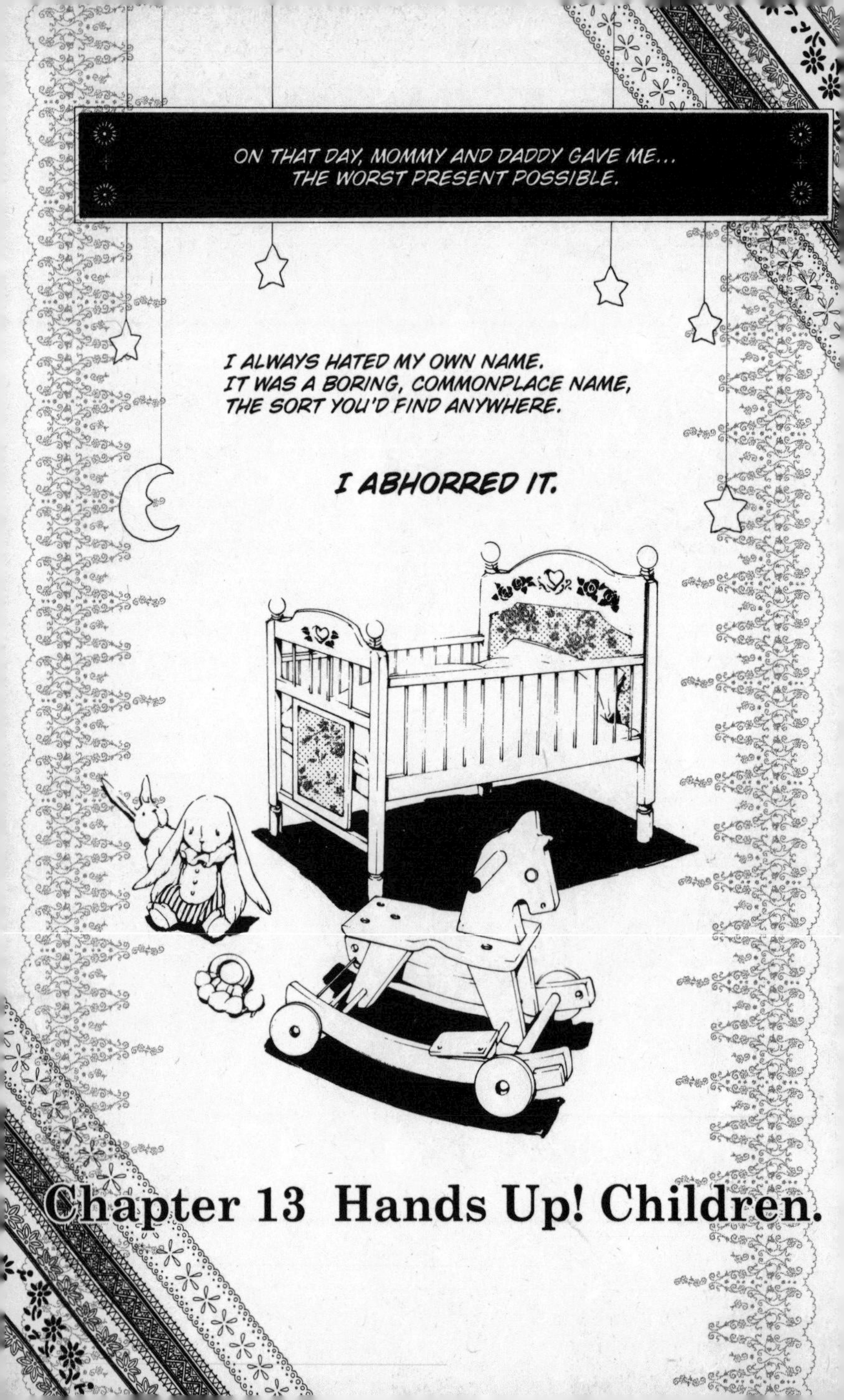
ON THAT DAY, MOMMY AND DADDY GAVE ME... THE WORST PRESENT POSSIBLE.
I ALWAYS HATED MY OWN NAME. IT WAS A BORING, COMMONPLACE NAME, THE SORT YOU'D FIND ANYWHERE.
I ABHORRED IT.

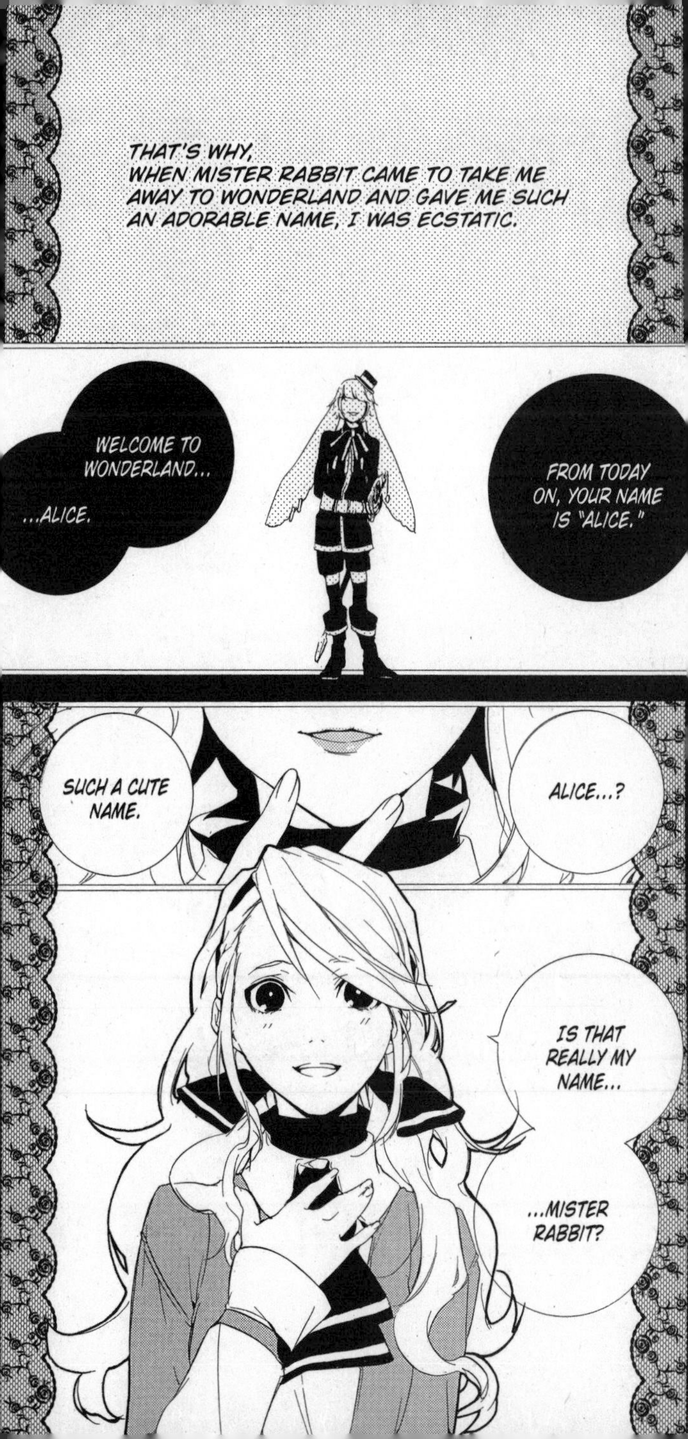
THAT'S WHY, WHEN MISTER RABBIT CAME TO TAKE ME AWAY TO WONDERLAND AND GAVE ME SUCH AN ADORABLE NAME, I WAS ECSTATIC.
FROM TODAY ON, YOUR NAME IS "ALICE."
WELCOME TO WONDERLAND...
...ALICE.
ALICE...?
SUCH A CUTE NAME.
IS THAT REALLY MY NAME...
...MISTER RABBIT?

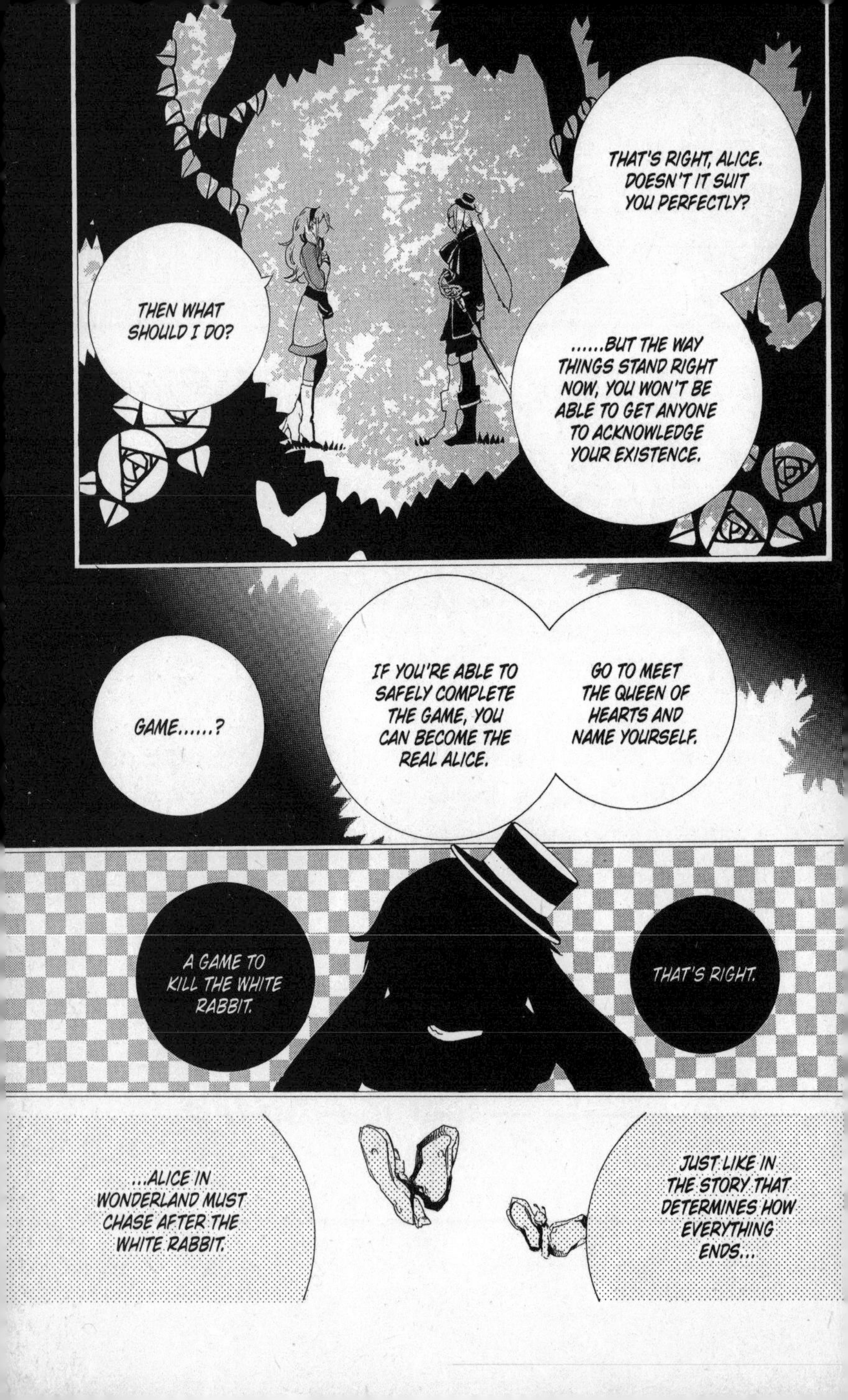
THAT'S RIGHT, ALICE. DOESN'T IT SUIT YOU PERFECTLY?
......BUT THE WAY THINGS STAND RIGHT NOW, YOU WON'T BE ABLE TO GET ANYONE TO ACKNOWLEDGE YOUR EXISTENCE.
THEN WHAT SHOULD I DO?
GO TO MEET THE QUEEN OF HEARTS AND NAME YOURSELF.
IF YOU'RE ABLE TO SAFELY COMPLETE THE GAME, YOU CAN BECOME THE REAL ALICE.
GAME......?
THAT'S RIGHT.
A GAME TO KILL THE WHITE RABBIT.
JUST LIKE IN THE STORY THAT DETERMINES HOW EVERYTHING ENDS...
...ALICE IN WONDERLAND MUST CHASE AFTER THE WHITE RABBIT.

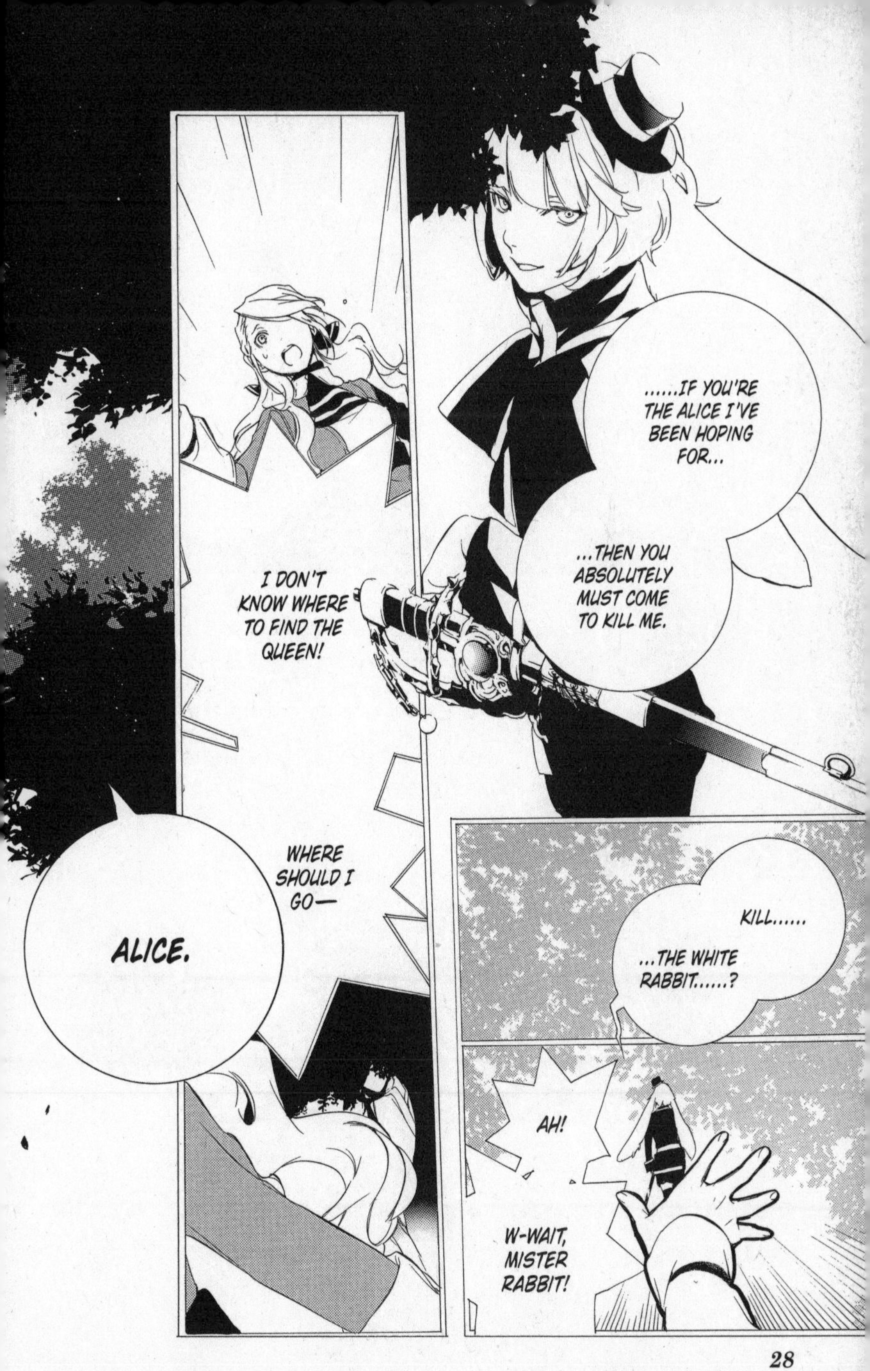
......IF YOU'RE THE ALICE I'VE BEEN HOPING FOR...
...THEN YOU ABSOLUTELY MUST COME TO KILL ME.
KILL......
...THE WHITE RABBIT......?
AH!
W-WAIT, MISTER RABBIT!
I DON'T KNOW WHERE TO FIND THE QUEEN!
WHERE SHOULD I GO—
ALICE.

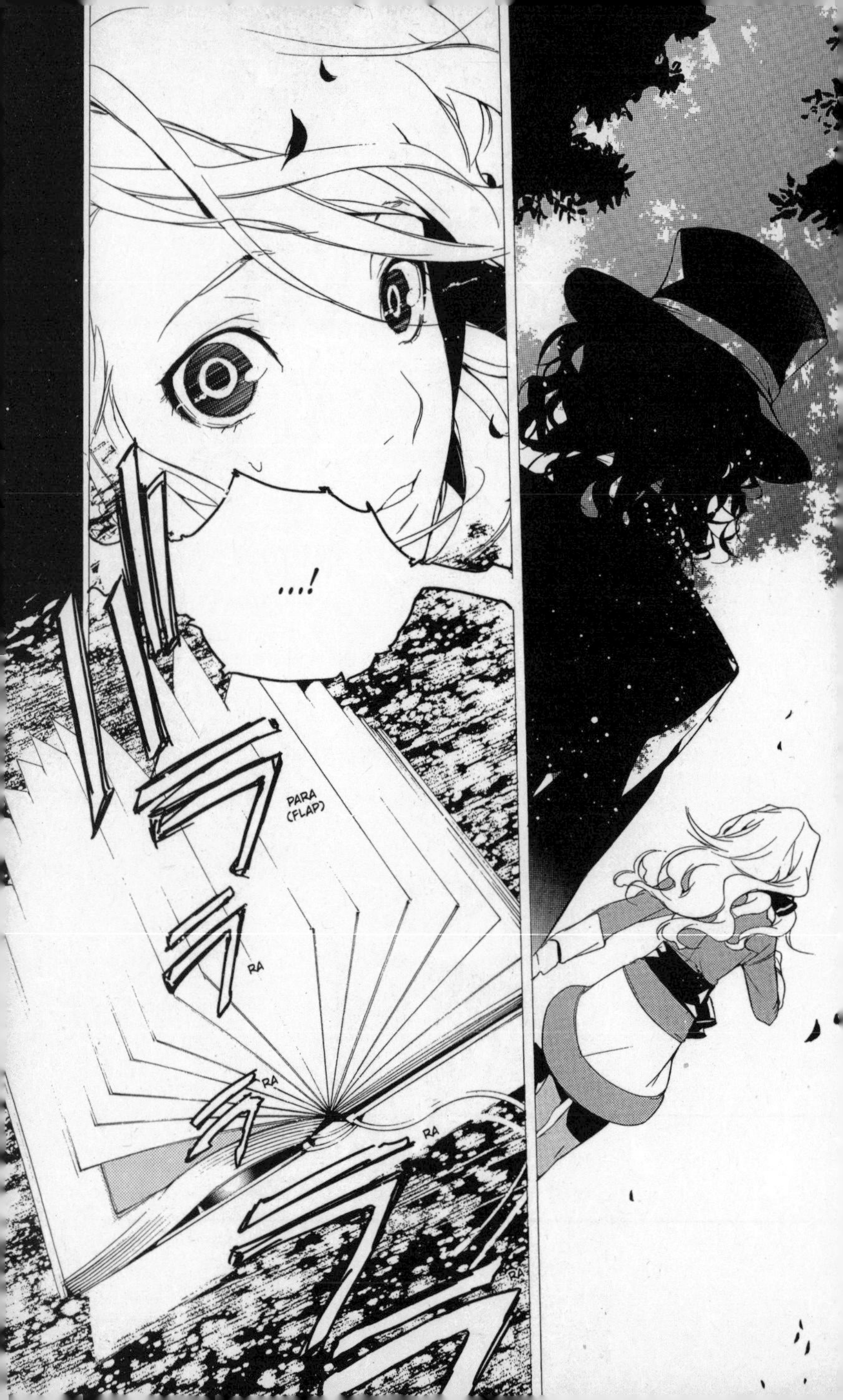
...!
PARA (FLAP)
RA
RA
RA
RA

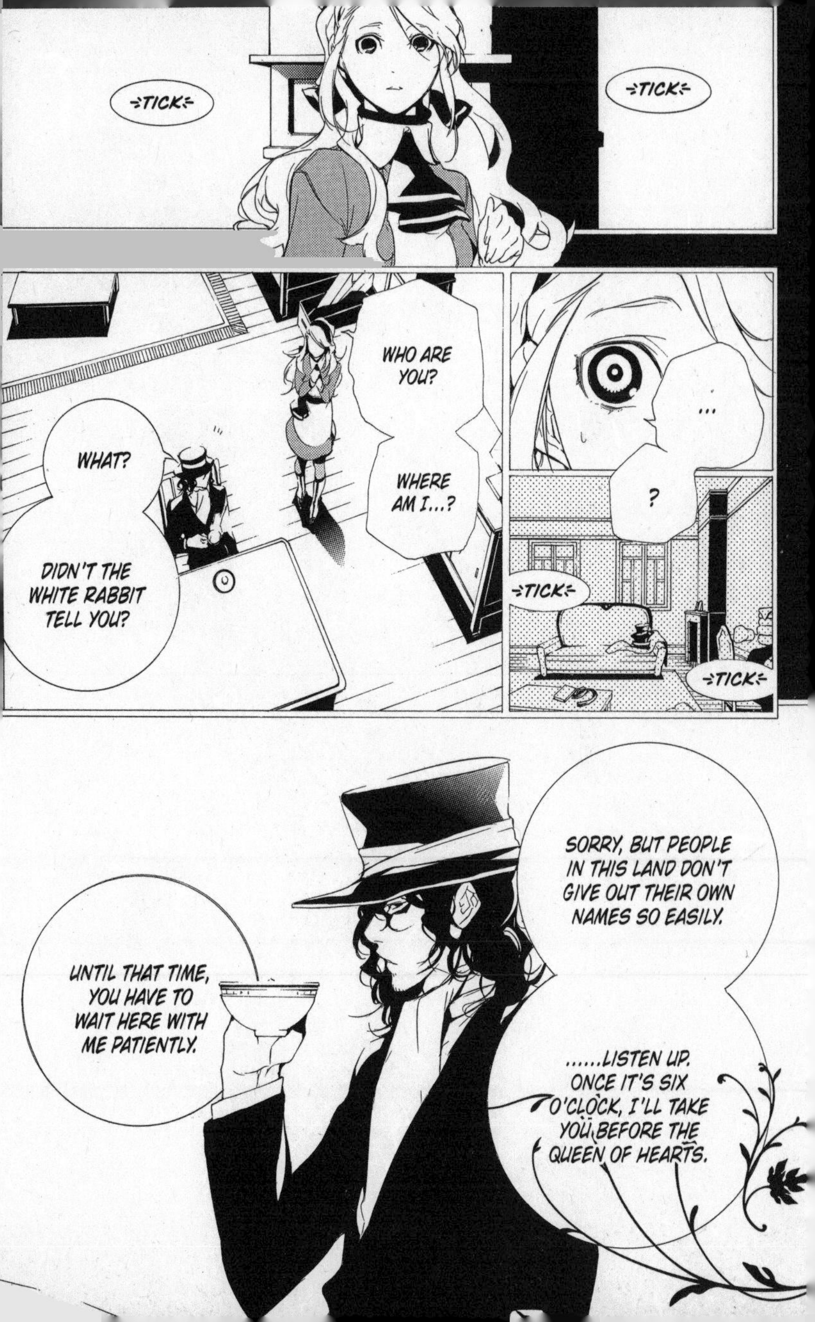

TICK
TICK
...
?
TICK
TICK
WHO ARE YOU?
WHERE AM I...?
WHAT?
DIDN'T THE WHITE RABBIT TELL YOU?
SORRY, BUT PEOPLE IN THIS LAND DON'T GIVE OUT THEIR OWN NAMES SO EASILY.
......LISTEN UP. ONCE IT'S SIX O'CLOCK, I'LL TAKE YOU BEFORE THE QUEEN OF HEARTS.
UNTIL THAT TIME, YOU HAVE TO WAIT HERE WITH ME PATIENTLY.

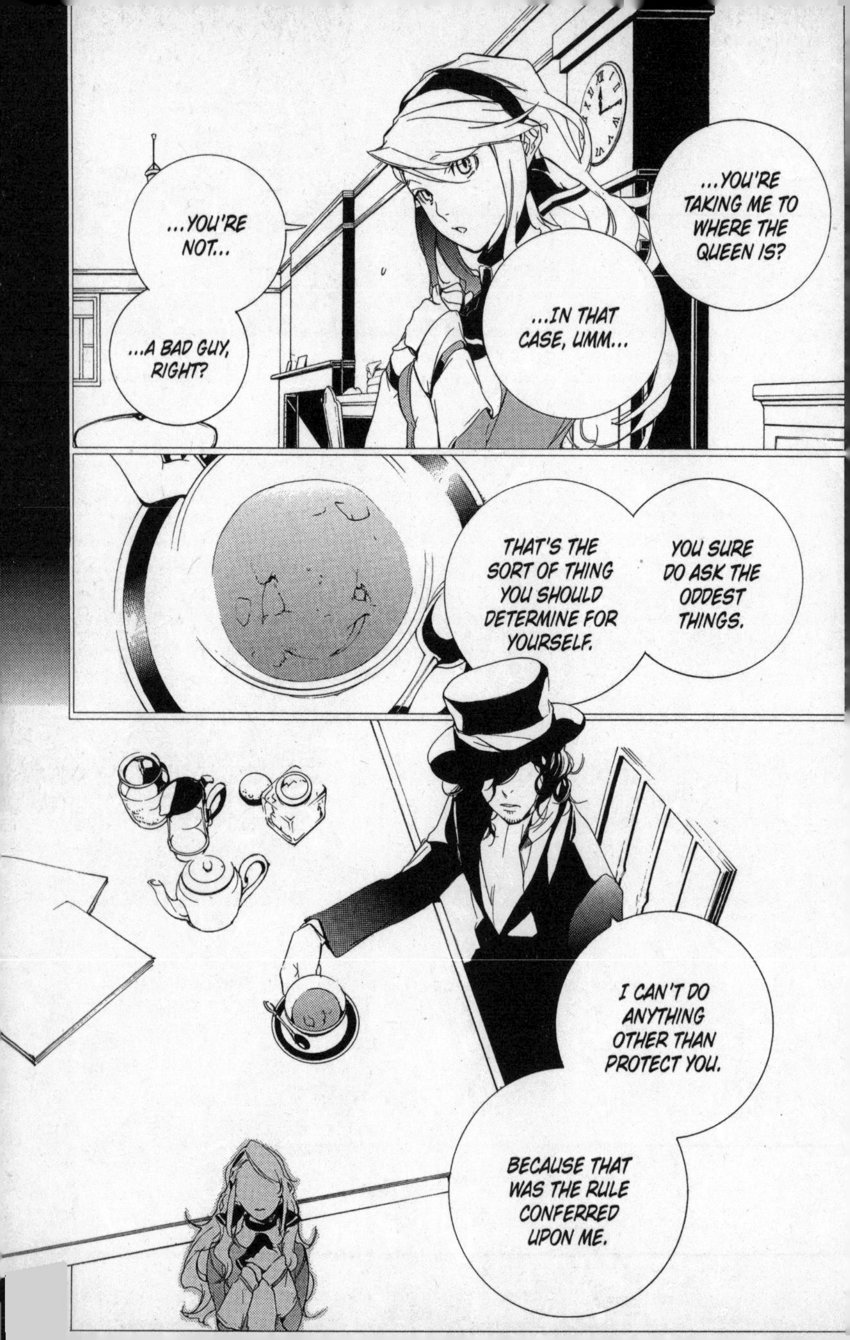
...YOU'RE TAKING ME TO WHERE THE QUEEN IS?
...IN THAT CASE, UMM...
...YOU'RE NOT...
...A BAD GUY, RIGHT?
YOU SURE DO ASK THE ODDEST THINGS.
THAT'S THE SORT OF THING YOU SHOULD DETERMINE FOR YOURSELF.
I CAN'T DO ANYTHING OTHER THAN PROTECT YOU.
BECAUSE THAT WAS THE RULE CONFERRED UPON ME.

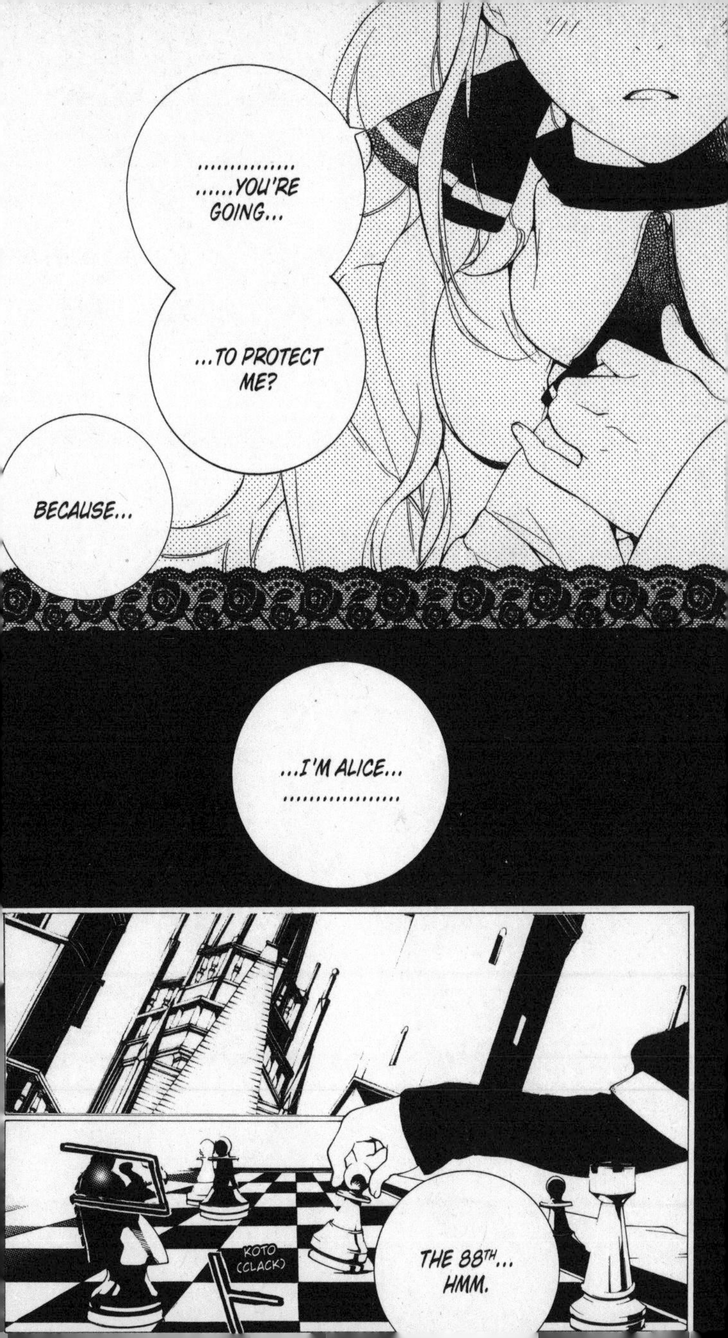

....YOU'RE GOING...
...TO PROTECT ME?
BECAUSE...
...I'M ALICE... ....
THE 88TH... HMM.
KOTO (CLACK)

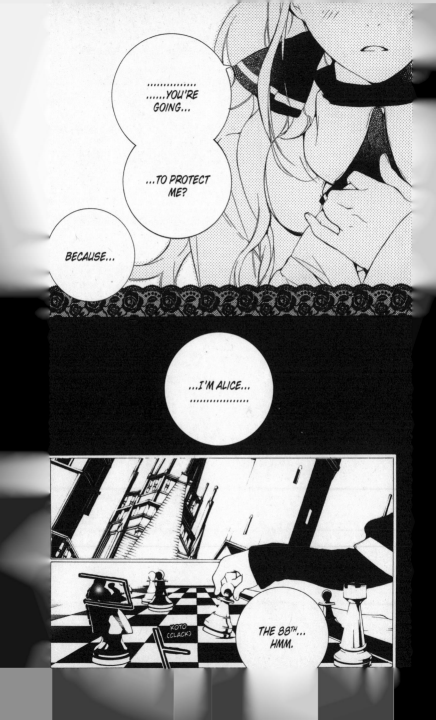

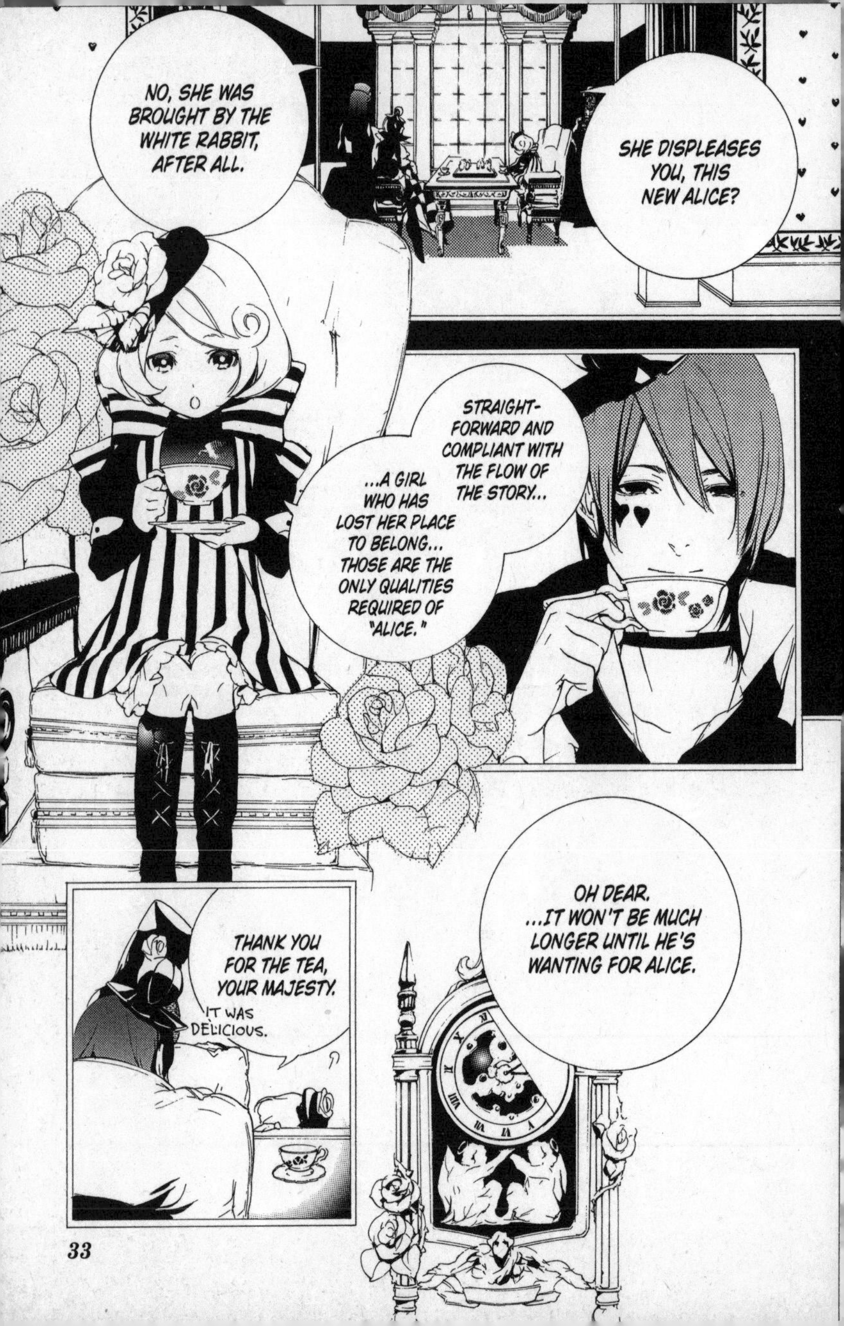
SHE DISPLEASES YOU, THIS NEW ALICE?
NO, SHE WAS BROUGHT BY THE WHITE RABBIT, AFTER ALL.
STRAIGHT-FORWARD AND COMPLIANT WITH THE FLOW OF THE STORY...
...A GIRL WHO HAS LOST HER PLACE TO BELONG... THOSE ARE THE ONLY QUALITIES REQUIRED OF "ALICE."
OH DEAR. ...IT WON'T BE MUCH LONGER UNTIL HE'S WANTING FOR ALICE.
THANK YOU FOR THE TEA, YOUR MAJESTY.
IT WAS DELICIOUS.

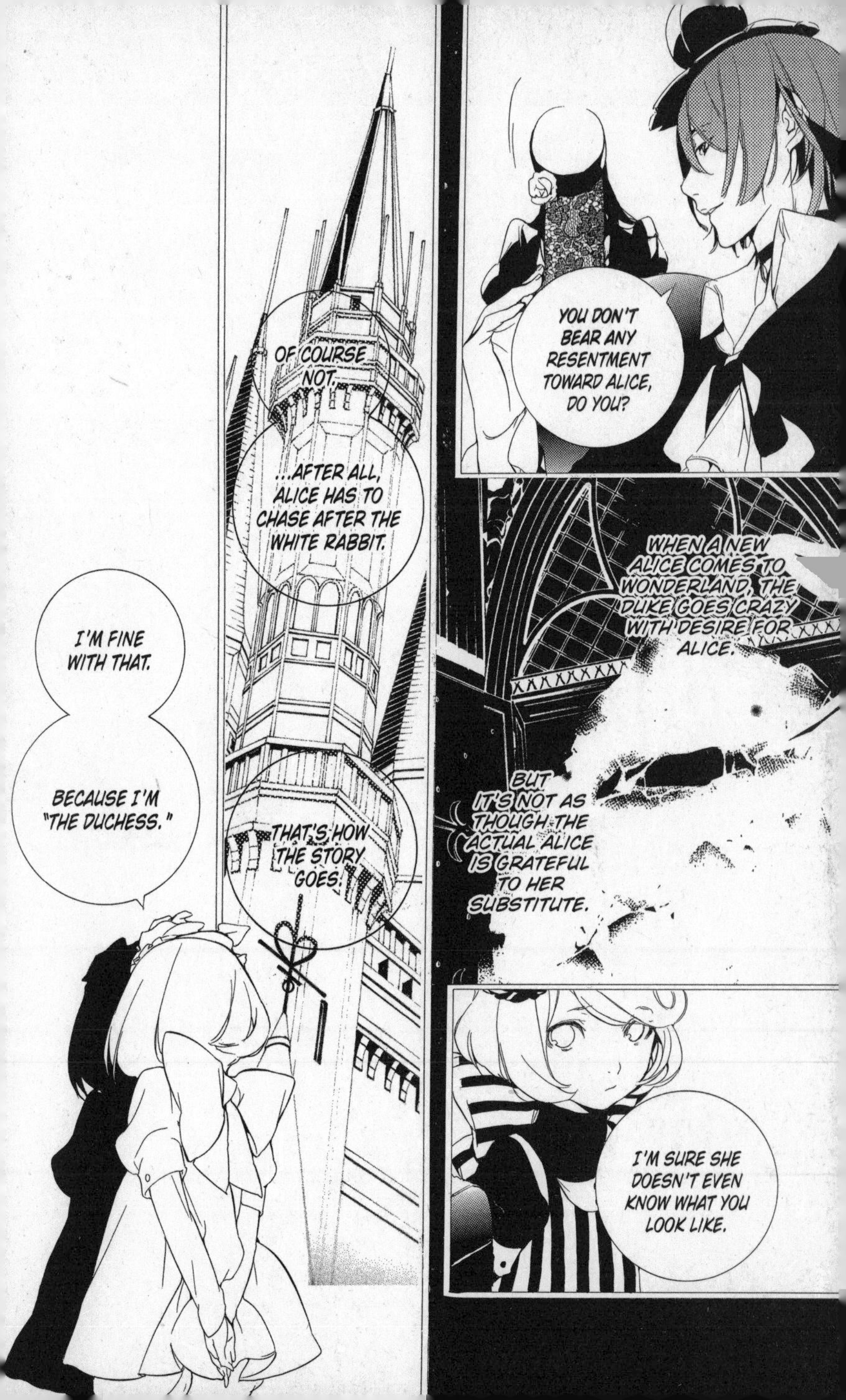
YOU DON'T BEAR ANY RESENTMENT TOWARD ALICE, DO YOU?
WHEN A NEW ALICE COMES TO WONDERLAND, THE DUKE GOES CRAZY WITH DESIRE FOR ALICE.
BUT IT'S NOT AS THOUGH THE ACTUAL ALICE IS GRATEFUL TO HER SUBSTITUTE.
I'M SURE SHE DOESN'T EVEN KNOW WHAT YOU LOOK LIKE.
OF COURSE NOT.
...AFTER ALL, ALICE HAS TO CHASE AFTER THE WHITE RABBIT.
THAT'S HOW THE STORY GOES.
I'M FINE WITH THAT.
BECAUSE I'M "THE DUCHESS."

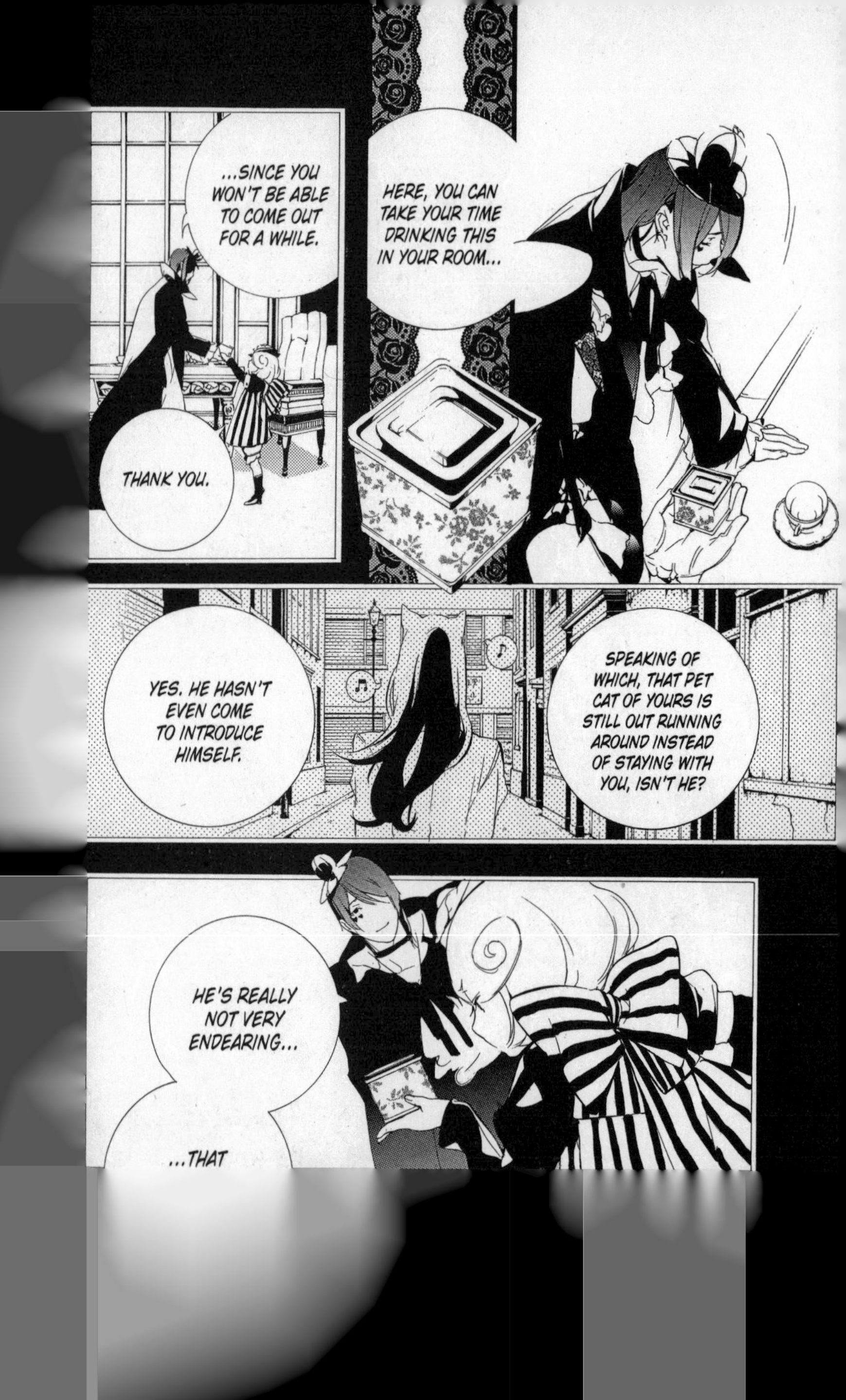
HERE, YOU CAN TAKE YOUR TIME DRINKING THIS IN YOUR ROOM...
...SINCE YOU WON'T BE ABLE TO COME OUT FOR A WHILE.
THANK YOU.
SPEAKING OF WHICH, THAT PET CAT OF YOURS IS STILL OUT RUNNING AROUND INSTEAD OF STAYING WITH YOU, ISN'T HE?
YES. HE HASN'T EVEN COME TO INTRODUCE HIMSELF.
HE'S REALLY NOT VERY ENDEARING...
...THAT

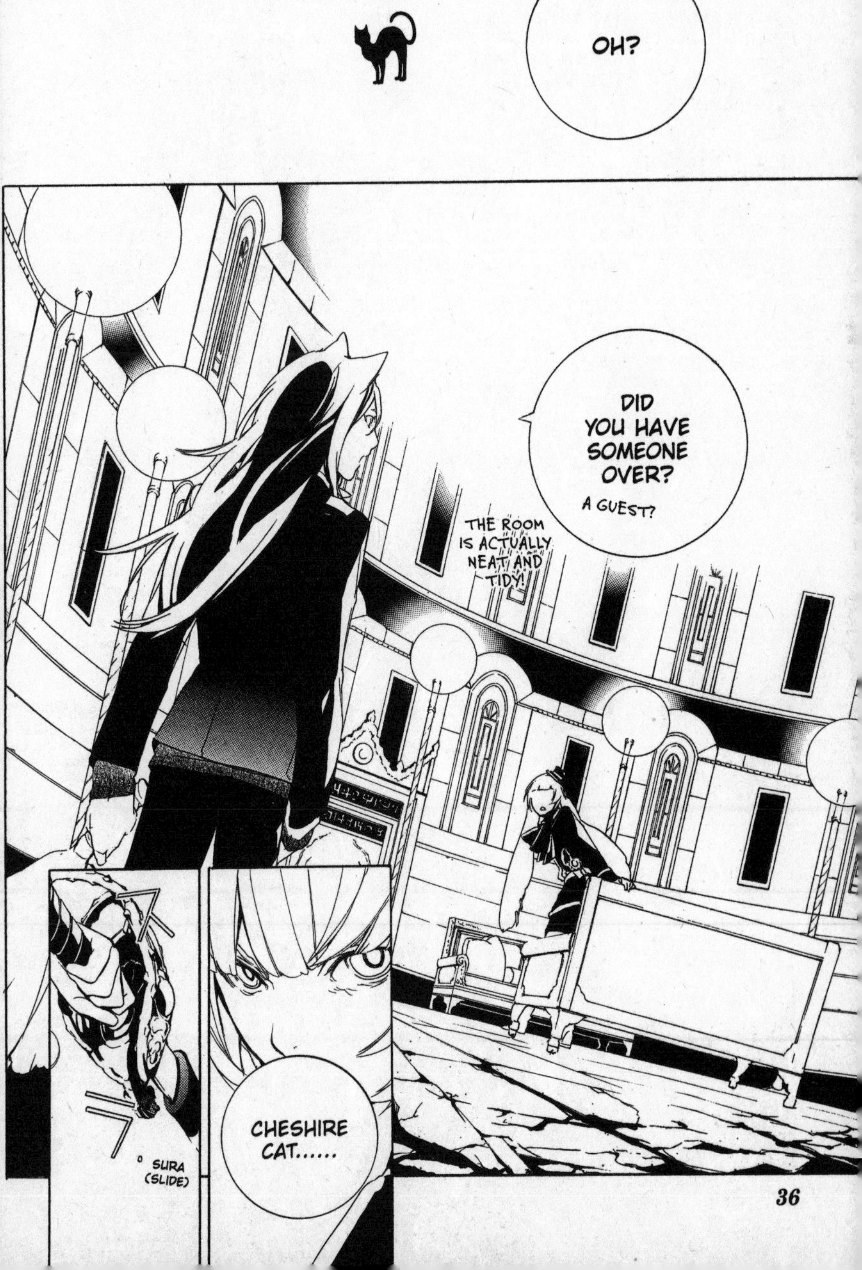
OH?
DID YOU HAVE SOMEONE OVER?
A GUEST?
THE ROOM IS ACTUALLY NEAT AND TIDY!
CHESHIRE CAT......
SURA (SLIDE)

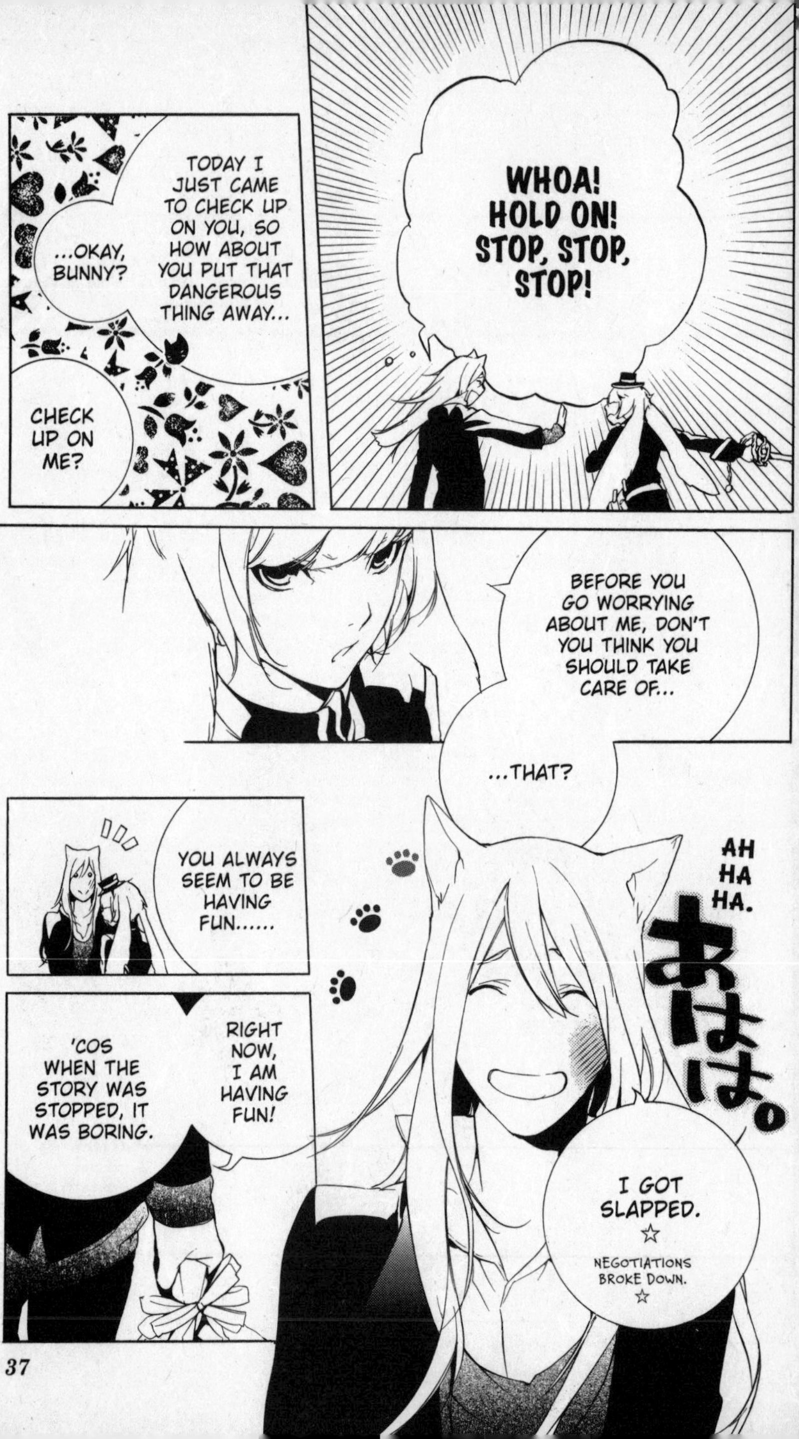
WHOA! HOLD ON! STOP, STOP, STOP!
TODAY I JUST CAME TO CHECK UP ON YOU, SO HOW ABOUT YOU PUT THAT DANGEROUS THING AWAY...
...OKAY, BUNNY?
CHECK UP ON ME?
BEFORE YOU GO WORRYING ABOUT ME, DON'T YOU THINK YOU SHOULD TAKE CARE OF...
...THAT?
AH HA HA.
あはは。
I GOT SLAPPED. ☆
NEGOTIATIONS BROKE DOWN. ☆
YOU ALWAYS SEEM TO BE HAVING FUN......
RIGHT NOW, I AM HAVING FUN!
'COS WHEN THE STORY WAS STOPPED, IT WAS BORING.

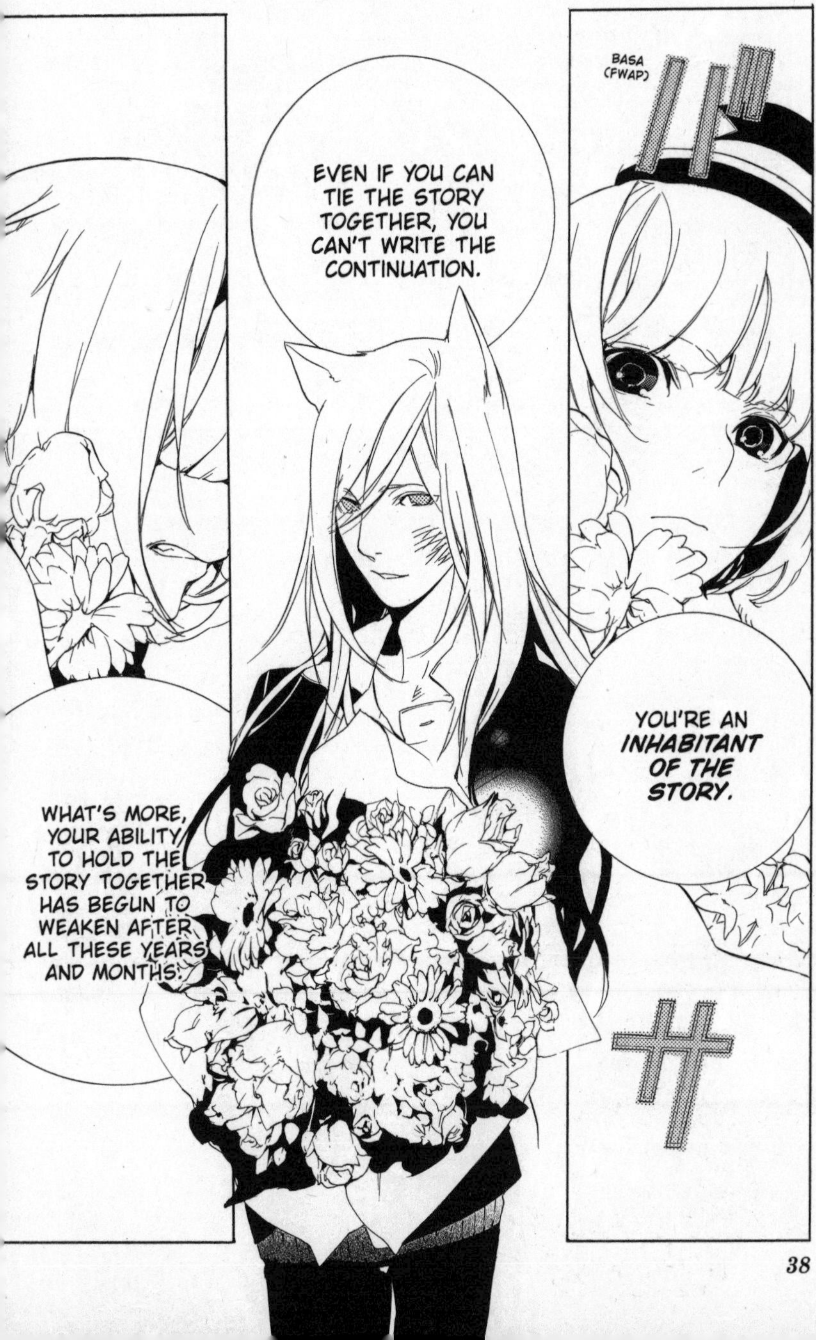
BASA (FWAP)
YOU'RE AN INHABITANT OF THE STORY.
EVEN IF YOU CAN TIE THE STORY TOGETHER, YOU CAN'T WRITE THE CONTINUATION.
WHAT'S MORE, YOUR ABILITY TO HOLD THE STORY TOGETHER HAS BEGUN TO WEAKEN AFTER ALL THESE YEARS AND MONTHS.

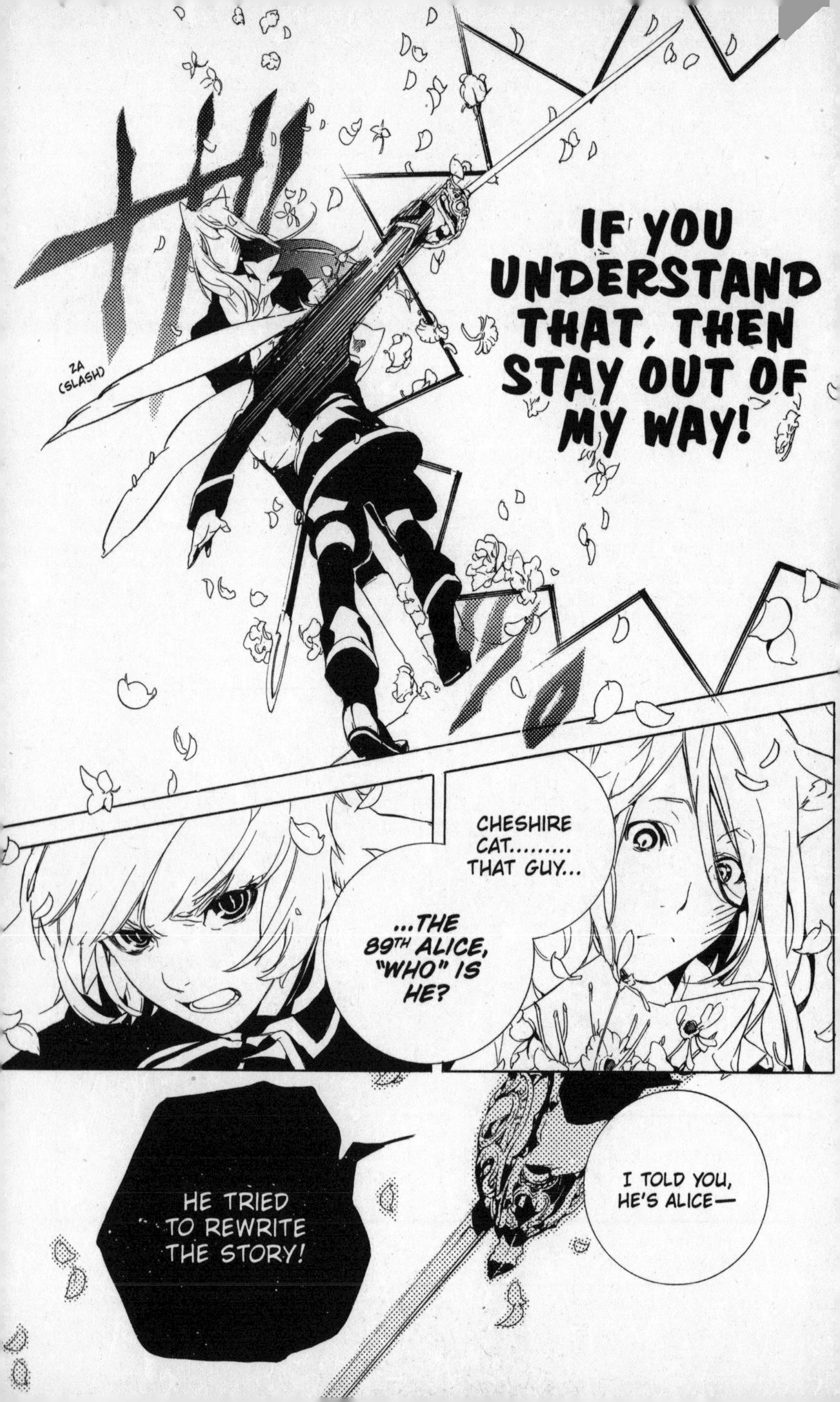
IF YOU UNDERSTAND THAT, THEN STAY OUT OF MY WAY!
ZA (SLASH)
CHESHIRE CAT......... THAT GUY...
...THE 89TH ALICE, "WHO" IS HE?
I TOLD YOU, HE'S ALICE—
HE TRIED TO REWRITE THE STORY!

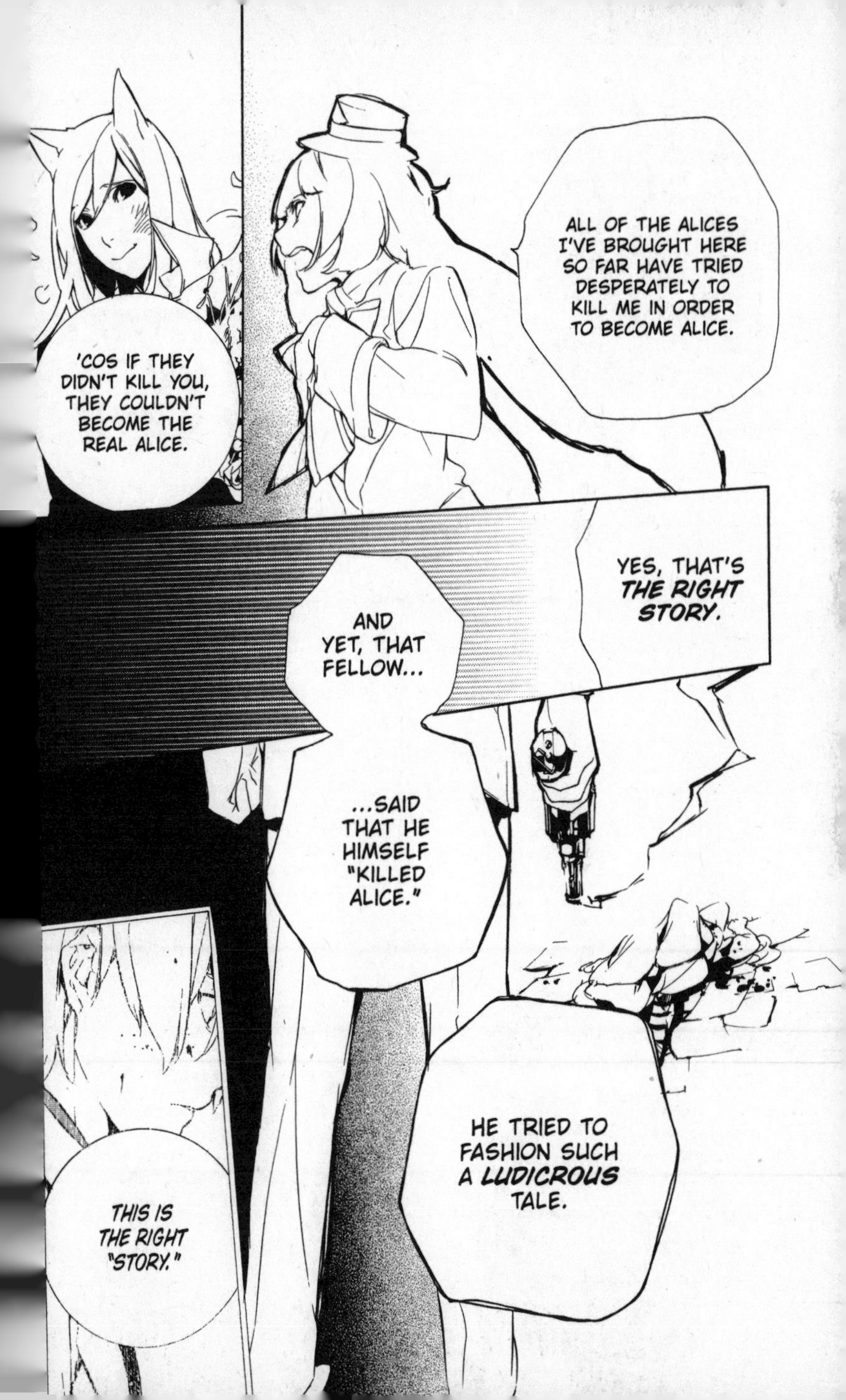
ALL OF THE ALICES I'VE BROUGHT HERE SO FAR HAVE TRIED DESPERATELY TO KILL ME IN ORDER TO BECOME ALICE.
'COS IF THEY DIDN'T KILL YOU, THEY COULDN'T BECOME THE REAL ALICE.
YES, THAT'S *THE RIGHT STORY.*
AND YET, THAT FELLOW...
...SAID THAT HE HIMSELF "KILLED ALICE."
HE TRIED TO FASHION SUCH A *LUDICROUS* TALE.
THIS IS THE RIGHT "STORY."

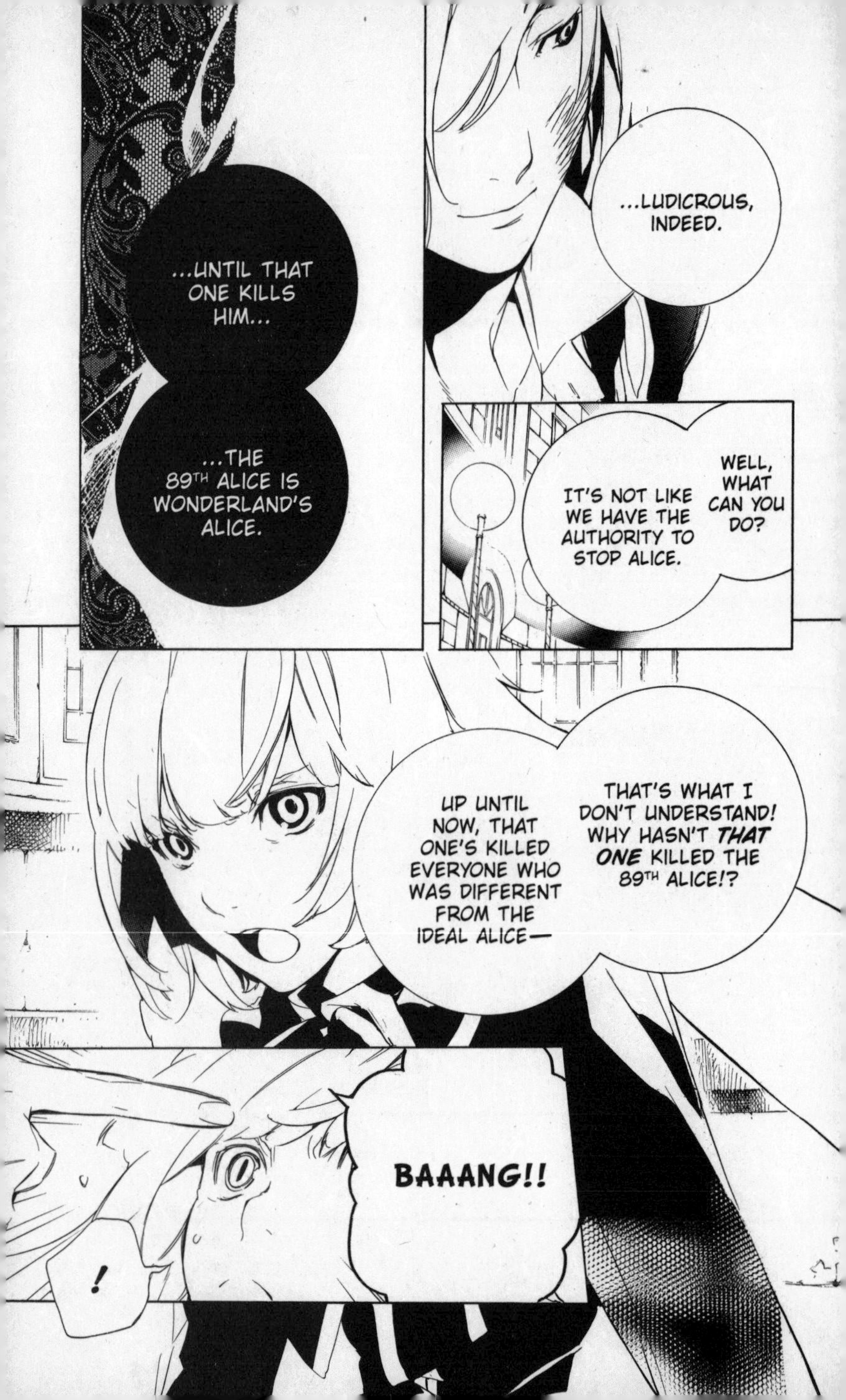

...LUDICROUS, INDEED.
WELL, WHAT CAN YOU DO?
IT'S NOT LIKE WE HAVE THE AUTHORITY TO STOP ALICE.
...UNTIL THAT ONE KILLS HIM...
...THE 89TH ALICE IS WONDERLAND'S ALICE.
THAT'S WHAT I DON'T UNDERSTAND! WHY HASN'T *THAT ONE* KILLED THE 89TH ALICE!?
UP UNTIL NOW, THAT ONE'S KILLED EVERYONE WHO WAS DIFFERENT FROM THE IDEAL ALICE—
BAAANG!!
!

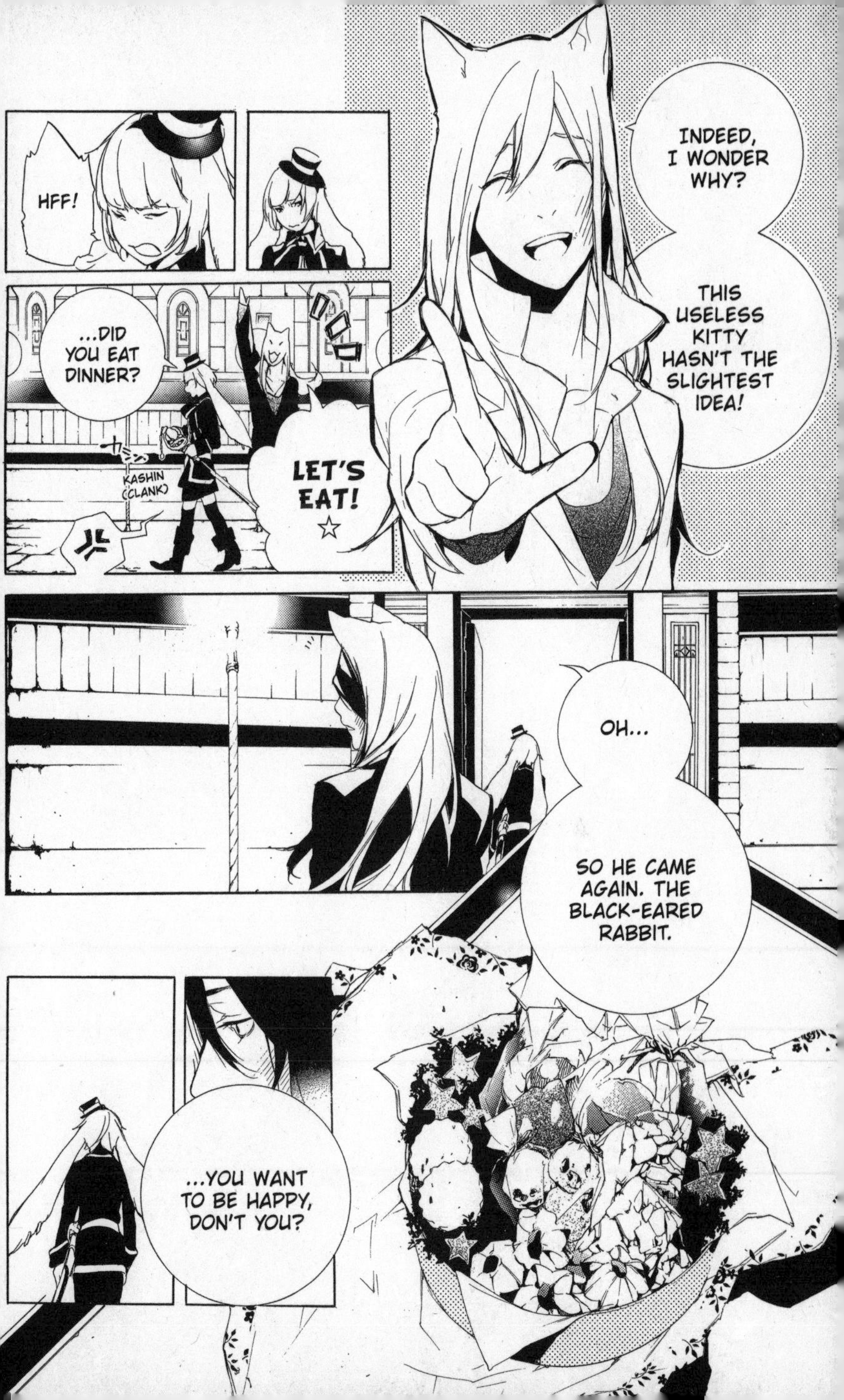
INDEED, I WONDER WHY?
THIS USELESS KITTY HASN'T THE SLIGHTEST IDEA!
HFF!
...DID YOU EAT DINNER?
LET'S EAT! ☆
KASHIN (CLANK)
OH...
SO HE CAME AGAIN. THE BLACK-EARED RABBIT.
...YOU WANT TO BE HAPPY, DON'T YOU?

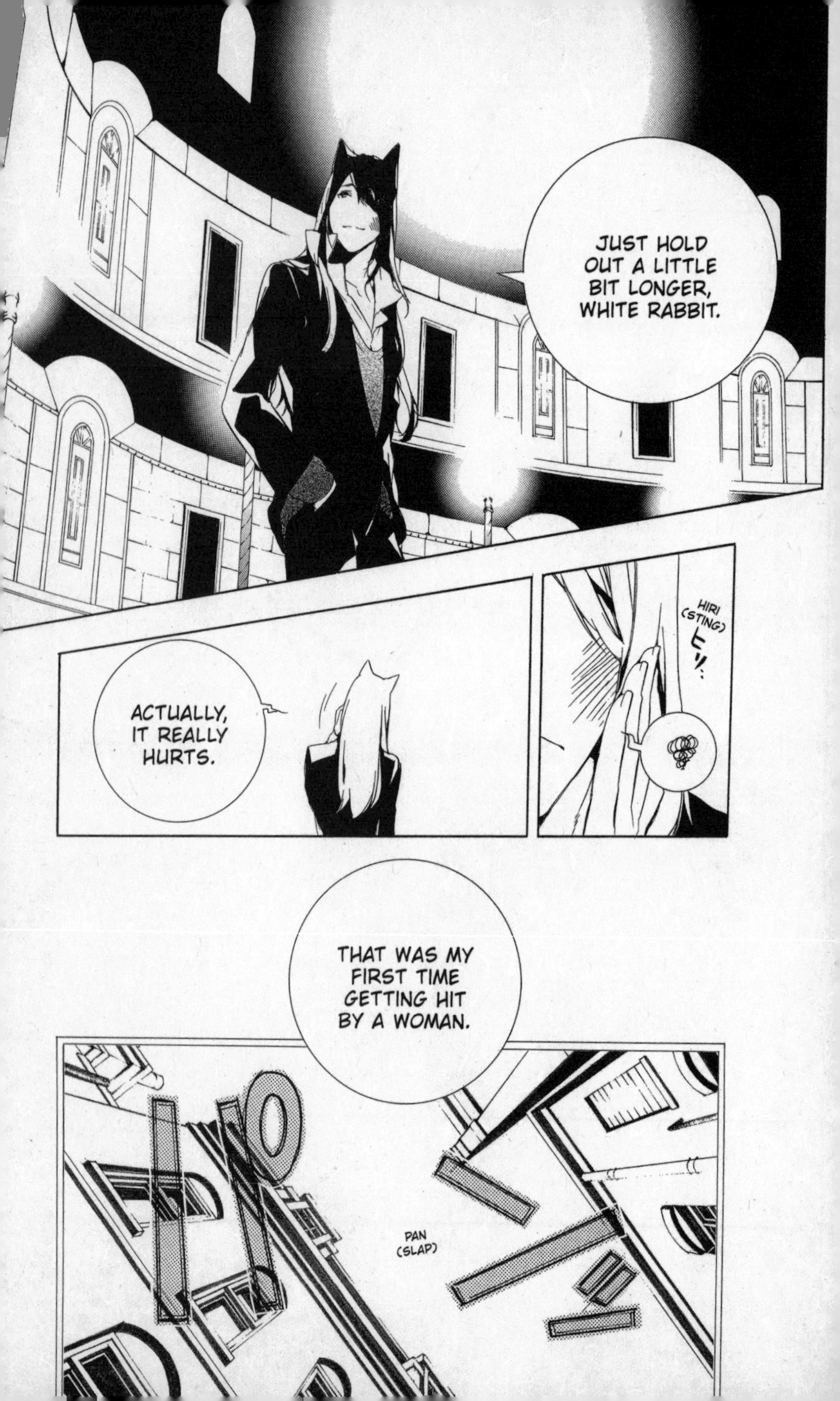
JUST HOLD OUT A LITTLE BIT LONGER, WHITE RABBIT.
HIRI (STING)
ヒリ
ACTUALLY, IT REALLY HURTS.
THAT WAS MY FIRST TIME GETTING HIT BY A WOMAN.
PAN (SLAP)

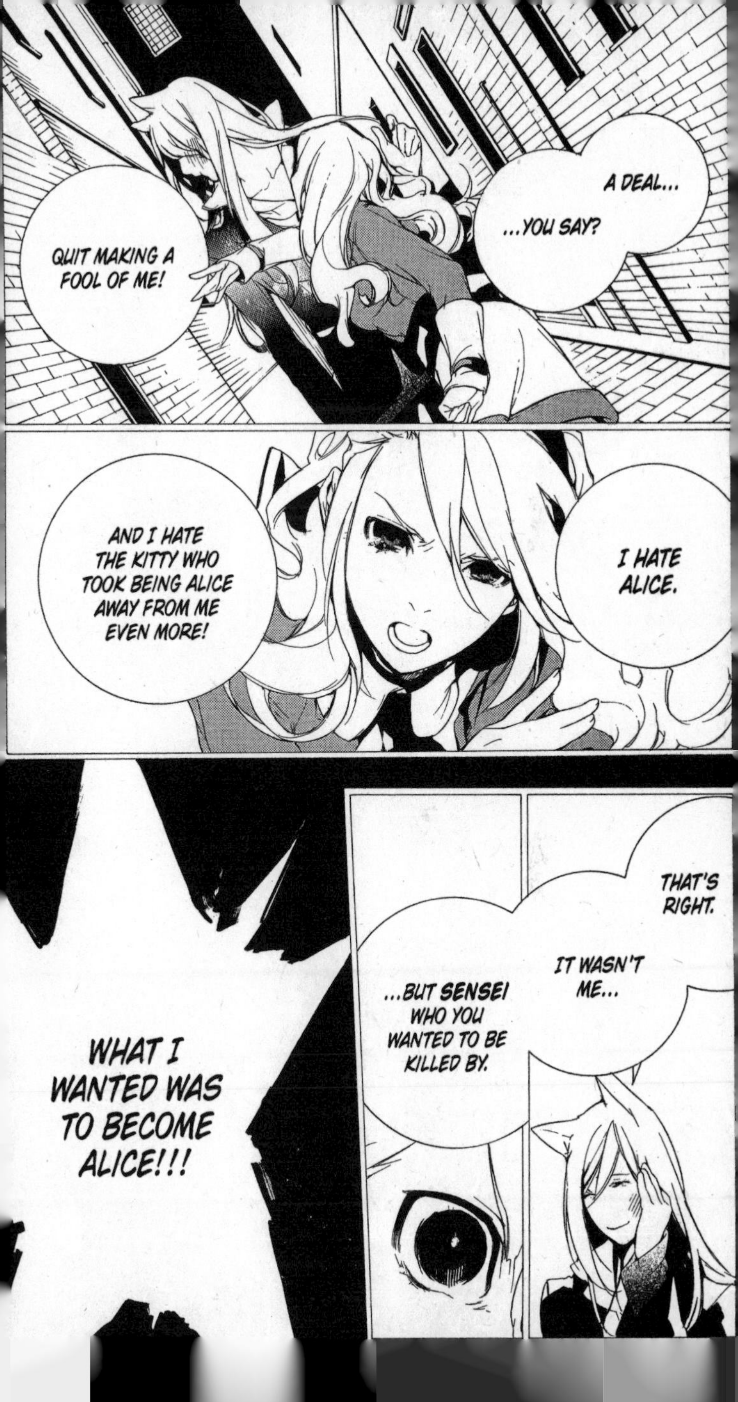
A DEAL...
...YOU SAY?
QUIT MAKING A FOOL OF ME!
I HATE ALICE.
AND I HATE THE KITTY WHO TOOK BEING ALICE AWAY FROM ME EVEN MORE!
THAT'S RIGHT.
IT WASN'T ME...
...BUT SENSEI WHO YOU WANTED TO BE KILLED BY.
WHAT I WANTED WAS TO BECOME ALICE!!!

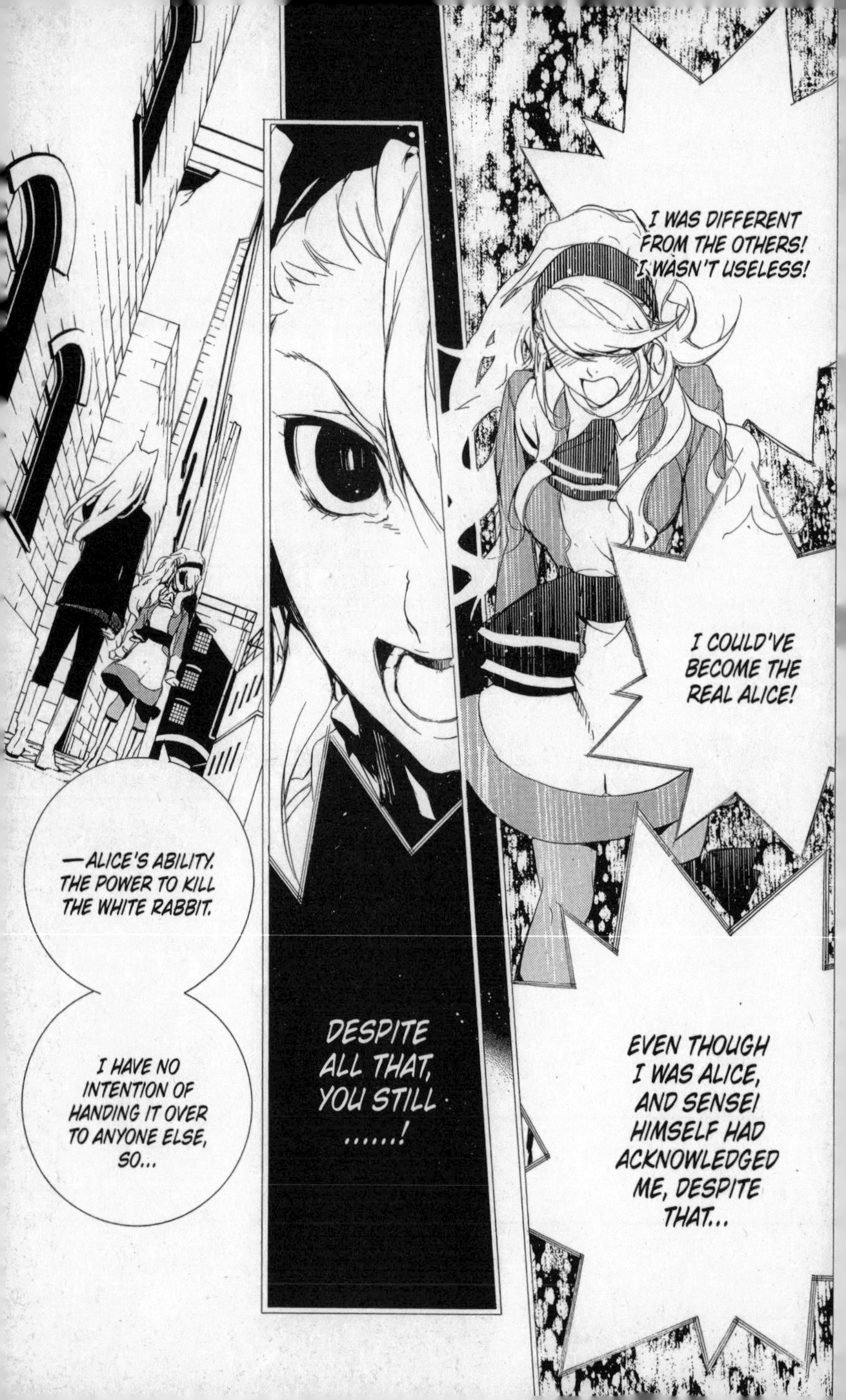
I WAS DIFFERENT FROM THE OTHERS! I WASN'T USELESS!
I COULD'VE BECOME THE REAL ALICE!
EVEN THOUGH I WAS ALICE, AND SENSEI HIMSELF HAD ACKNOWLEDGED ME, DESPITE THAT...
DESPITE ALL THAT, YOU STILL ......!
—ALICE'S ABILITY. THE POWER TO KILL THE WHITE RABBIT.
I HAVE NO INTENTION OF HANDING IT OVER TO ANYONE ELSE, SO...

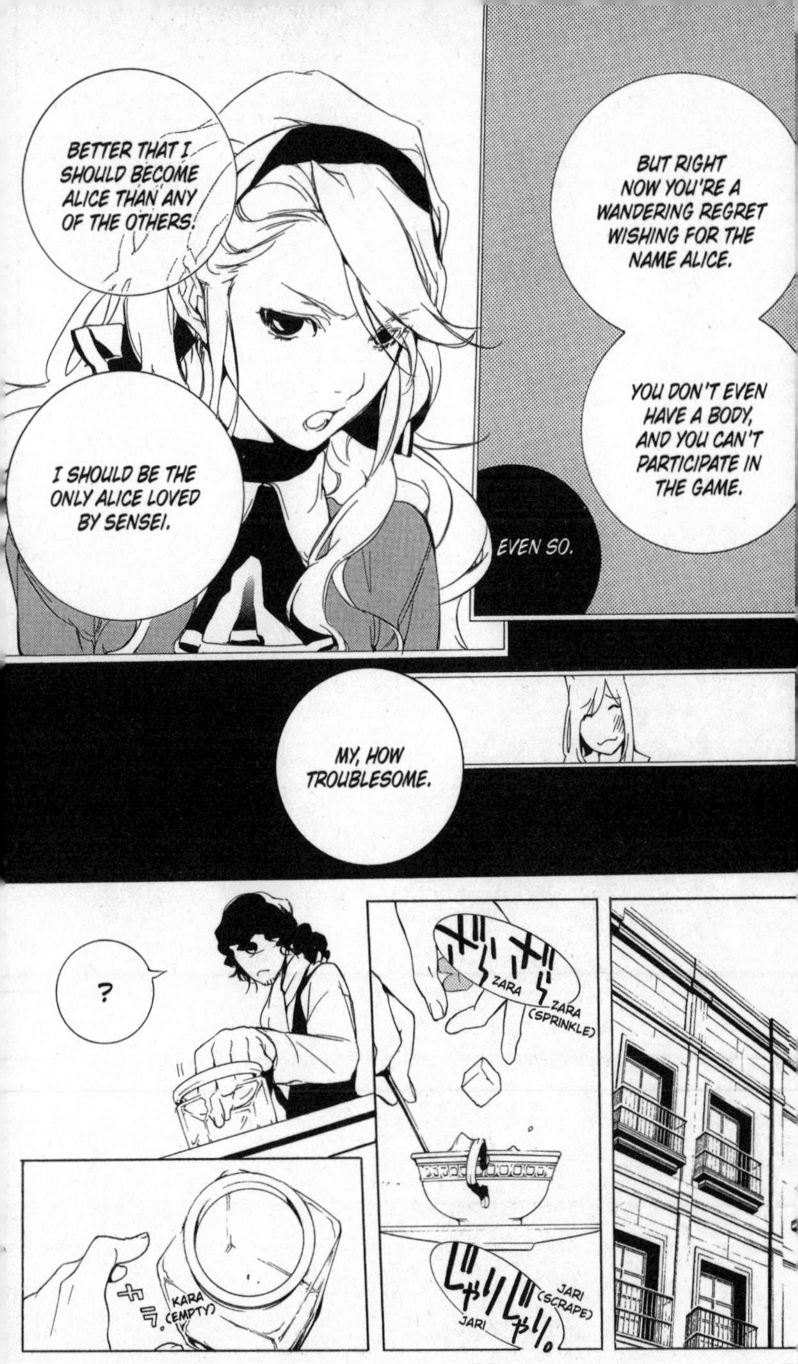
BUT RIGHT NOW YOU'RE A WANDERING REGRET WISHING FOR THE NAME ALICE.
YOU DON'T EVEN HAVE A BODY, AND YOU CAN'T PARTICIPATE IN THE GAME.
EVEN SO.
BETTER THAT I SHOULD BECOME ALICE THAN ANY OF THE OTHERS.
I SHOULD BE THE ONLY ALICE LOVED BY SENSEI.
MY, HOW TROUBLESOME.
ZARA
ZARA (SPRINKLE)
JARI (SCRAPE)
JARI
?
KARA (EMPTY)

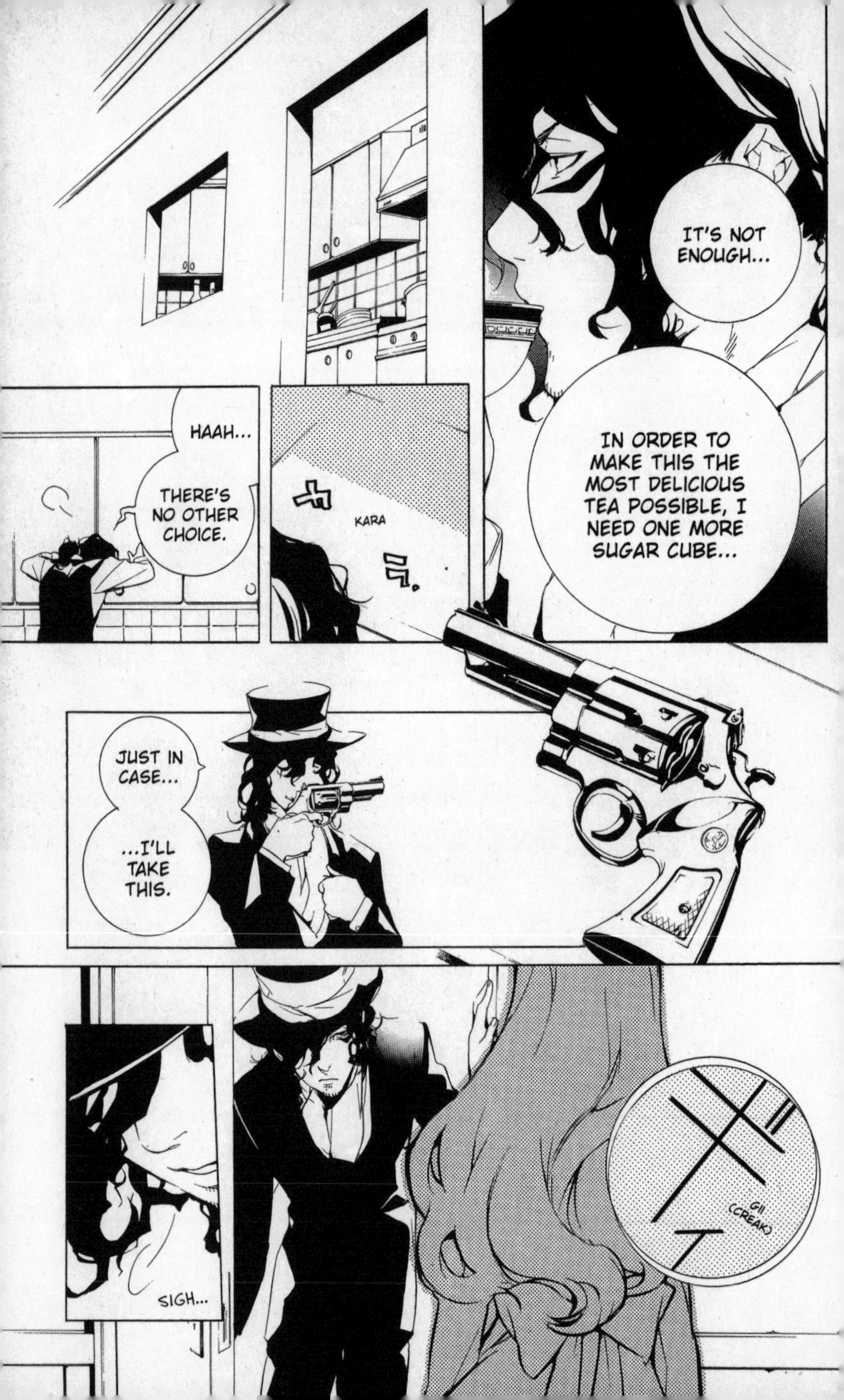
IT'S NOT ENOUGH...
IN ORDER TO MAKE THIS THE MOST DELICIOUS TEA POSSIBLE, I NEED ONE MORE SUGAR CUBE...
KARA
HAAH...
THERE'S NO OTHER CHOICE.
JUST IN CASE...
...I'LL TAKE THIS.
GII (CREAK)
SIGH...

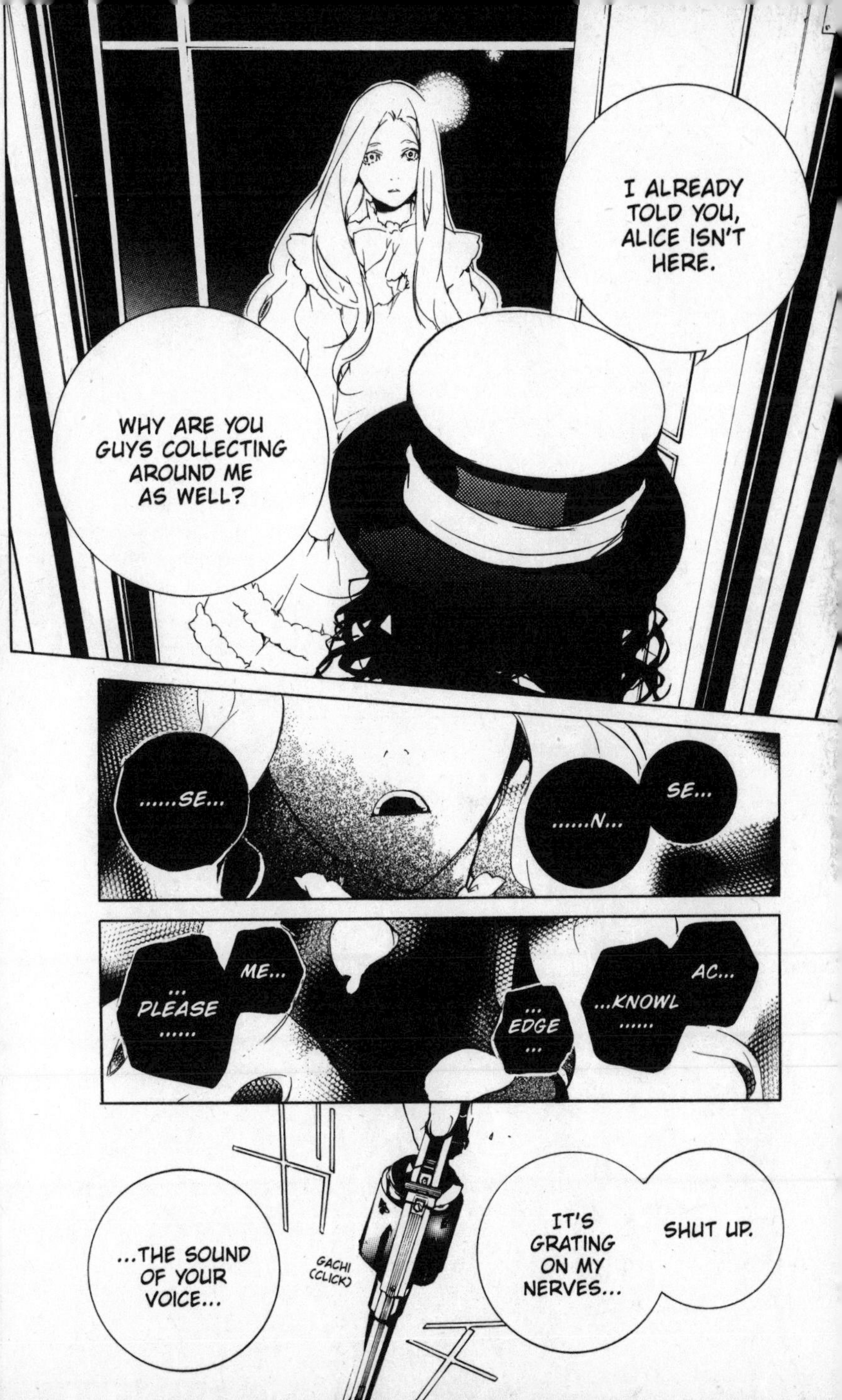
I ALREADY TOLD YOU, ALICE ISN'T HERE.
WHY ARE YOU GUYS COLLECTING AROUND ME AS WELL?
SE...
......N...
......SE...
AC... ...KNOWL ......
... EDGE ...
ME... ... PLEASE ......
SHUT UP.
IT'S GRATING ON MY NERVES...
GACHI (CLICK)
...THE SOUND OF YOUR VOICE...

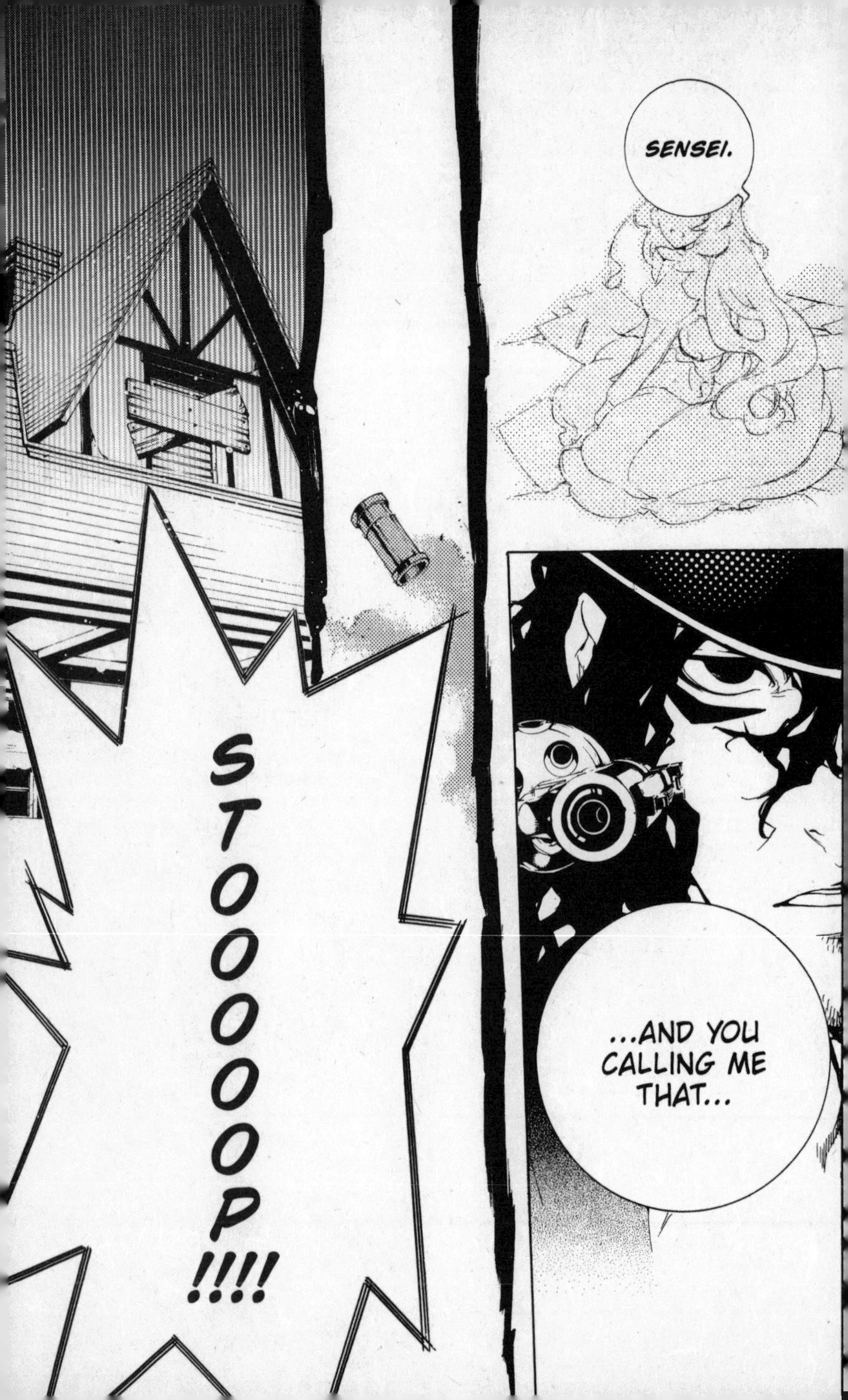
SENSEI.
...AND YOU CALLING ME THAT...
STOOOOOP!!!!

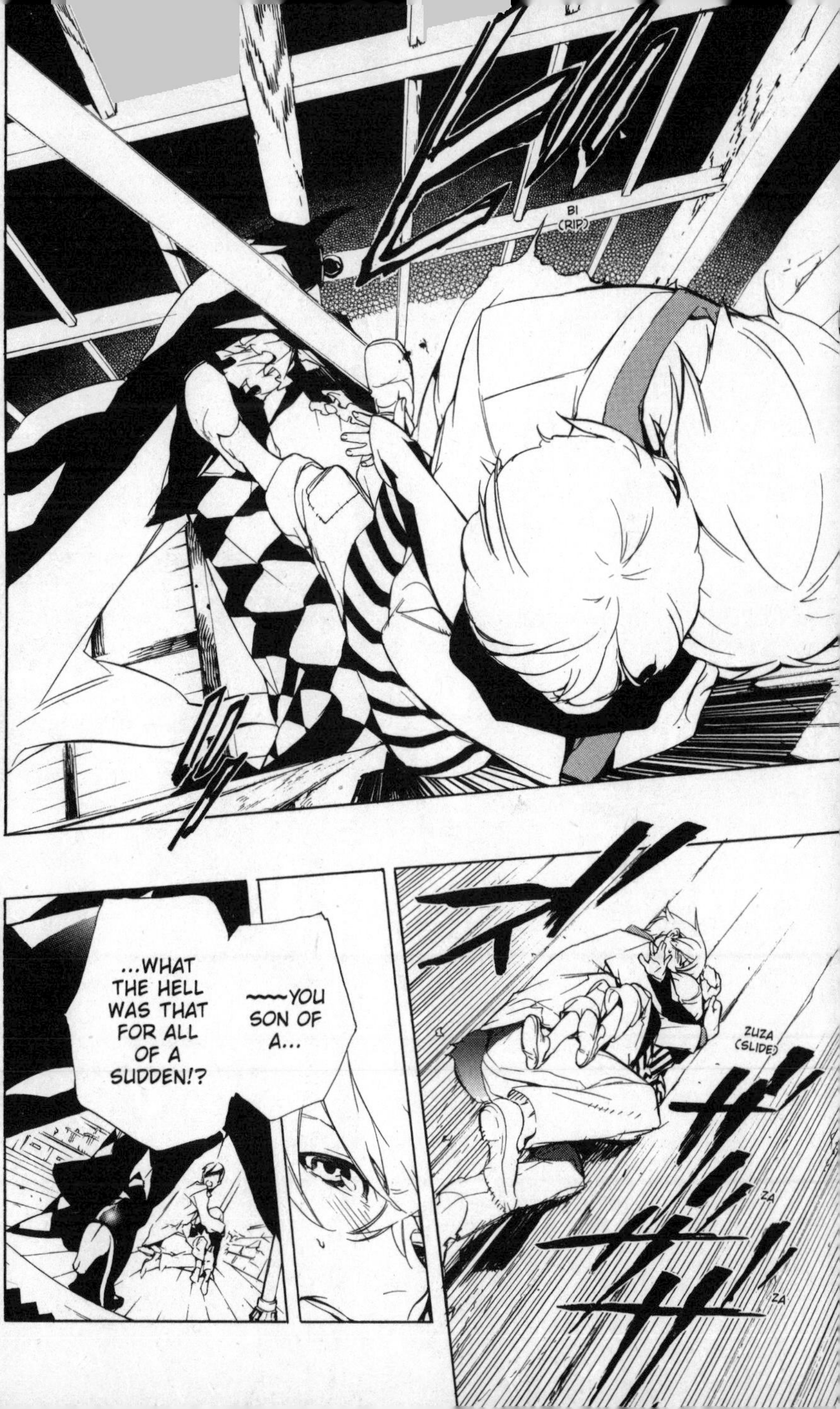
BI
(RIP)
ZUZA
(SLIDE)
ZA
ZA
~~~~YOU SON OF A...
...WHAT THE HELL WAS THAT FOR ALL OF A SUDDEN!?
~~~~

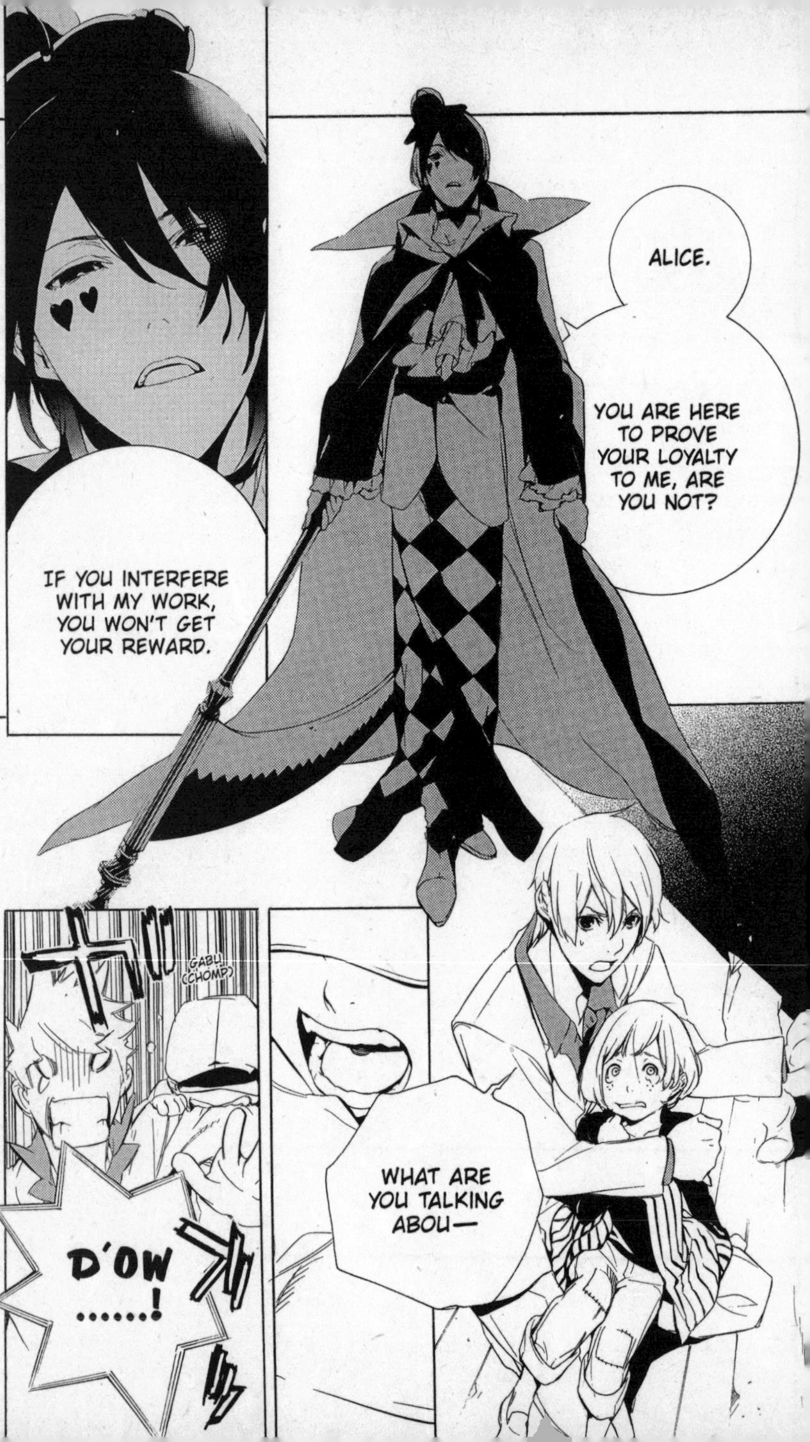
ALICE.
YOU ARE HERE TO PROVE YOUR LOYALTY TO ME, ARE YOU NOT?
IF YOU INTERFERE WITH MY WORK, YOU WON'T GET YOUR REWARD.
WHAT ARE YOU TALKING ABOU—
GABU (CHOMP)
D'OW ......!

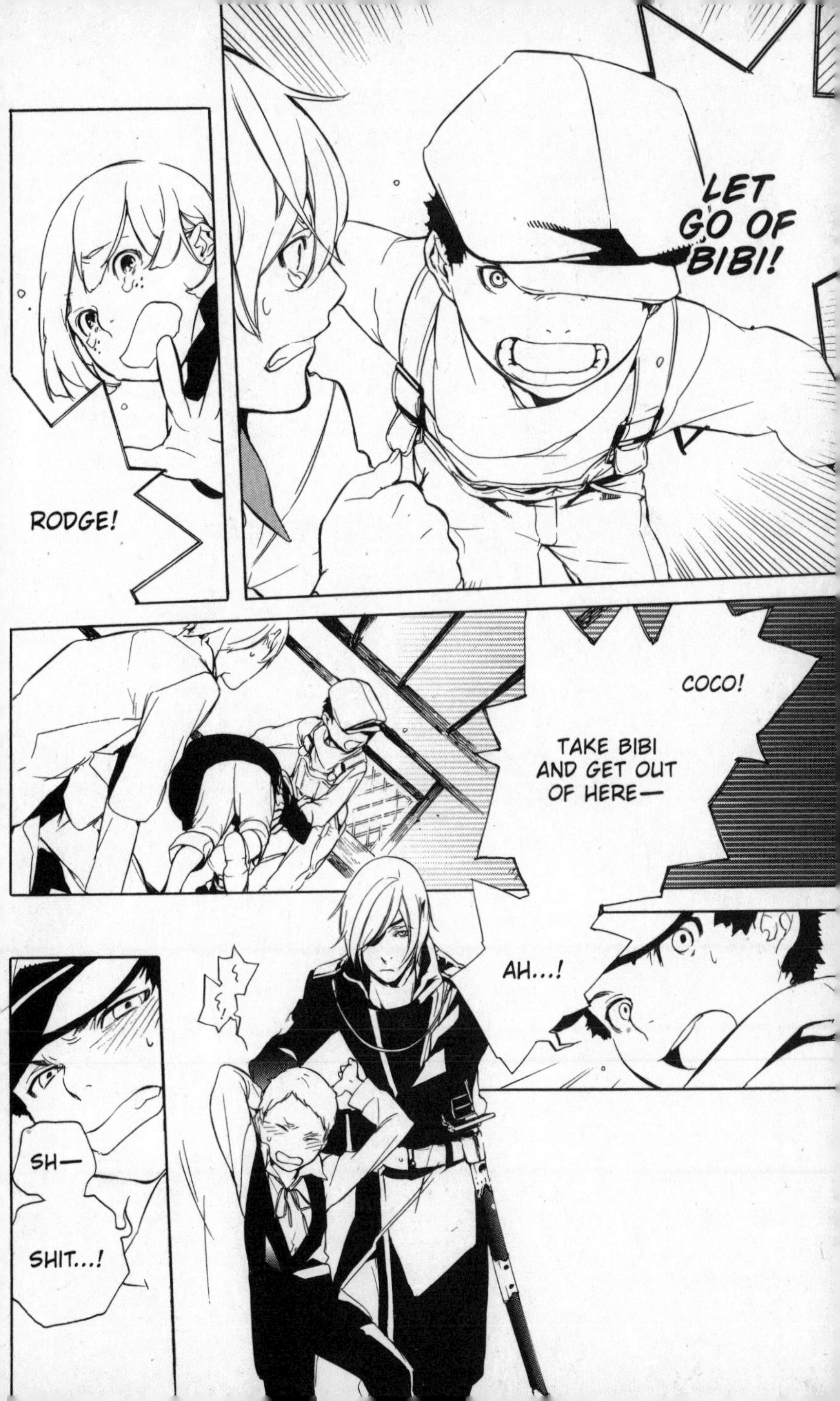
LET GO OF BIBI!
RODGE!
COCO!
TAKE BIBI AND GET OUT OF HERE—
AH...!
SH—
SHIT...!

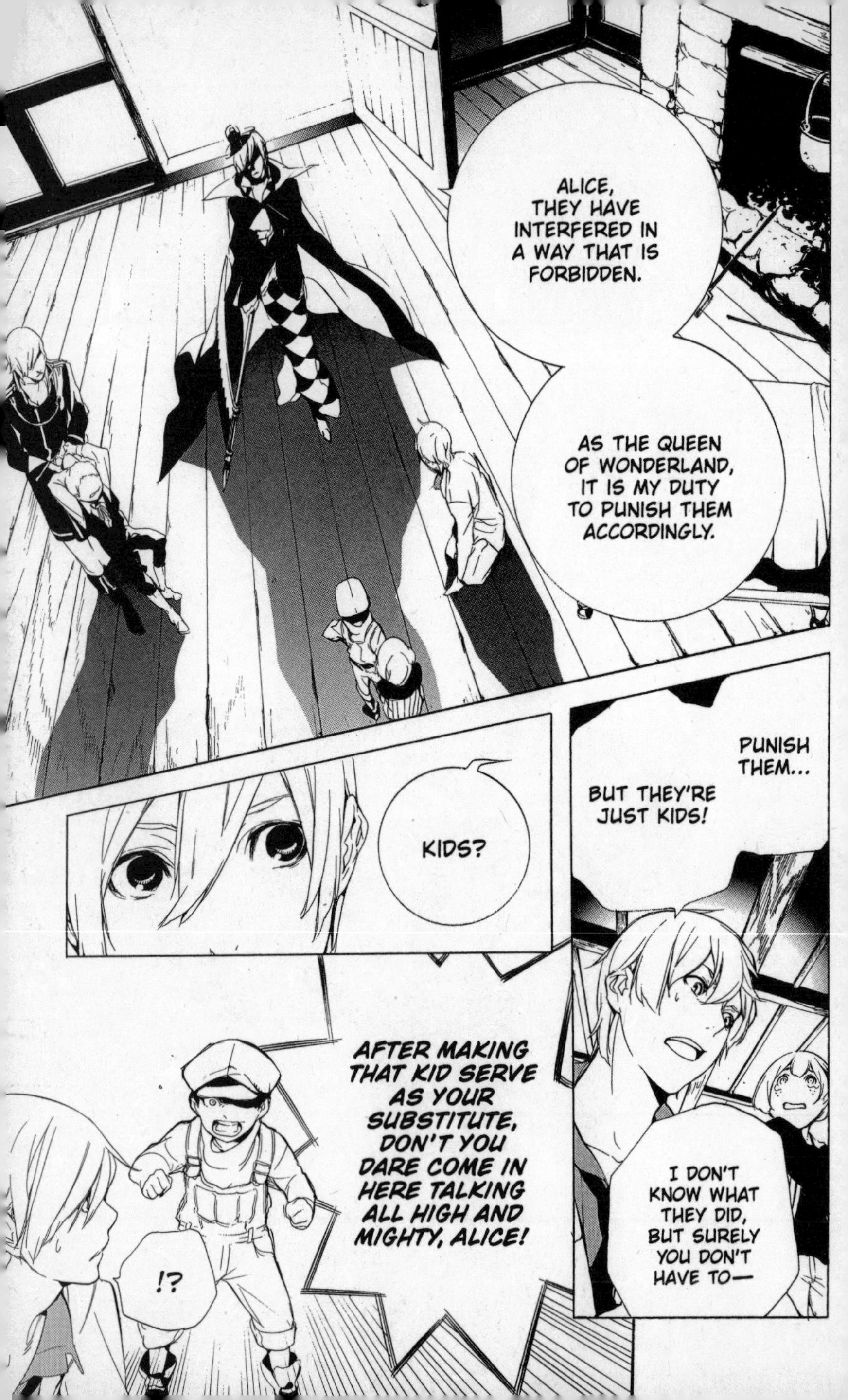
ALICE, THEY HAVE INTERFERED IN A WAY THAT IS FORBIDDEN.
AS THE QUEEN OF WONDERLAND, IT IS MY DUTY TO PUNISH THEM ACCORDINGLY.
PUNISH THEM...
BUT THEY'RE JUST KIDS!
I DON'T KNOW WHAT THEY DID, BUT SURELY YOU DON'T HAVE TO—
KIDS?
AFTER MAKING THAT KID SERVE AS YOUR SUBSTITUTE, DON'T YOU DARE COME IN HERE TALKING ALL HIGH AND MIGHTY, ALICE!
!?

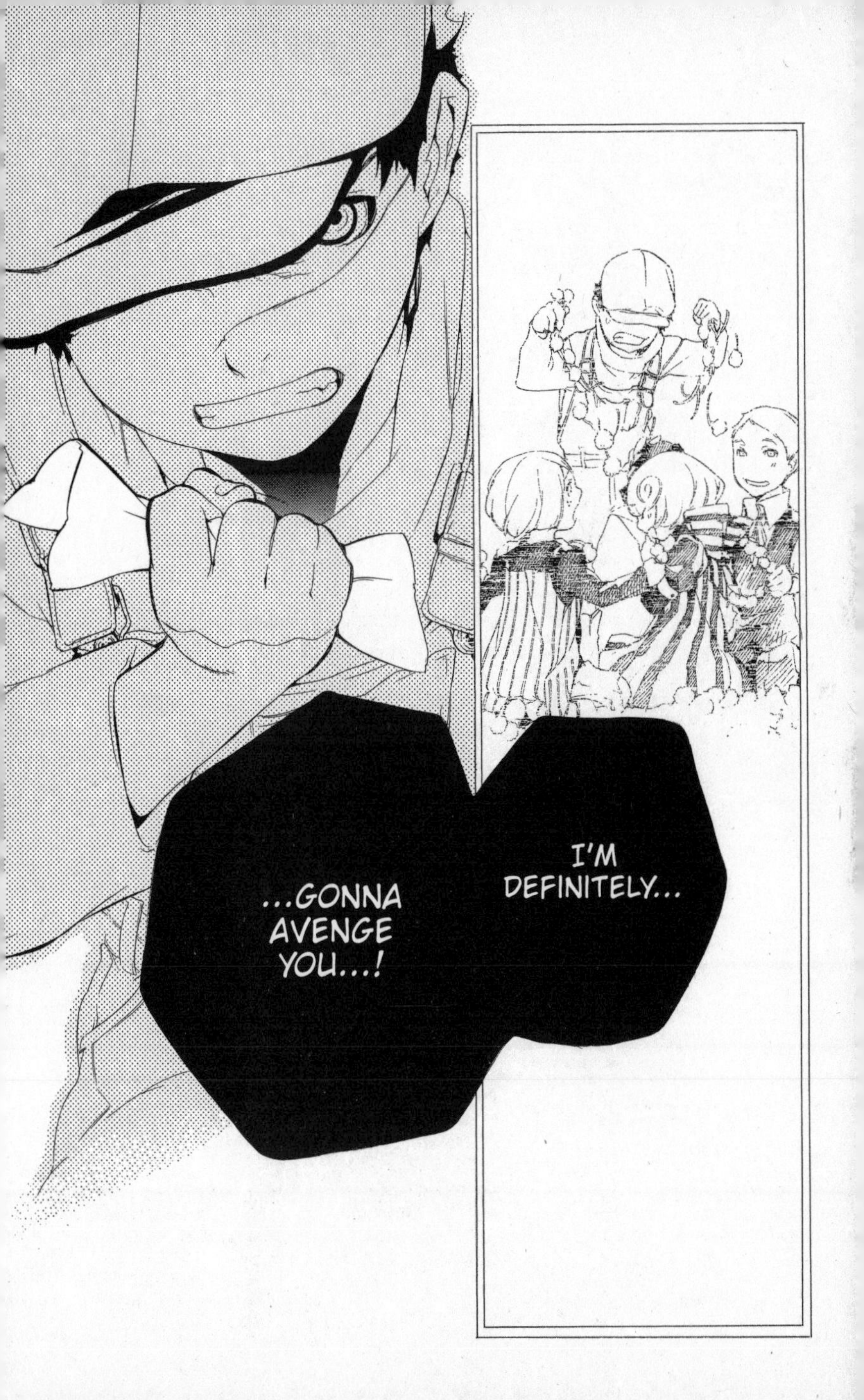
I'M DEFINITELY...
...GONNA AVENGE YOU...!

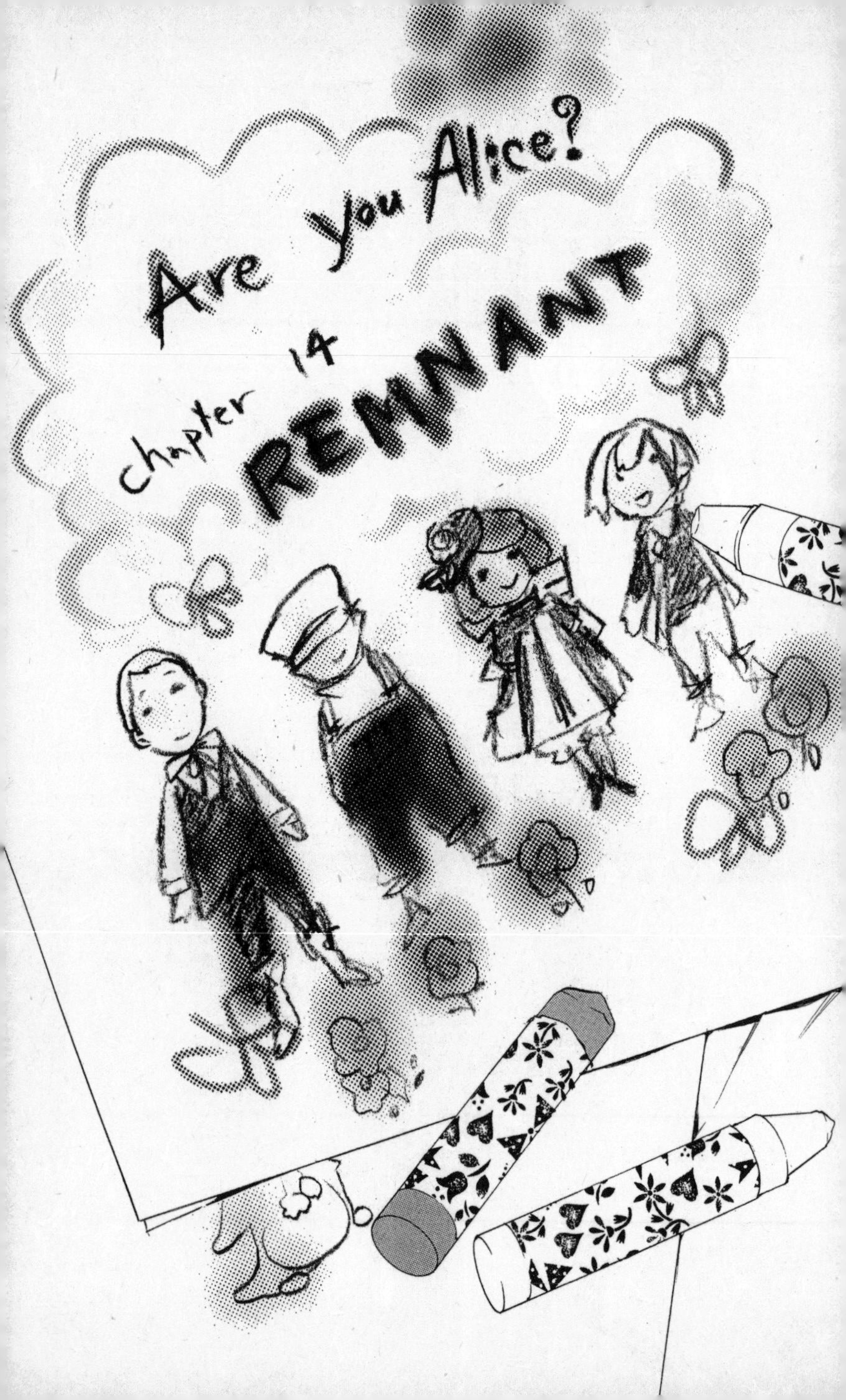
Are you Alice?
chapter 14
REMNANT

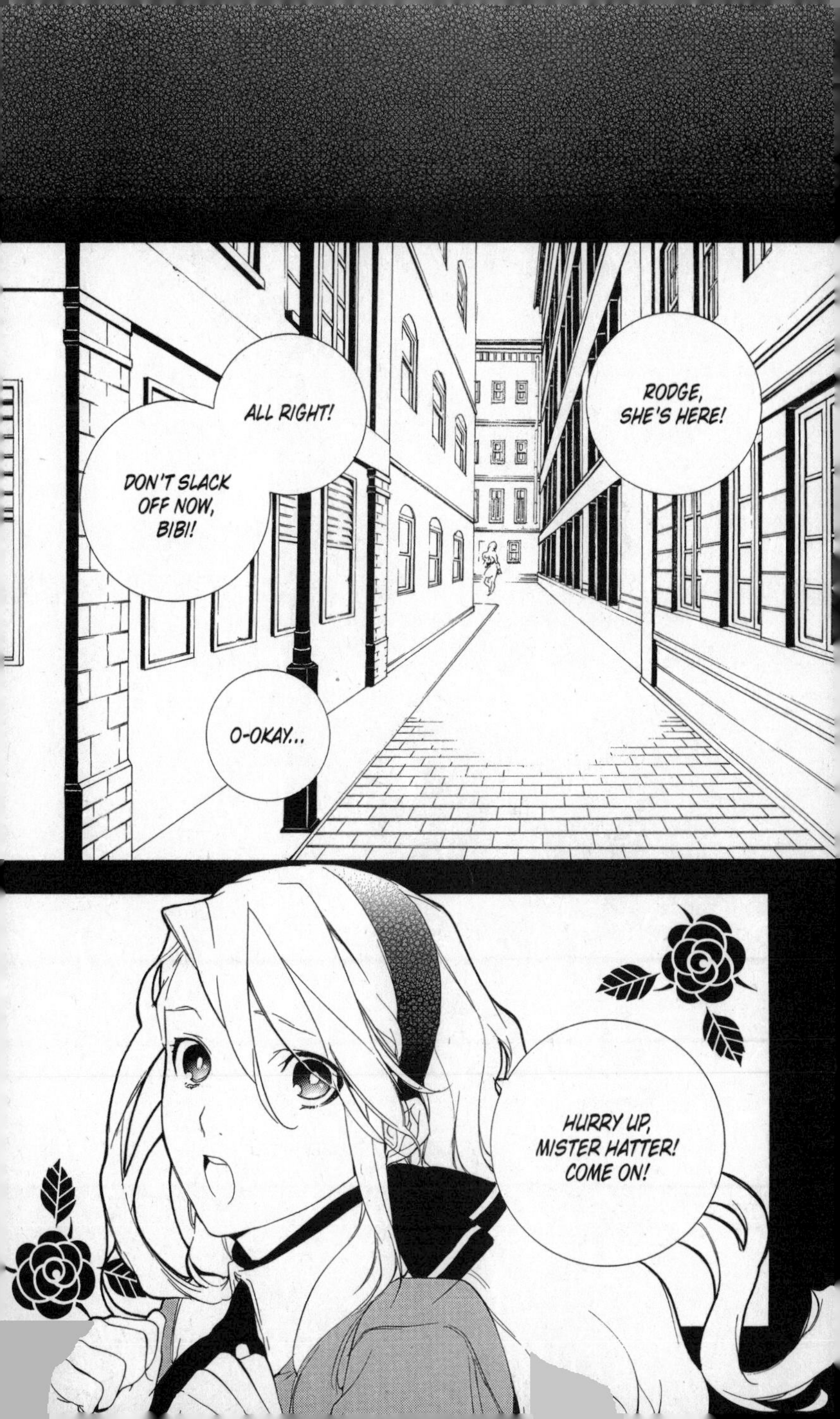
RODGE, SHE'S HERE!
ALL RIGHT!
DON'T SLACK OFF NOW, BIBI!
O-OKAY...
HURRY UP, MISTER HATTER! COME ON!

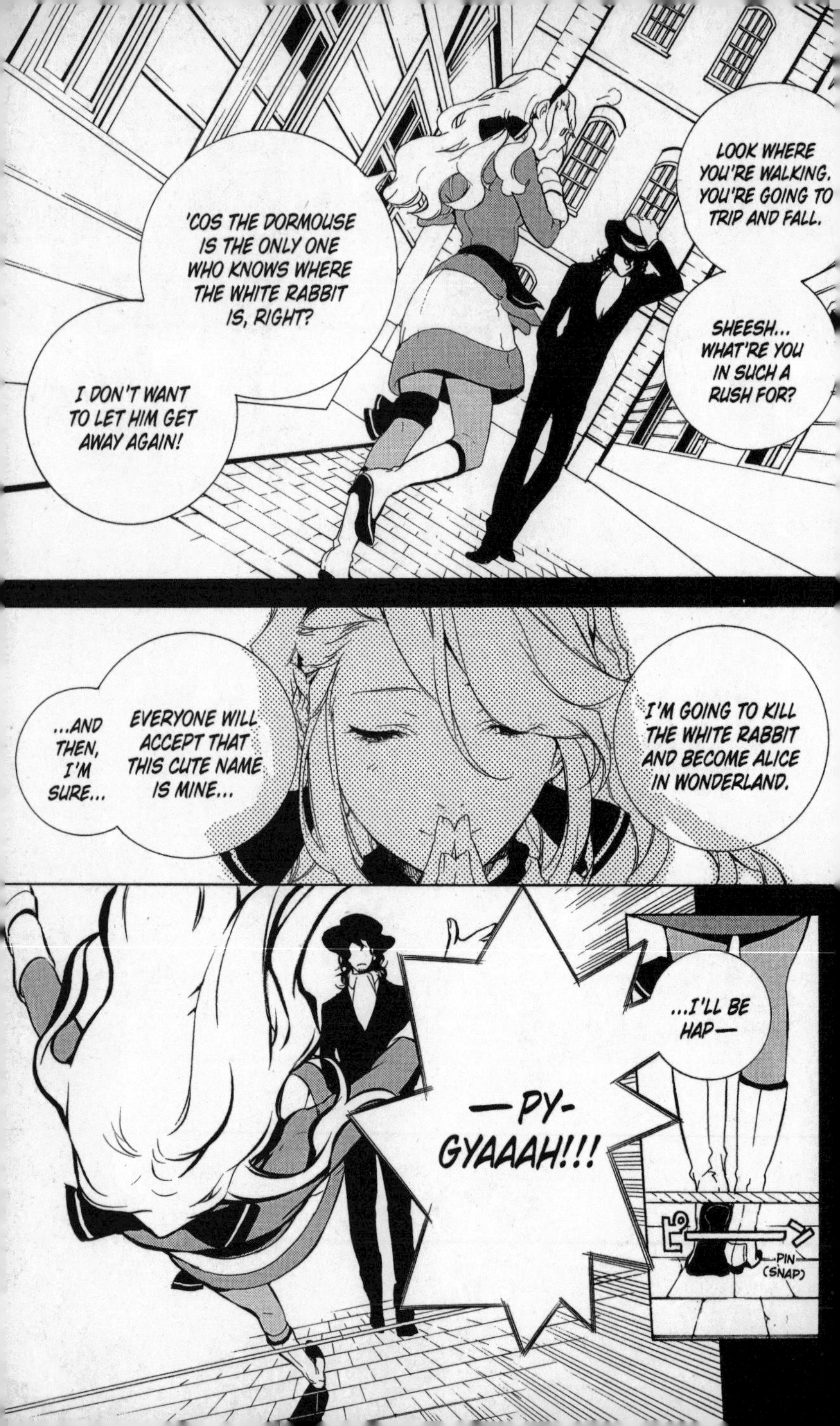
LOOK WHERE YOU'RE WALKING. YOU'RE GOING TO TRIP AND FALL.
SHEESH... WHAT'RE YOU IN SUCH A RUSH FOR?
'COS THE DORMOUSE IS THE ONLY ONE WHO KNOWS WHERE THE WHITE RABBIT IS, RIGHT?
I DON'T WANT TO LET HIM GET AWAY AGAIN!
I'M GOING TO KILL THE WHITE RABBIT AND BECOME ALICE IN WONDERLAND.
EVERYONE WILL ACCEPT THAT THIS CUTE NAME IS MINE...
...AND THEN, I'M SURE...
...I'LL BE HAP—
PIN (SNAP)
—PY-GYAAAH!!!

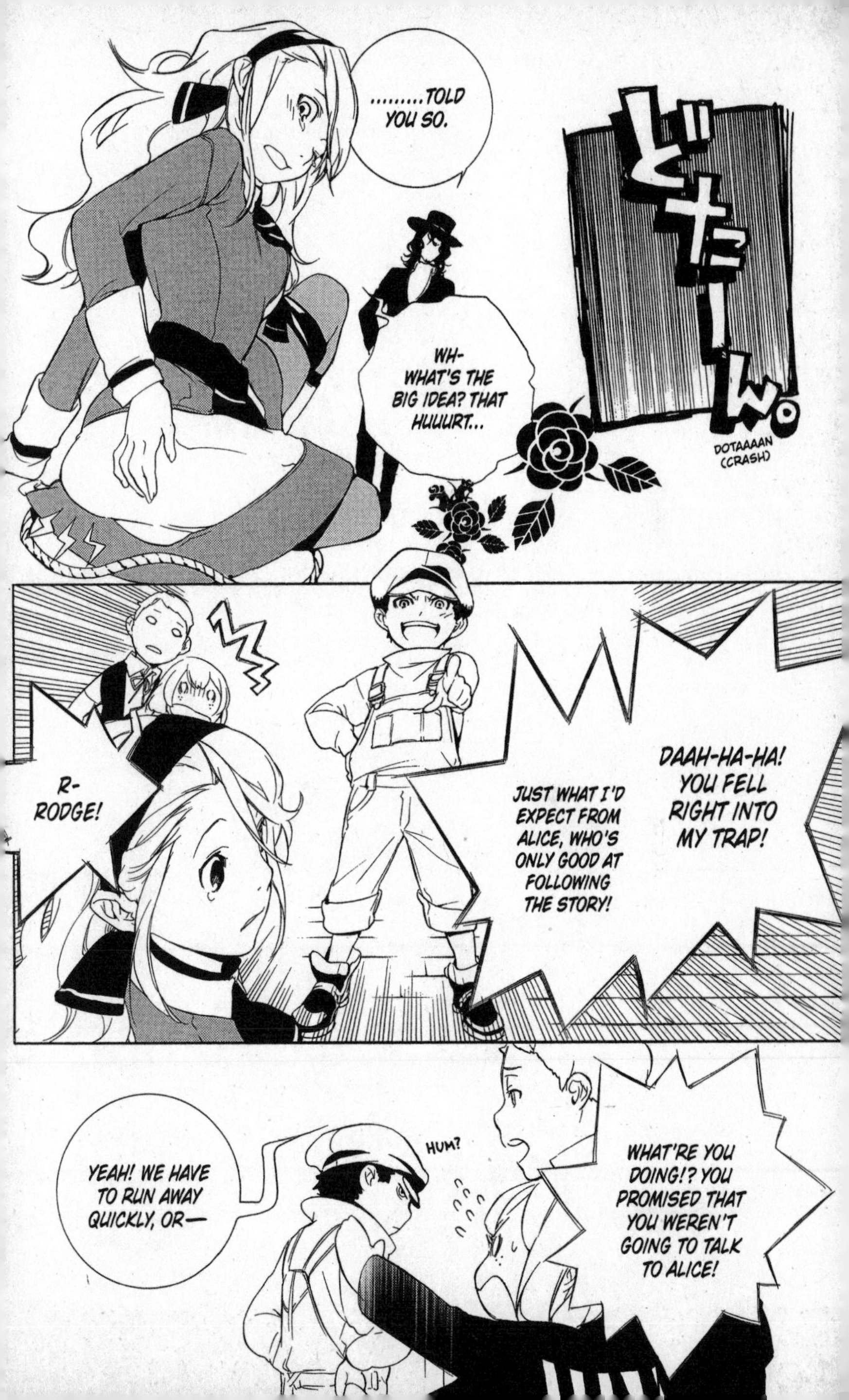
どたーん。
DOTAAAAN (CRASH)
.........TOLD YOU SO.
WH- WHAT'S THE BIG IDEA? THAT HUUURT...
DAAH-HA-HA! YOU FELL RIGHT INTO MY TRAP!
JUST WHAT I'D EXPECT FROM ALICE, WHO'S ONLY GOOD AT FOLLOWING THE STORY!
R- RODGE!
WHAT'RE YOU DOING!? YOU PROMISED THAT YOU WEREN'T GOING TO TALK TO ALICE!
HUM?
YEAH! WE HAVE TO RUN AWAY QUICKLY, OR—

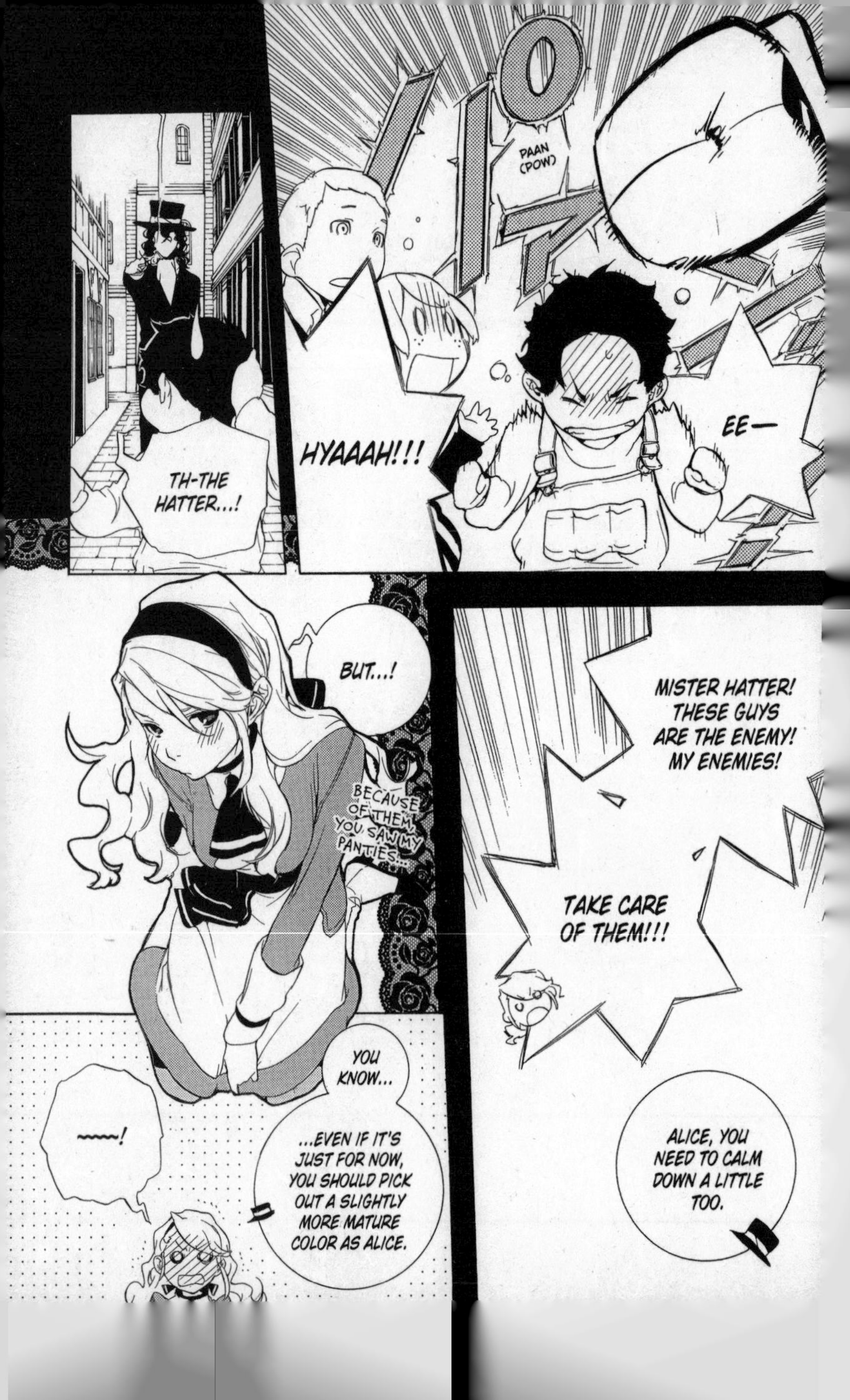
PAAN (POW)
EE—
HYAAAH!!!
TH-THE HATTER...!
MISTER HATTER! THESE GUYS ARE THE ENEMY! MY ENEMIES!
TAKE CARE OF THEM!!!
ALICE, YOU NEED TO CALM DOWN A LITTLE TOO.
BUT...!
BECAUSE OF THEM, YOU SAW MY PANTIES...
YOU KNOW...
...EVEN IF IT'S JUST FOR NOW, YOU SHOULD PICK OUT A SLIGHTLY MORE MATURE COLOR AS ALICE.
~~~!
~~~

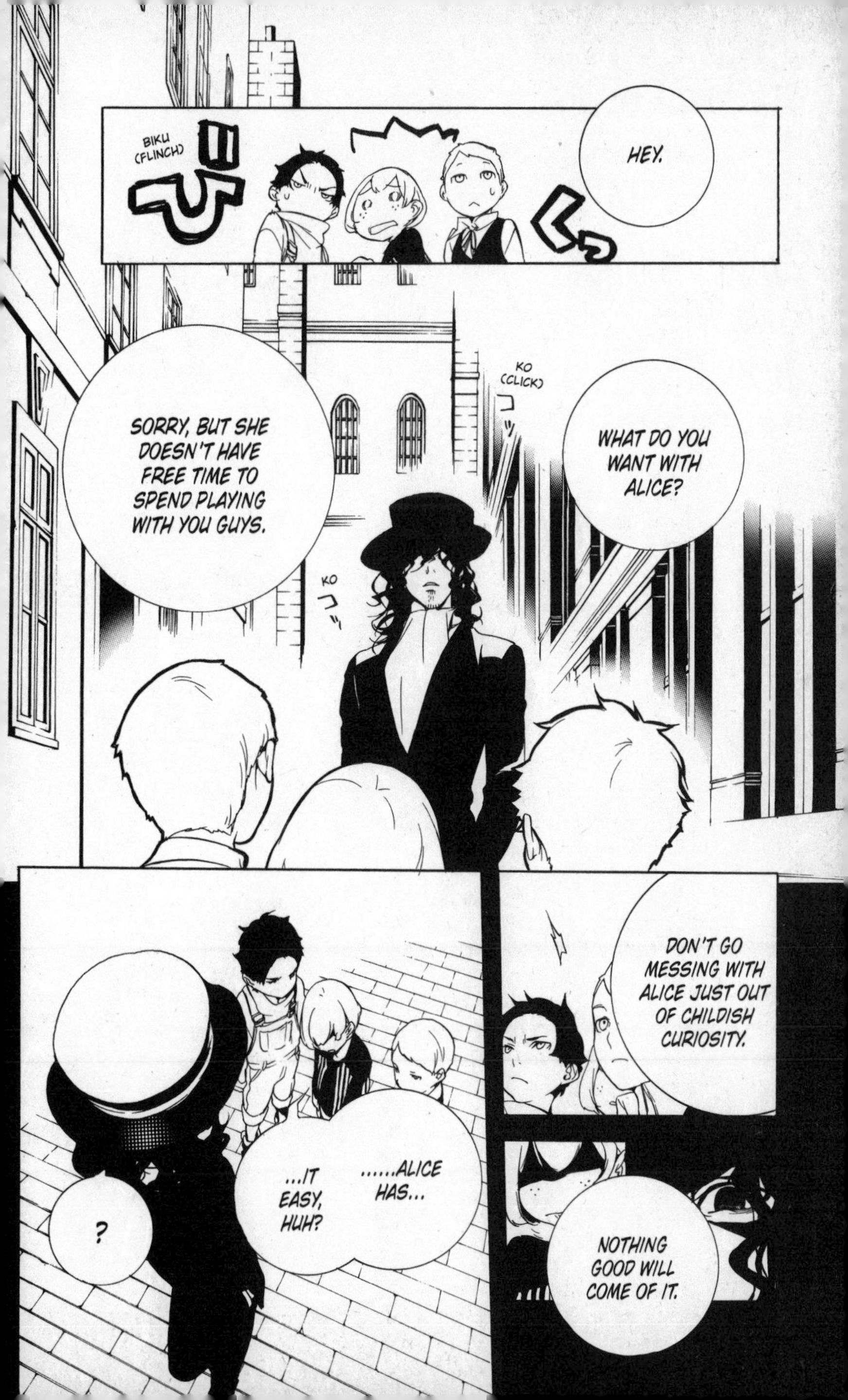
HEY.
BIKU (FLINCH)
KO (CLICK)
WHAT DO YOU WANT WITH ALICE?
KO
SORRY, BUT SHE DOESN'T HAVE FREE TIME TO SPEND PLAYING WITH YOU GUYS.
DON'T GO MESSING WITH ALICE JUST OUT OF CHILDISH CURIOSITY.
NOTHING GOOD WILL COME OF IT.
......ALICE HAS...
...IT EASY, HUH?
?

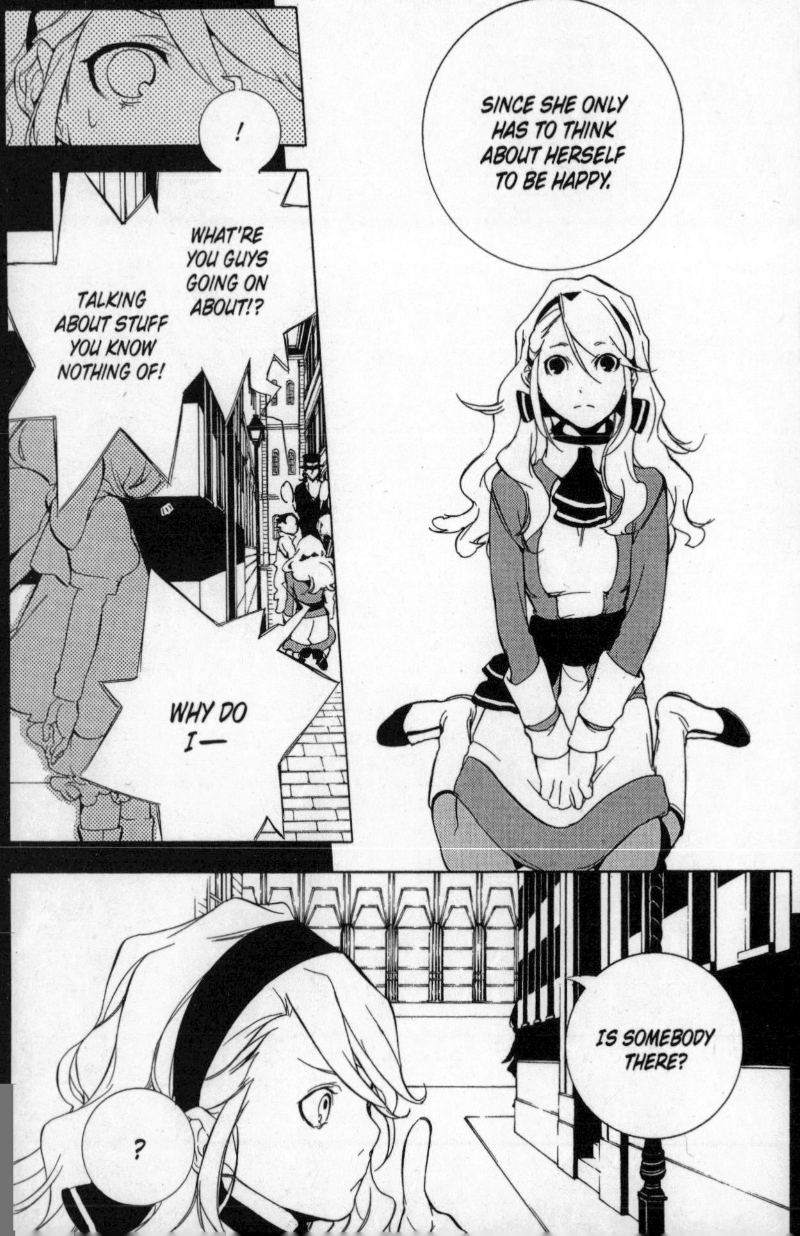
SINCE SHE ONLY HAS TO THINK ABOUT HERSELF TO BE HAPPY.
!
WHAT'RE YOU GUYS GOING ON ABOUT!?
TALKING ABOUT STUFF YOU KNOW NOTHING OF!
WHY DO I—
IS SOMEBODY THERE?
?

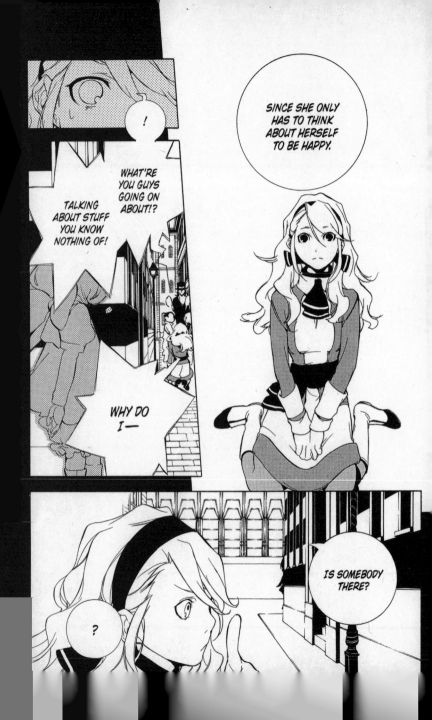

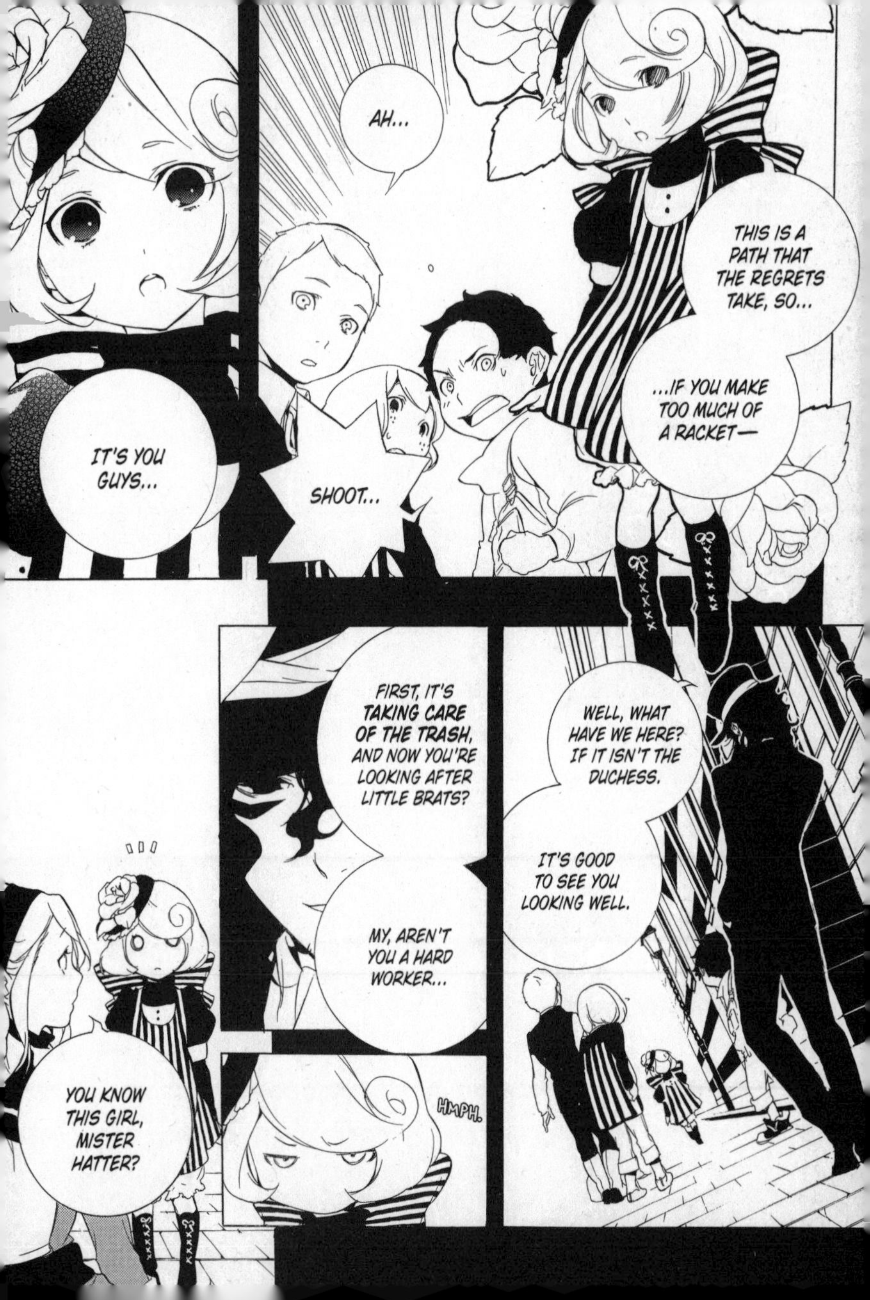
THIS IS A PATH THAT THE REGRETS TAKE, SO...
...IF YOU MAKE TOO MUCH OF A RACKET—
AH...
SHOOT...
IT'S YOU GUYS...
WELL, WHAT HAVE WE HERE? IF IT ISN'T THE DUCHESS.
IT'S GOOD TO SEE YOU LOOKING WELL.
FIRST, IT'S **TAKING CARE OF THE TRASH**, AND NOW YOU'RE LOOKING AFTER LITTLE BRATS?
MY, AREN'T YOU A HARD WORKER...
HMPH.
YOU KNOW THIS GIRL, MISTER HATTER?

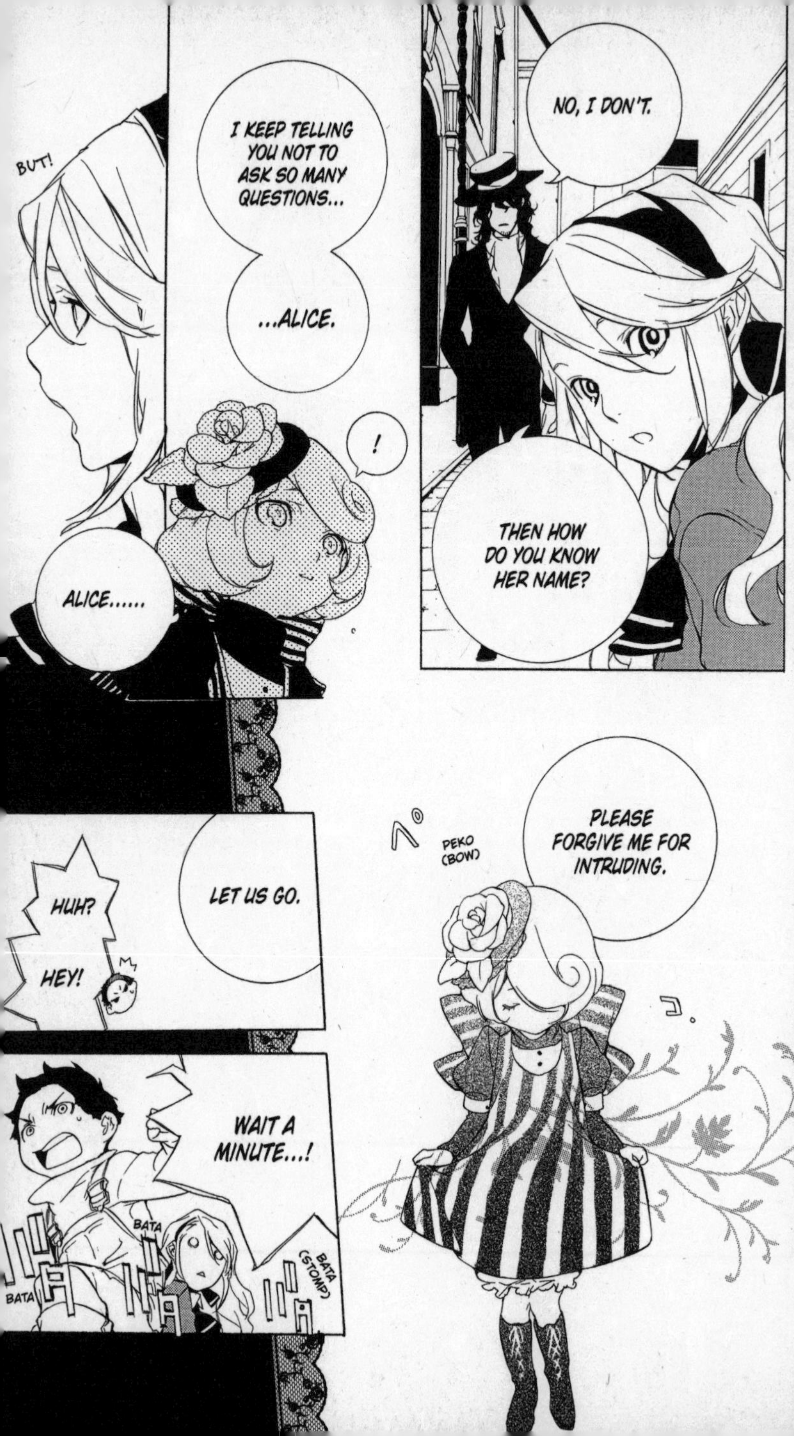
NO, I DON'T.
THEN HOW DO YOU KNOW HER NAME?
I KEEP TELLING YOU NOT TO ASK SO MANY QUESTIONS...
...ALICE.
!
BUT!
ALICE......
PLEASE FORGIVE ME FOR INTRUDING.
PEKO (BOW)
LET US GO.
HUH?
HEY!
WAIT A MINUTE...!
BATA (STOMP)
BATA
BATA

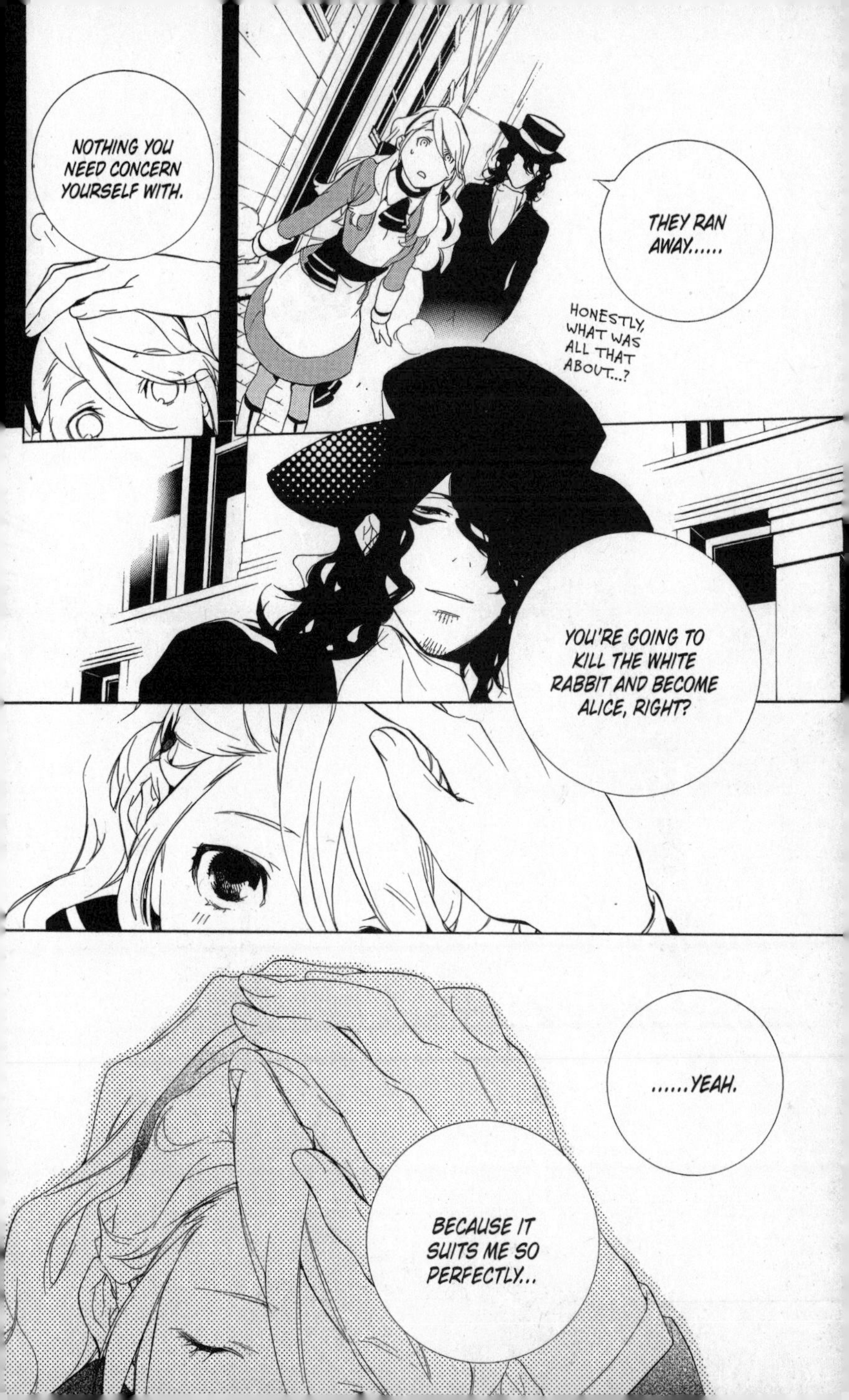
THEY RAN AWAY......
HONESTLY, WHAT WAS ALL THAT ABOUT...?
NOTHING YOU NEED CONCERN YOURSELF WITH.
YOU'RE GOING TO KILL THE WHITE RABBIT AND BECOME ALICE, RIGHT?
......YEAH.
BECAUSE IT SUITS ME SO PERFECTLY...

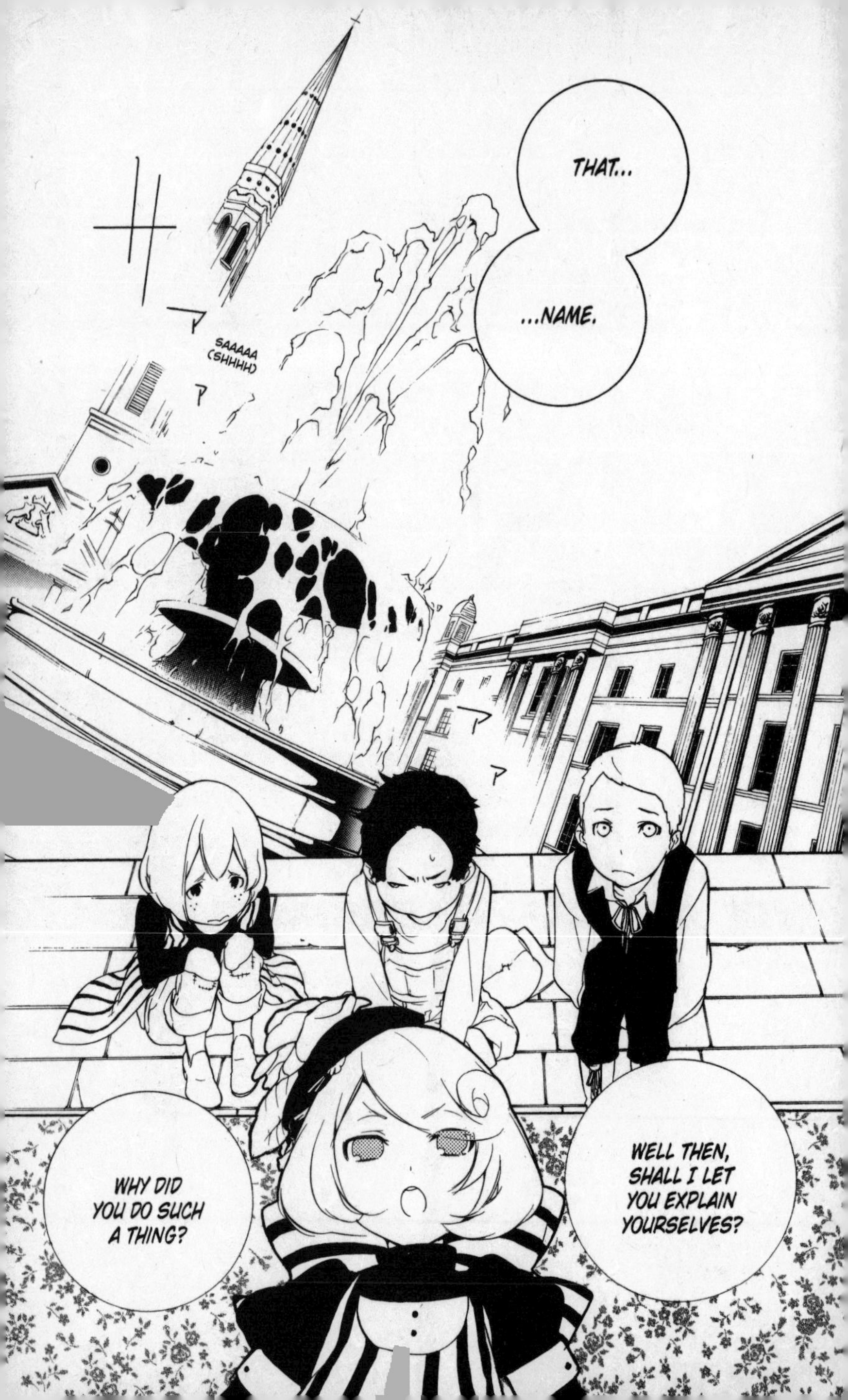
THAT...
...NAME.
SAAAAA (SHHHH)
WELL THEN, SHALL I LET YOU EXPLAIN YOURSELVES?
WHY DID YOU DO SUCH A THING?

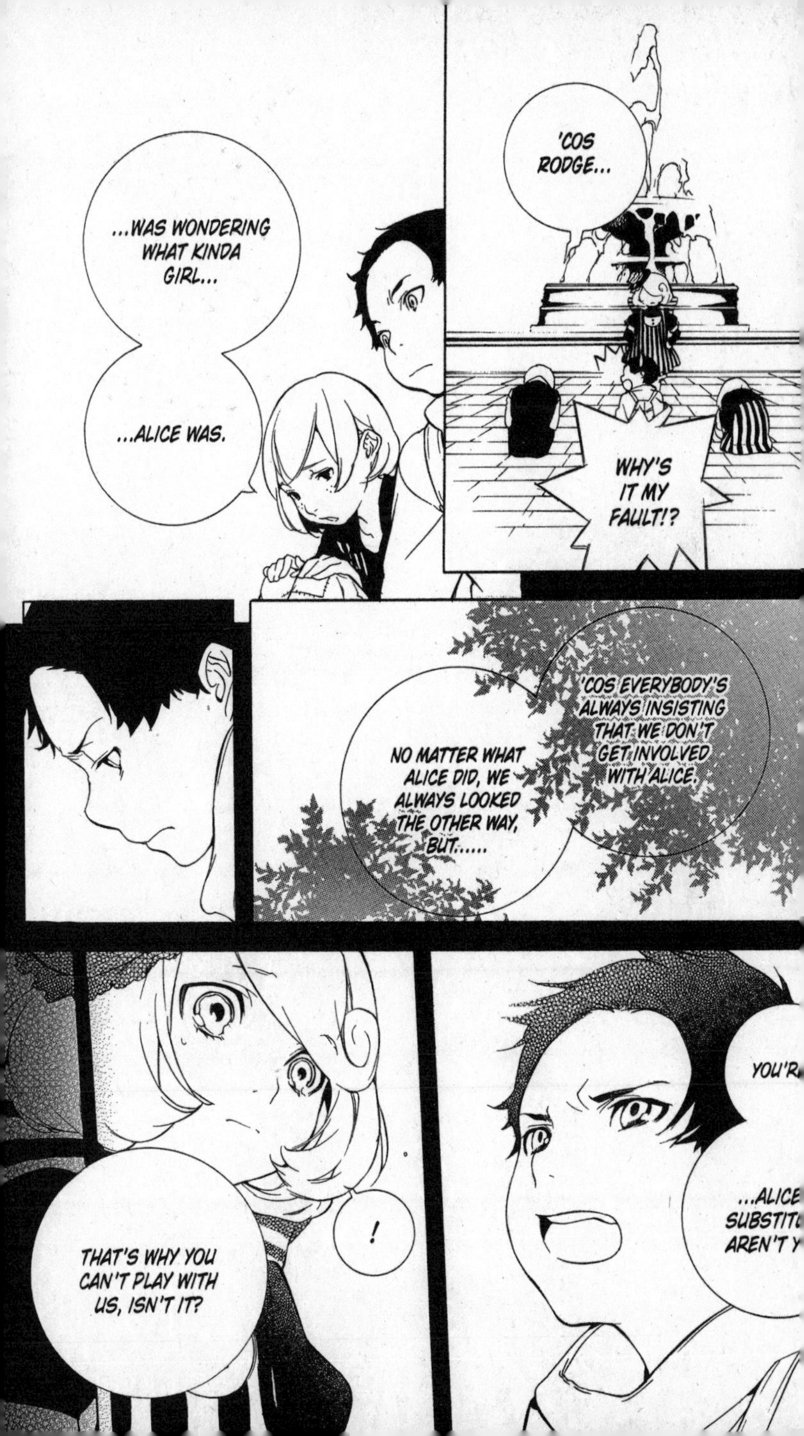
'COS RODGE...
WHY'S IT MY FAULT!?
...WAS WONDERING WHAT KINDA GIRL...
...ALICE WAS.
'COS EVERYBODY'S ALWAYS INSISTING THAT WE DON'T GET INVOLVED WITH ALICE.
NO MATTER WHAT ALICE DID, WE ALWAYS LOOKED THE OTHER WAY, BUT......
YOU'R
...ALICE SUBSTIT AREN'T Y
!
THAT'S WHY YOU CAN'T PLAY WITH US, ISN'T IT?

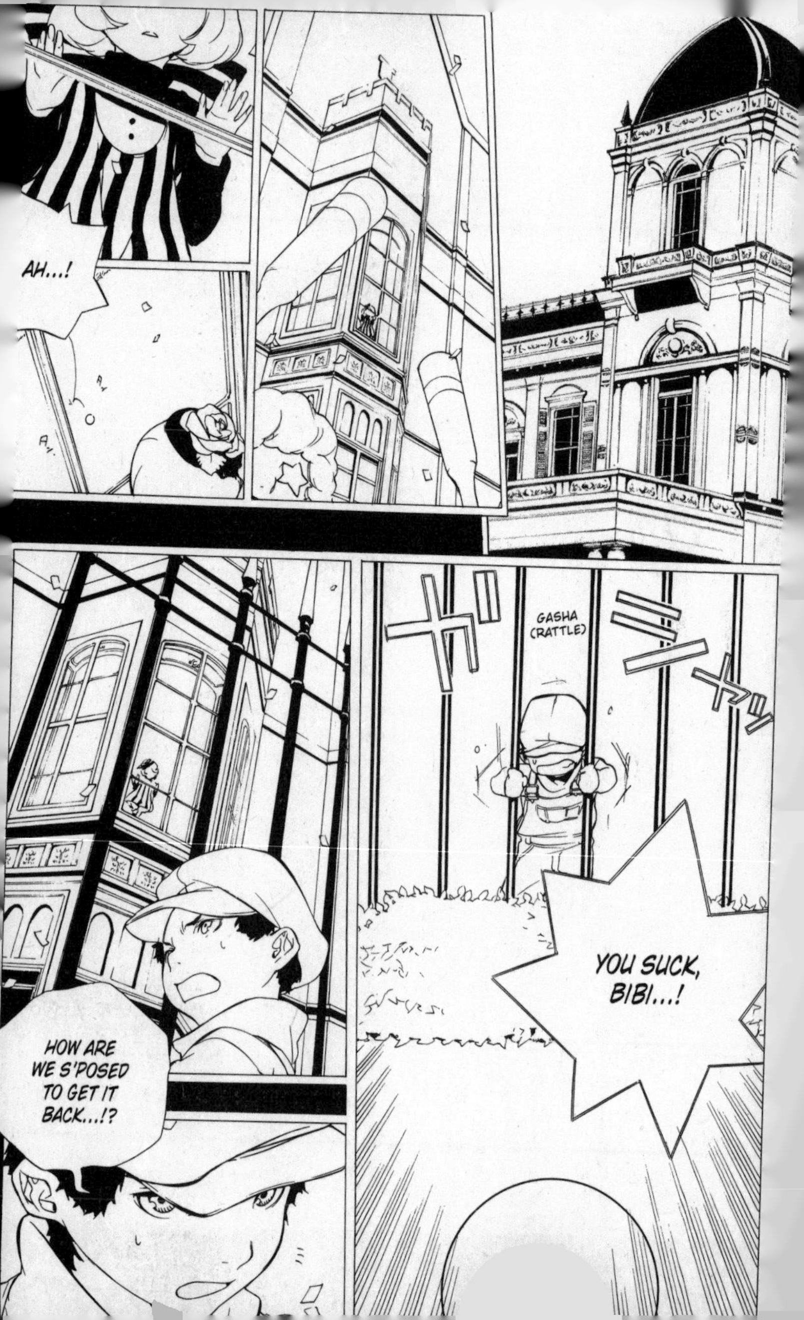
AH...!
GASHA (RATTLE)
YOU SUCK, BIBI...!
HOW ARE WE S'POSED TO GET IT BACK...!?

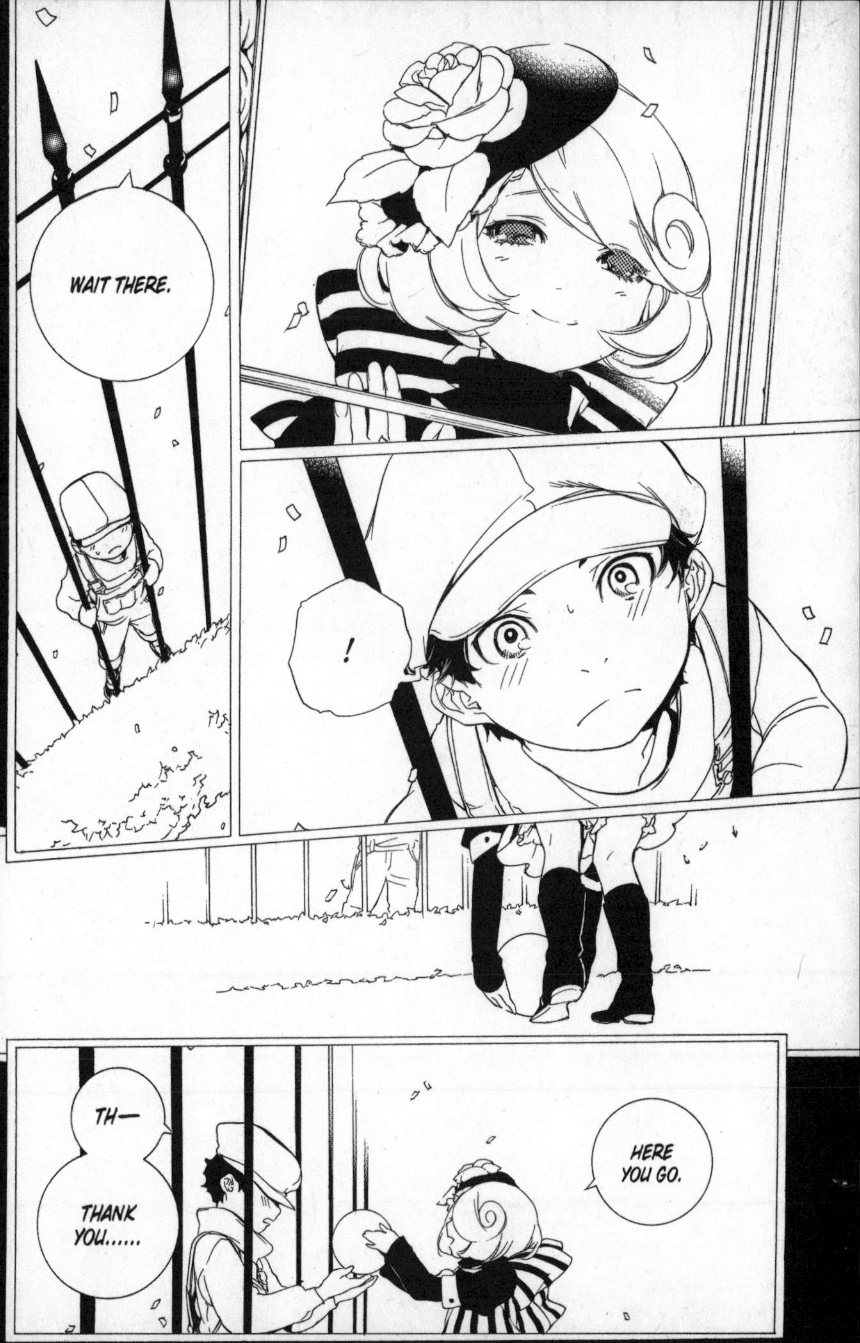
!
WAIT THERE.
HERE YOU GO.
TH—
THANK YOU......

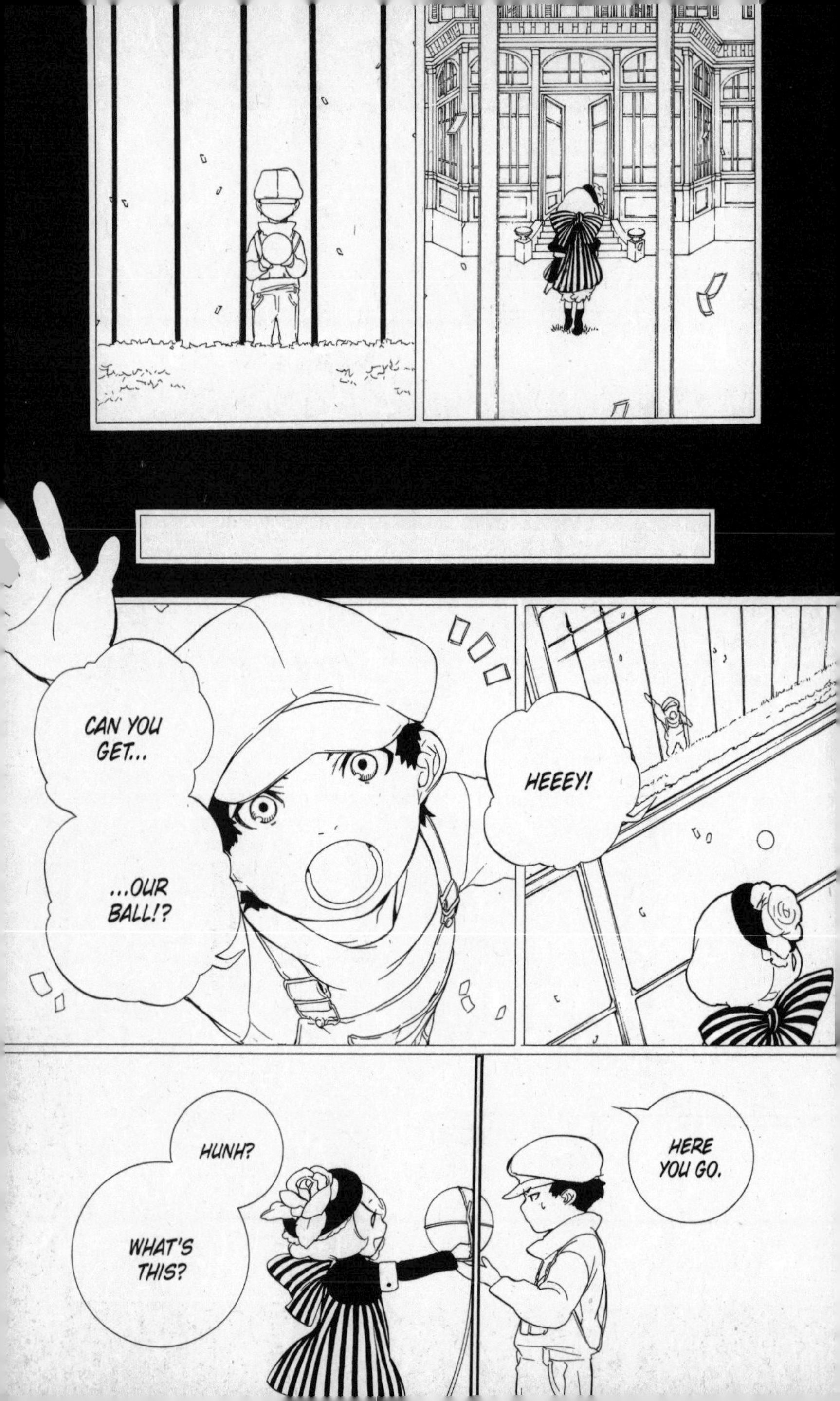
HEEEY!
CAN YOU GET... ...OUR BALL!?
HERE YOU GO.
HUNH? WHAT'S THIS?

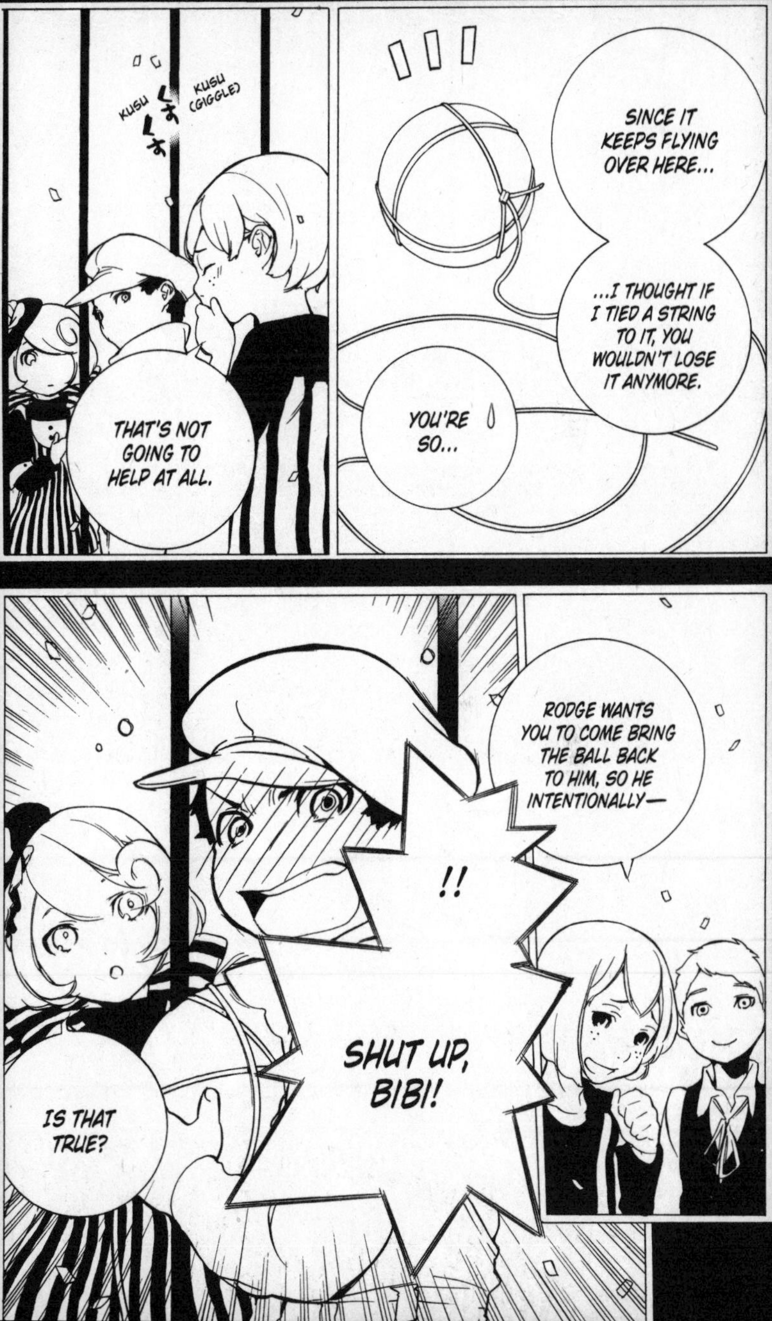
SINCE IT KEEPS FLYING OVER HERE...
...I THOUGHT IF I TIED A STRING TO IT, YOU WOULDN'T LOSE IT ANYMORE.
YOU'RE SO...
KUSU くす くす KUSU (GIGGLE)
THAT'S NOT GOING TO HELP AT ALL.
RODGE WANTS YOU TO COME BRING THE BALL BACK TO HIM, SO HE INTENTIONALLY—
!!
SHUT UP, BIBI!
IS THAT TRUE?

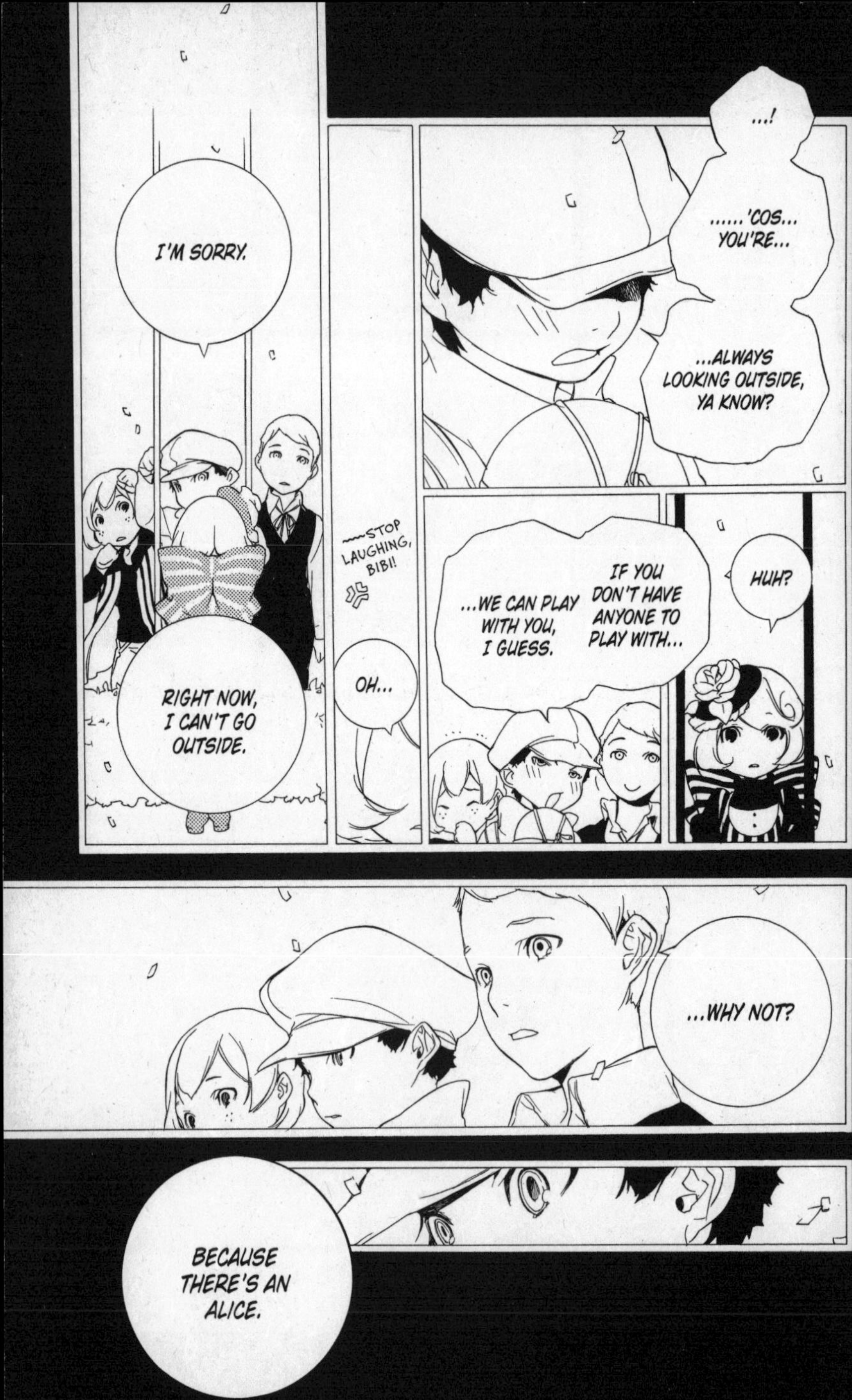
...!
......'COS... YOU'RE...
...ALWAYS LOOKING OUTSIDE, YA KNOW?
HUH?
IF YOU DON'T HAVE ANYONE TO PLAY WITH...
...WE CAN PLAY WITH YOU, I GUESS.
STOP LAUGHING, BIBI!
OH...
I'M SORRY.
RIGHT NOW, I CAN'T GO OUTSIDE.
...WHY NOT?
BECAUSE THERE'S AN ALICE.

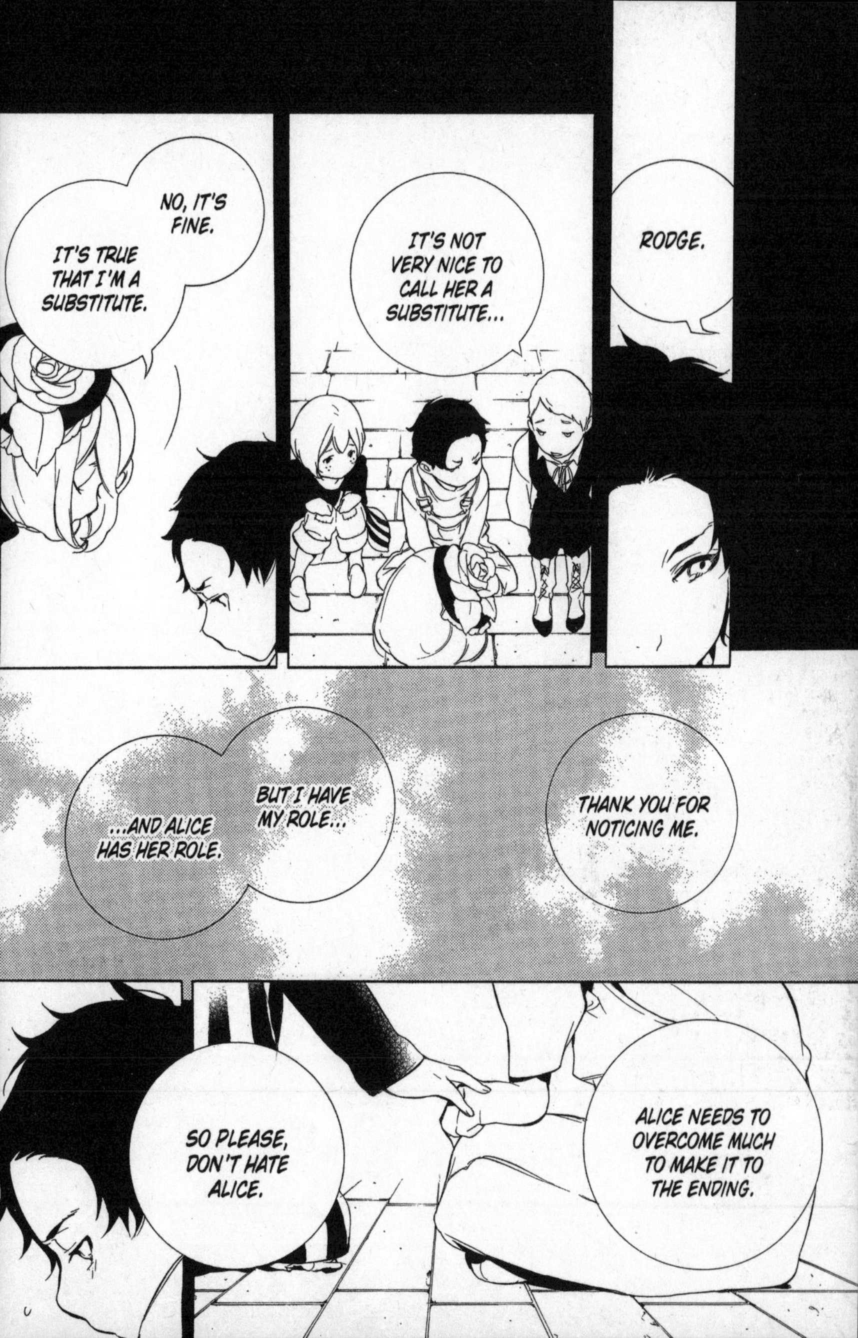
RODGE.
IT'S NOT VERY NICE TO CALL HER A SUBSTITUTE...
NO, IT'S FINE.
IT'S TRUE THAT I'M A SUBSTITUTE.
THANK YOU FOR NOTICING ME.
BUT I HAVE MY ROLE...
...AND ALICE HAS HER ROLE.
ALICE NEEDS TO OVERCOME MUCH TO MAKE IT TO THE ENDING.
SO PLEASE, DON'T HATE ALICE.

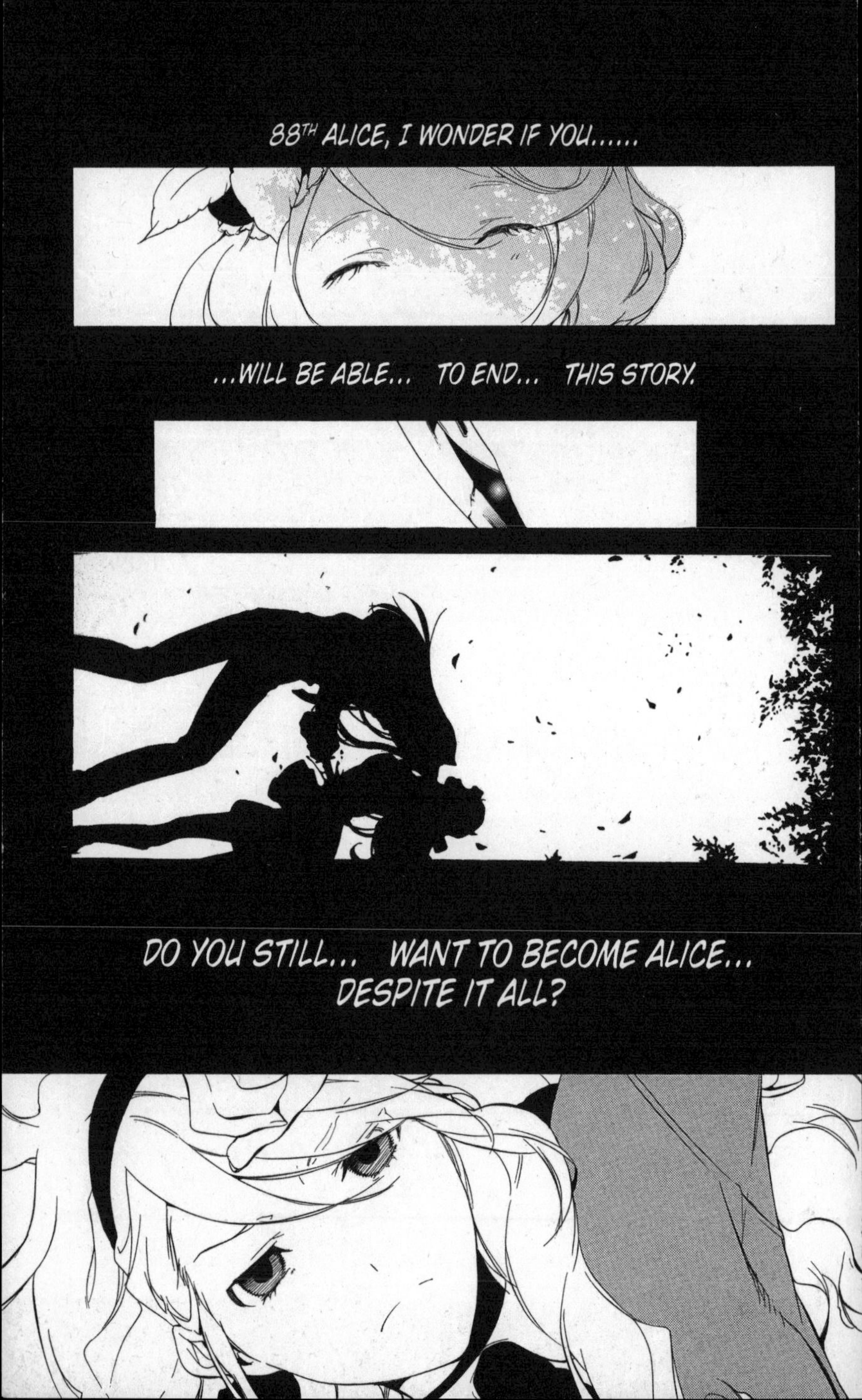
88TH ALICE, I WONDER IF YOU......
...WILL BE ABLE... TO END... THIS STORY.
DO YOU STILL... WANT TO BECOME ALICE... DESPITE IT ALL?

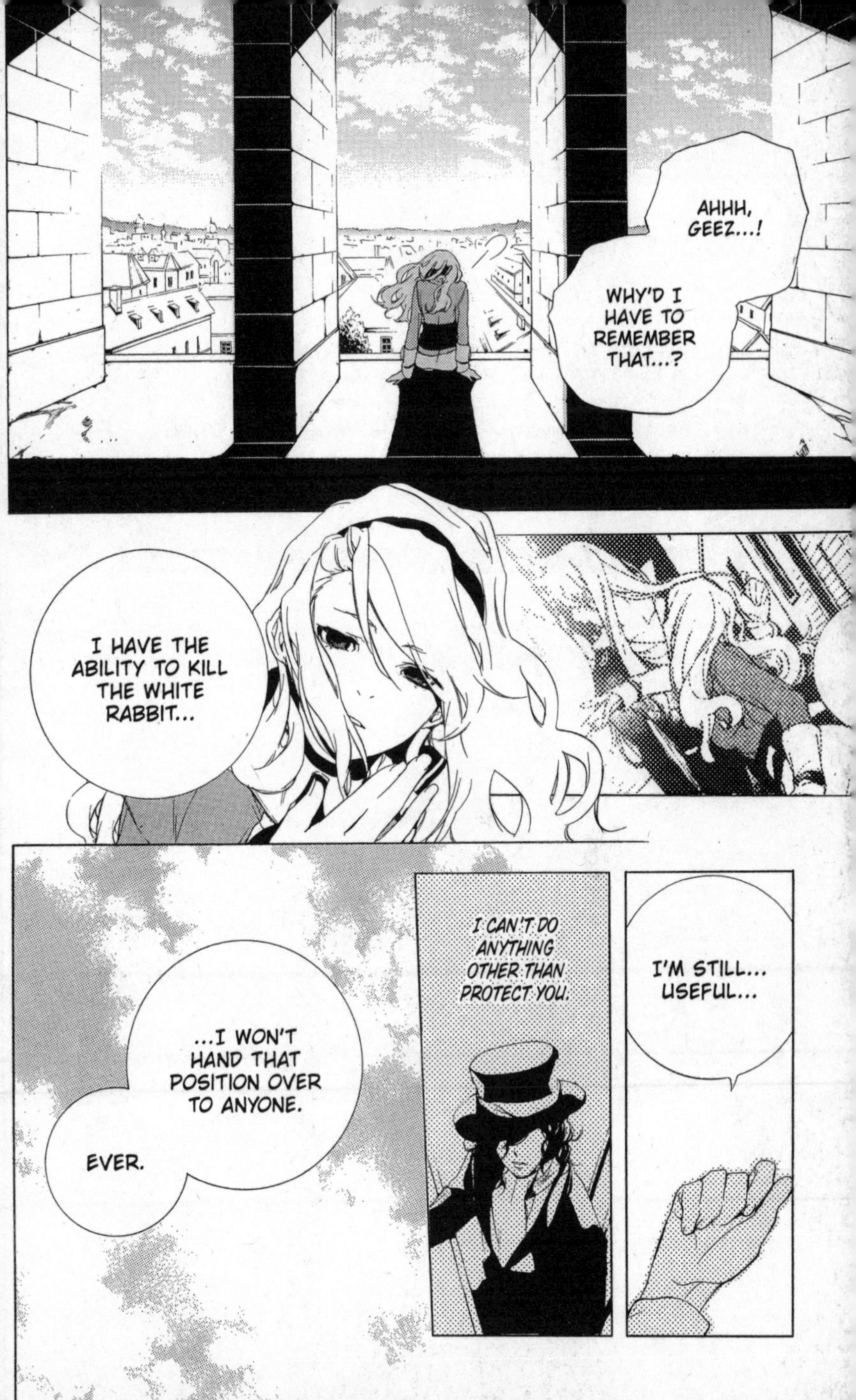
AHHH, GEEZ...!
WHY'D I HAVE TO REMEMBER THAT...?
I HAVE THE ABILITY TO KILL THE WHITE RABBIT...
I'M STILL... USEFUL...
I CAN'T DO ANYTHING OTHER THAN PROTECT YOU.
...I WON'T HAND THAT POSITION OVER TO ANYONE.
EVER.

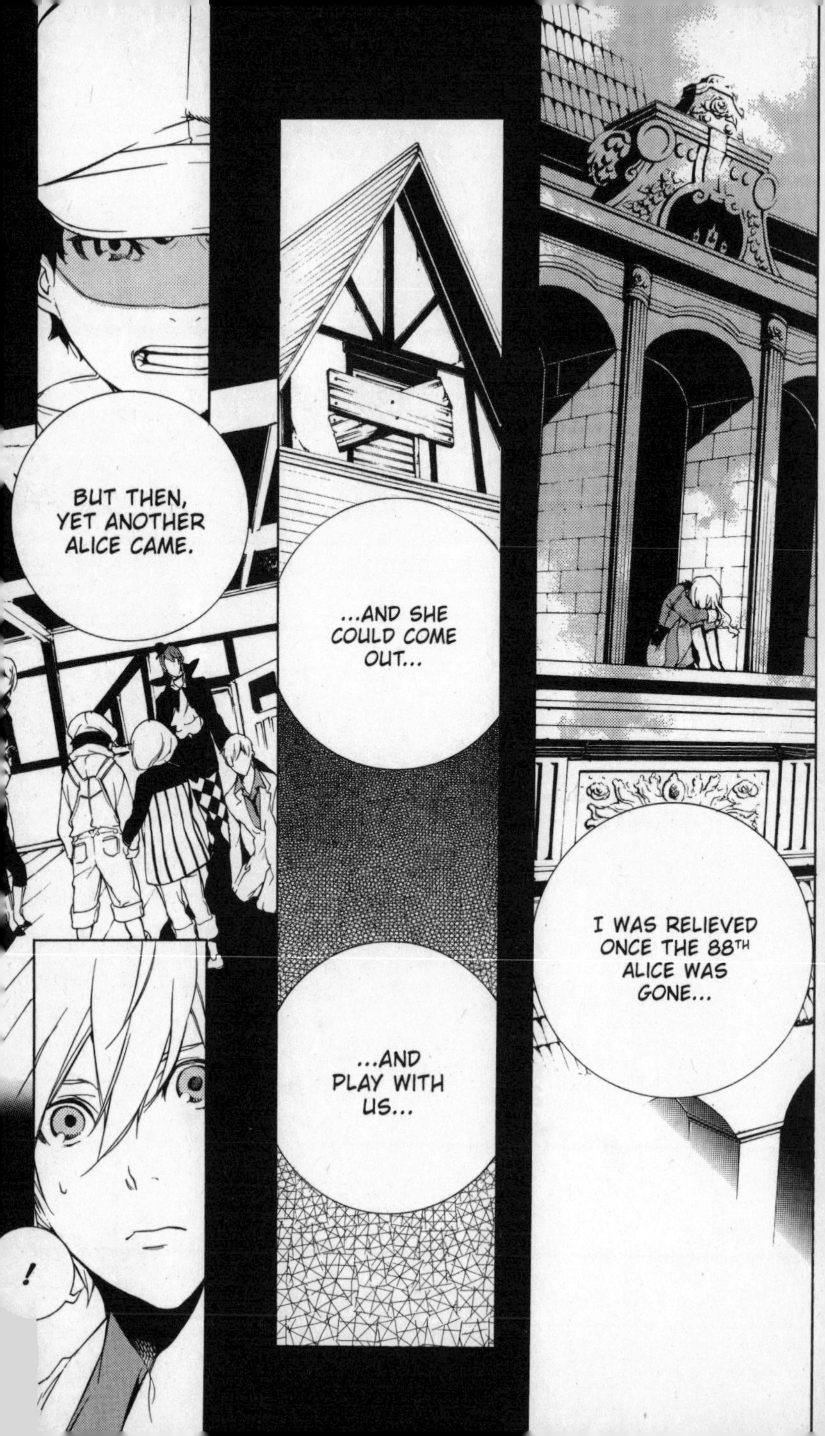
I WAS RELIEVED ONCE THE 88TH ALICE WAS GONE...
...AND SHE COULD COME OUT...
...AND PLAY WITH US...
BUT THEN, YET ANOTHER ALICE CAME.
!

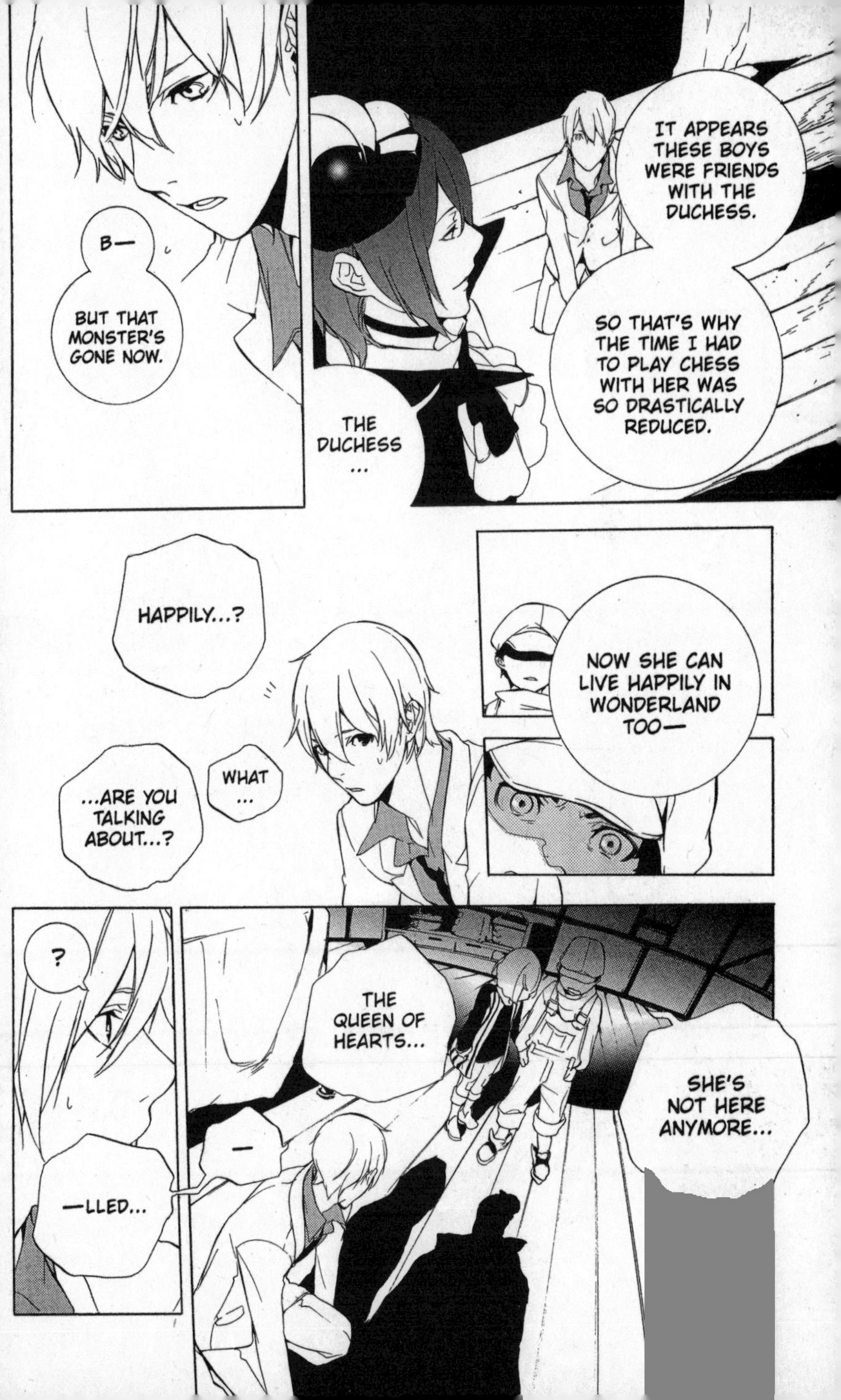
IT APPEARS THESE BOYS WERE FRIENDS WITH THE DUCHESS.
SO THAT'S WHY THE TIME I HAD TO PLAY CHESS WITH HER WAS SO DRASTICALLY REDUCED.
THE DUCHESS...
B—
BUT THAT MONSTER'S GONE NOW.
NOW SHE CAN LIVE HAPPILY IN WONDERLAND TOO—
HAPPILY...?
WHAT...
...ARE YOU TALKING ABOUT...?
SHE'S NOT HERE ANYMORE...
THE QUEEN OF HEARTS...
—
—LLED...
?

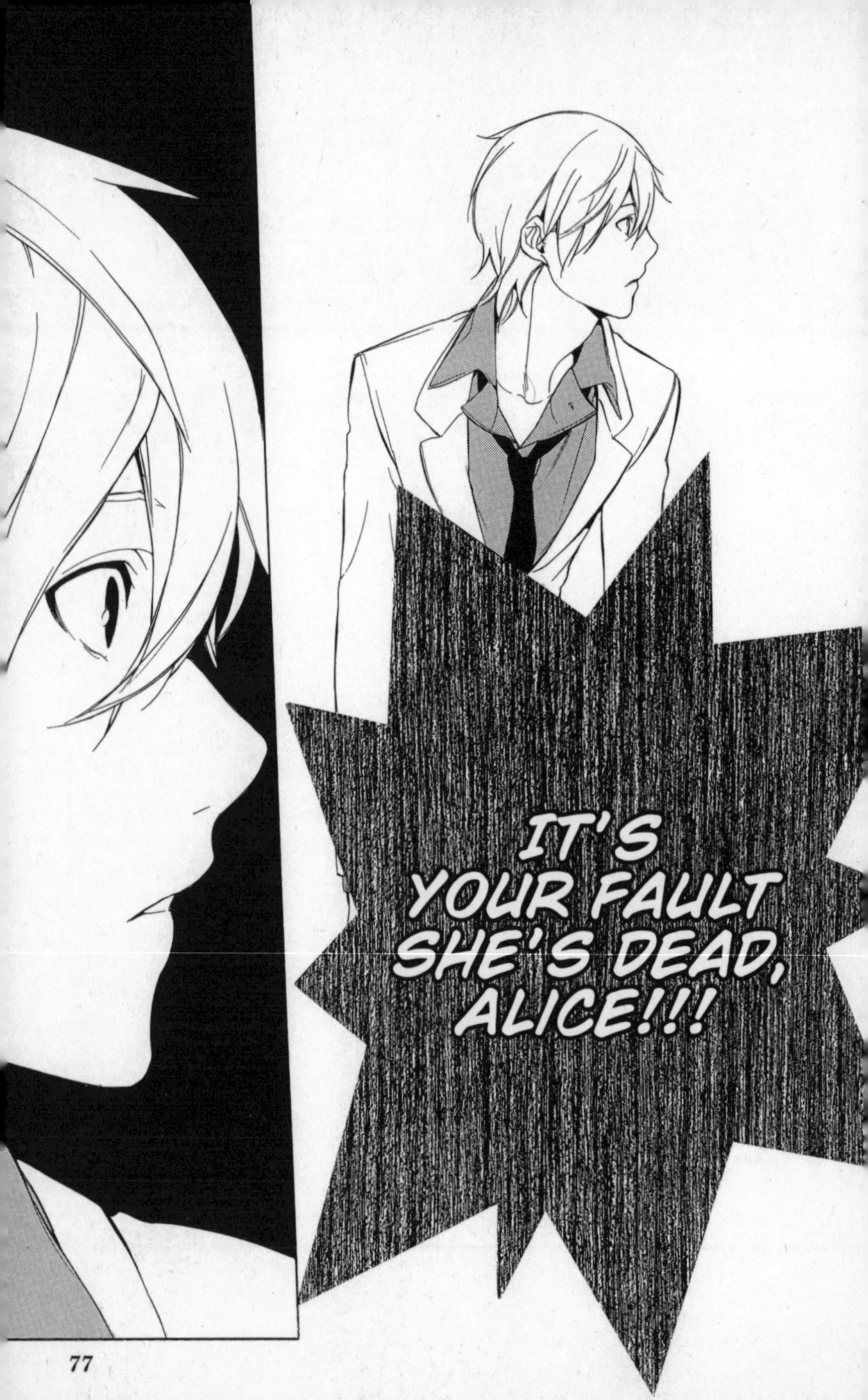
IT'S YOUR FAULT SHE'S DEAD, ALICE!!!

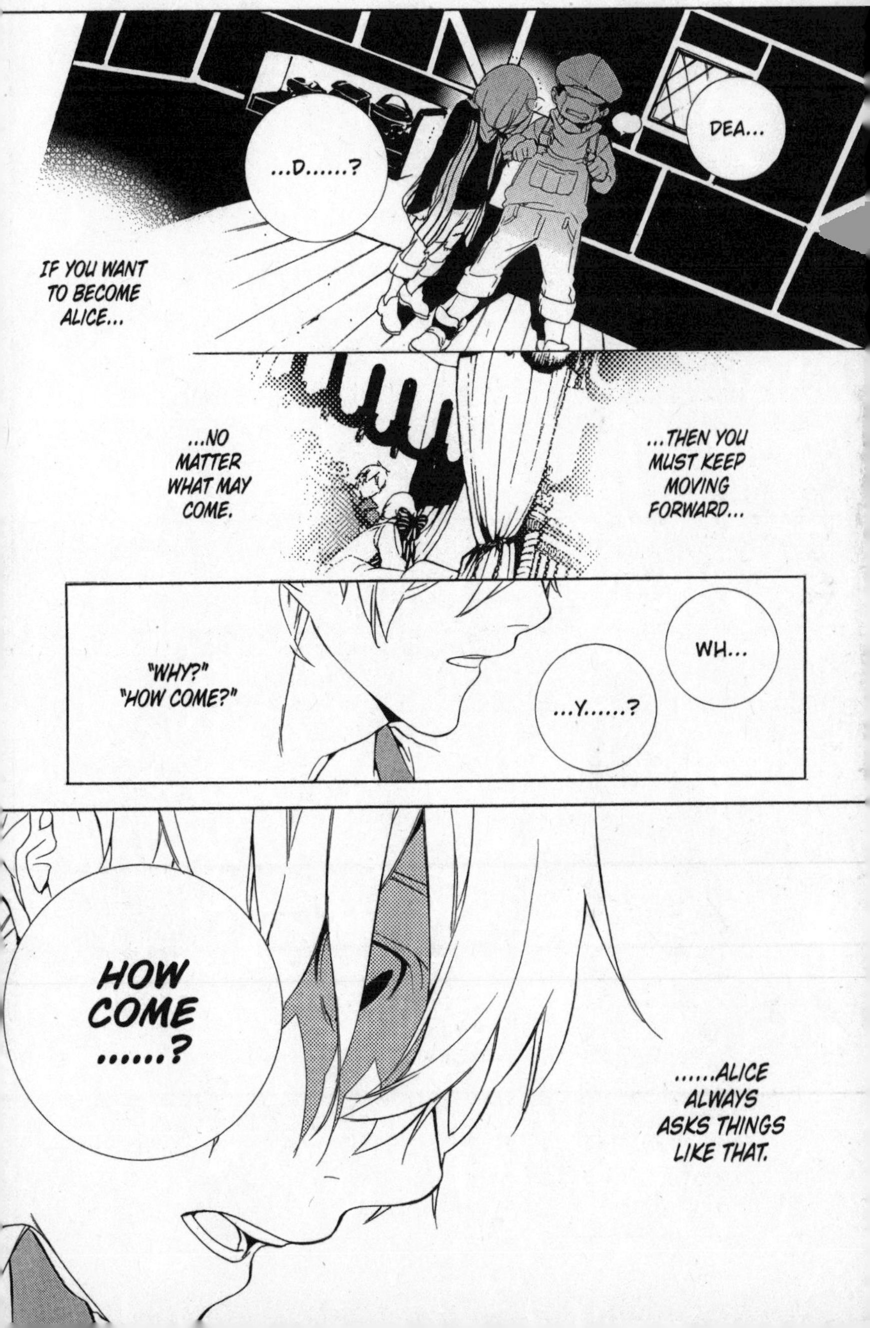
DEA...
...D......?
IF YOU WANT TO BECOME ALICE...
...THEN YOU MUST KEEP MOVING FORWARD...
...NO MATTER WHAT MAY COME.
WH...
...Y......?
"WHY?" "HOW COME?"
HOW COME ......?
......ALICE ALWAYS ASKS THINGS LIKE THAT.

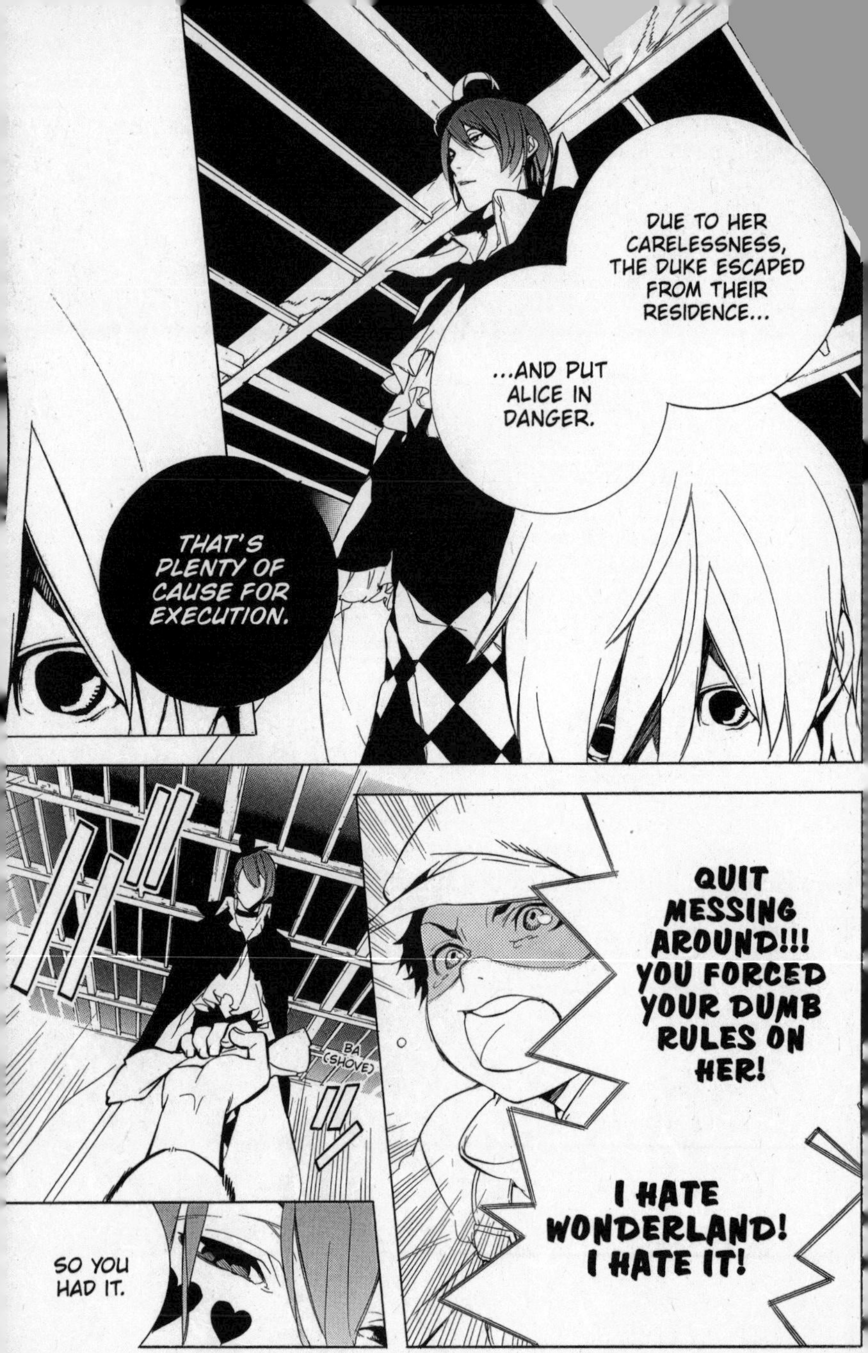
DUE TO HER CARELESSNESS, THE DUKE ESCAPED FROM THEIR RESIDENCE...
...AND PUT ALICE IN DANGER.
THAT'S PLENTY OF CAUSE FOR EXECUTION.
QUIT MESSING AROUND!!! YOU FORCED YOUR DUMB RULES ON HER!
I HATE WONDERLAND! I HATE IT!
BA (SHOVE)
SO YOU HAD IT.

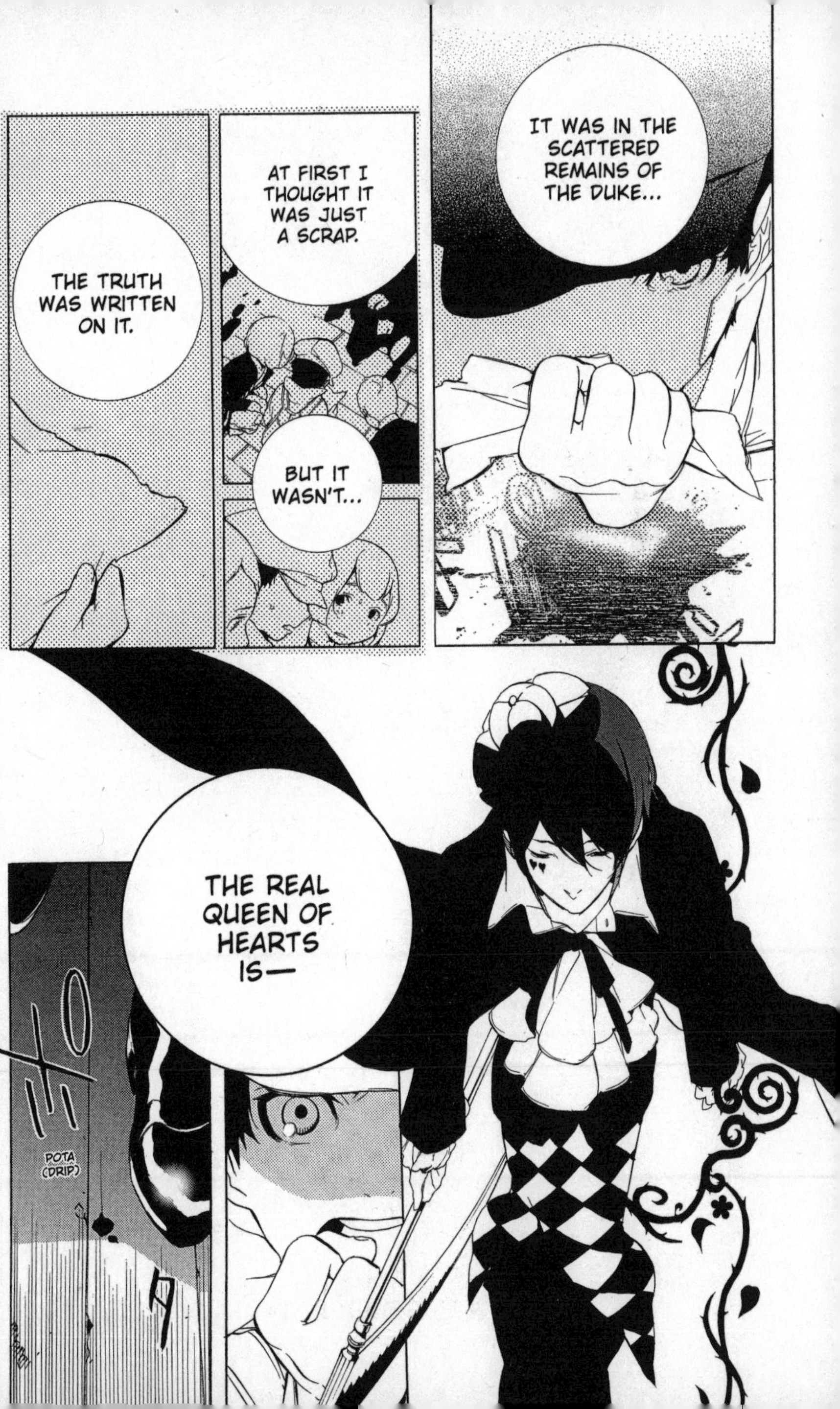
IT WAS IN THE SCATTERED REMAINS OF THE DUKE...
AT FIRST I THOUGHT IT WAS JUST A SCRAP.
BUT IT WASN'T...
THE TRUTH WAS WRITTEN ON IT.
THE REAL QUEEN OF HEARTS IS—
POTA (DRIP)

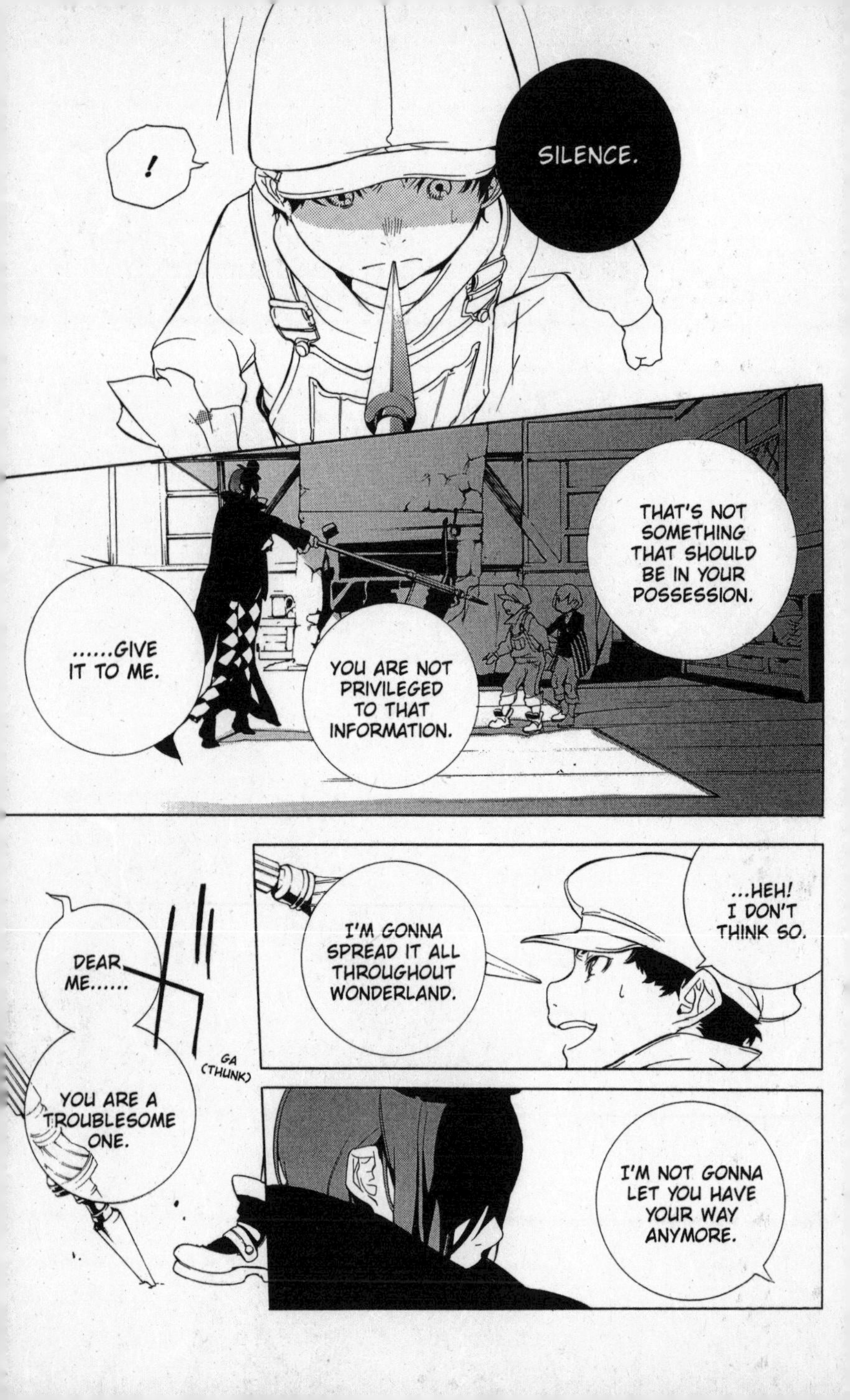
SILENCE.
!
THAT'S NOT SOMETHING THAT SHOULD BE IN YOUR POSSESSION.
YOU ARE NOT PRIVILEGED TO THAT INFORMATION.
......GIVE IT TO ME.
...HEH! I DON'T THINK SO.
I'M GONNA SPREAD IT ALL THROUGHOUT WONDERLAND.
I'M NOT GONNA LET YOU HAVE YOUR WAY ANYMORE.
DEAR ME......
GA (THUNK)
YOU ARE A TROUBLESOME ONE.

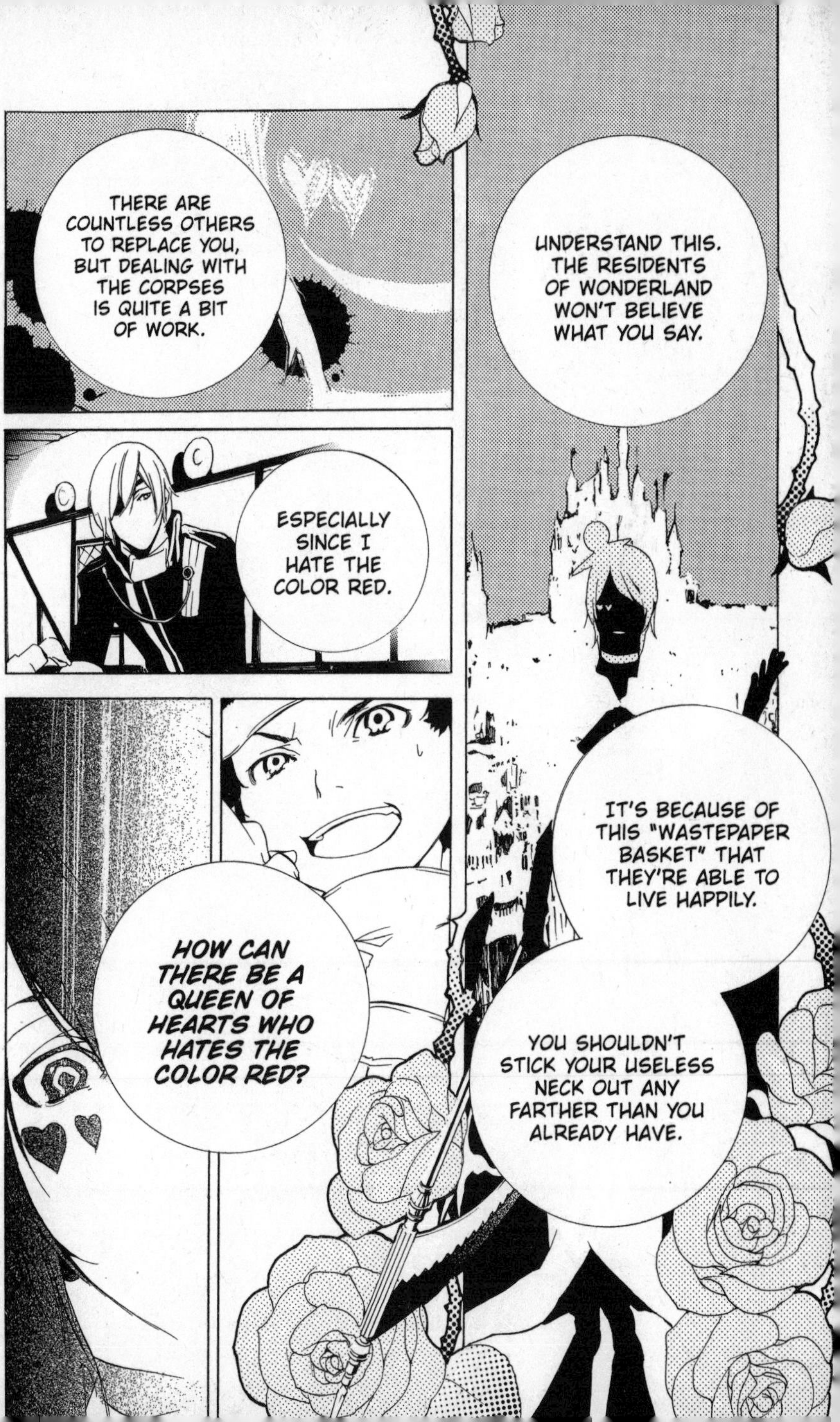
UNDERSTAND THIS. THE RESIDENTS OF WONDERLAND WON'T BELIEVE WHAT YOU SAY.
IT'S BECAUSE OF THIS "WASTEPAPER BASKET" THAT THEY'RE ABLE TO LIVE HAPPILY.
YOU SHOULDN'T STICK YOUR USELESS NECK OUT ANY FARTHER THAN YOU ALREADY HAVE.
THERE ARE COUNTLESS OTHERS TO REPLACE YOU, BUT DEALING WITH THE CORPSES IS QUITE A BIT OF WORK.
ESPECIALLY SINCE I HATE THE COLOR RED.
HOW CAN THERE BE A QUEEN OF HEARTS WHO HATES THE COLOR RED?

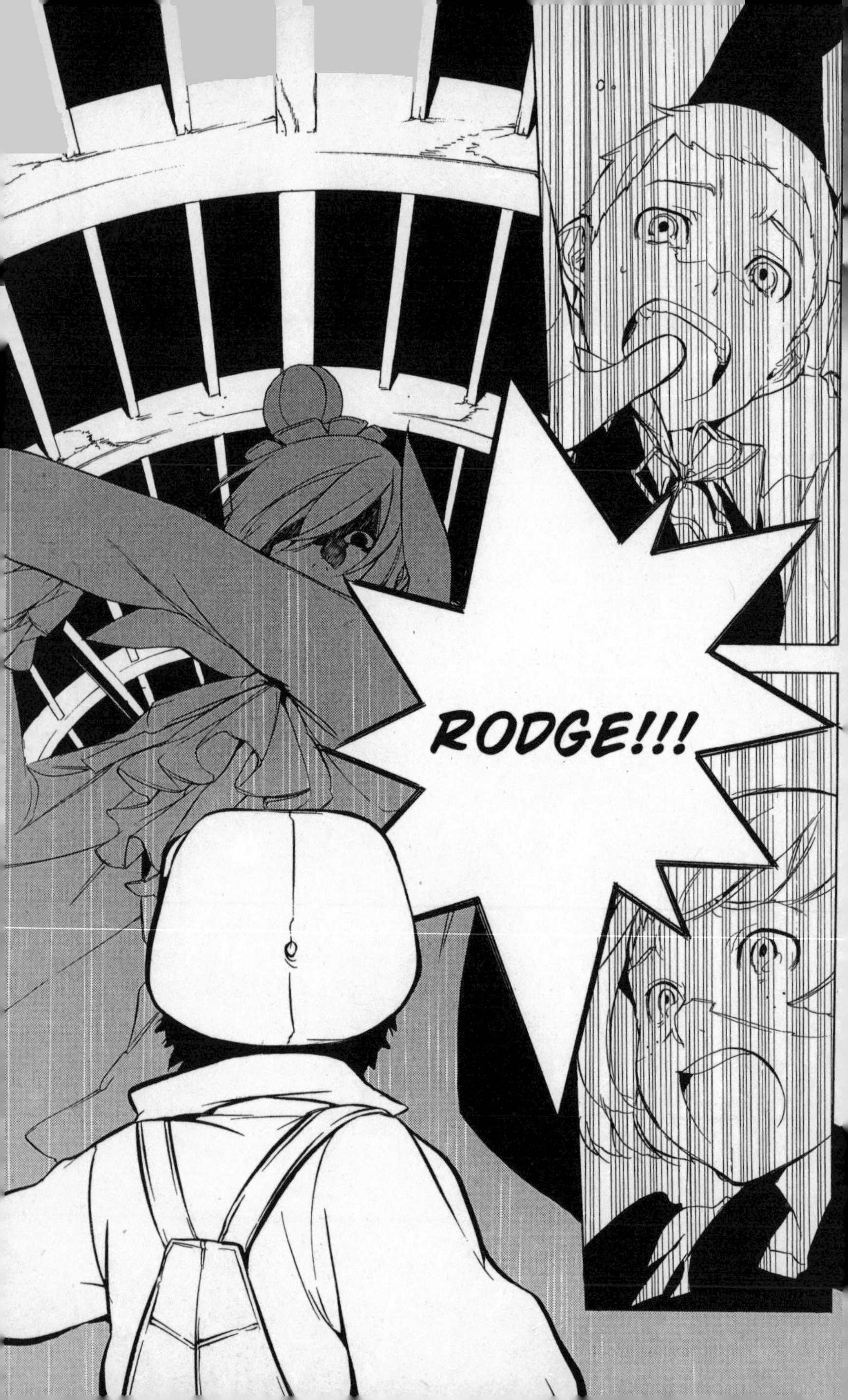
RODGE!!!

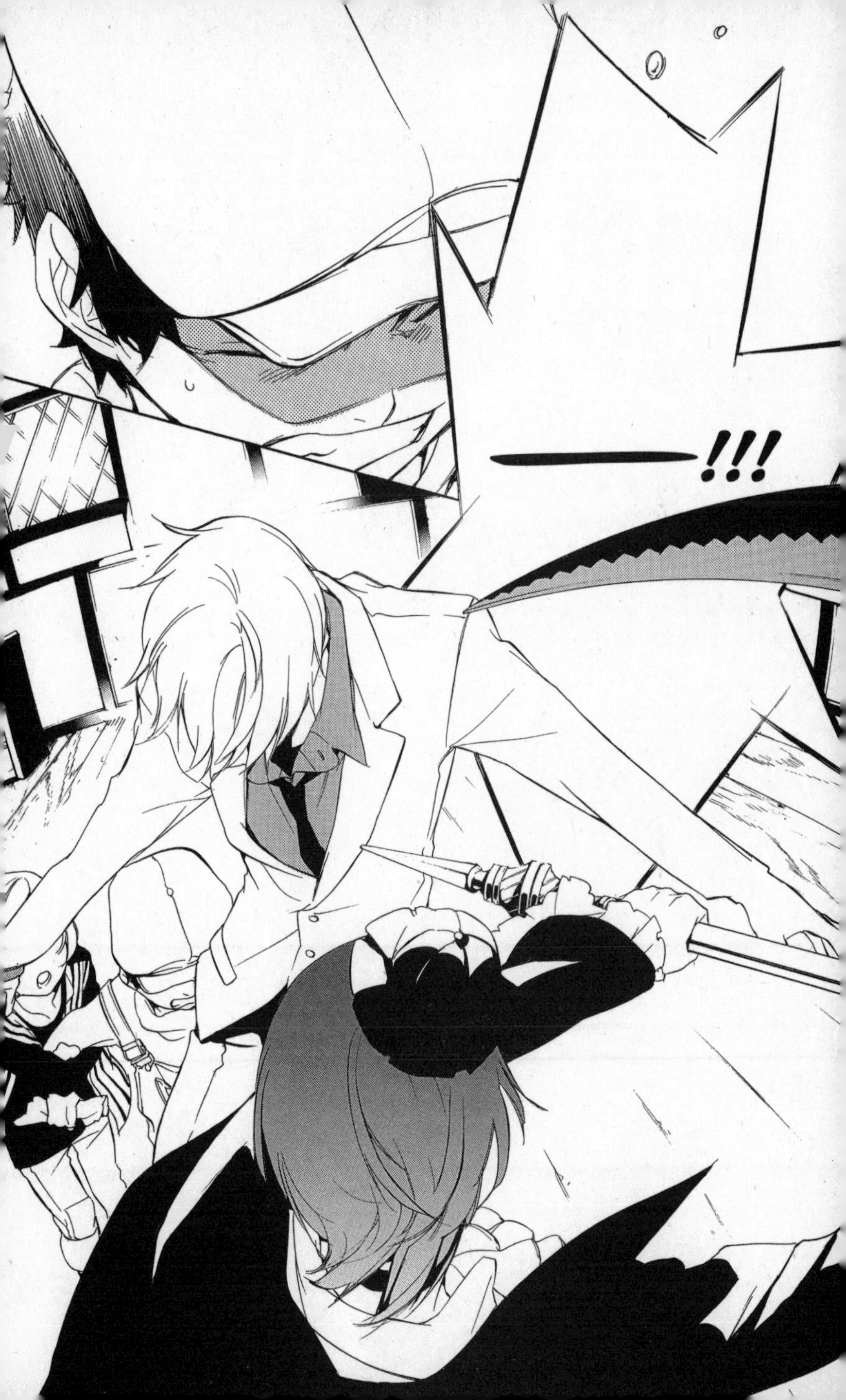
—!!!

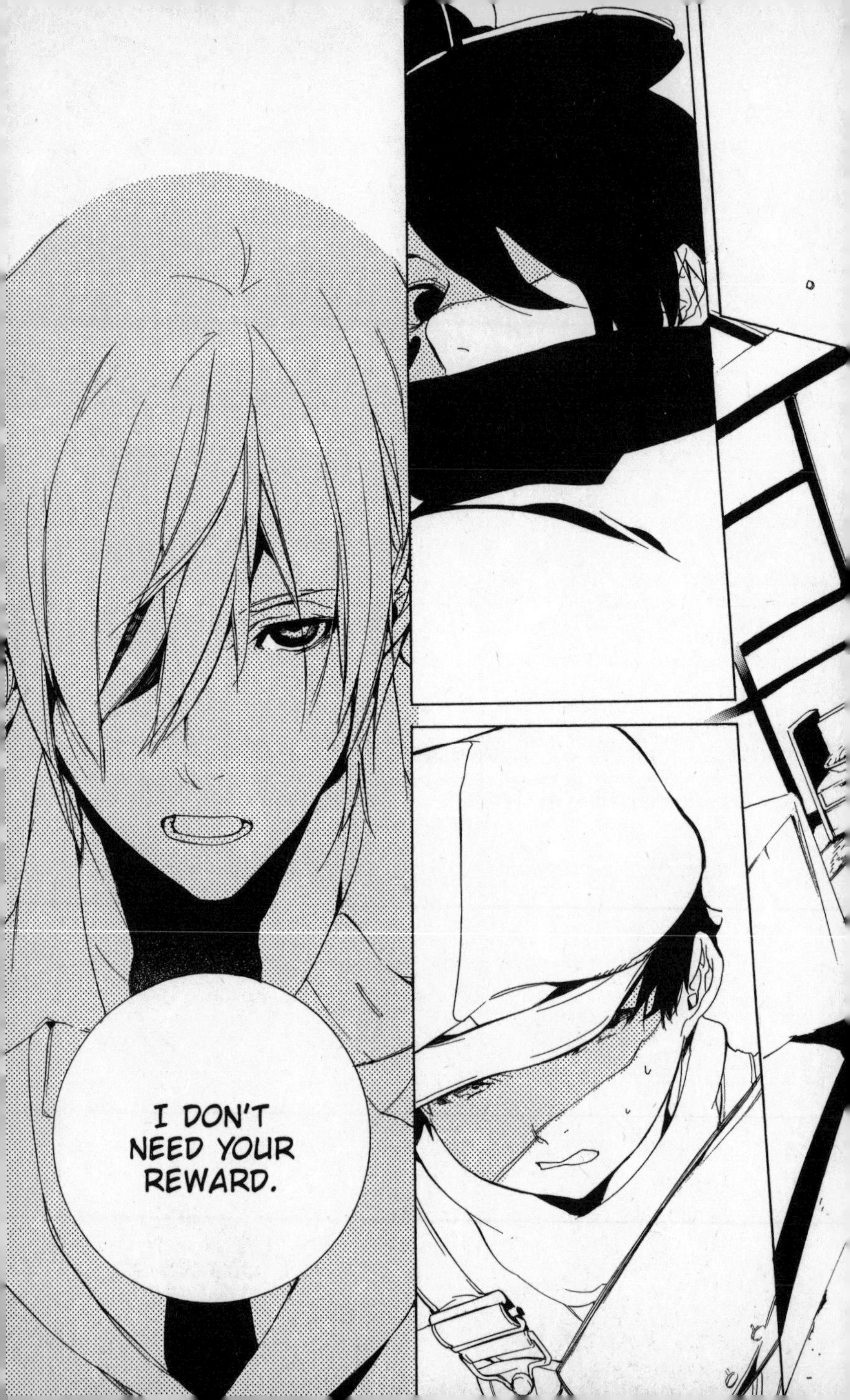
I DON'T NEED YOUR REWARD.

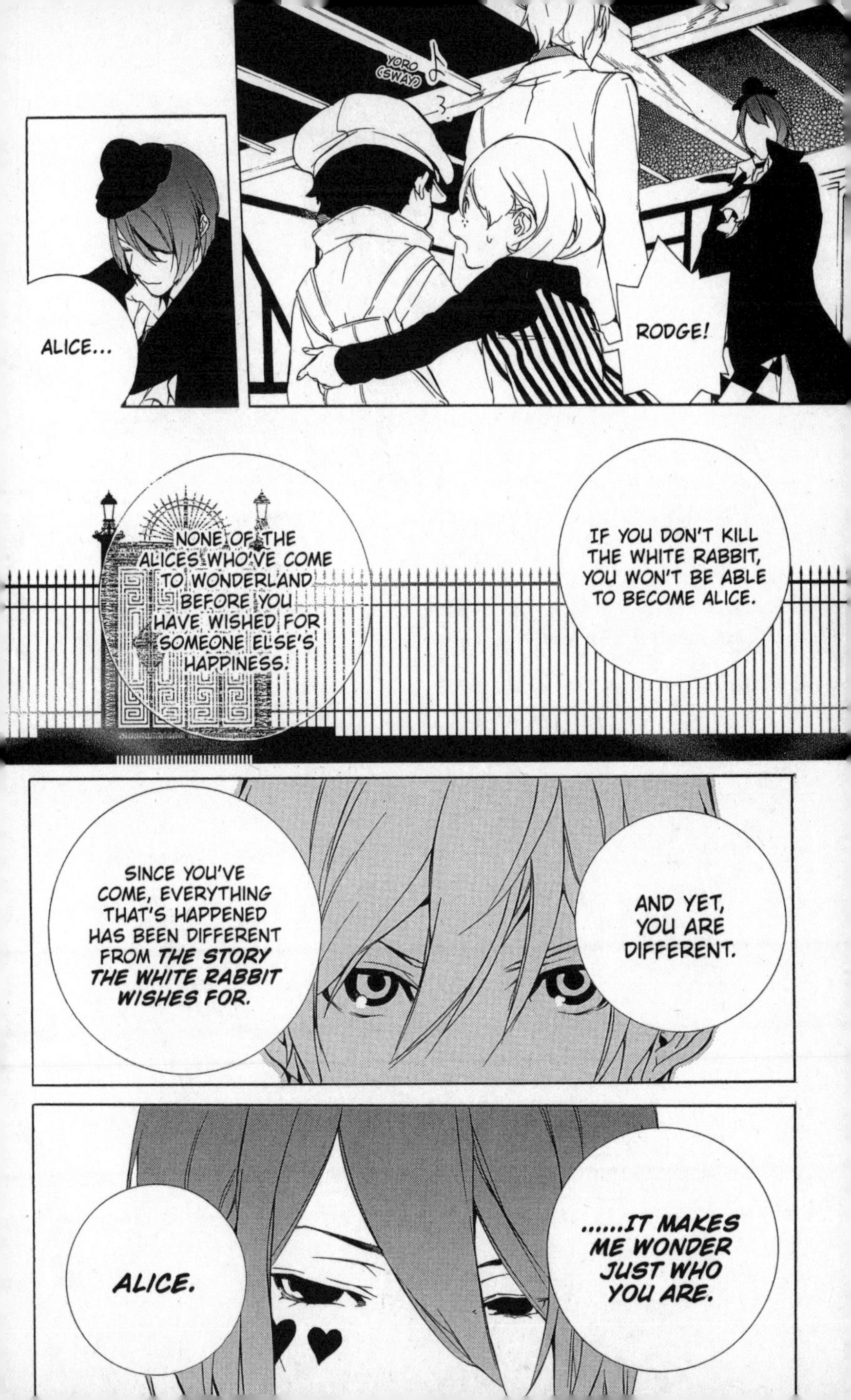
YORO (SWAY)
RODGE!
ALICE...
IF YOU DON'T KILL THE WHITE RABBIT, YOU WON'T BE ABLE TO BECOME ALICE.
NONE OF THE ALICES WHO'VE COME TO WONDERLAND BEFORE YOU HAVE WISHED FOR SOMEONE ELSE'S HAPPINESS.
AND YET, YOU ARE DIFFERENT.
SINCE YOU'VE COME, EVERYTHING THAT'S HAPPENED HAS BEEN DIFFERENT FROM THE STORY THE WHITE RABBIT WISHES FOR.
......IT MAKES ME WONDER JUST WHO YOU ARE.
ALICE.

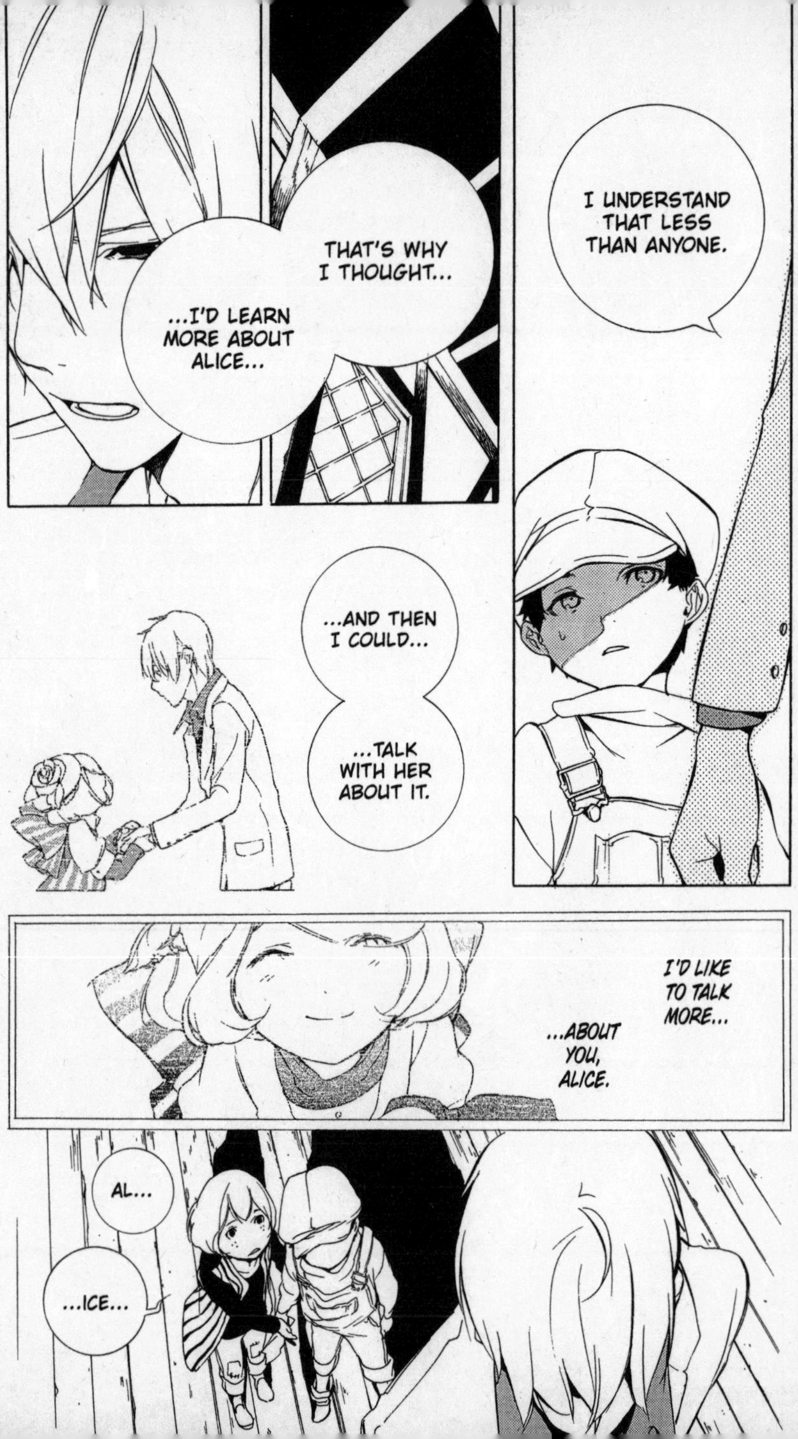
I UNDERSTAND THAT LESS THAN ANYONE.
THAT'S WHY I THOUGHT...
...I'D LEARN MORE ABOUT ALICE...
...AND THEN I COULD...
...TALK WITH HER ABOUT IT.
I'D LIKE TO TALK MORE...
...ABOUT YOU, ALICE.
AL...
...ICE...

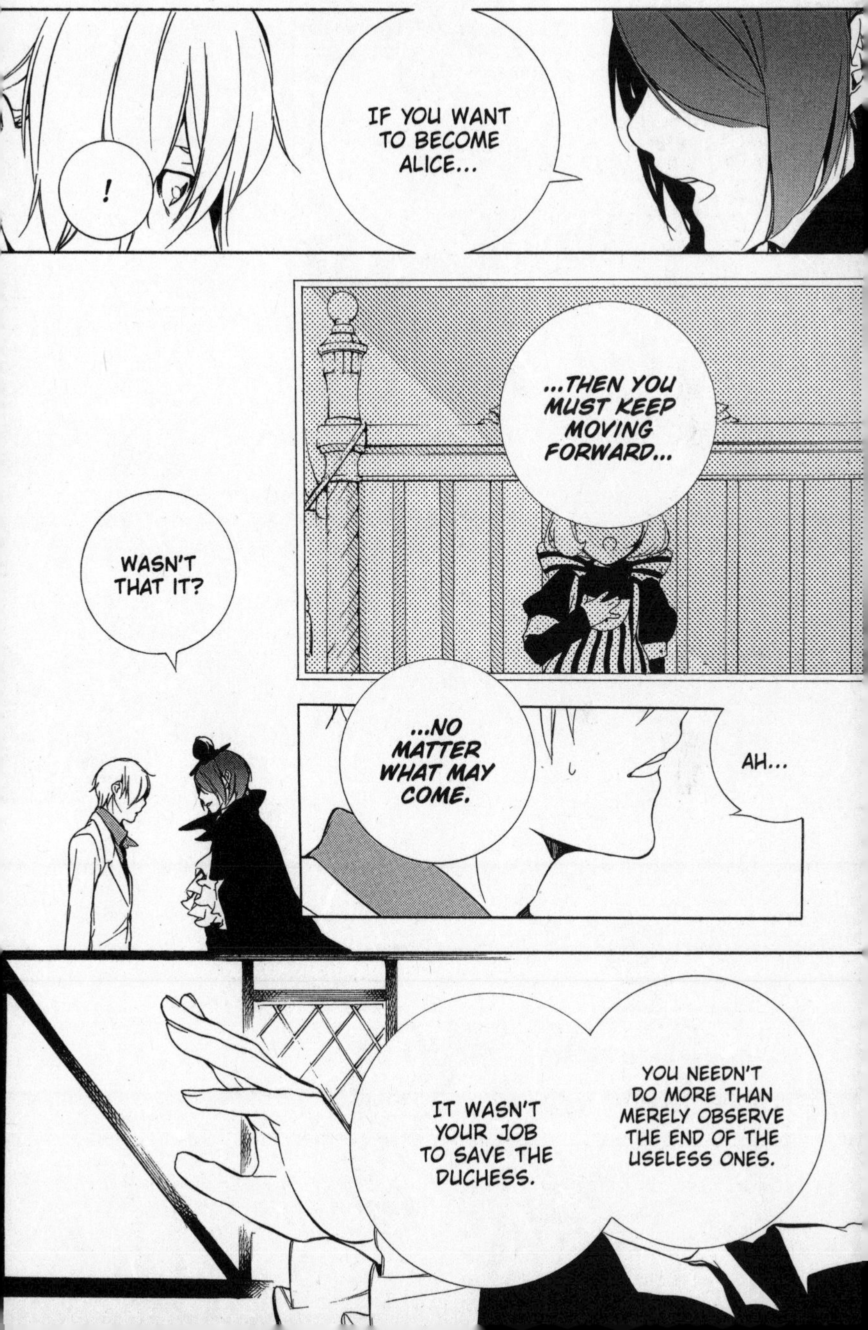
IF YOU WANT TO BECOME ALICE...
!
...THEN YOU MUST KEEP MOVING FORWARD...
...NO MATTER WHAT MAY COME.
AH...
WASN'T THAT IT?
YOU NEEDN'T DO MORE THAN MERELY OBSERVE THE END OF THE USELESS ONES.
IT WASN'T YOUR JOB TO SAVE THE DUCHESS.

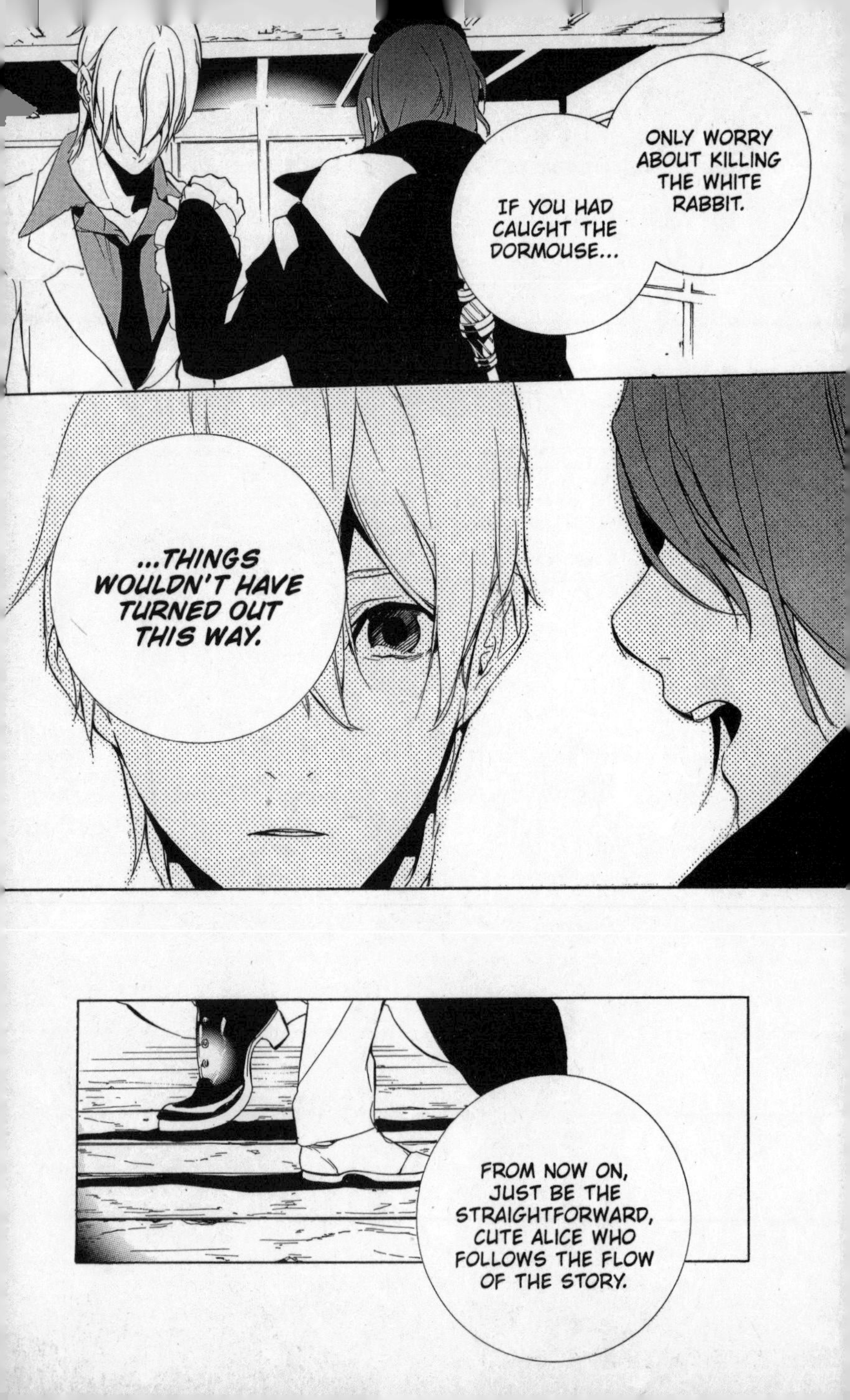
ONLY WORRY ABOUT KILLING THE WHITE RABBIT.
IF YOU HAD CAUGHT THE DORMOUSE...
...THINGS WOULDN'T HAVE TURNED OUT THIS WAY.
FROM NOW ON, JUST BE THE STRAIGHTFORWARD, CUTE ALICE WHO FOLLOWS THE FLOW OF THE STORY.

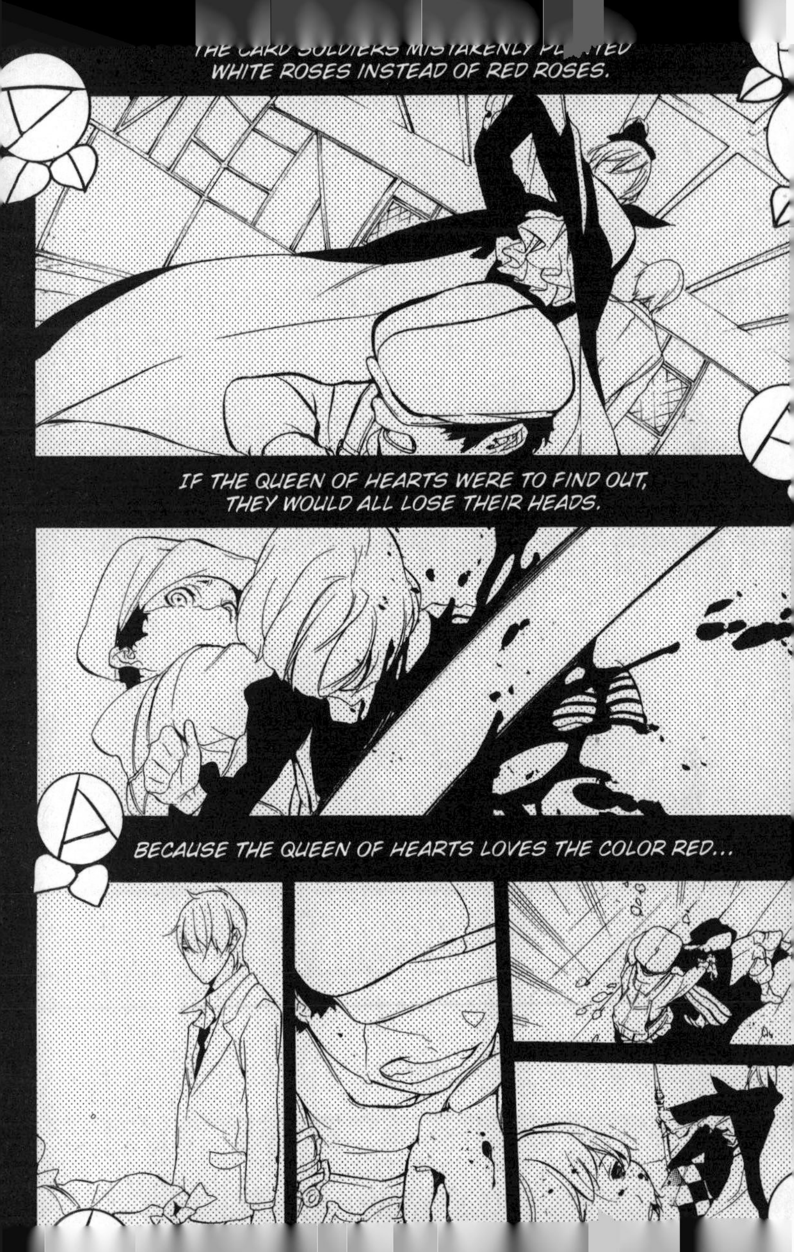
THE CARD SOLDIERS MISTAKENLY PLANTED WHITE ROSES INSTEAD OF RED ROSES.
IF THE QUEEN OF HEARTS WERE TO FIND OUT, THEY WOULD ALL LOSE THEIR HEADS.
BECAUSE THE QUEEN OF HEARTS LOVES THE COLOR RED...

SPLAT, SPLAT, SPLAT, SPLAT GOES THE RED PAINT.

THE CARD SOLDIERS DO THEIR BEST,
COLORING THE WHITE ROSES RED.

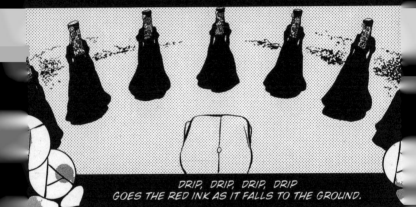

DRIP, DRIP, DRIP, DRIP
GOES THE RED INK AS IT FALLS TO THE GROUND.

IT LOOKS ALMOST LIKE

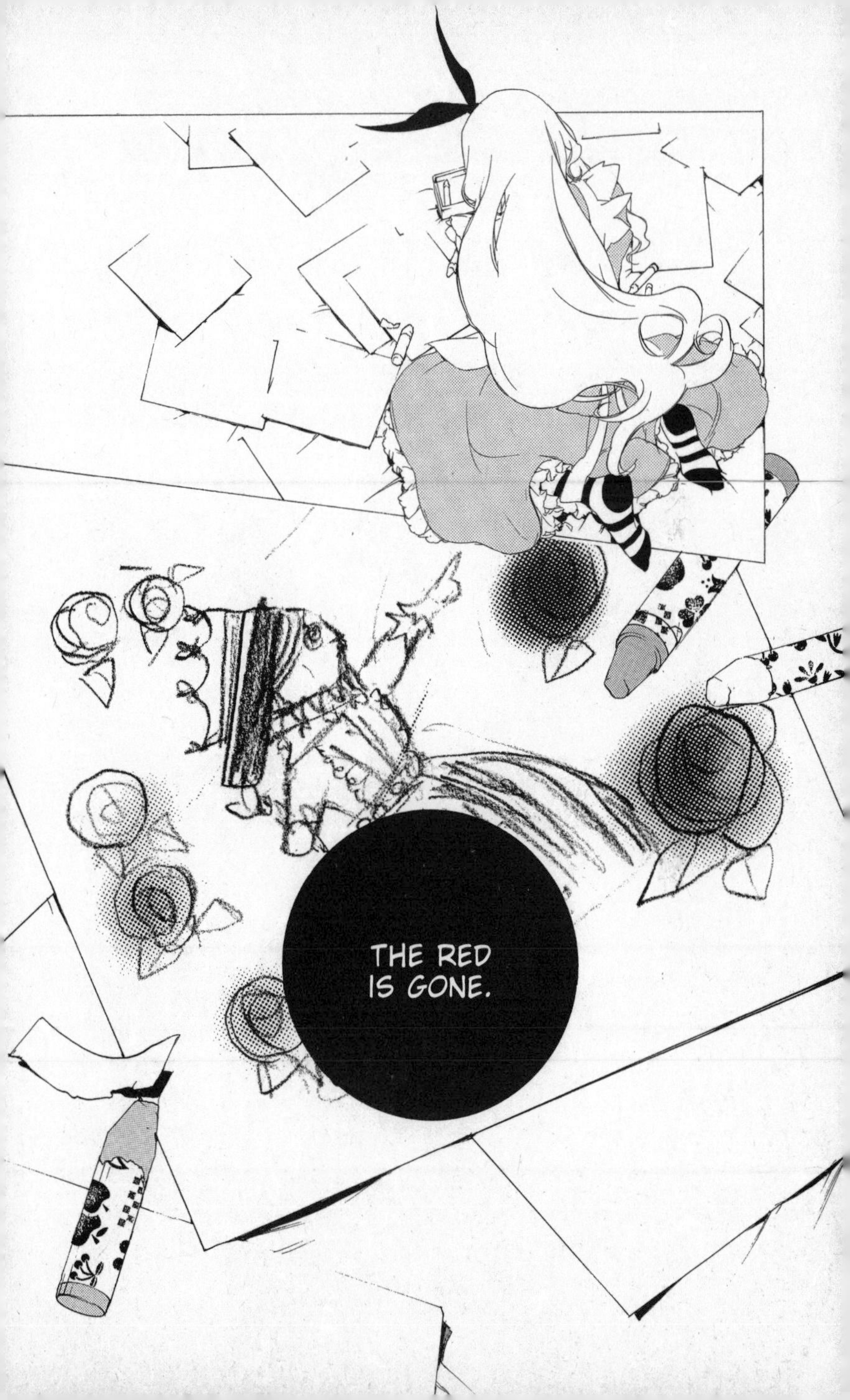
THE RED
IS GONE.

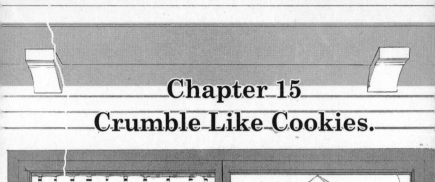

Chapter 15
Crumble Like Cookies.

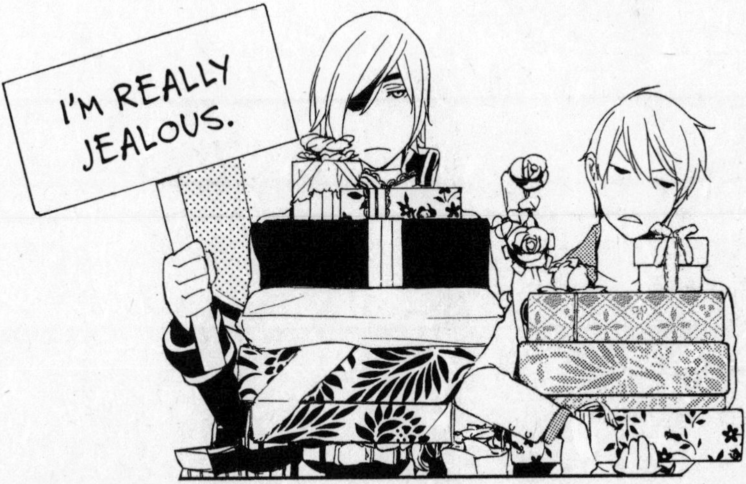
I'M REALLY JEALOUS.

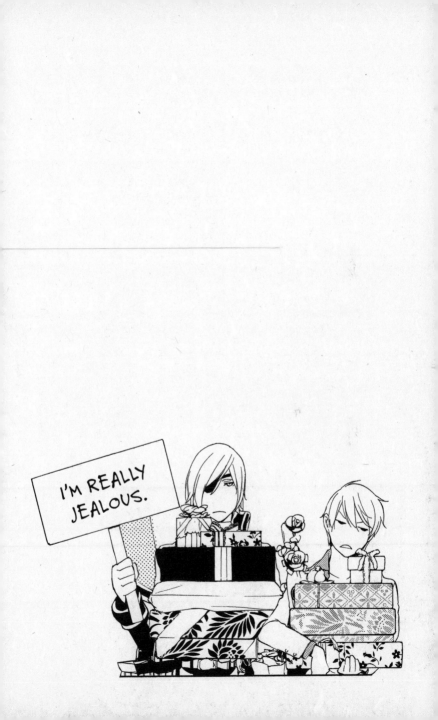

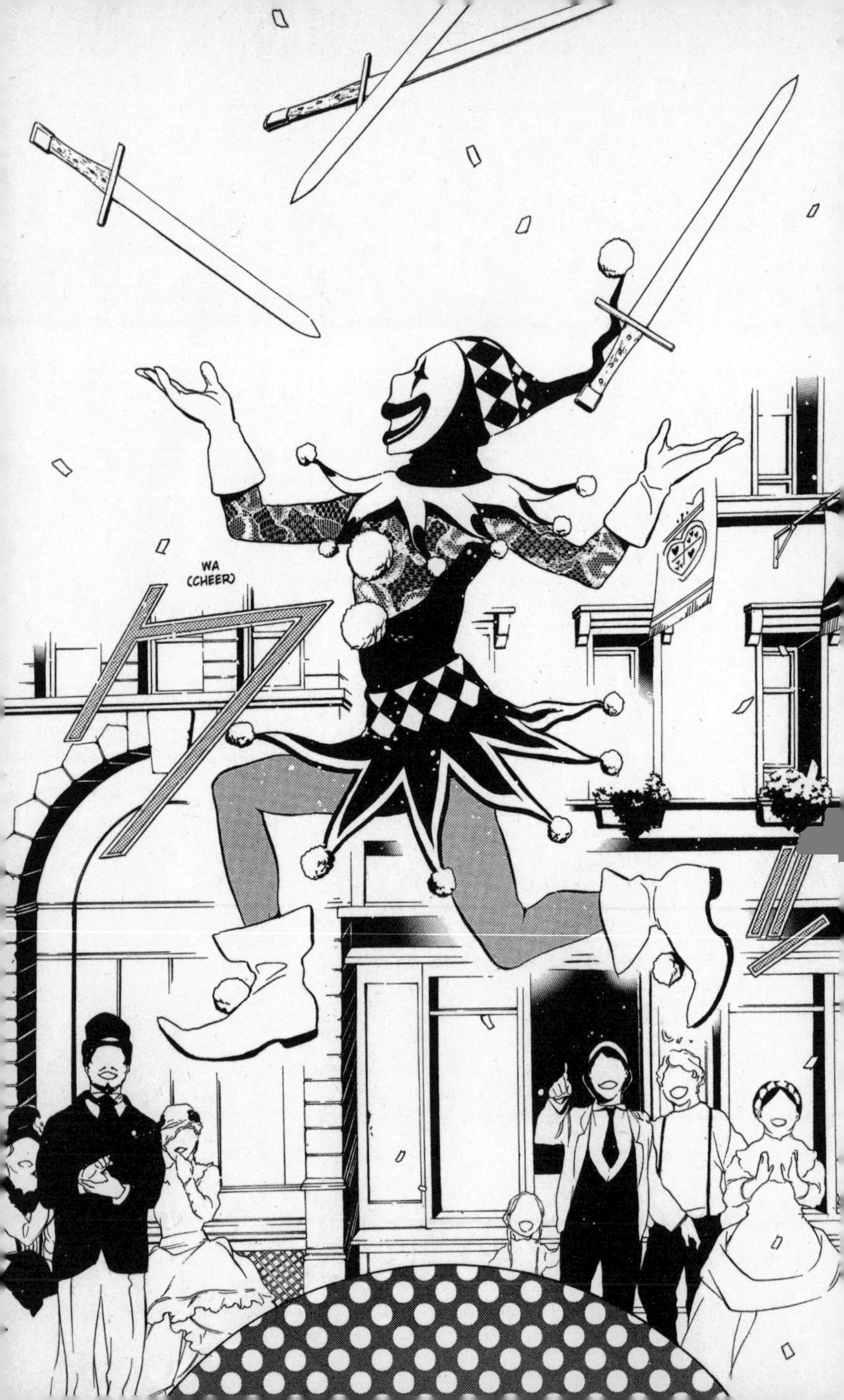
WA
(CHEER)

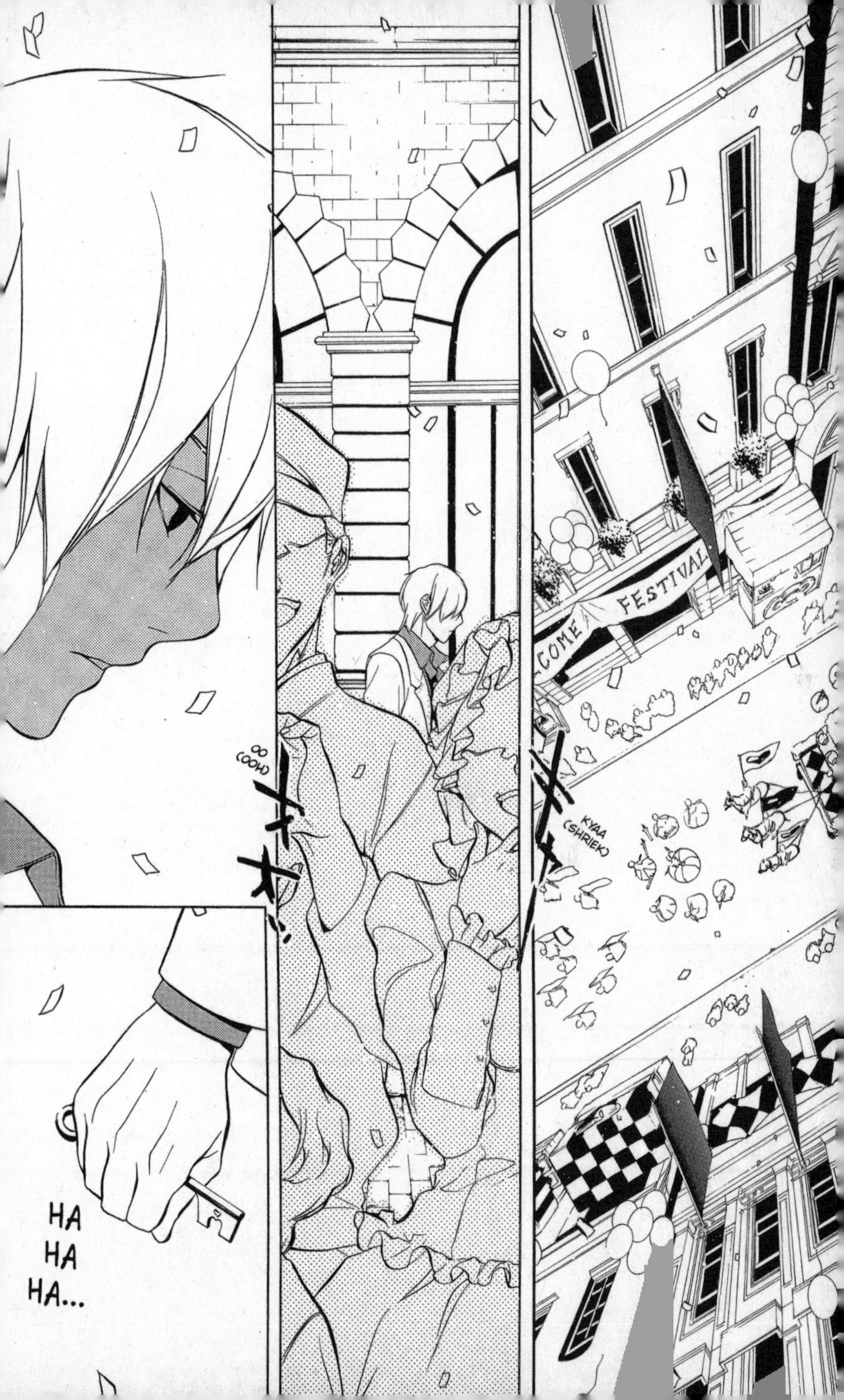
COME FESTIVAL
KYAA (SHRIEK)
OO (OOH)
HA HA HA...

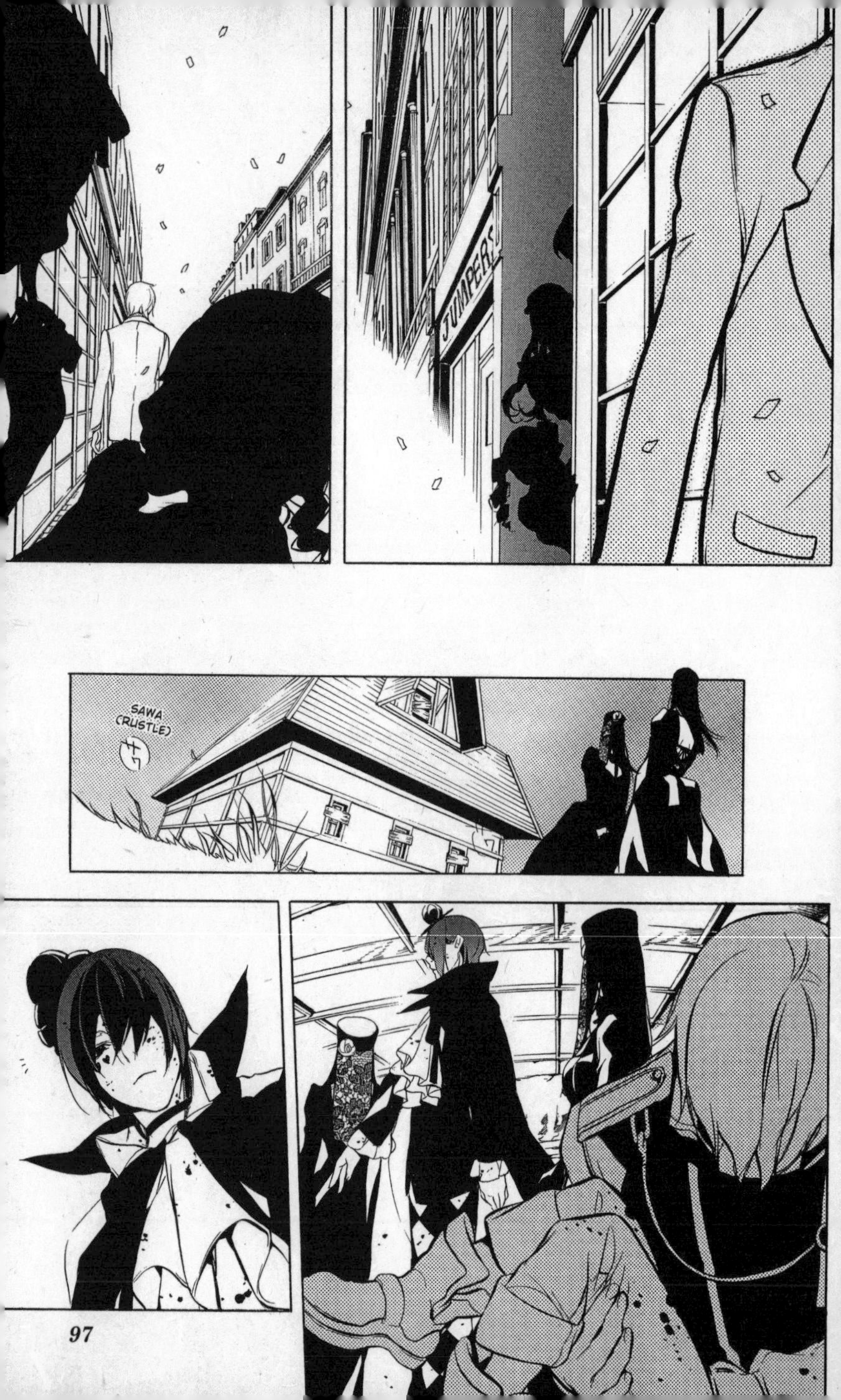
JUMPERS
SAWA (RUSTLE)

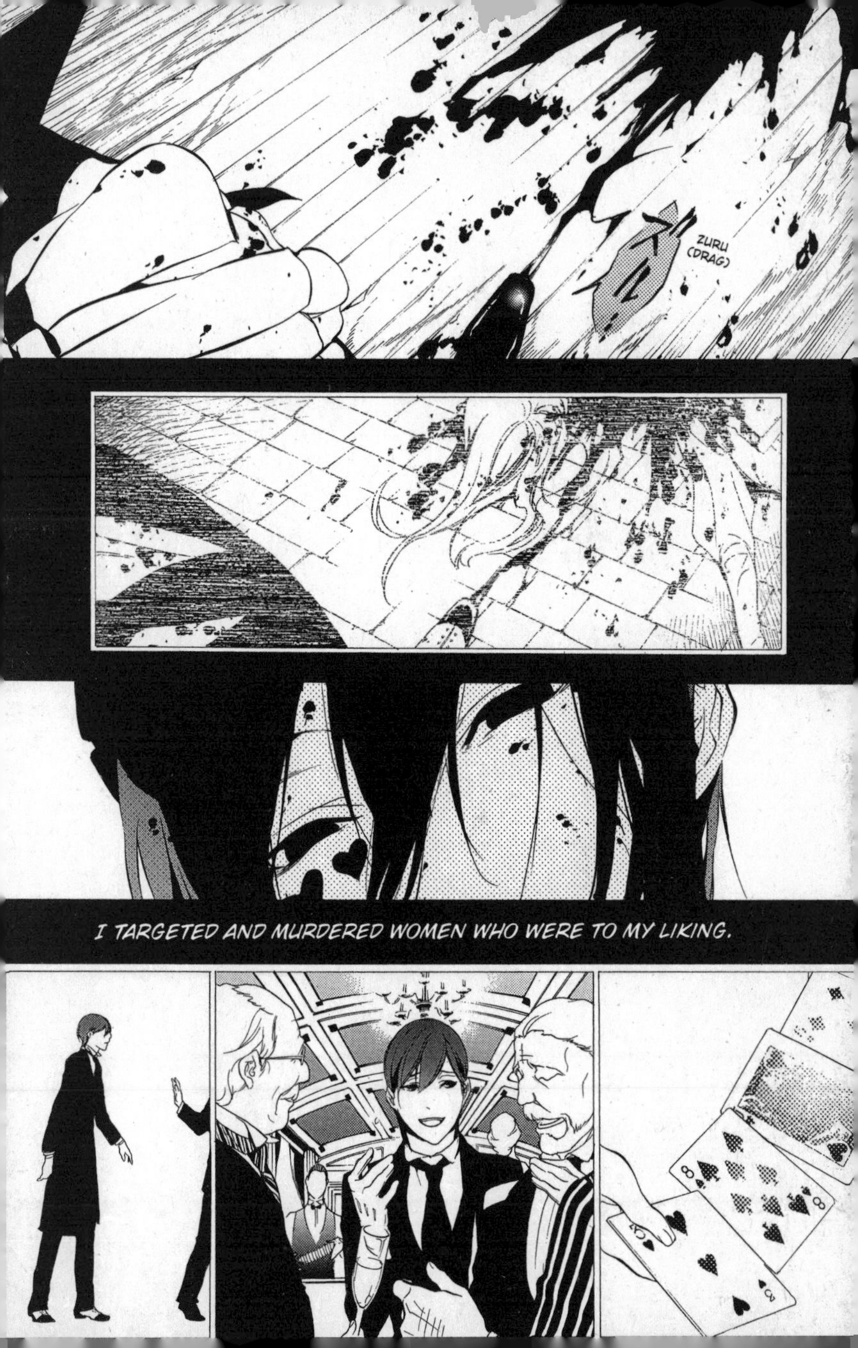
ZURU (DRAG)
I TARGETED AND MURDERED WOMEN WHO WERE TO MY LIKING.

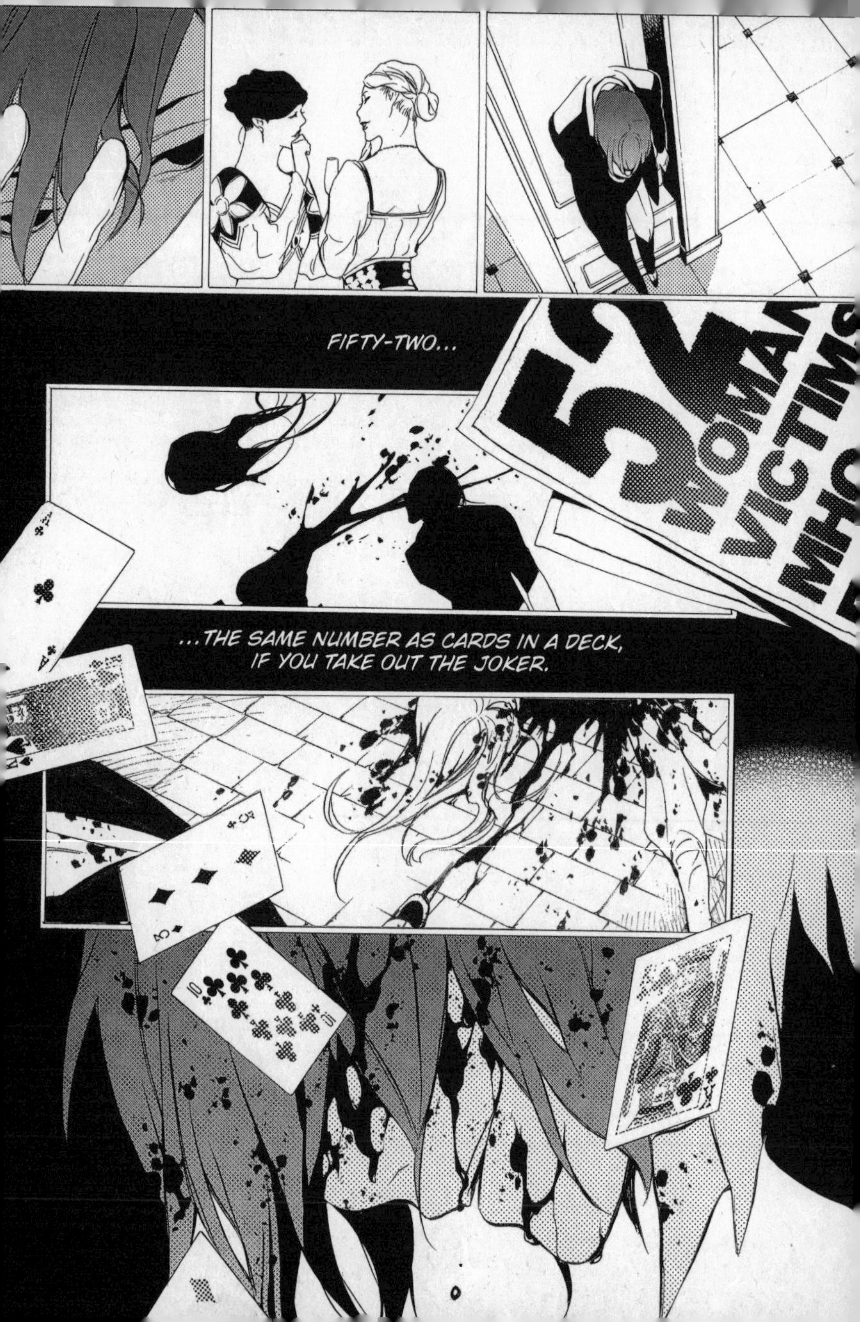
FIFTY-TWO...
...THE SAME NUMBER AS CARDS IN A DECK, IF YOU TAKE OUT THE JOKER.

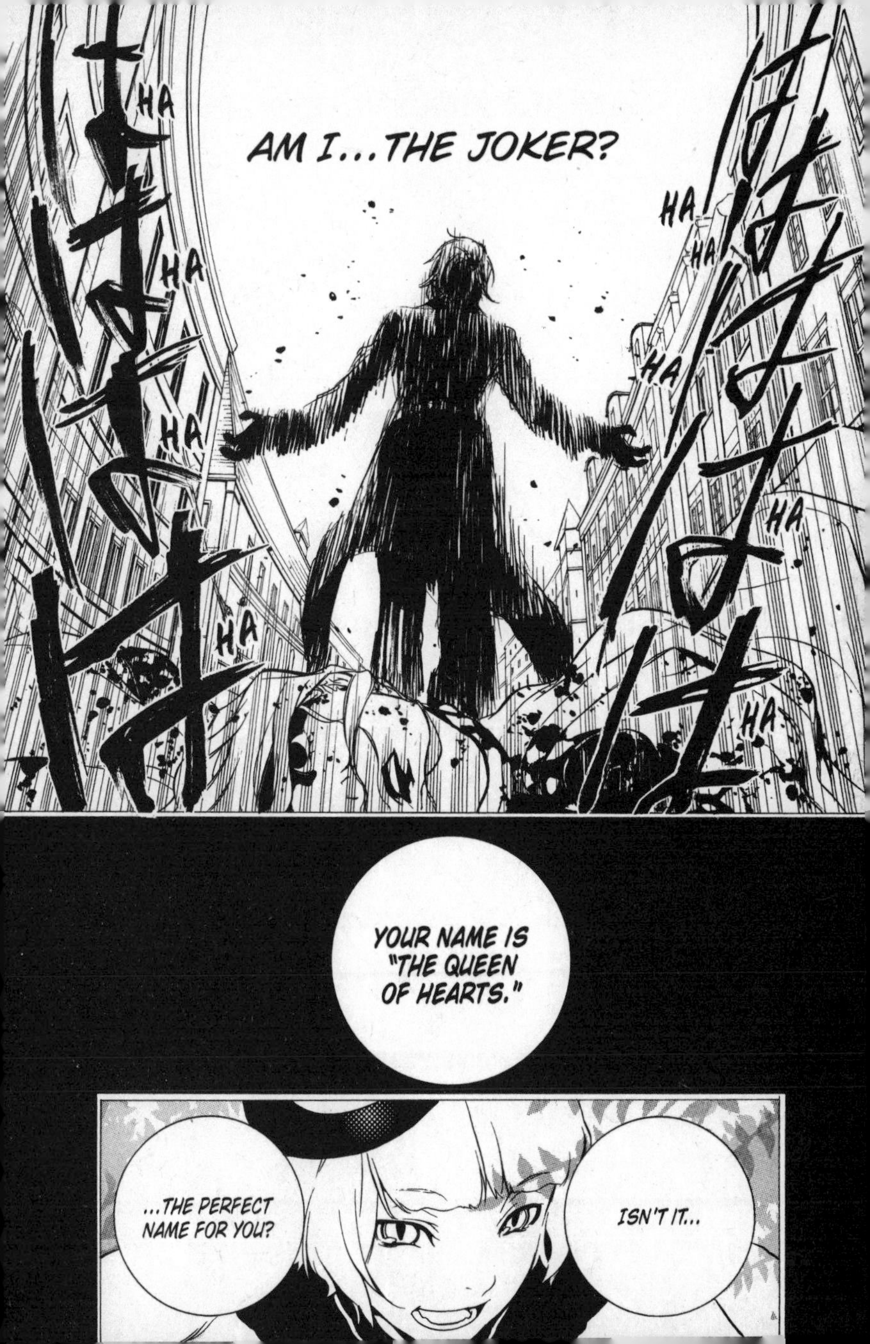
AM I...THE JOKER?
HA HA HA HA HA HA
HA HA HA HA
YOUR NAME IS "THE QUEEN OF HEARTS."
ISN'T IT...
...THE PERFECT NAME FOR YOU?

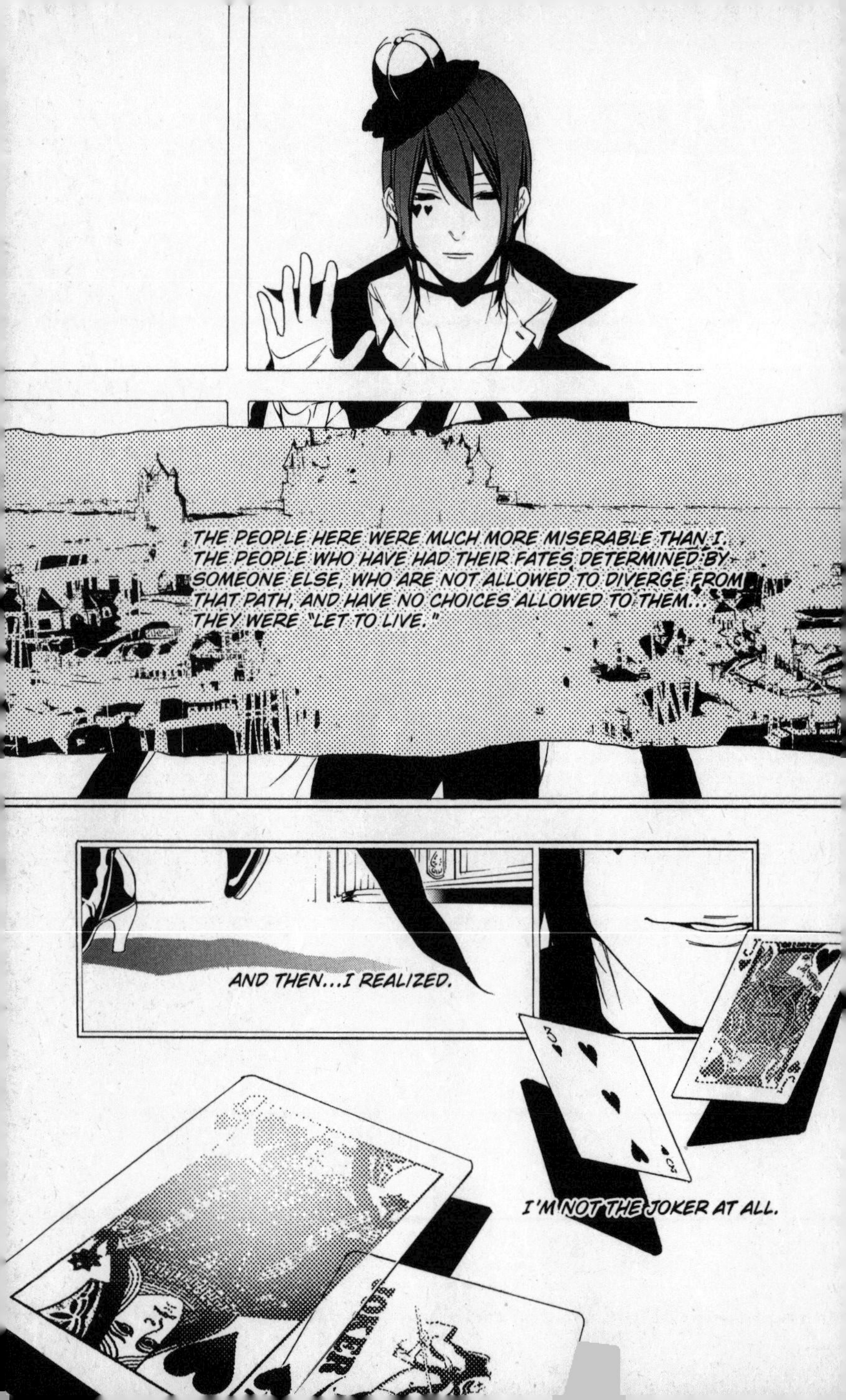
THE PEOPLE HERE WERE MUCH MORE MISERABLE THAN I. THE PEOPLE WHO HAVE HAD THEIR FATES DETERMINED BY SOMEONE ELSE, WHO ARE NOT ALLOWED TO DIVERGE FROM THAT PATH, AND HAVE NO CHOICES ALLOWED TO THEM... THEY WERE "LET TO LIVE."
AND THEN...I REALIZED.
I'M NOT THE JOKER AT ALL.
JOKER

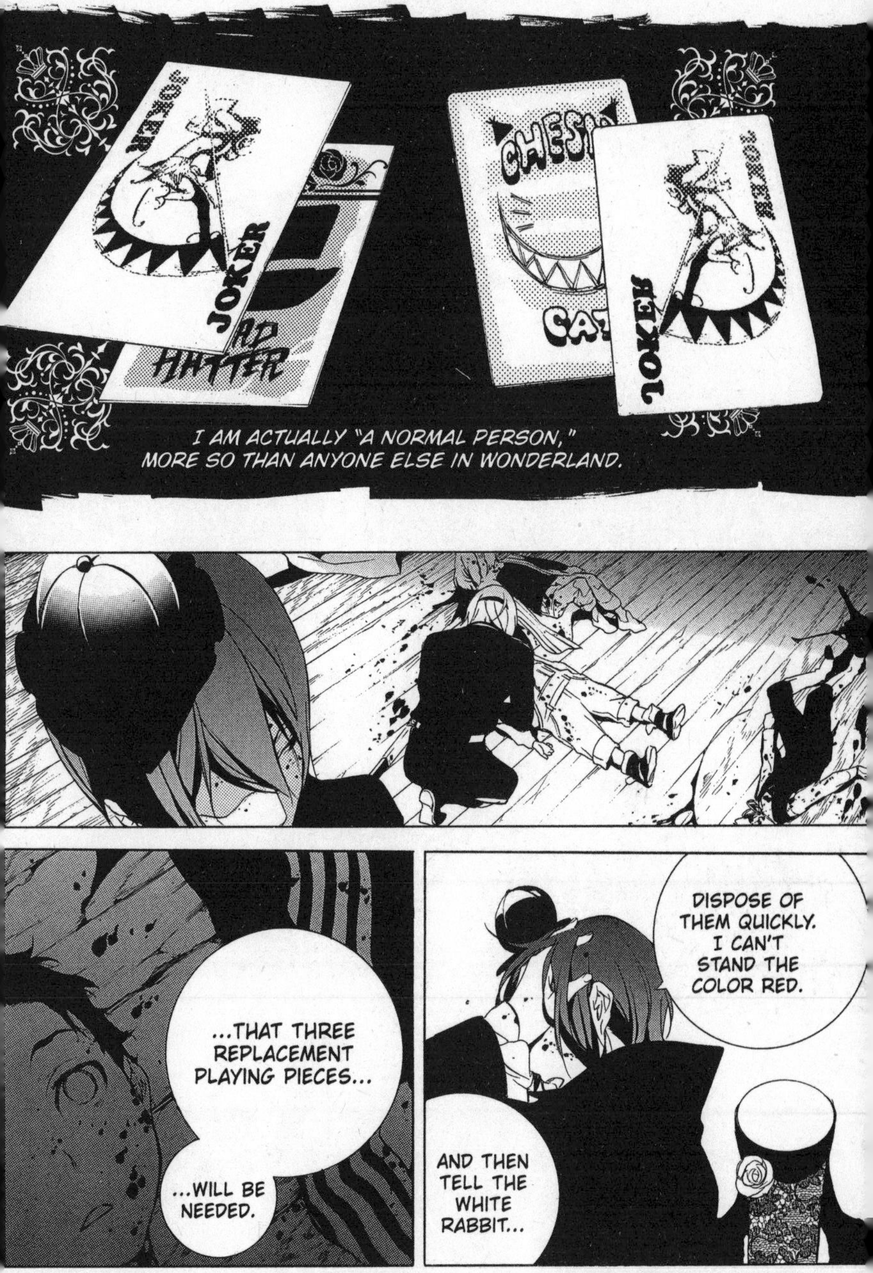
JOKER
HATTER
JOKER
I AM ACTUALLY "A NORMAL PERSON," MORE SO THAN ANYONE ELSE IN WONDERLAND.
DISPOSE OF THEM QUICKLY. I CAN'T STAND THE COLOR RED.
AND THEN TELL THE WHITE RABBIT...
...THAT THREE REPLACEMENT PLAYING PIECES...
...WILL BE NEEDED.

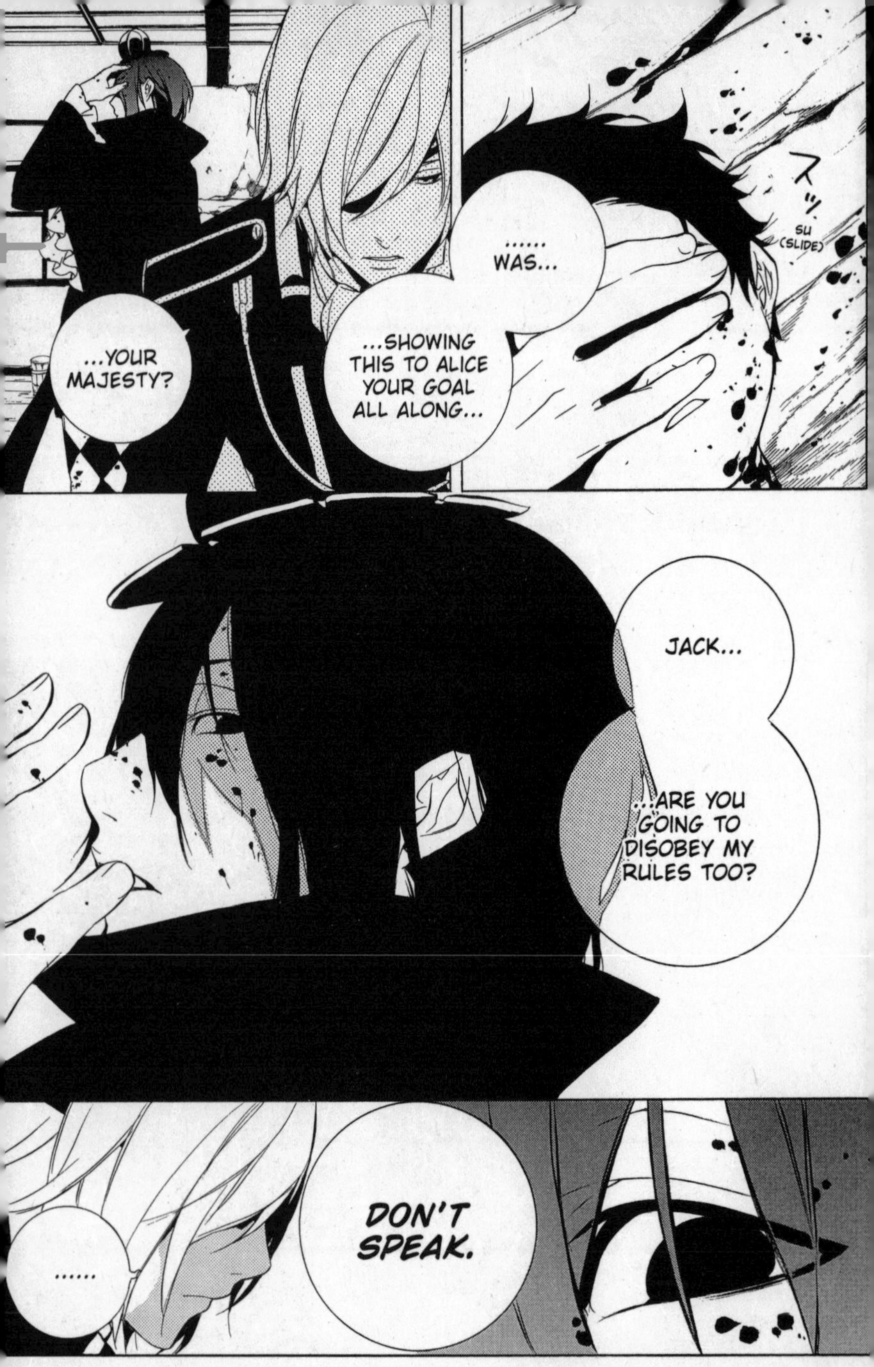
SU (SLIDE)
......WAS...
...SHOWING THIS TO ALICE YOUR GOAL ALL ALONG...
...YOUR MAJESTY?
JACK...
...ARE YOU GOING TO DISOBEY MY RULES TOO?
DON'T SPEAK.
......

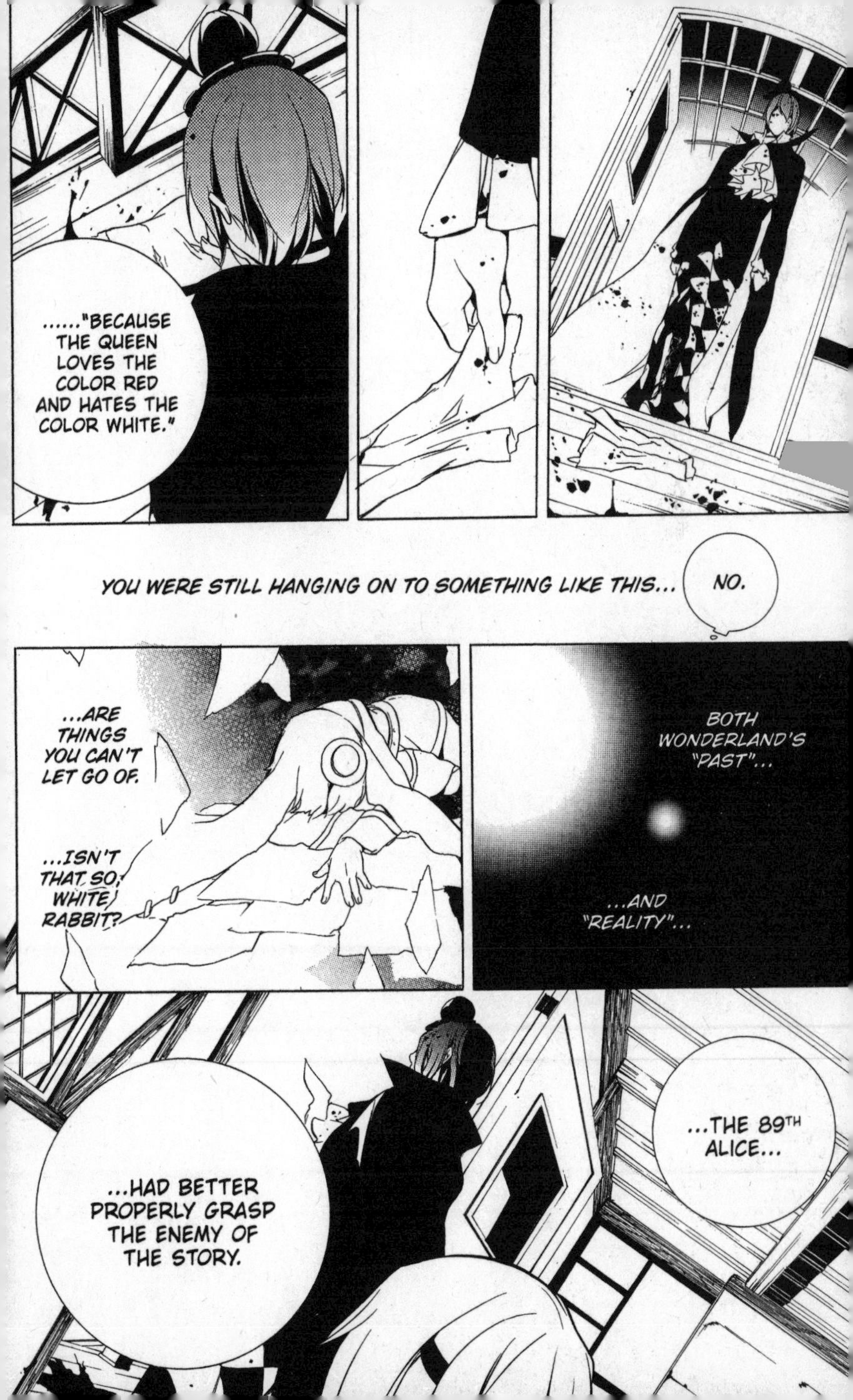
......"BECAUSE THE QUEEN LOVES THE COLOR RED AND HATES THE COLOR WHITE."
NO.
YOU WERE STILL HANGING ON TO SOMETHING LIKE THIS...
BOTH WONDERLAND'S "PAST"...
...AND "REALITY"...
...ARE THINGS YOU CAN'T LET GO OF.
...ISN'T THAT SO, WHITE RABBIT?
...THE 89TH ALICE...
...HAD BETTER PROPERLY GRASP THE ENEMY OF THE STORY.

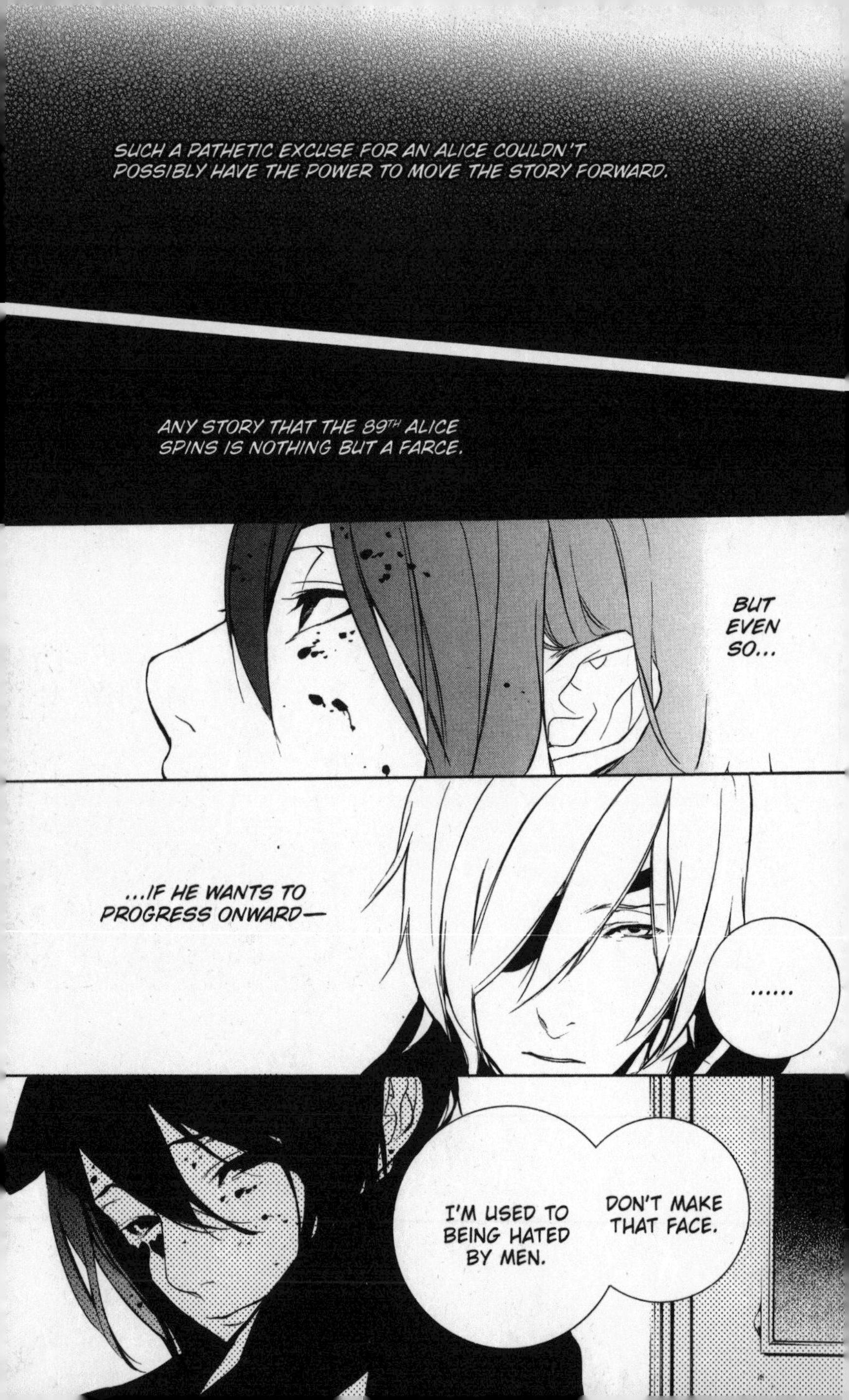
SUCH A PATHETIC EXCUSE FOR AN ALICE COULDN'T POSSIBLY HAVE THE POWER TO MOVE THE STORY FORWARD.
ANY STORY THAT THE 89TH ALICE SPINS IS NOTHING BUT A FARCE.
BUT EVEN SO...
...IF HE WANTS TO PROGRESS ONWARD—
......
DON'T MAKE THAT FACE.
I'M USED TO BEING HATED BY MEN.

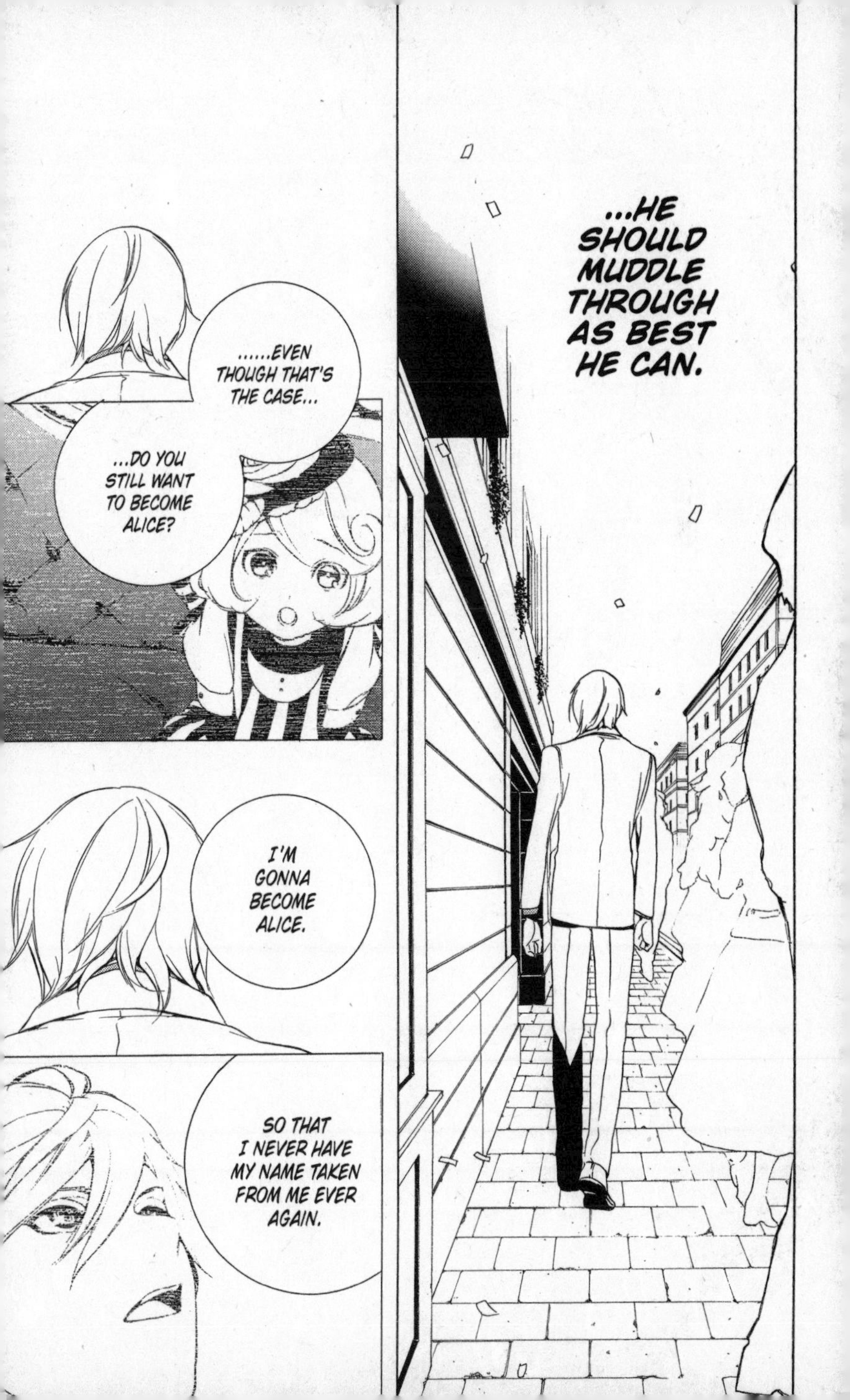
...HE SHOULD MUDDLE THROUGH AS BEST HE CAN.
......EVEN THOUGH THAT'S THE CASE...
...DO YOU STILL WANT TO BECOME ALICE?
I'M GONNA BECOME ALICE.
SO THAT I NEVER HAVE MY NAME TAKEN FROM ME EVER AGAIN.

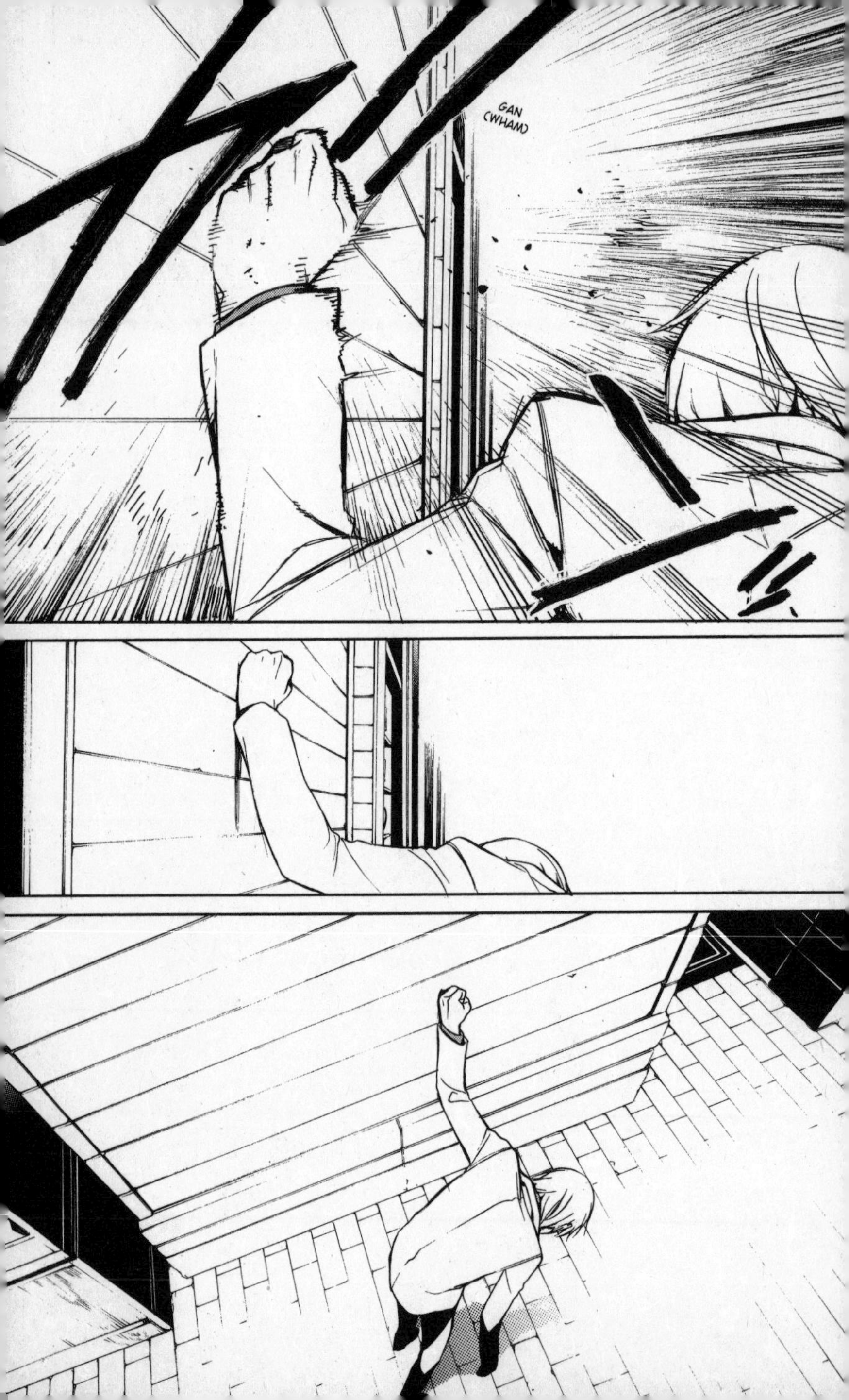
GAN
(WHAM)

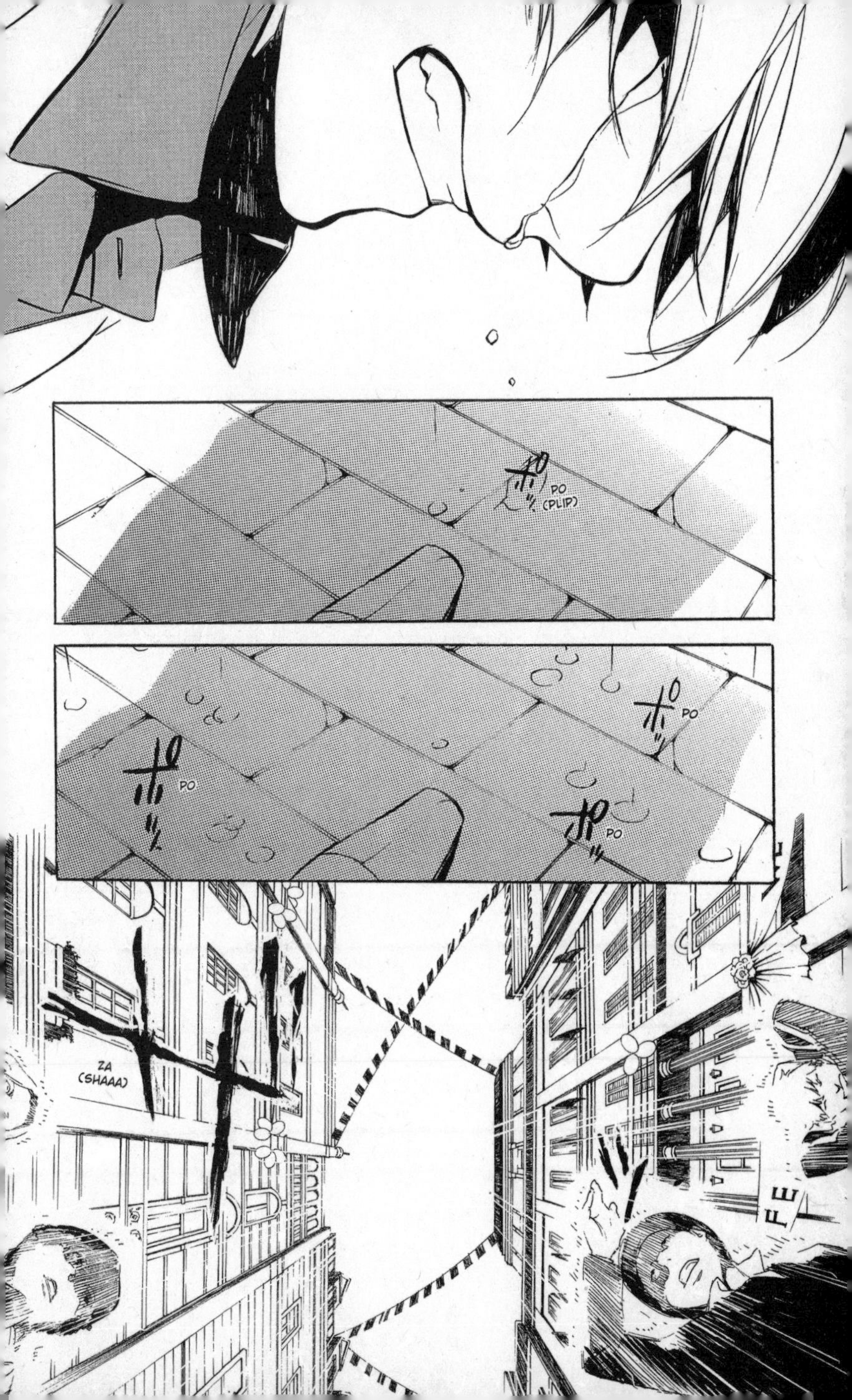
PO (PLIP)
PO
PO
PO
FE
ZA (SHAAA)

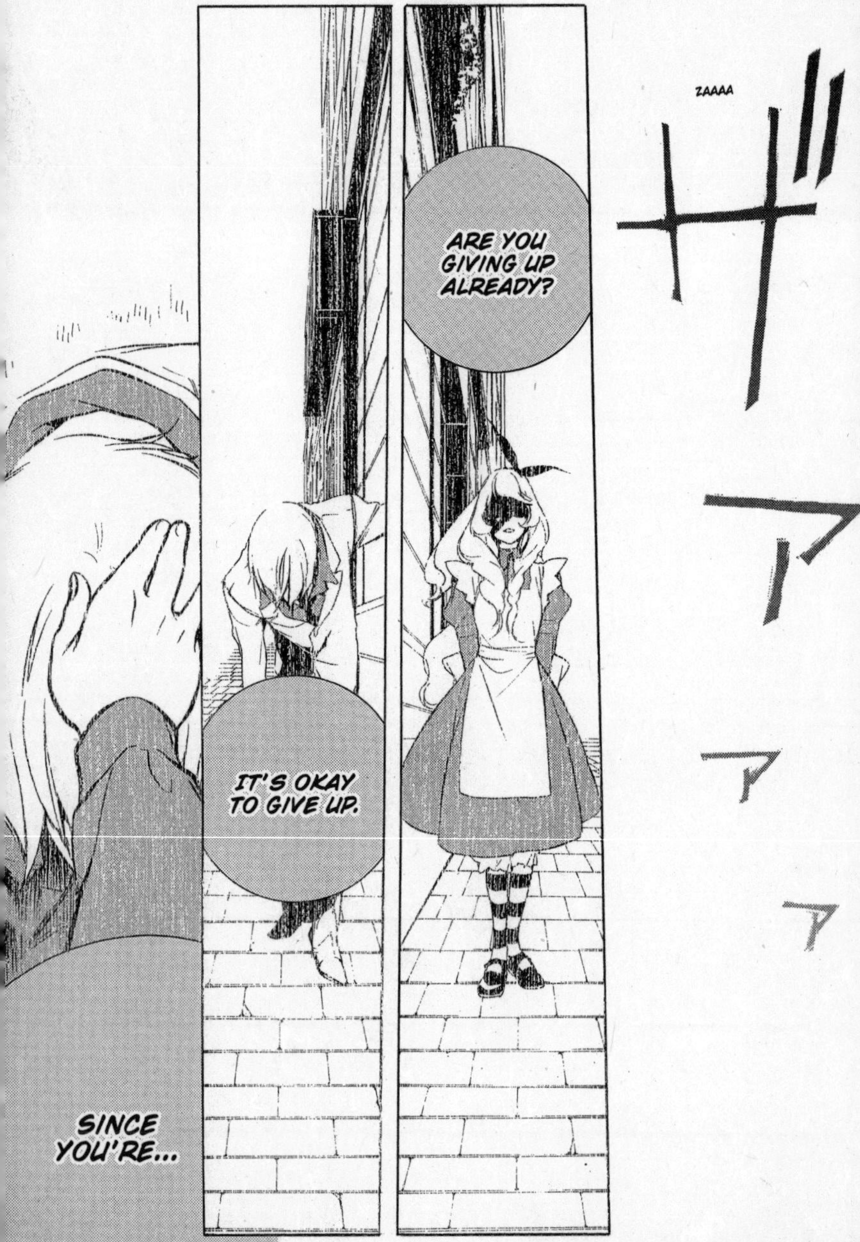
ZAAAA
ARE YOU GIVING UP ALREADY?
IT'S OKAY TO GIVE UP.
SINCE YOU'RE...

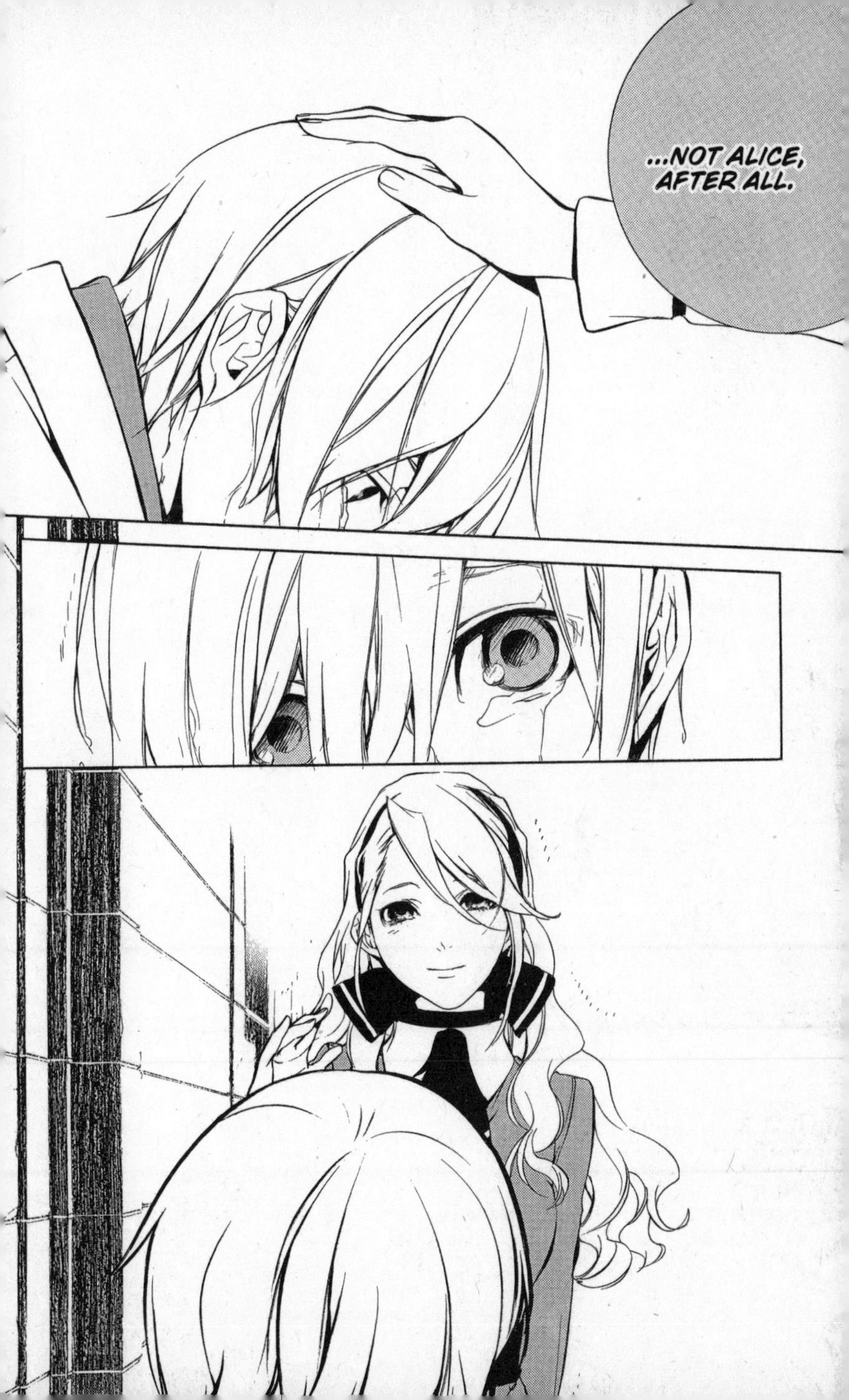
...NOT ALICE, AFTER ALL.

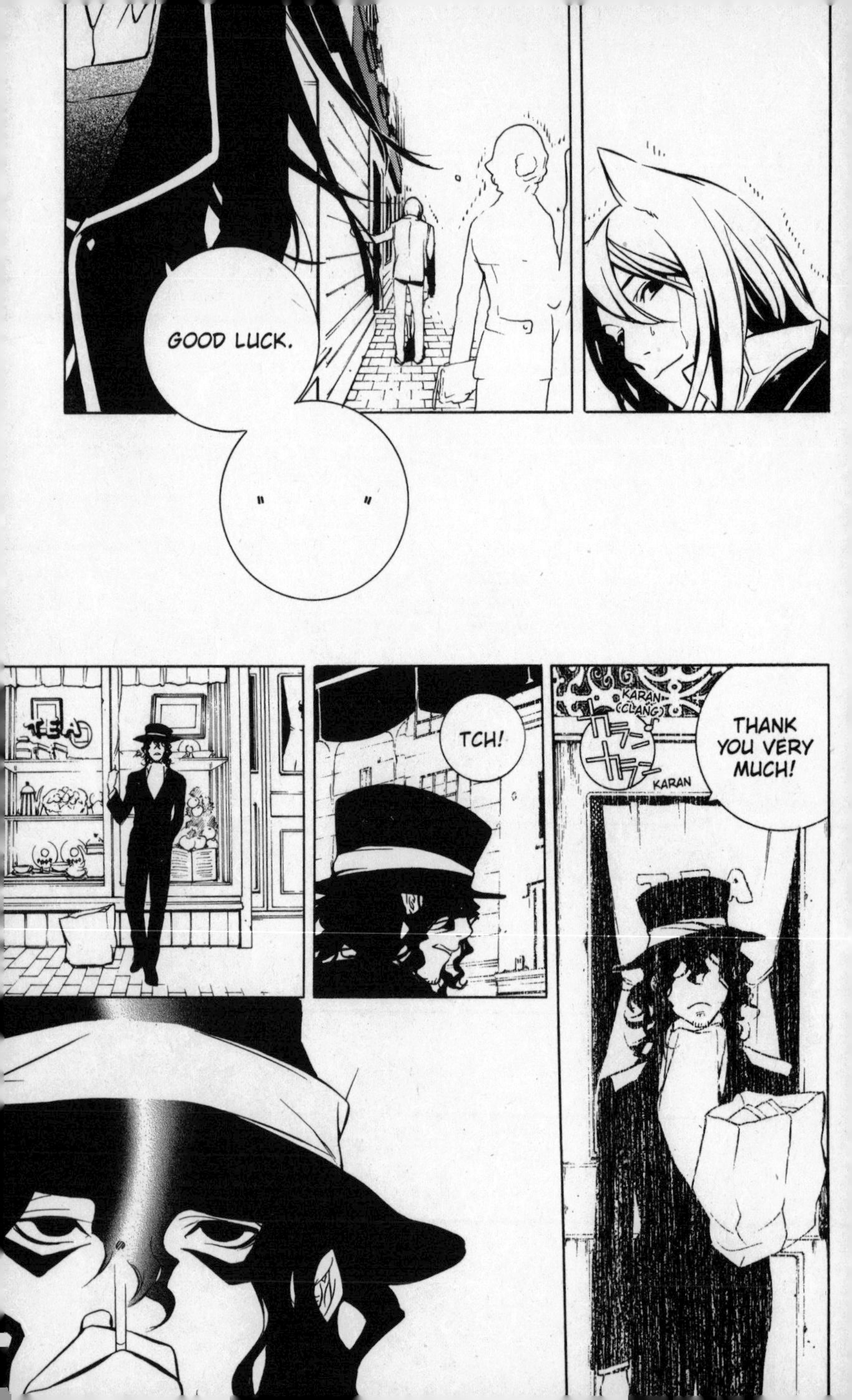
GOOD LUCK.
KARAN (CLANG) KARAN
THANK YOU VERY MUCH!
TCH!

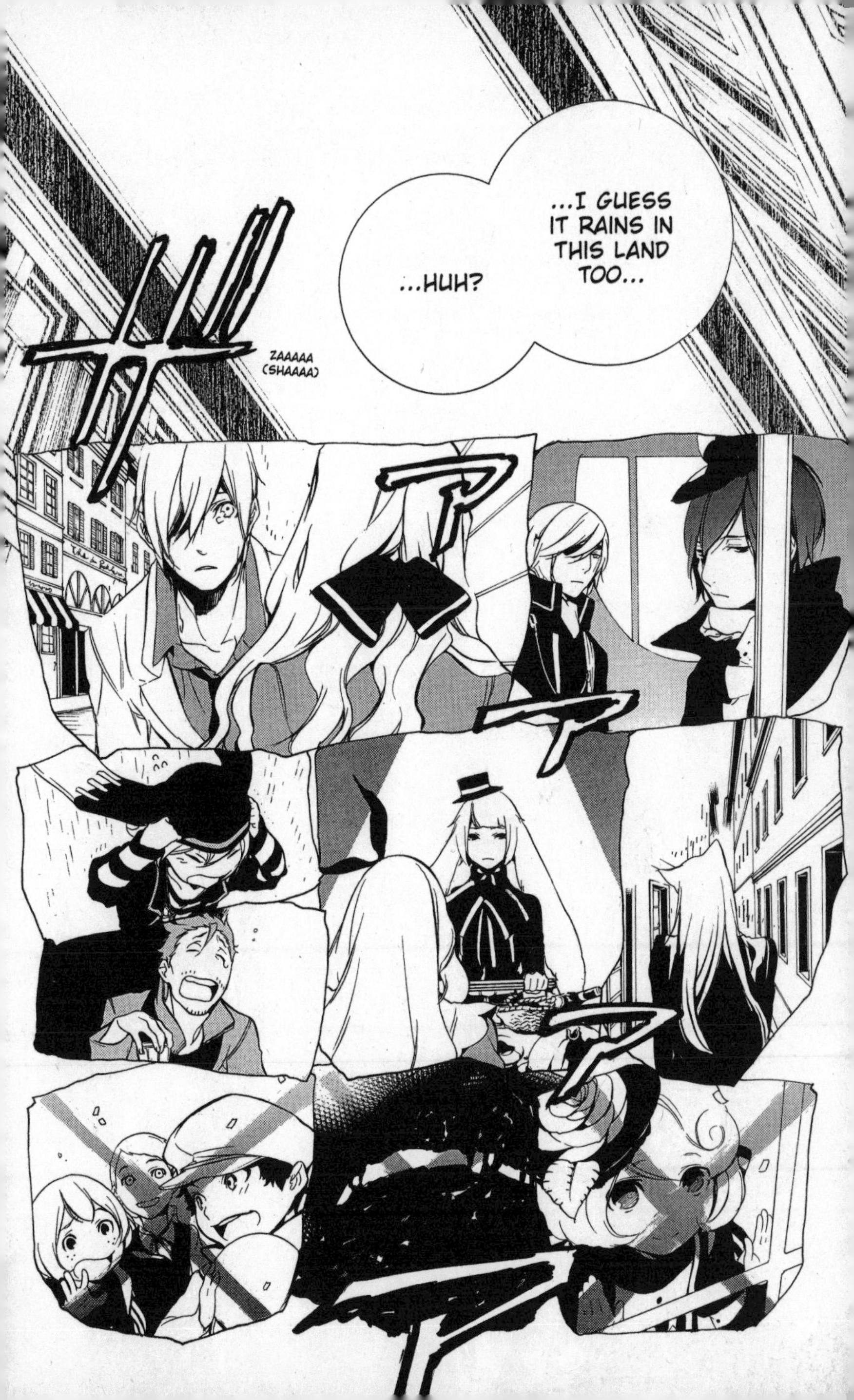
...I GUESS IT RAINS IN THIS LAND TOO...
...HUH?
ZAAAAA (SHAAAA)

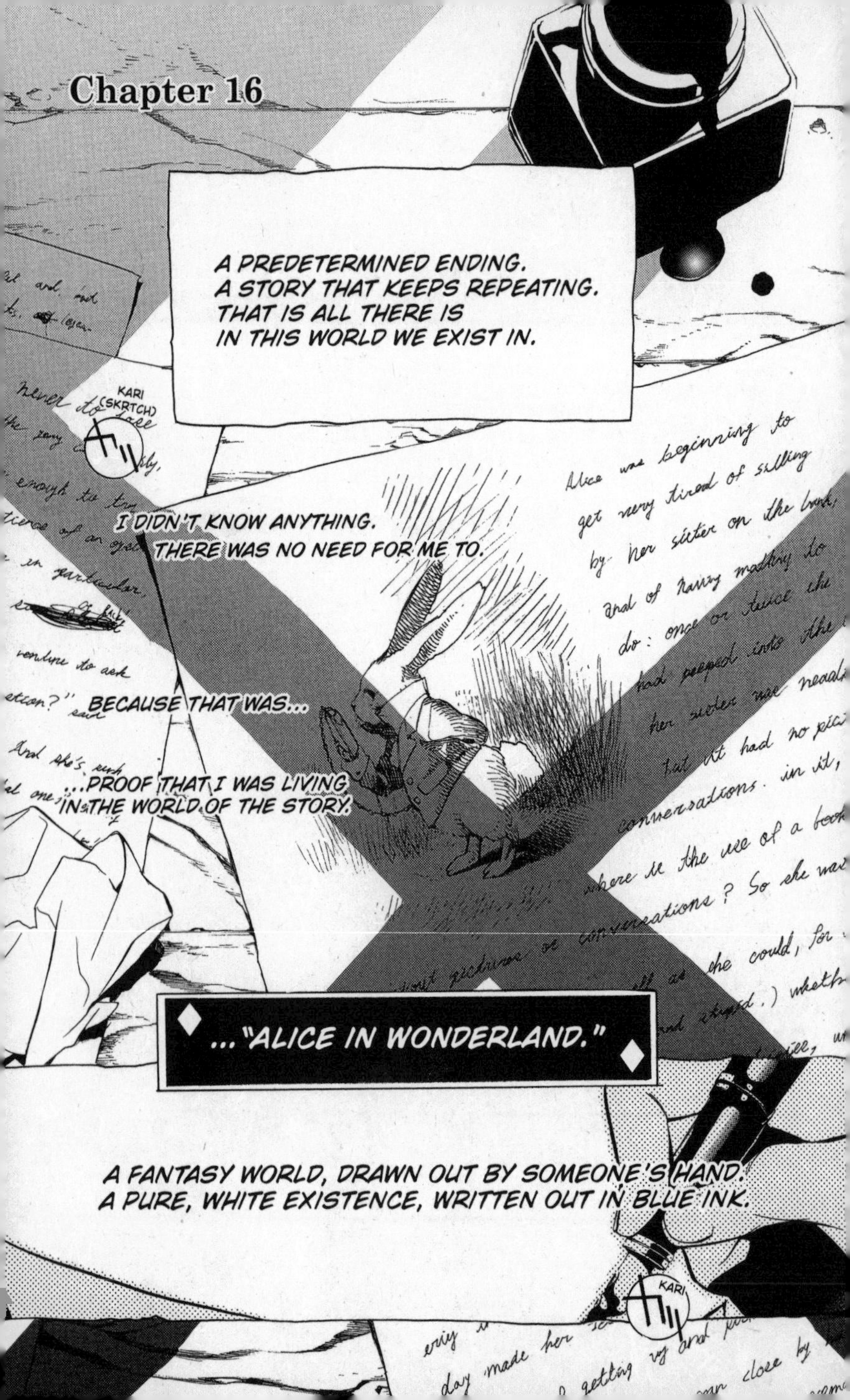
Chapter 16
A PREDETERMINED ENDING. A STORY THAT KEEPS REPEATING. THAT IS ALL THERE IS IN THIS WORLD WE EXIST IN.
KARI (SKRTCH)
I DIDN'T KNOW ANYTHING. THERE WAS NO NEED FOR ME TO.
BECAUSE THAT WAS...
...PROOF THAT I WAS LIVING IN THE WORLD OF THE STORY.
..."ALICE IN WONDERLAND."
A FANTASY WORLD, DRAWN OUT BY SOMEONE'S HAND. A PURE, WHITE EXISTENCE, WRITTEN OUT IN BLUE INK.
KARI

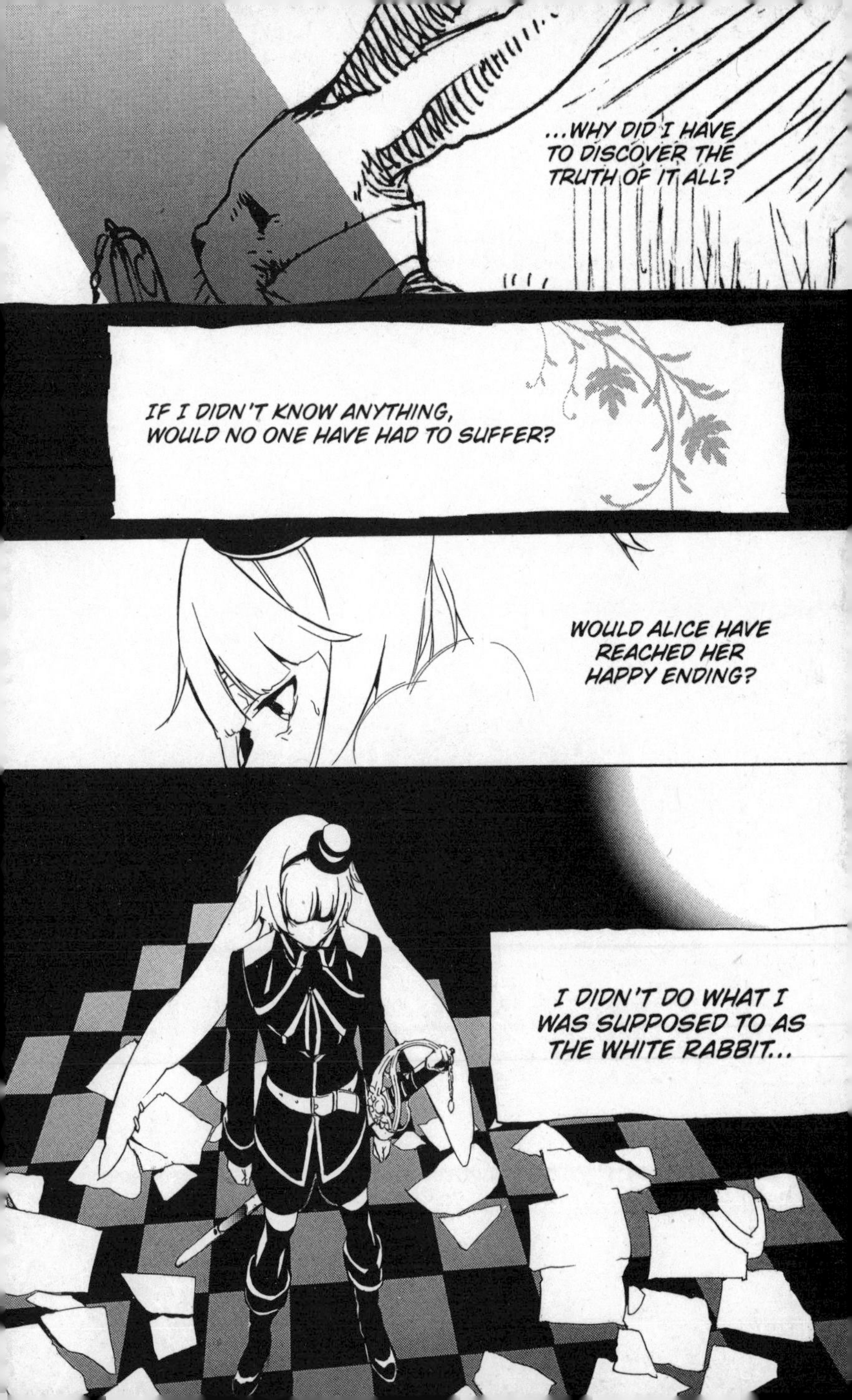
...WHY DID I HAVE TO DISCOVER THE TRUTH OF IT ALL?
IF I DIDN'T KNOW ANYTHING, WOULD NO ONE HAVE HAD TO SUFFER?
WOULD ALICE HAVE REACHED HER HAPPY ENDING?
I DIDN'T DO WHAT I WAS SUPPOSED TO AS THE WHITE RABBIT...

Are you Alice?

Chapter 16

be lost in reverie

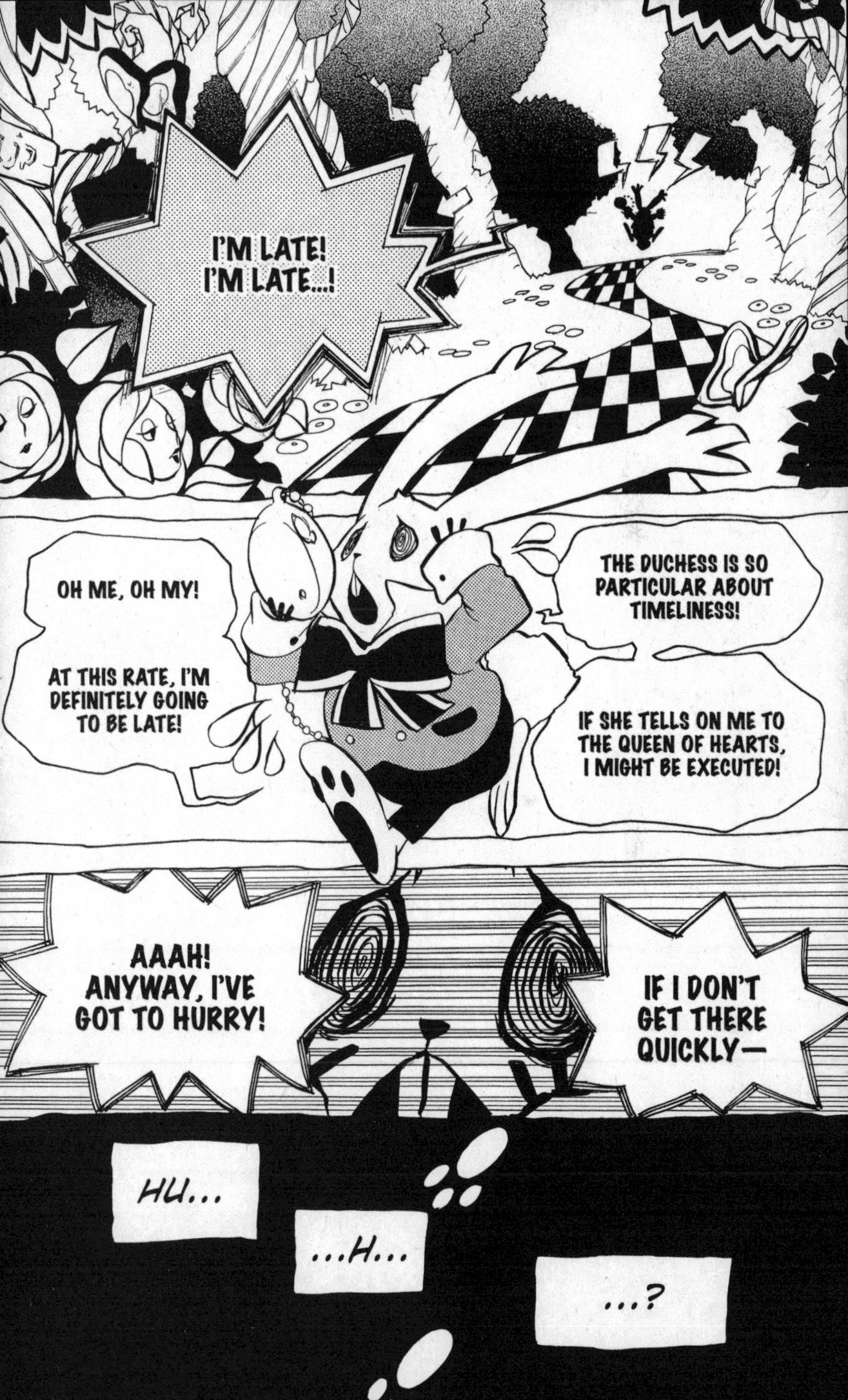
I'M LATE!
I'M LATE...!
THE DUCHESS IS SO PARTICULAR ABOUT TIMELINESS!
IF SHE TELLS ON ME TO THE QUEEN OF HEARTS, I MIGHT BE EXECUTED!
OH ME, OH MY!
AT THIS RATE, I'M DEFINITELY GOING TO BE LATE!
IF I DON'T GET THERE QUICKLY—
AAAH! ANYWAY, I'VE GOT TO HURRY!
HU...
...H...
...?

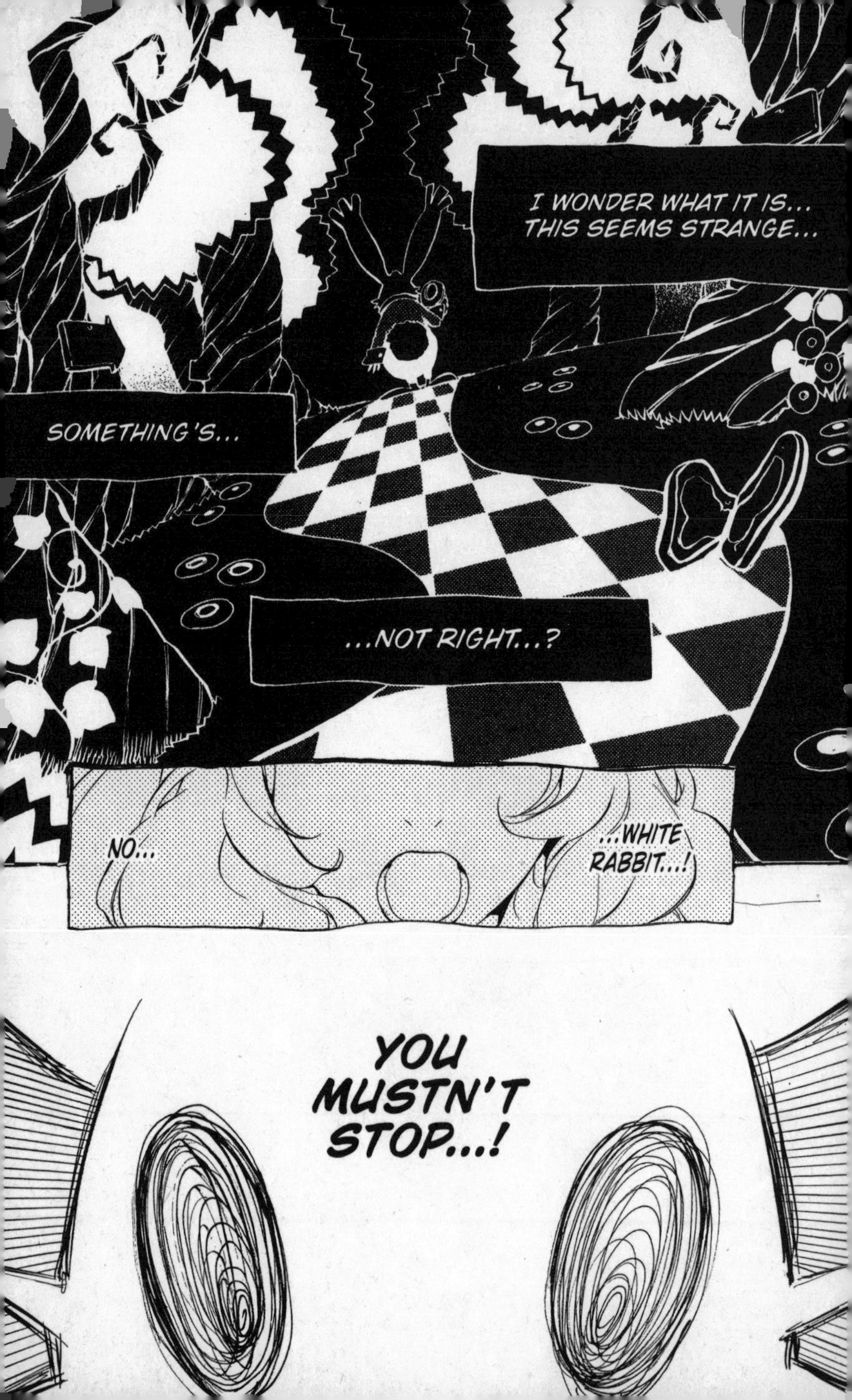
I WONDER WHAT IT IS... THIS SEEMS STRANGE...
SOMETHING'S...
...NOT RIGHT...?
...WHITE RABBIT...!
NO...
YOU MUSTN'T STOP...!

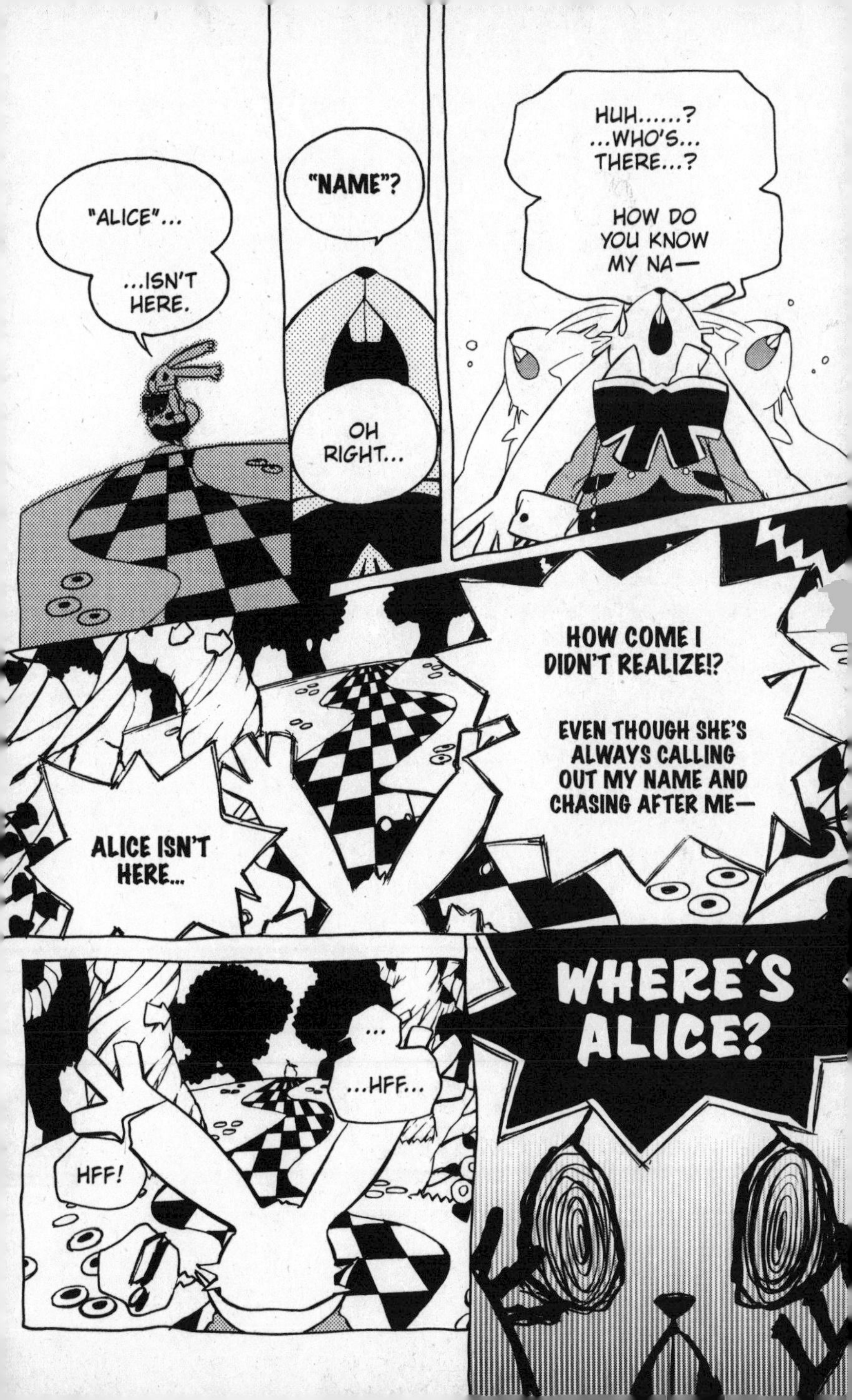
HUH......? ...WHO'S... THERE...?
HOW DO YOU KNOW MY NA—
"NAME"?
OH RIGHT...
"ALICE"...
...ISN'T HERE.
HOW COME I DIDN'T REALIZE!?
EVEN THOUGH SHE'S ALWAYS CALLING OUT MY NAME AND CHASING AFTER ME—
ALICE ISN'T HERE...
WHERE'S ALICE?
...
...HFF...
HFF!

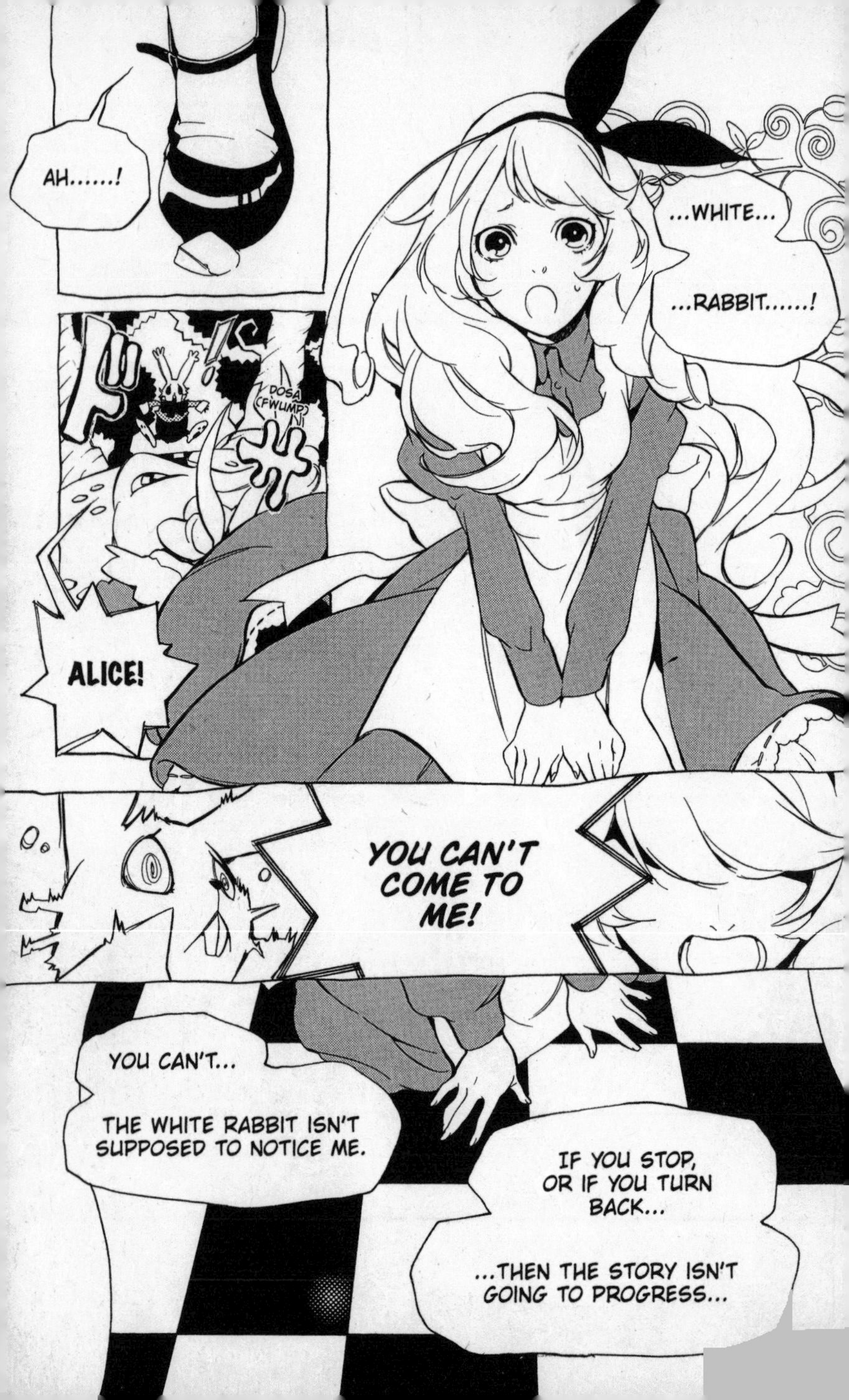
...WHITE...
...RABBIT......!
AH......!
DOSA (FWUMP)
ALICE!
YOU CAN'T COME TO ME!
YOU CAN'T...
THE WHITE RABBIT ISN'T SUPPOSED TO NOTICE ME.
IF YOU STOP, OR IF YOU TURN BACK...
...THEN THE STORY ISN'T GOING TO PROGRESS...

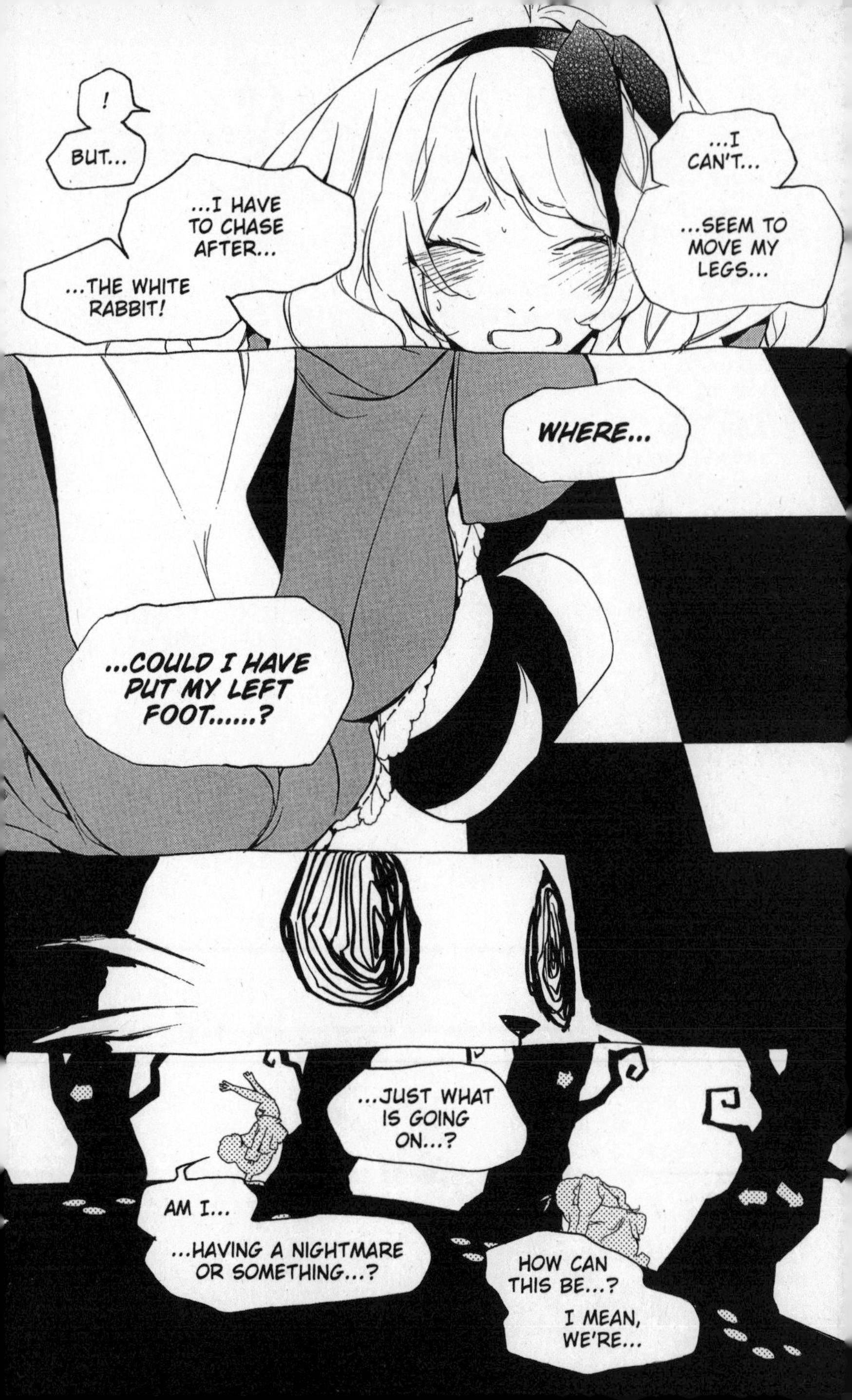
...I CAN'T...
...SEEM TO MOVE MY LEGS...
!
BUT...
...I HAVE TO CHASE AFTER...
...THE WHITE RABBIT!
WHERE...
...COULD I HAVE PUT MY LEFT FOOT......?
...JUST WHAT IS GOING ON...?
AM I...
...HAVING A NIGHTMARE OR SOMETHING...?
HOW CAN THIS BE...?
I MEAN, WE'RE...

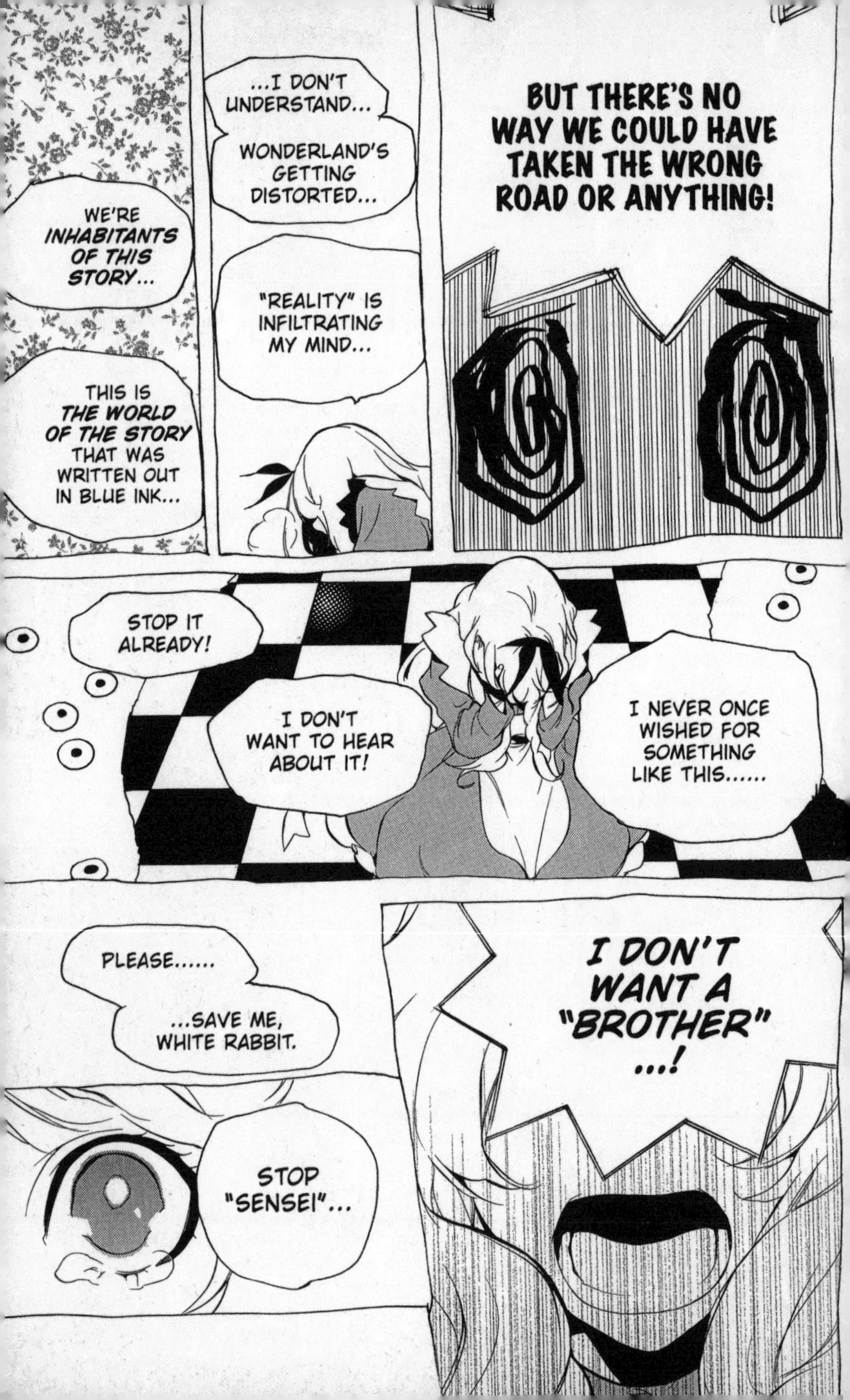
BUT THERE'S NO WAY WE COULD HAVE TAKEN THE WRONG ROAD OR ANYTHING!
...I DON'T UNDERSTAND...
WONDERLAND'S GETTING DISTORTED...
"REALITY" IS INFILTRATING MY MIND...
WE'RE *INHABITANTS OF THIS STORY*...
THIS IS *THE WORLD OF THE STORY* THAT WAS WRITTEN OUT IN BLUE INK...
I NEVER ONCE WISHED FOR SOMETHING LIKE THIS......
I DON'T WANT TO HEAR ABOUT IT!
STOP IT ALREADY!
I DON'T WANT A "BROTHER" ...!
PLEASE......
...SAVE ME, WHITE RABBIT.
STOP "SENSEI"...

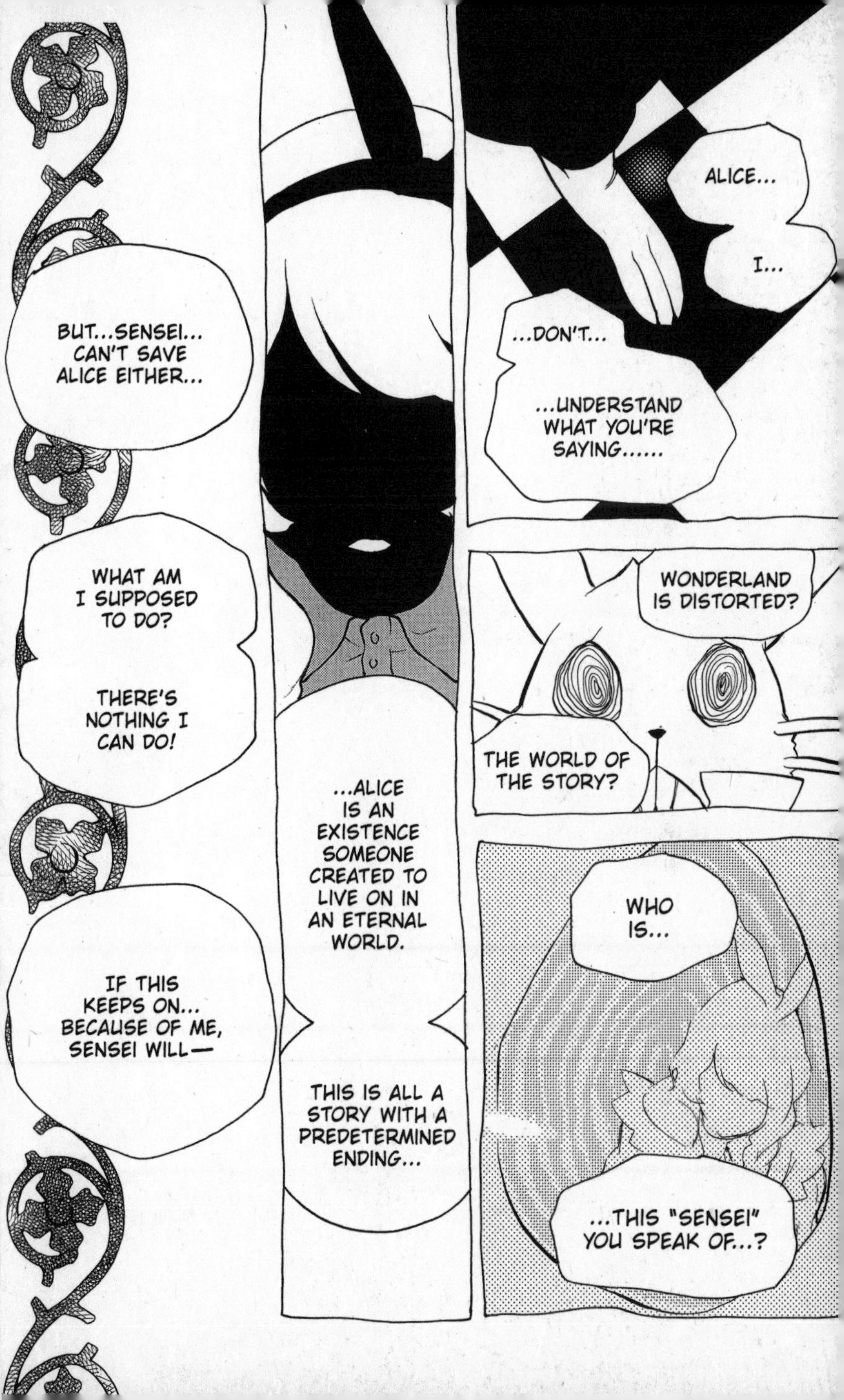
ALICE...
I...
...DON'T...
...UNDERSTAND WHAT YOU'RE SAYING......
WONDERLAND IS DISTORTED?
THE WORLD OF THE STORY?
WHO IS...
...THIS "SENSEI" YOU SPEAK OF...?
...ALICE IS AN EXISTENCE SOMEONE CREATED TO LIVE ON IN AN ETERNAL WORLD.
THIS IS ALL A STORY WITH A PREDETERMINED ENDING...
BUT...SENSEI... CAN'T SAVE ALICE EITHER...
WHAT AM I SUPPOSED TO DO?
THERE'S NOTHING I CAN DO!
IF THIS KEEPS ON... BECAUSE OF ME, SENSEI WILL—

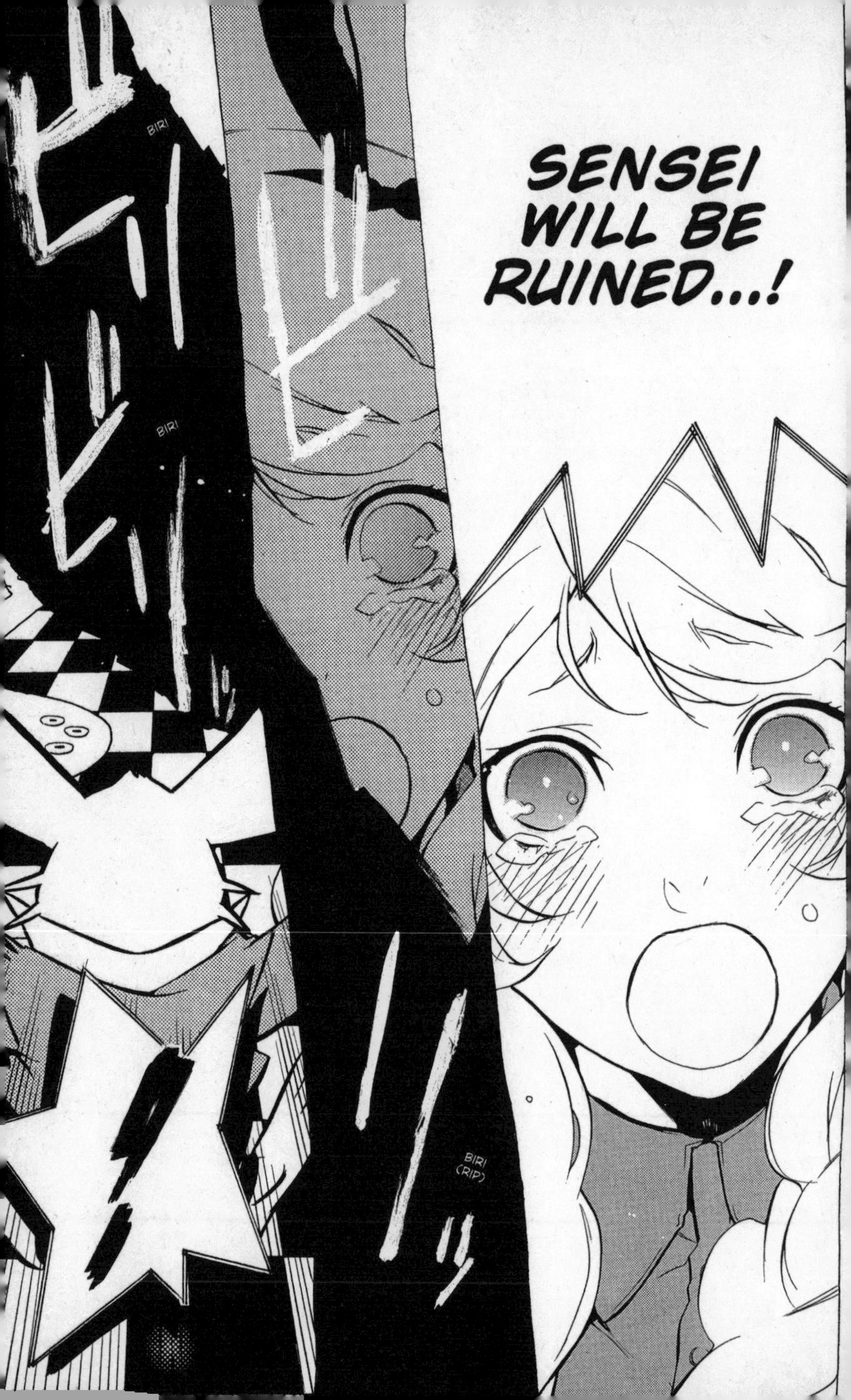
SENSEI WILL BE RUINED...!
BIRI
BIRI
BIRI (RIP)

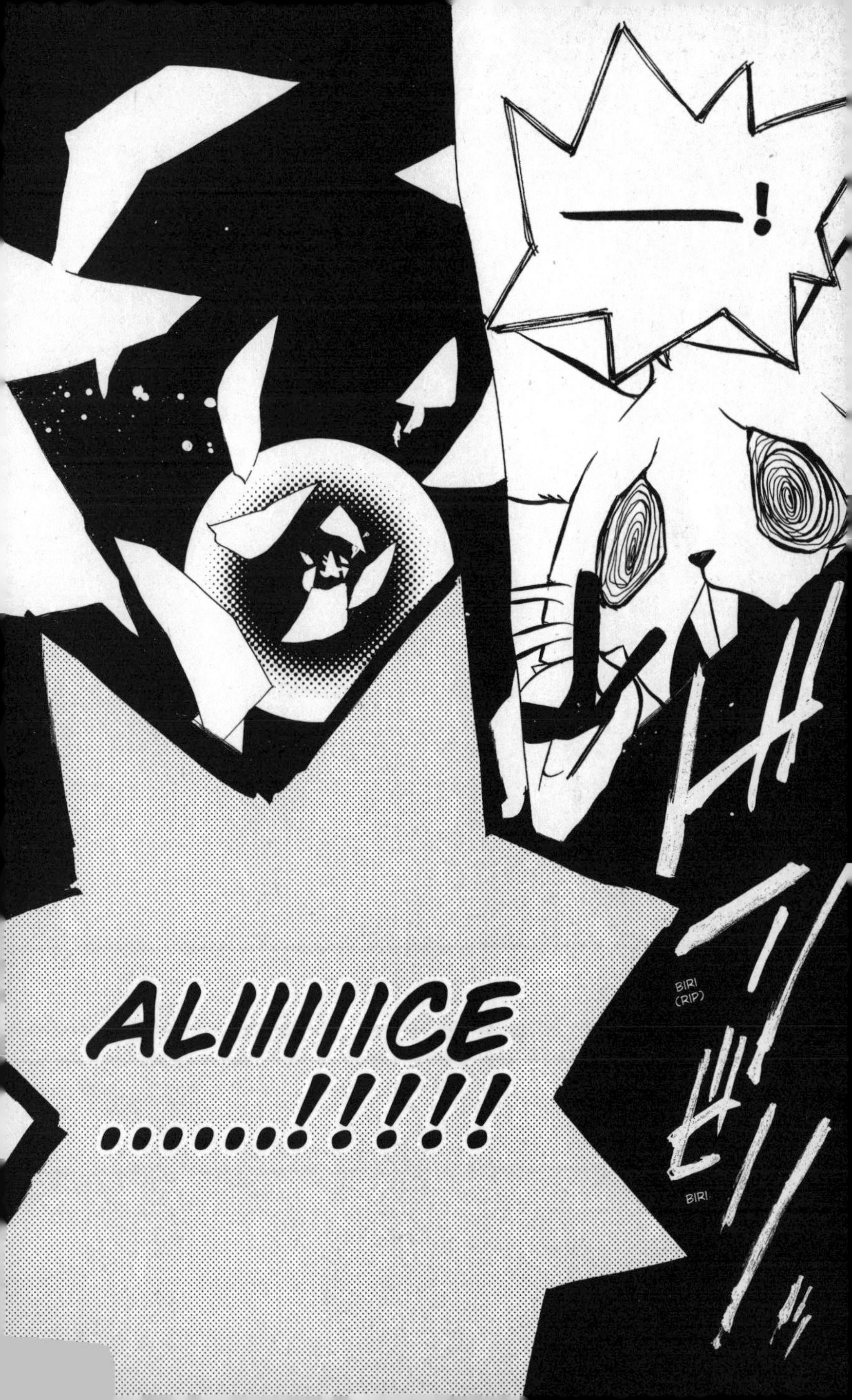
—!
BIRI (RIP)
BIRI
ALIIIIICE ......!!!!!

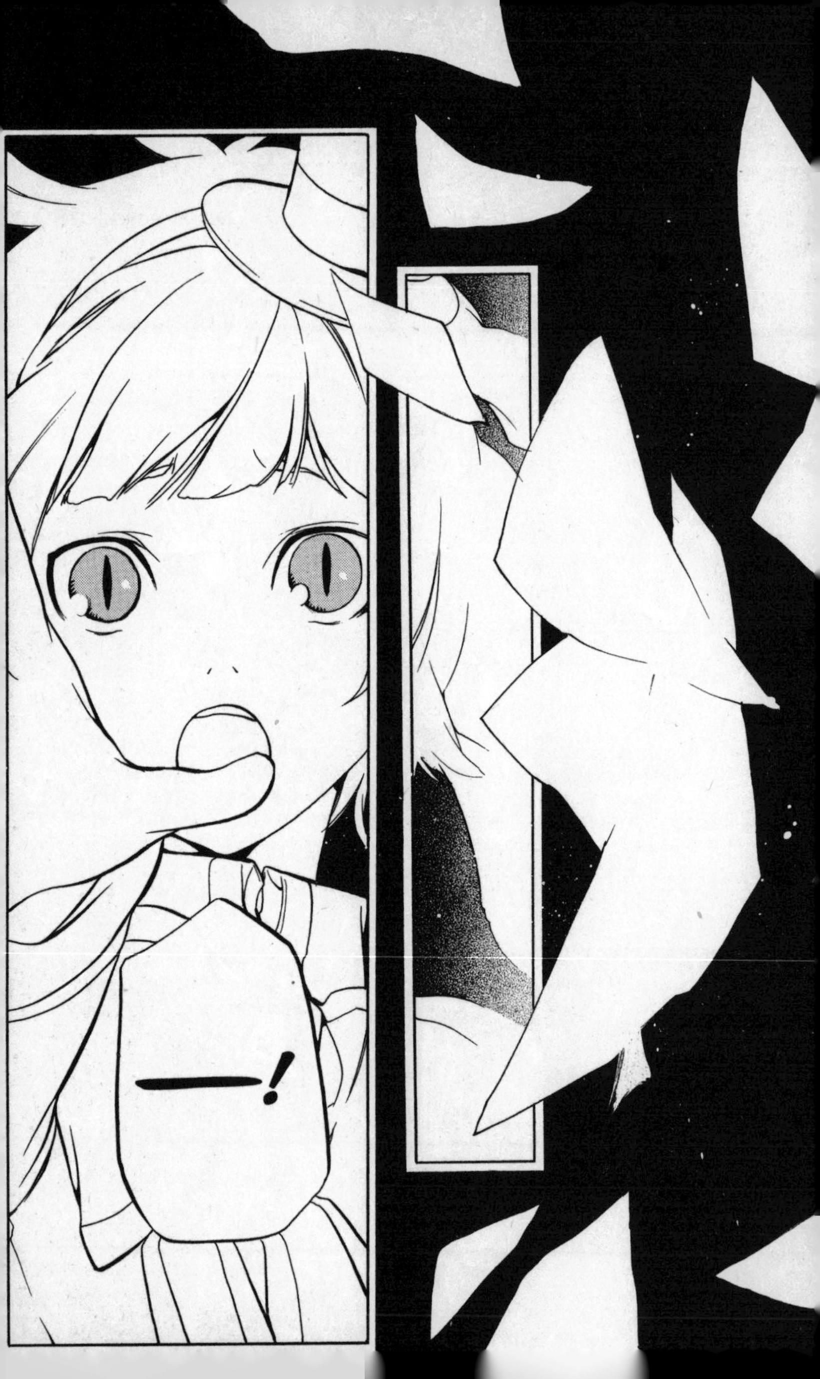
——!

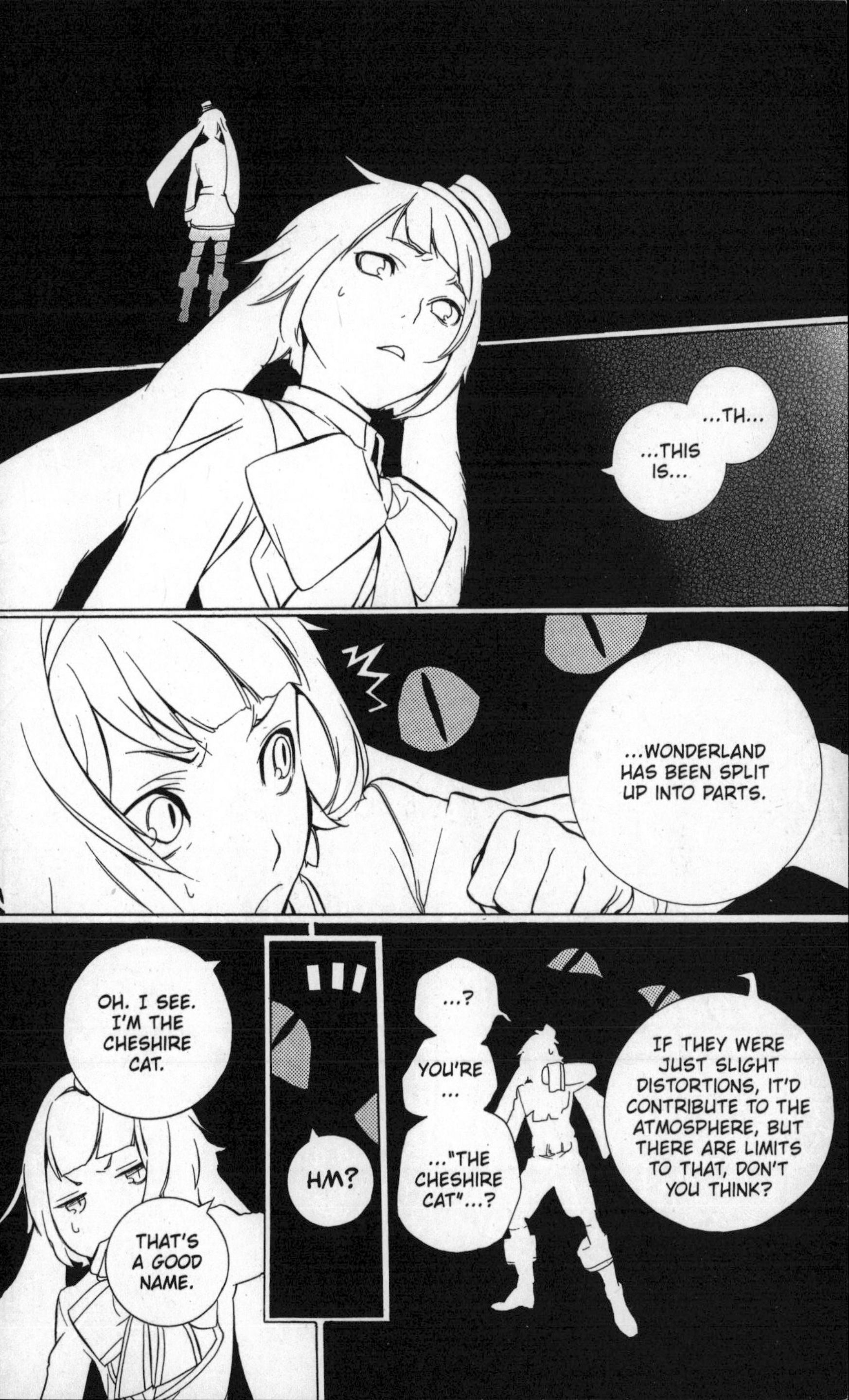
...TH...
...THIS IS...
...WONDERLAND HAS BEEN SPLIT UP INTO PARTS.
IF THEY WERE JUST SLIGHT DISTORTIONS, IT'D CONTRIBUTE TO THE ATMOSPHERE, BUT THERE ARE LIMITS TO THAT, DON'T YOU THINK?
...?
YOU'RE ...
..."THE CHESHIRE CAT"...?
HM?
OH. I SEE. I'M THE CHESHIRE CAT.
THAT'S A GOOD NAME.

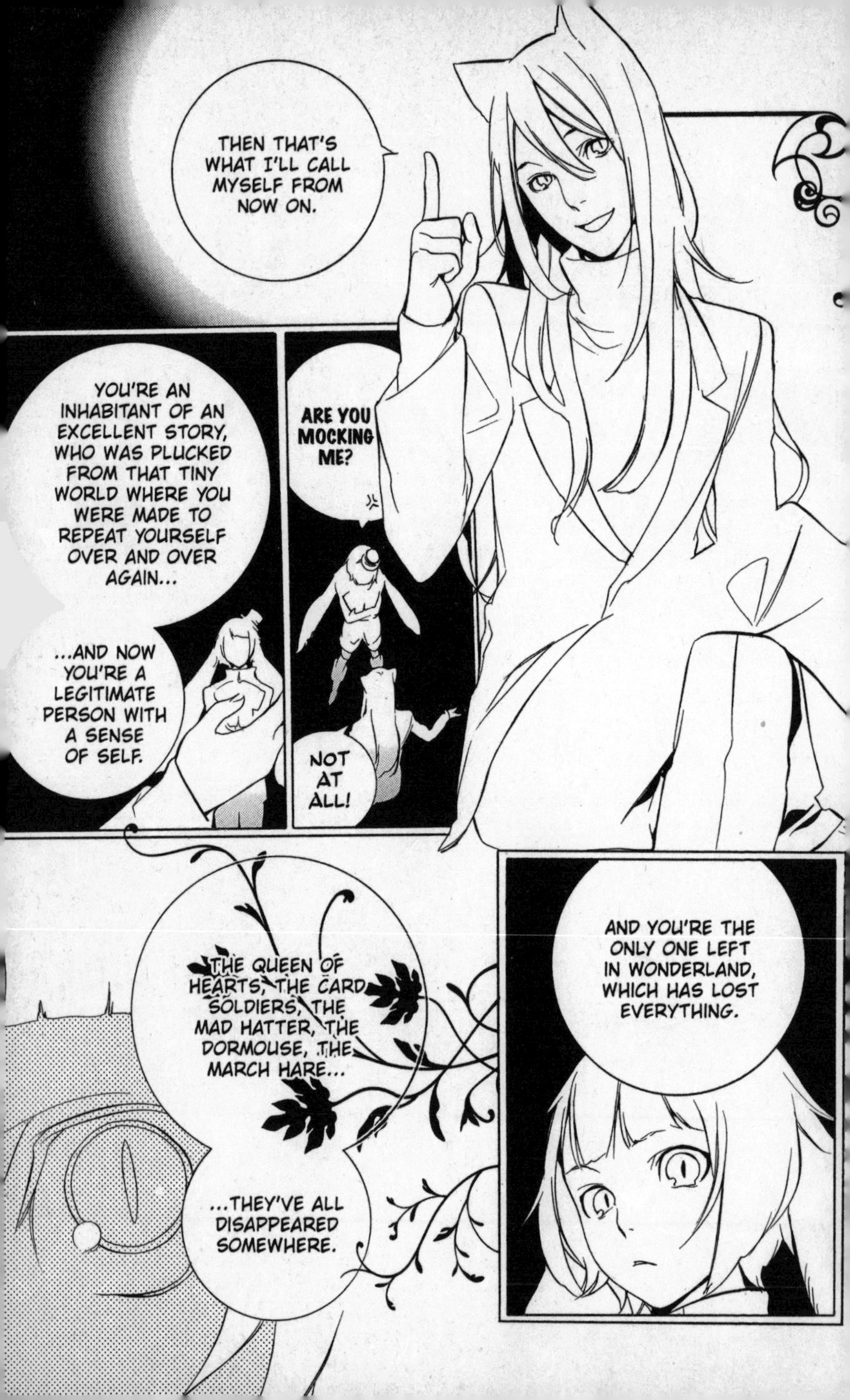
THEN THAT'S WHAT I'LL CALL MYSELF FROM NOW ON.
ARE YOU MOCKING ME?
NOT AT ALL!
YOU'RE AN INHABITANT OF AN EXCELLENT STORY, WHO WAS PLUCKED FROM THAT TINY WORLD WHERE YOU WERE MADE TO REPEAT YOURSELF OVER AND OVER AGAIN...
...AND NOW YOU'RE A LEGITIMATE PERSON WITH A SENSE OF SELF.
AND YOU'RE THE ONLY ONE LEFT IN WONDERLAND, WHICH HAS LOST EVERYTHING.
THE QUEEN OF HEARTS, THE CARD SOLDIERS, THE MAD HATTER, THE DORMOUSE, THE MARCH HARE...
...THEY'VE ALL DISAPPEARED SOMEWHERE.

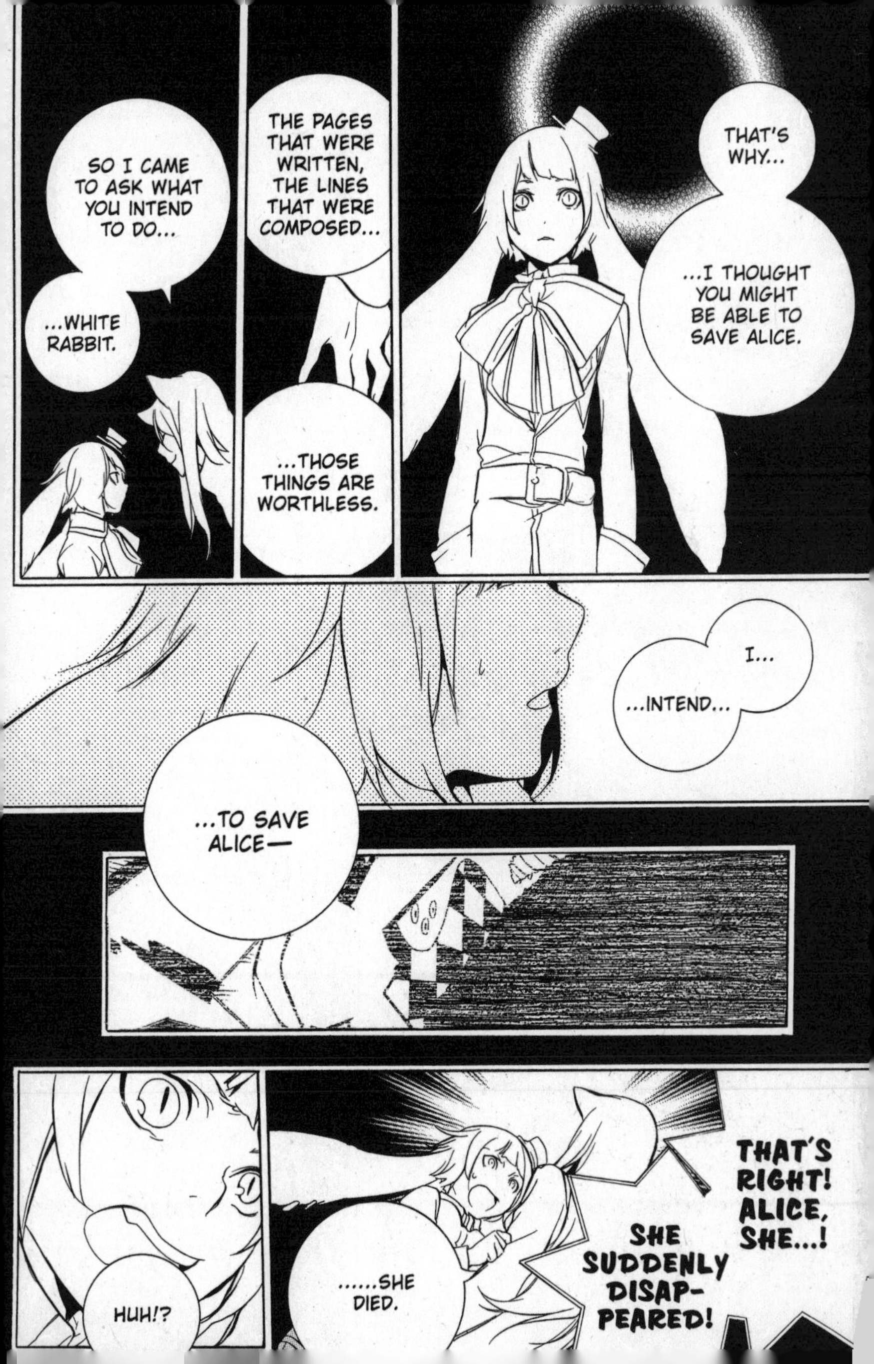
THAT'S WHY...
...I THOUGHT YOU MIGHT BE ABLE TO SAVE ALICE.
THE PAGES THAT WERE WRITTEN, THE LINES THAT WERE COMPOSED...
...THOSE THINGS ARE WORTHLESS.
SO I CAME TO ASK WHAT YOU INTEND TO DO...
...WHITE RABBIT.
I...
...INTEND...
...TO SAVE ALICE—
THAT'S RIGHT! ALICE, SHE...!
SHE SUDDENLY DISAP-PEARED!
......SHE DIED.
HUH!?

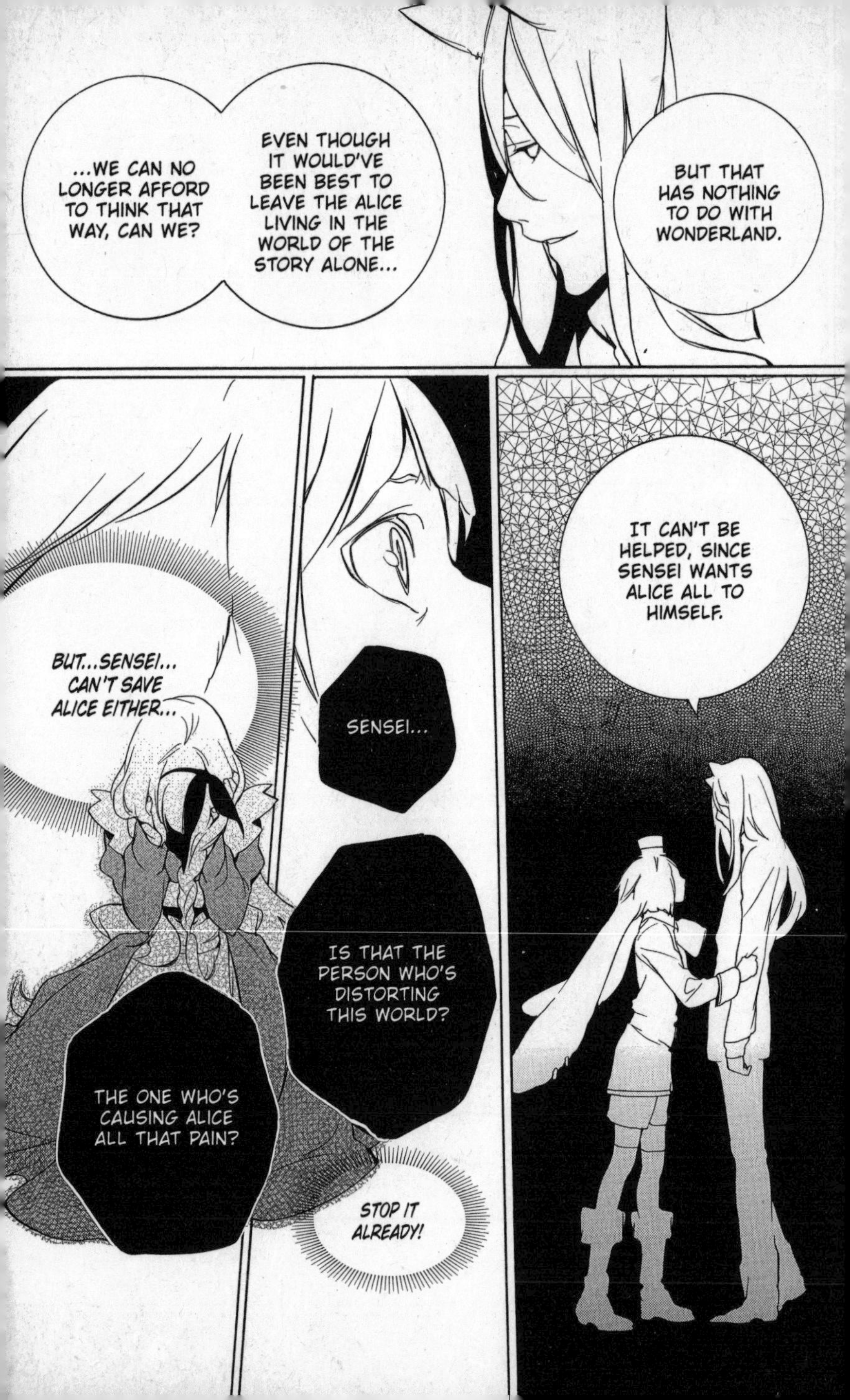
BUT THAT HAS NOTHING TO DO WITH WONDERLAND.
EVEN THOUGH IT WOULD'VE BEEN BEST TO LEAVE THE ALICE LIVING IN THE WORLD OF THE STORY ALONE...
...WE CAN NO LONGER AFFORD TO THINK THAT WAY, CAN WE?
IT CAN'T BE HELPED, SINCE SENSEI WANTS ALICE ALL TO HIMSELF.
SENSEI...
IS THAT THE PERSON WHO'S DISTORTING THIS WORLD?
BUT...SENSEI... CAN'T SAVE ALICE EITHER...
THE ONE WHO'S CAUSING ALICE ALL THAT PAIN?
STOP IT ALREADY!

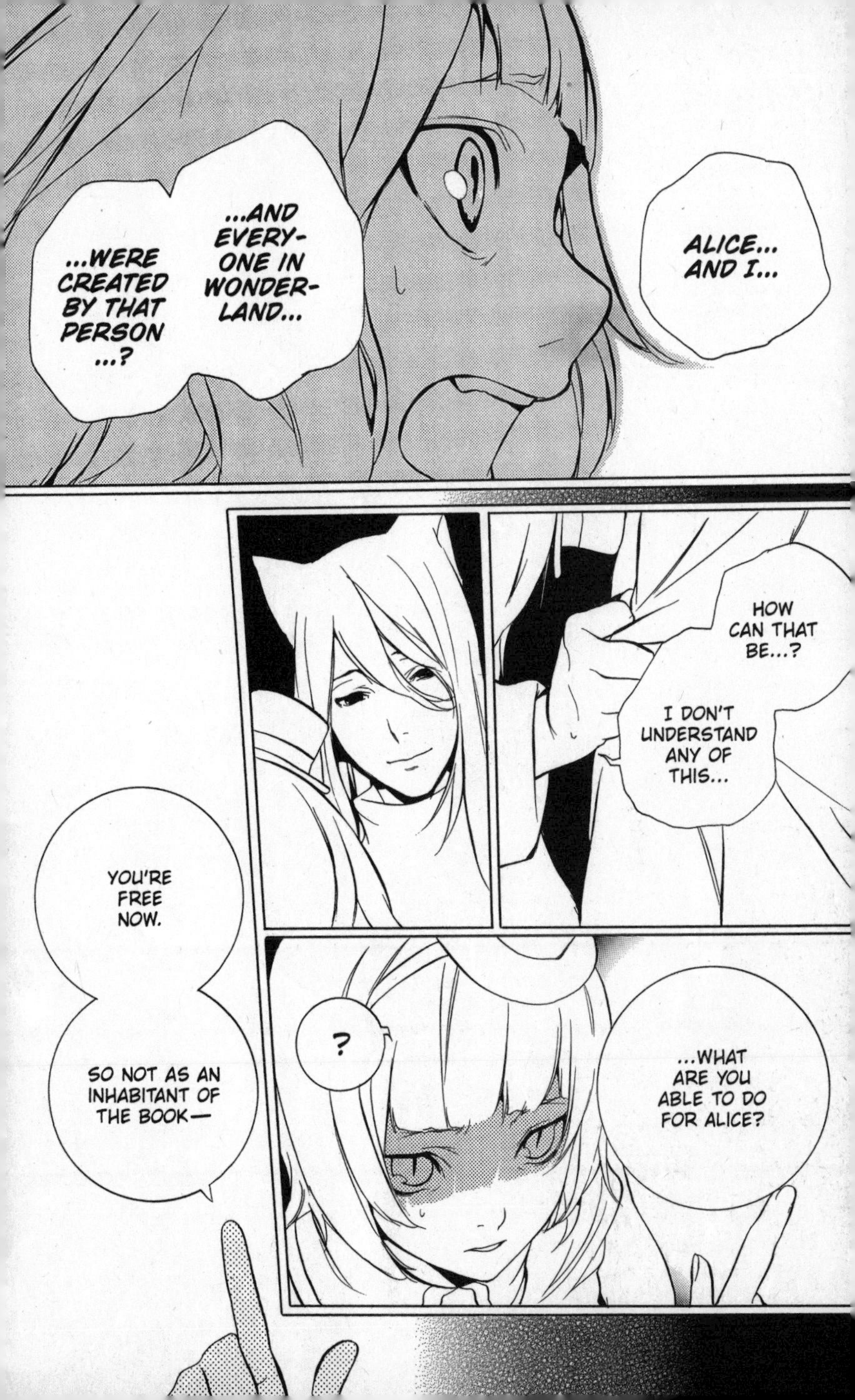
ALICE... AND I...
...AND EVERYONE IN WONDERLAND...
...WERE CREATED BY THAT PERSON ...?
HOW CAN THAT BE...?
I DON'T UNDERSTAND ANY OF THIS...
YOU'RE FREE NOW.
SO NOT AS AN INHABITANT OF THE BOOK—
?
...WHAT ARE YOU ABLE TO DO FOR ALICE?

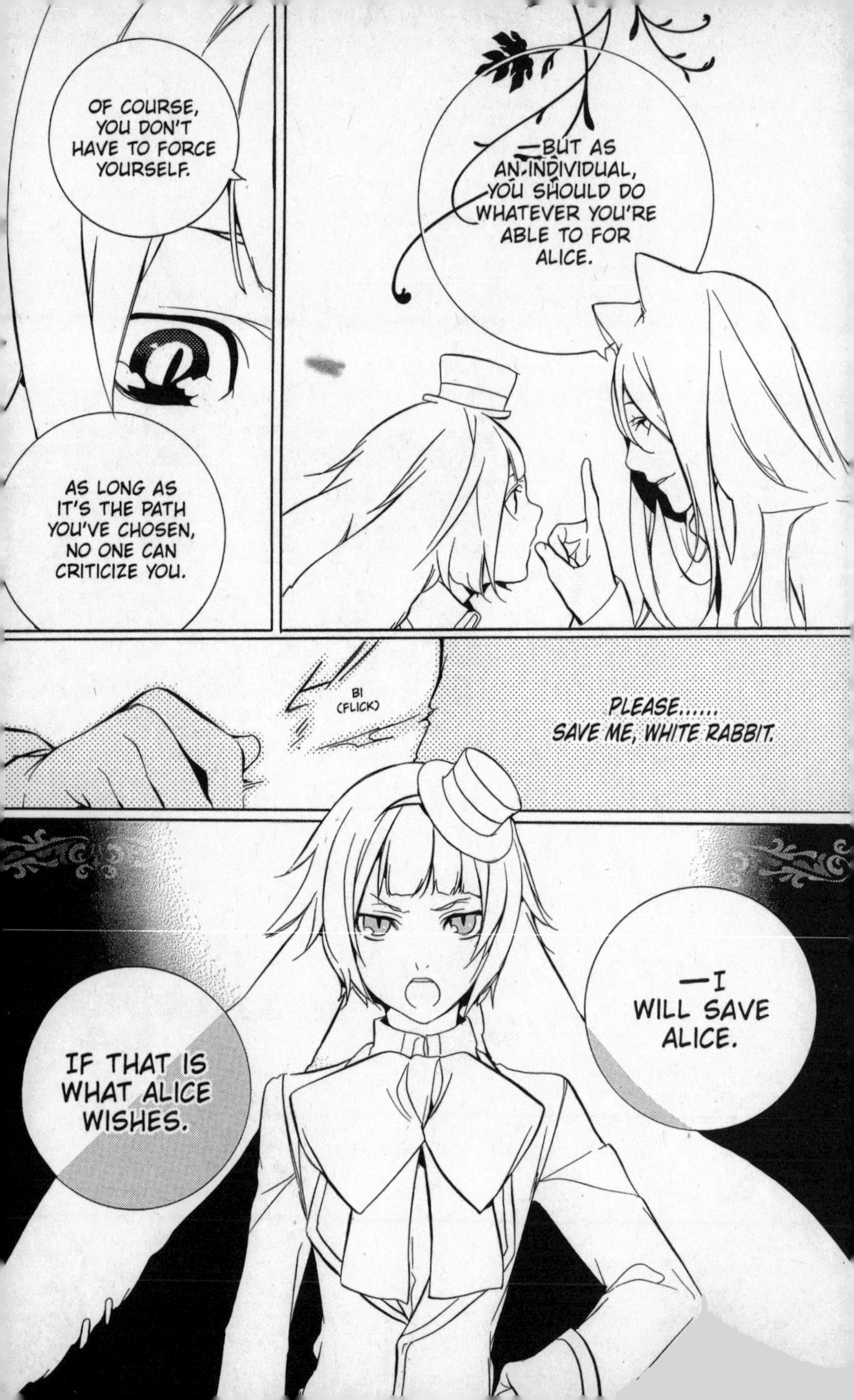
—BUT AS AN INDIVIDUAL, YOU SHOULD DO WHATEVER YOU'RE ABLE TO FOR ALICE.
OF COURSE, YOU DON'T HAVE TO FORCE YOURSELF.
AS LONG AS IT'S THE PATH YOU'VE CHOSEN, NO ONE CAN CRITICIZE YOU.
PLEASE...... SAVE ME, WHITE RABBIT.
BI (FLICK)
—I WILL SAVE ALICE.
IF THAT IS WHAT ALICE WISHES.

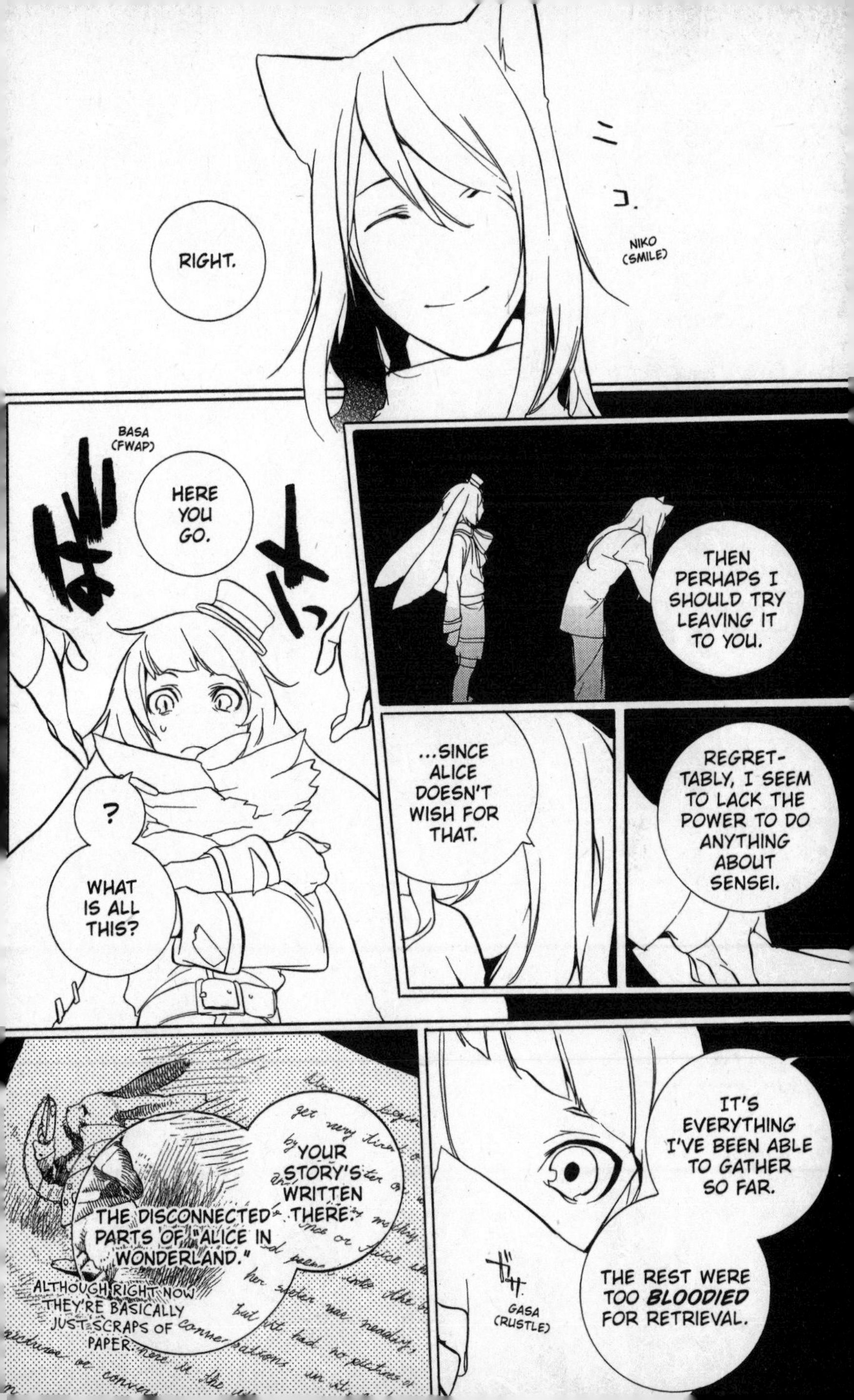
ニコ
NIKO (SMILE)
RIGHT.
THEN PERHAPS I SHOULD TRY LEAVING IT TO YOU.
REGRET-TABLY, I SEEM TO LACK THE POWER TO DO ANYTHING ABOUT SENSEI.
...SINCE ALICE DOESN'T WISH FOR THAT.
ばさっ
BASA (FWAP)
HERE YOU GO.
?
WHAT IS ALL THIS?
IT'S EVERYTHING I'VE BEEN ABLE TO GATHER SO FAR.
ガサ
GASA (RUSTLE)
THE REST WERE TOO *BLOODIED* FOR RETRIEVAL.
YOUR STORY'S WRITTEN THERE.
THE DISCONNECTED PARTS OF "ALICE IN WONDERLAND."
ALTHOUGH RIGHT NOW THEY'RE BASICALLY JUST SCRAPS OF PAPER.

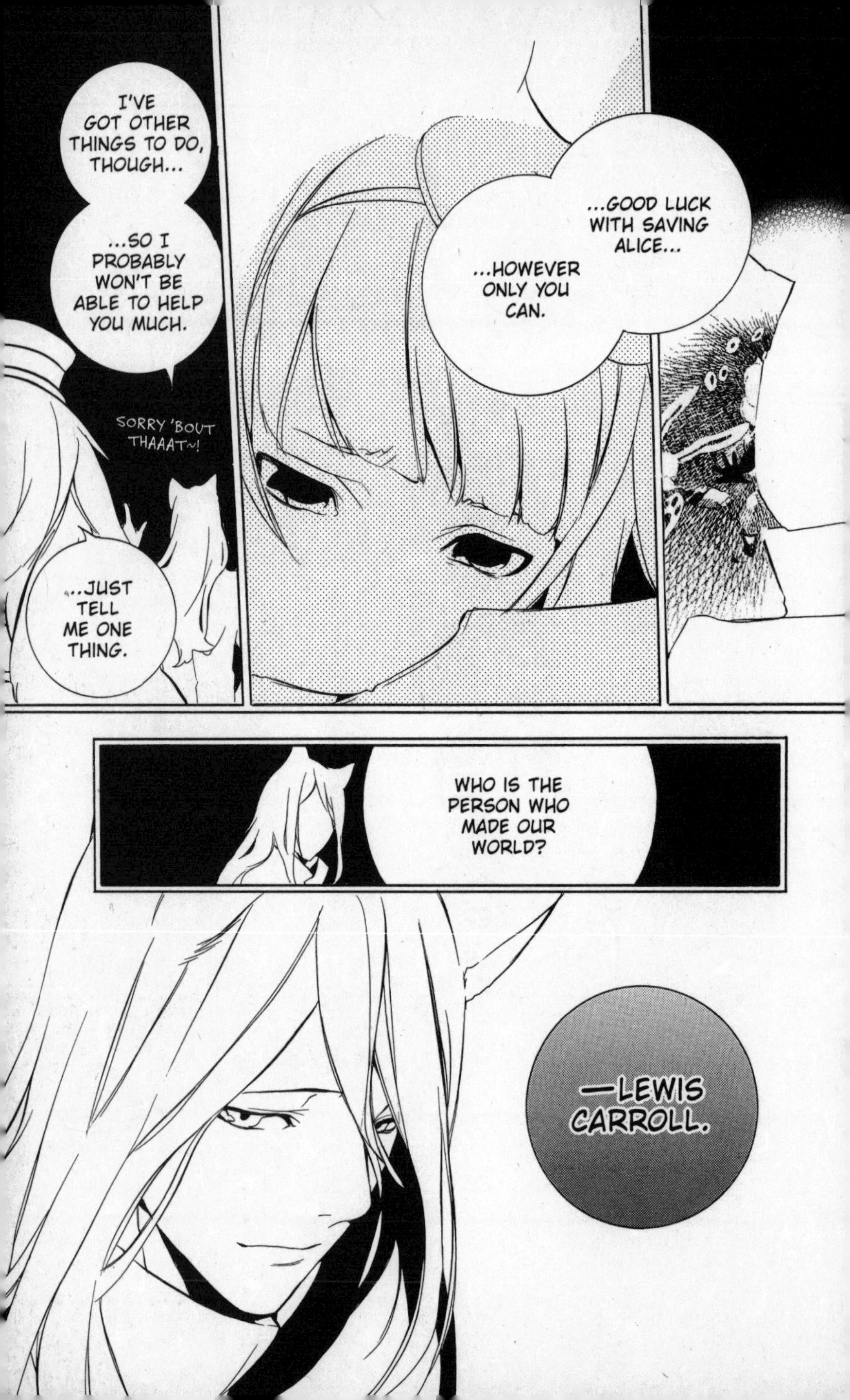
...GOOD LUCK WITH SAVING ALICE...
...HOWEVER ONLY YOU CAN.
I'VE GOT OTHER THINGS TO DO, THOUGH...
...SO I PROBABLY WON'T BE ABLE TO HELP YOU MUCH.
SORRY 'BOUT THAAAT~!
...JUST TELL ME ONE THING.
WHO IS THE PERSON WHO MADE OUR WORLD?
—LEWIS CARROLL.

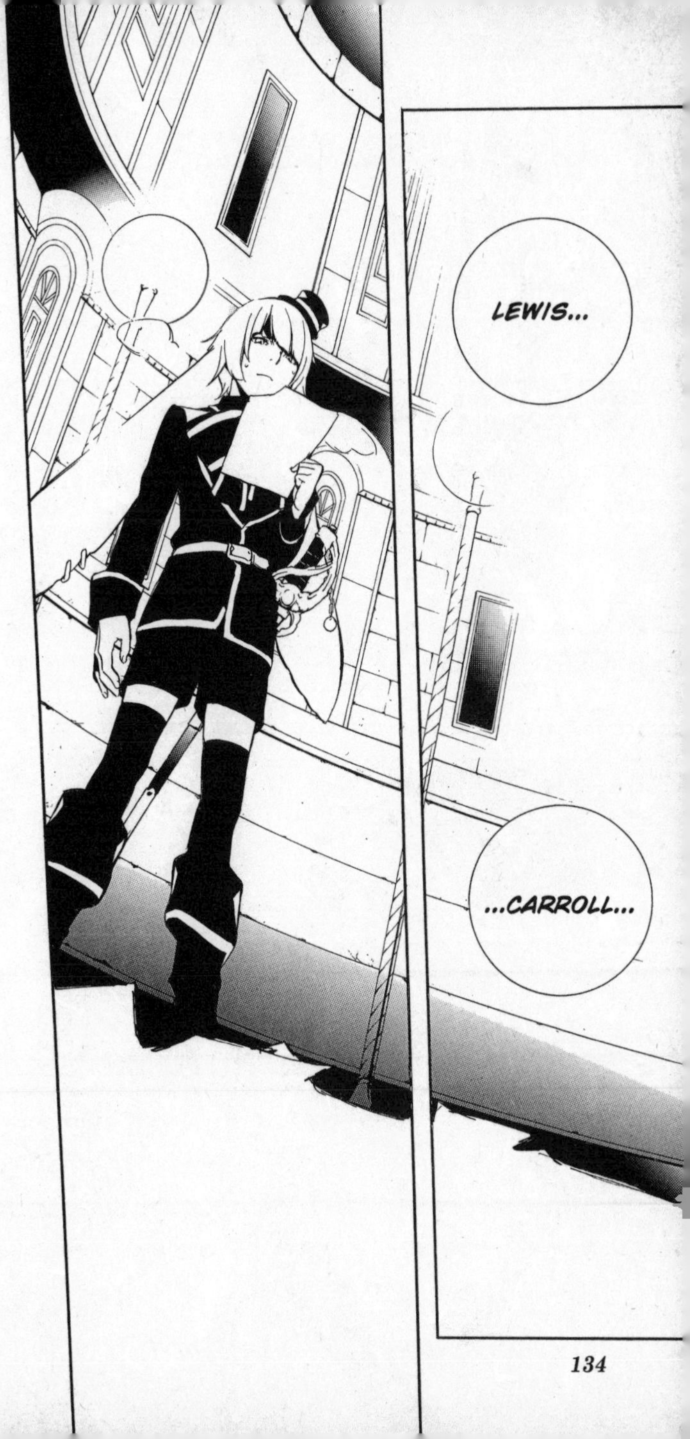
LEWIS...
...CARROLL...

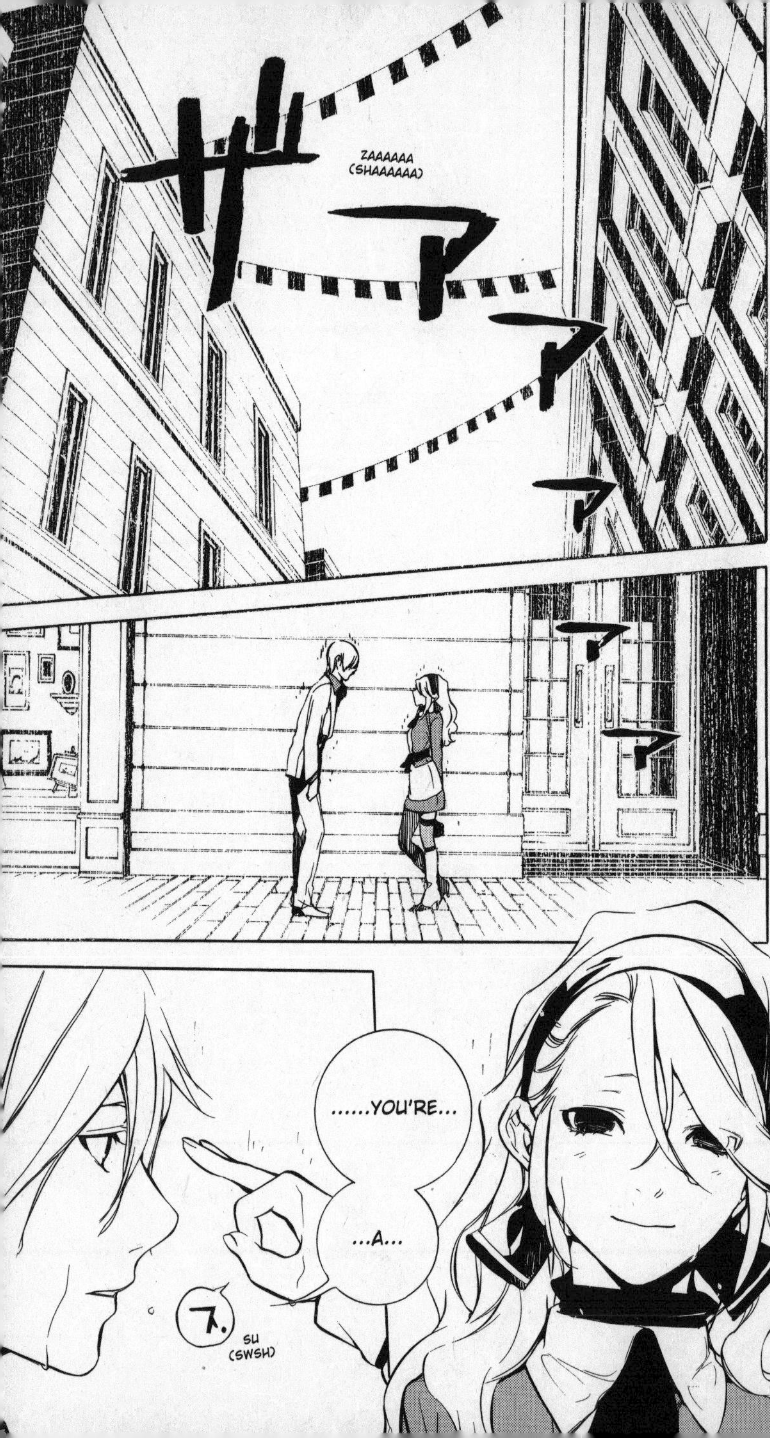
ZAAAAAA
(SHAAAAAA)
......YOU'RE...
...A...
SU
(SWSH)

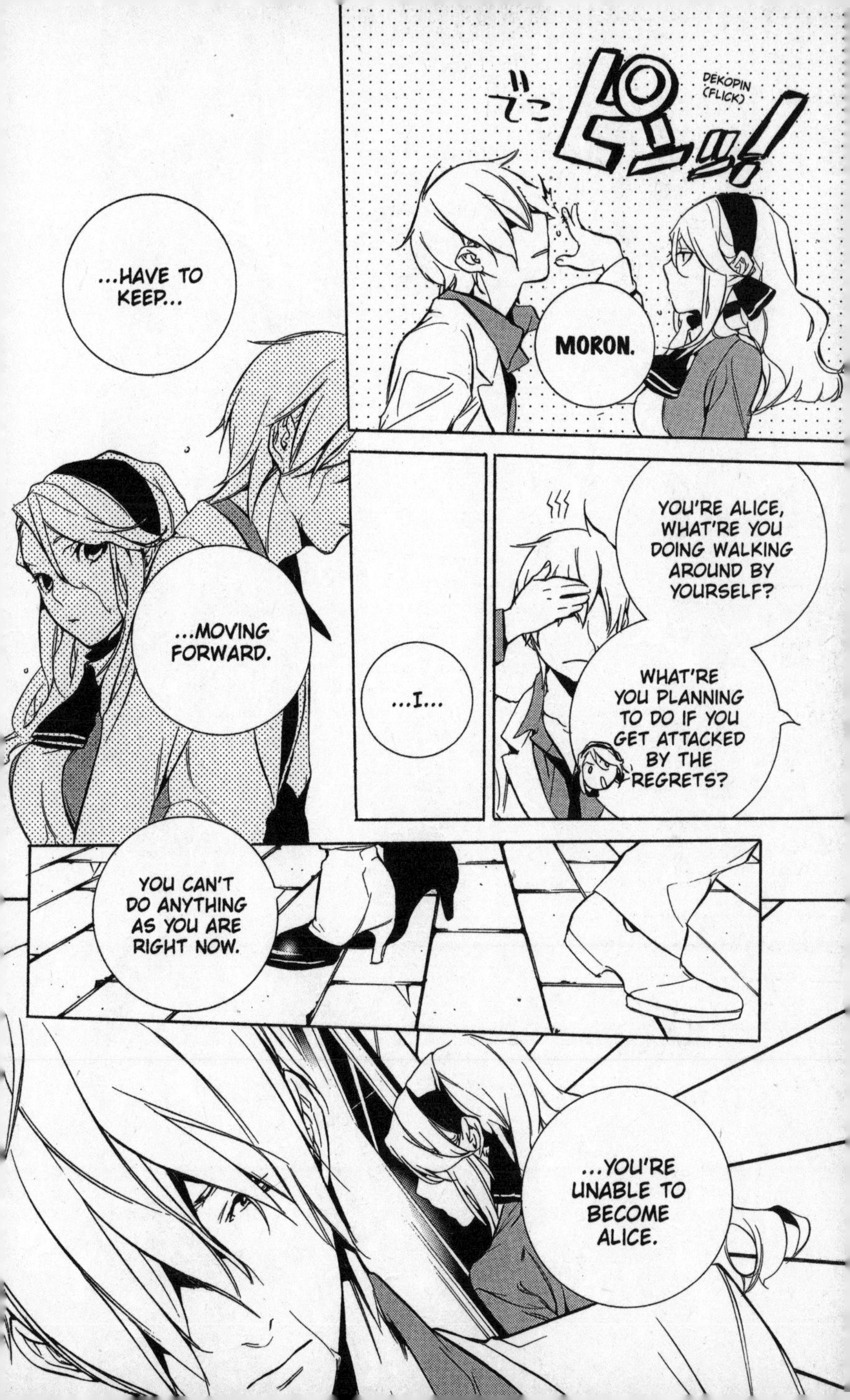
でこピンッ!
DEKOPIN (FLICK)
MORON.
YOU'RE ALICE, WHAT'RE YOU DOING WALKING AROUND BY YOURSELF?
WHAT'RE YOU PLANNING TO DO IF YOU GET ATTACKED BY THE REGRETS?
...I...
...HAVE TO KEEP...
...MOVING FORWARD.
YOU CAN'T DO ANYTHING AS YOU ARE RIGHT NOW.
...YOU'RE UNABLE TO BECOME ALICE.

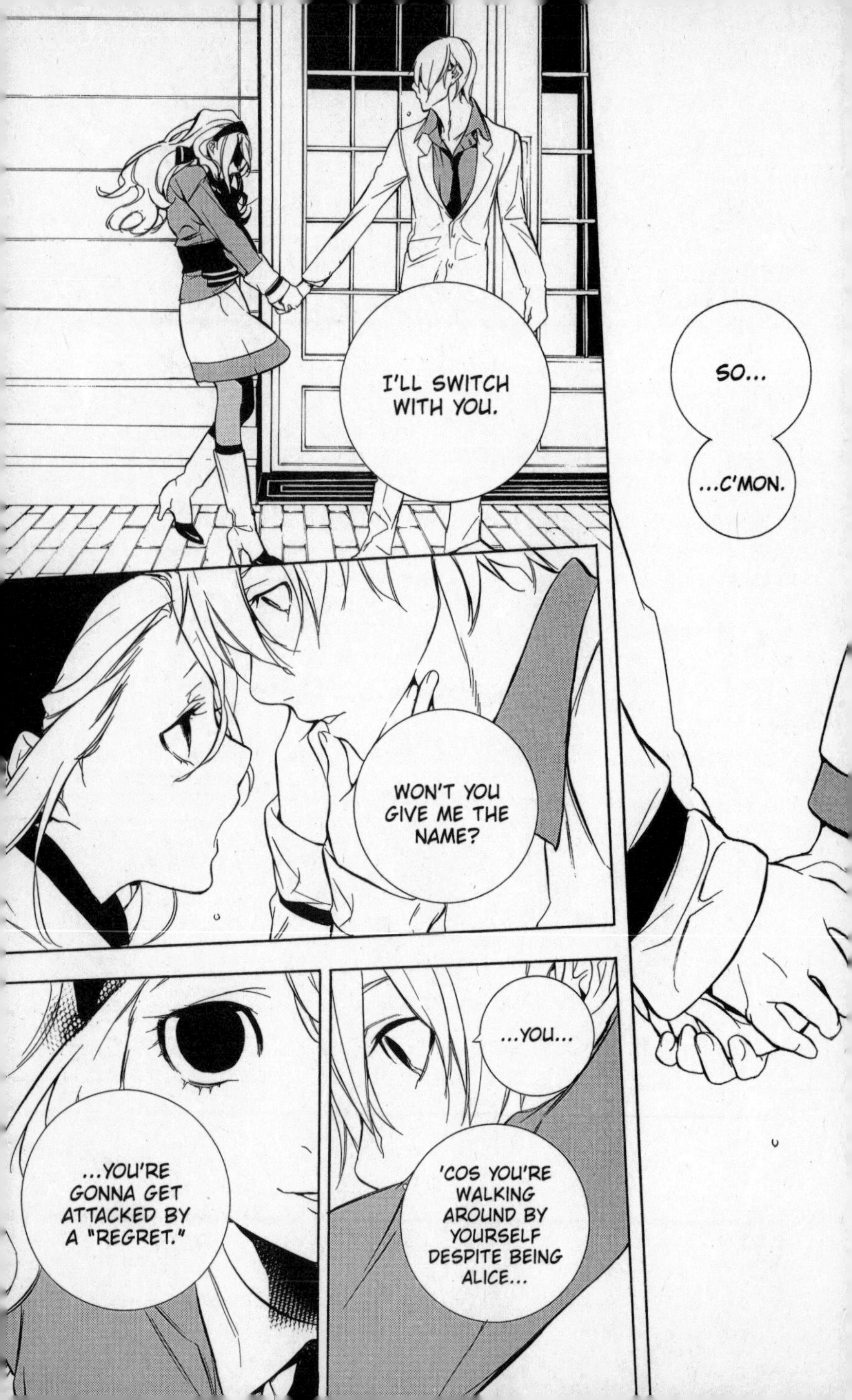
SO...
...C'MON.
I'LL SWITCH WITH YOU.
WON'T YOU GIVE ME THE NAME?
...YOU...
'COS YOU'RE WALKING AROUND BY YOURSELF DESPITE BEING ALICE...
...YOU'RE GONNA GET ATTACKED BY A "REGRET."

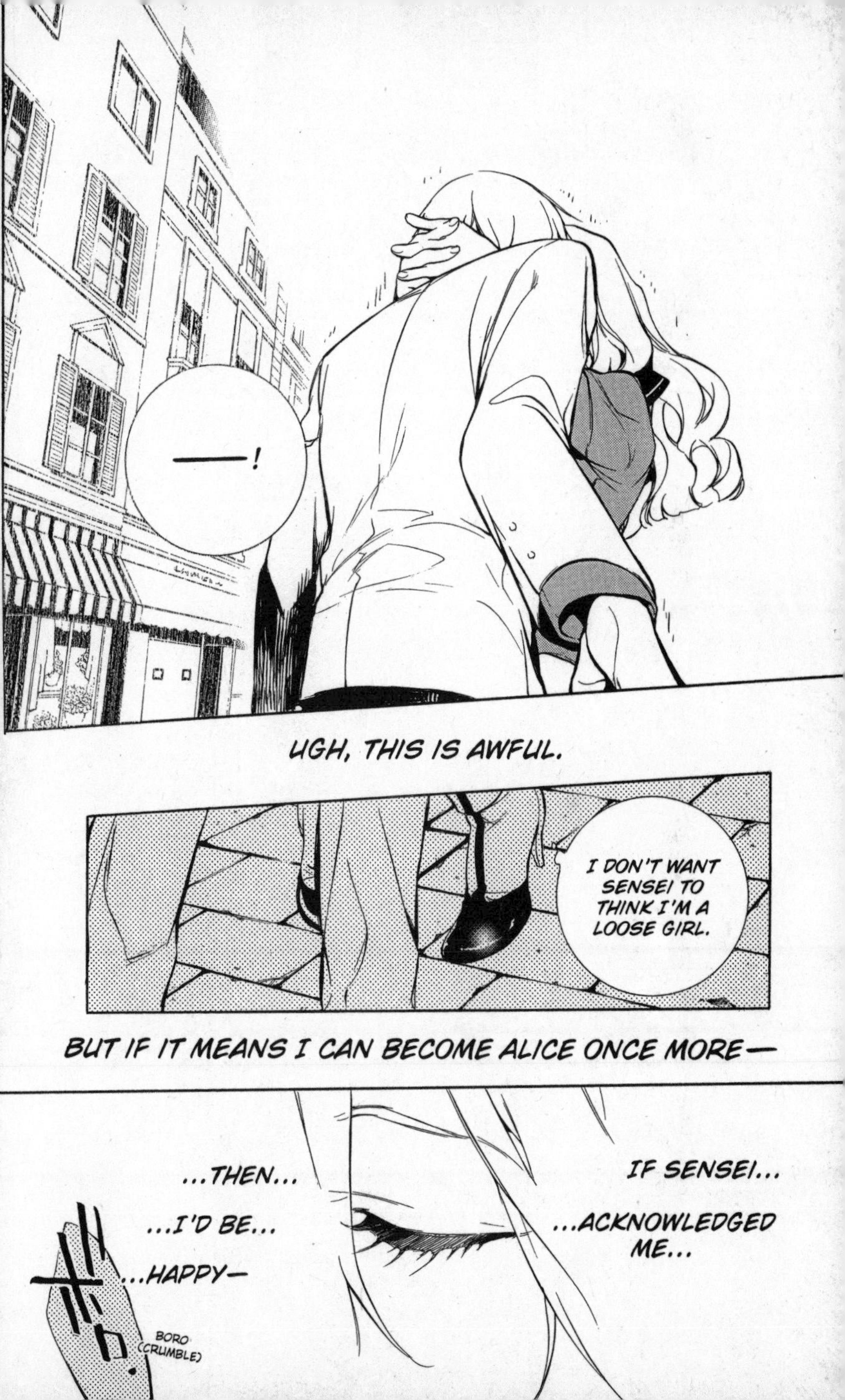
—!
UGH, THIS IS AWFUL.
I DON'T WANT SENSEI TO THINK I'M A LOOSE GIRL.
BUT IF IT MEANS I CAN BECOME ALICE ONCE MORE—
IF SENSEI...
...ACKNOWLEDGED ME...
...THEN...
...I'D BE...
...HAPPY—
BORO (CRUMBLE)

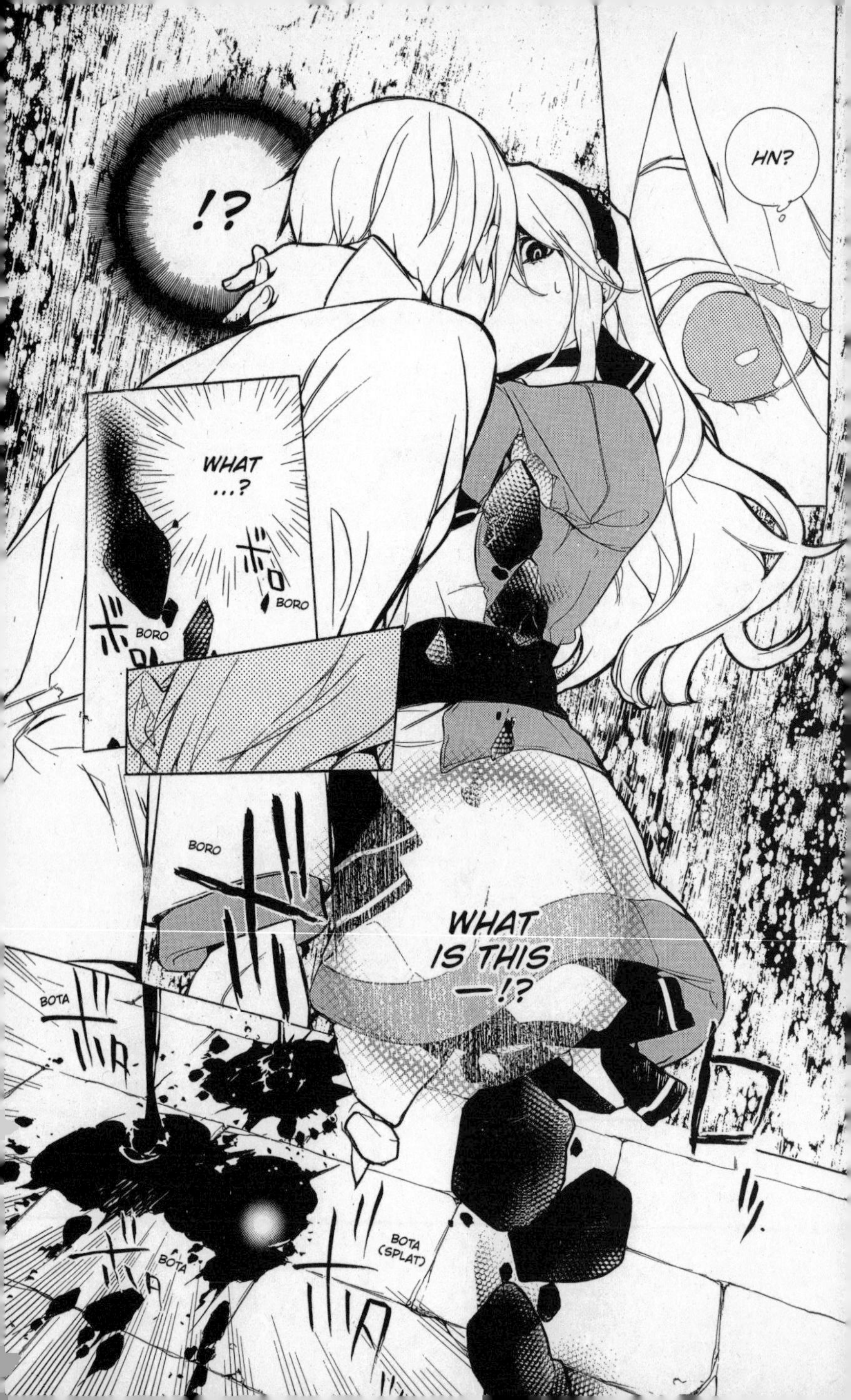

HN?
!?
WHAT ...?
BORO
BORO
WHAT IS THIS —!?
BORO
BOTA (SPLAT)
BOTA
BOTA

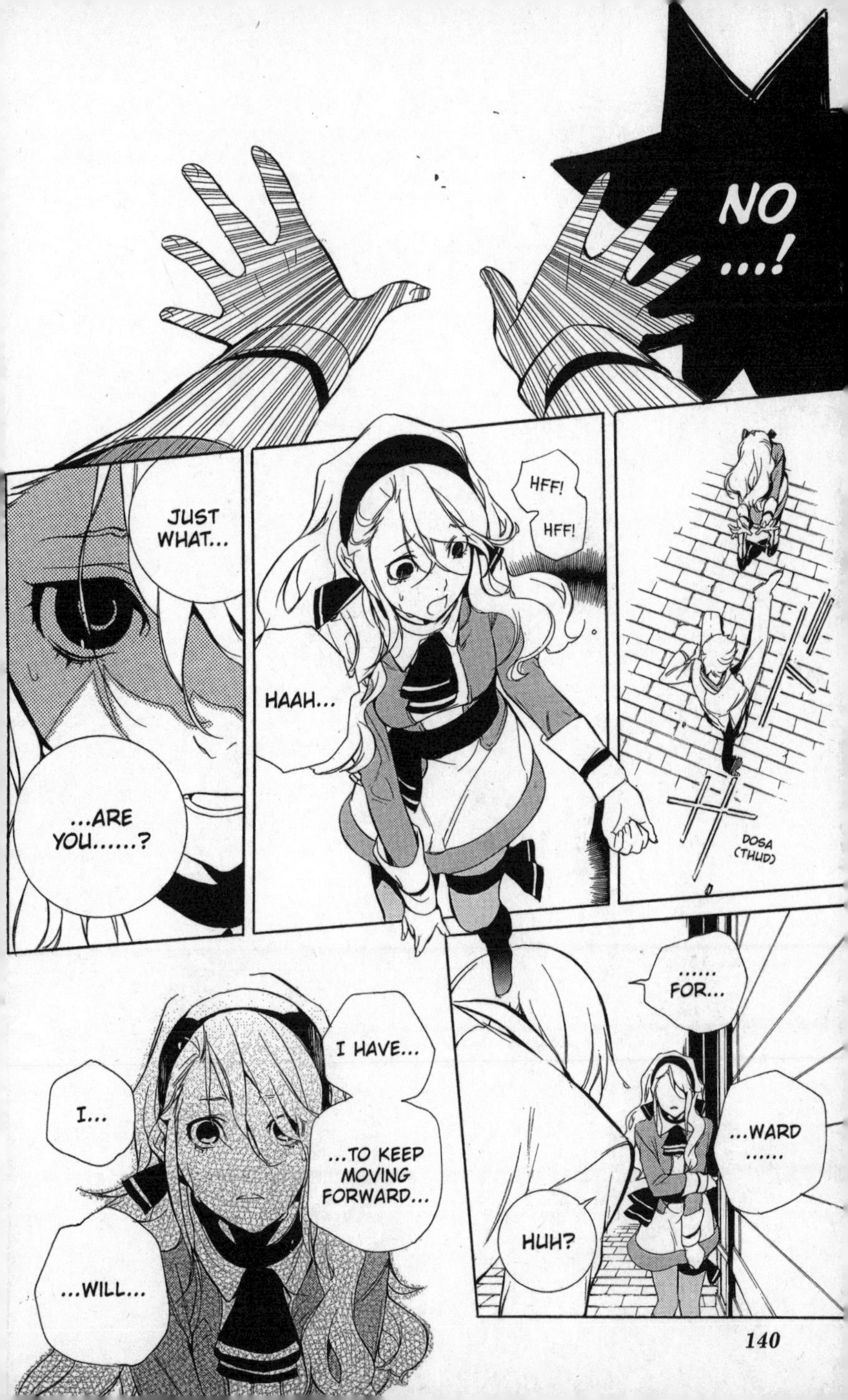
NO ...!
DOSA (THUD)
HFF!
HFF!
HAAH...
JUST WHAT...
...ARE YOU......?
......FOR...
...WARD......
HUH?
I HAVE...
...TO KEEP MOVING FORWARD...
I...
...WILL...

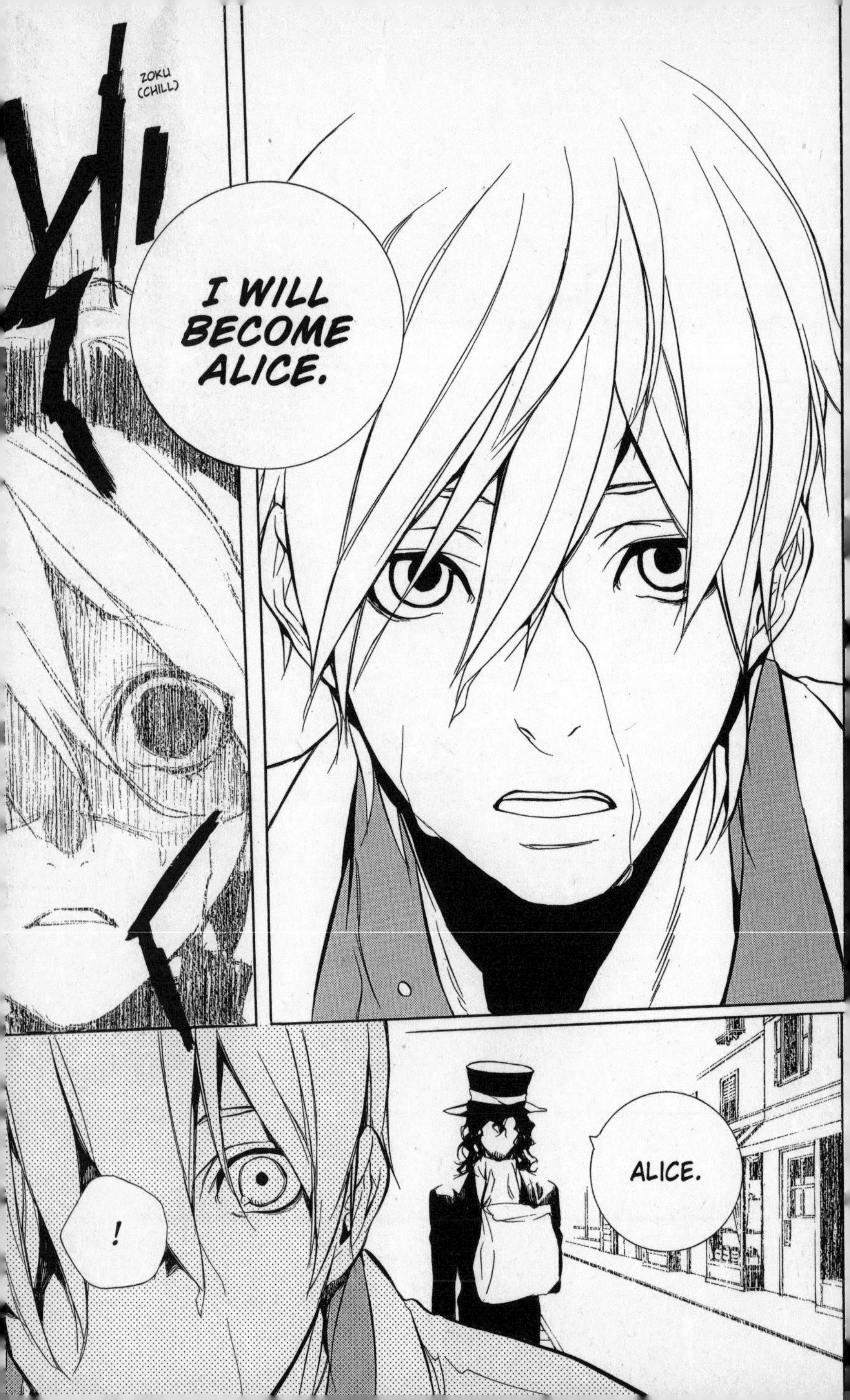
I WILL BECOME ALICE.
ZOKU (CHILL)
ALICE.
!

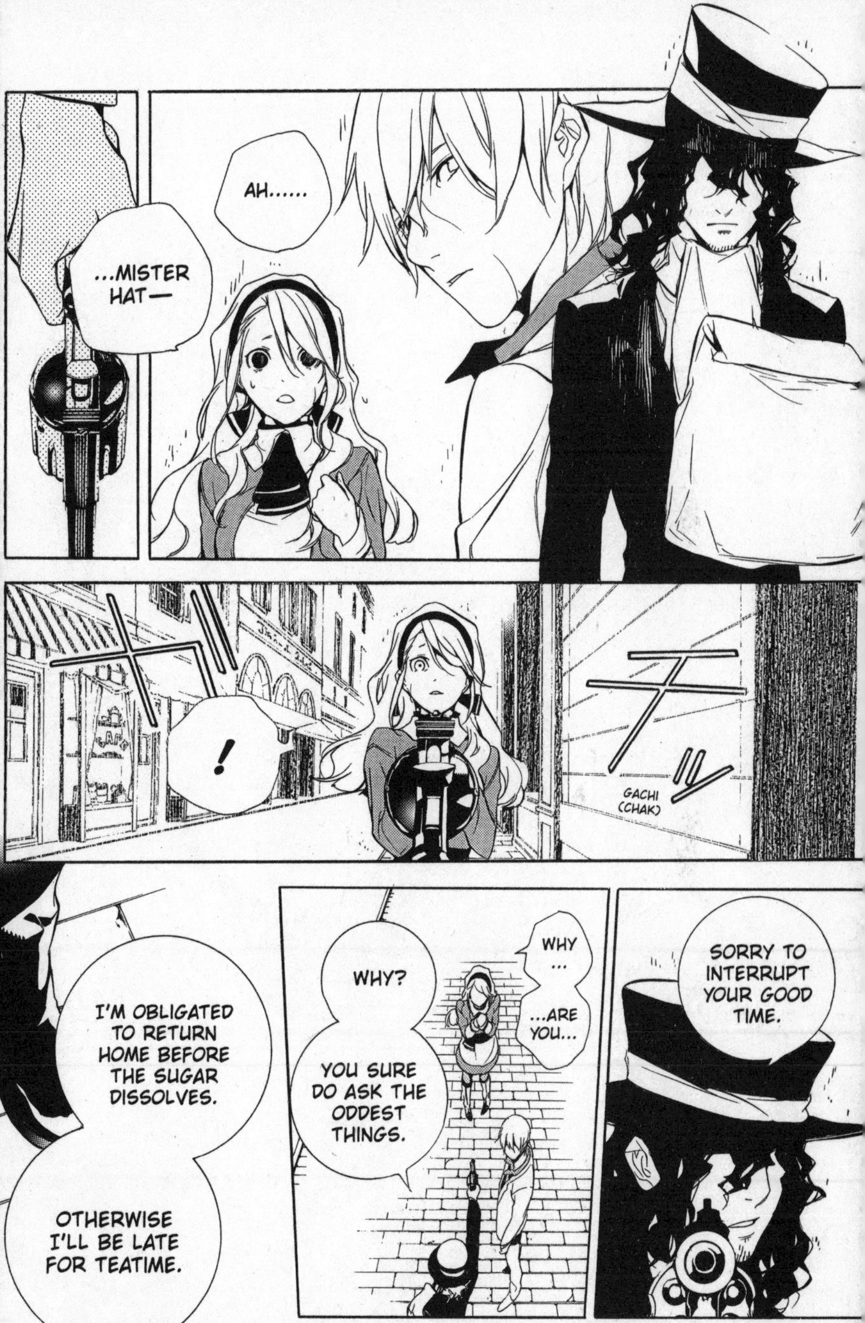

AH......
...MISTER HAT—
GACHI (CHAK)
!
SORRY TO INTERRUPT YOUR GOOD TIME.
WHY ...
...ARE YOU...
WHY?
YOU SURE DO ASK THE ODDEST THINGS.
I'M OBLIGATED TO RETURN HOME BEFORE THE SUGAR DISSOLVES.
OTHERWISE I'LL BE LATE FOR TEATIME.

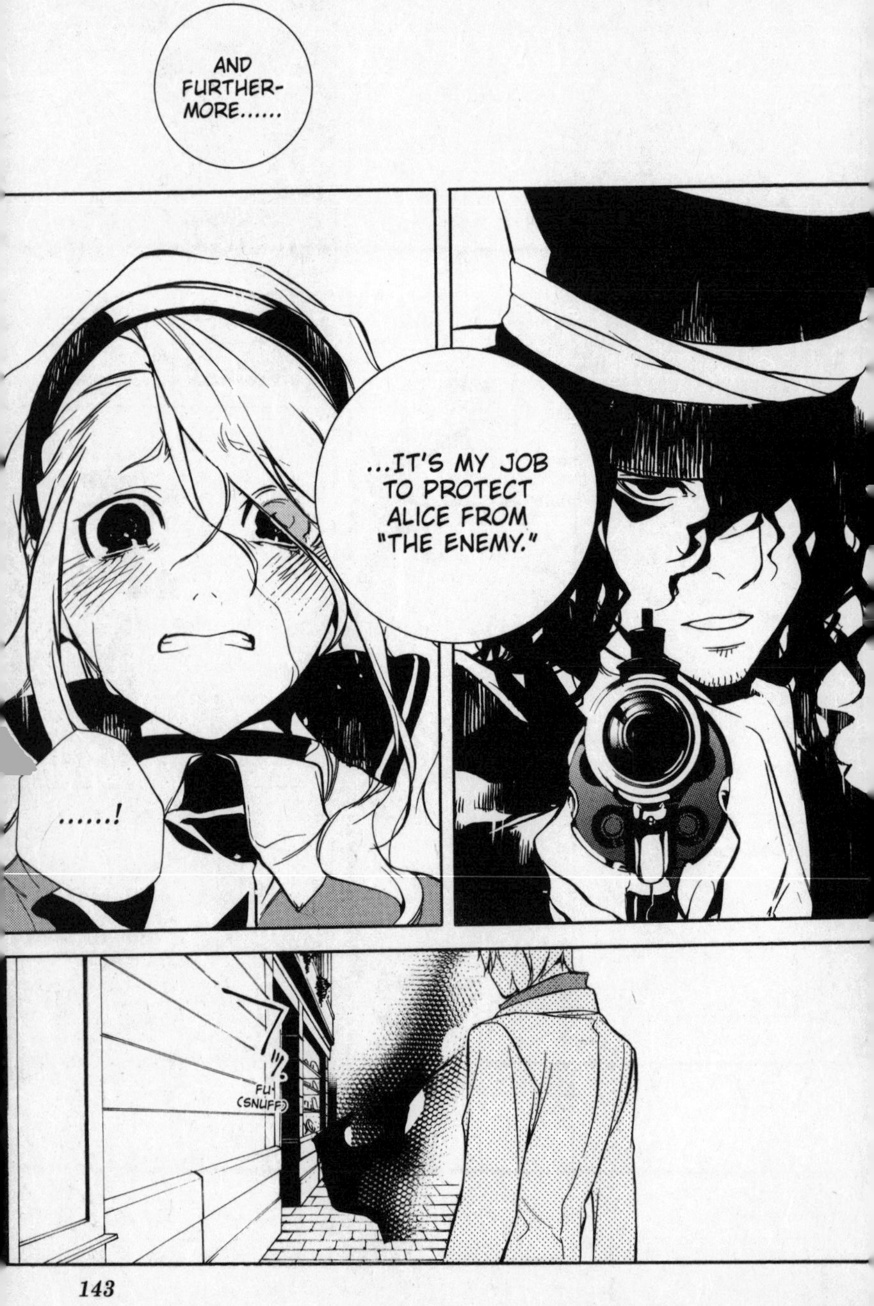
AND FURTHER-MORE......
...IT'S MY JOB TO PROTECT ALICE FROM "THE ENEMY."
......!
FU (SNUFF)

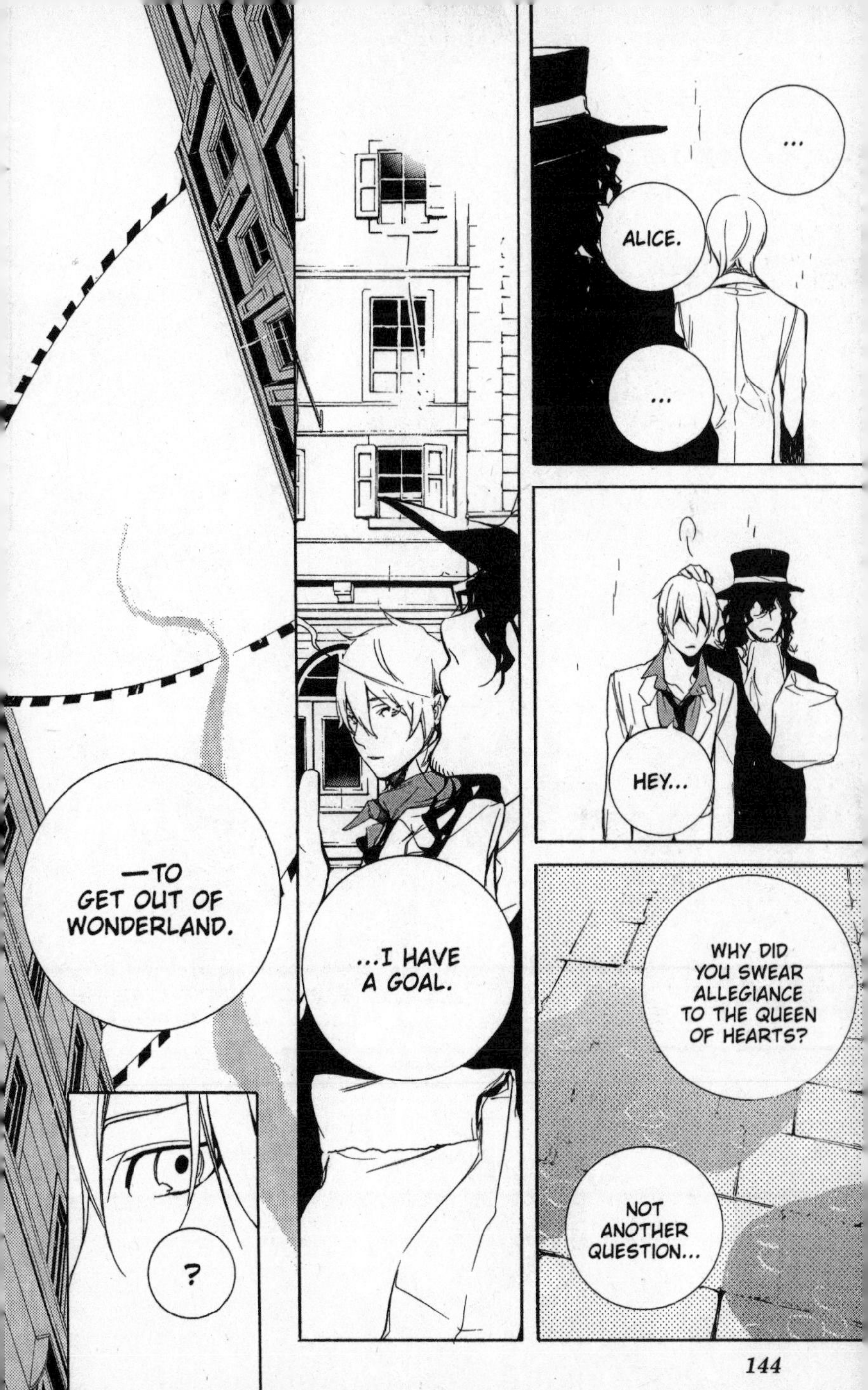
...
ALICE.
...
HEY...
WHY DID YOU SWEAR ALLEGIANCE TO THE QUEEN OF HEARTS?
NOT ANOTHER QUESTION...
...I HAVE A GOAL.
—TO GET OUT OF WONDERLAND.
?

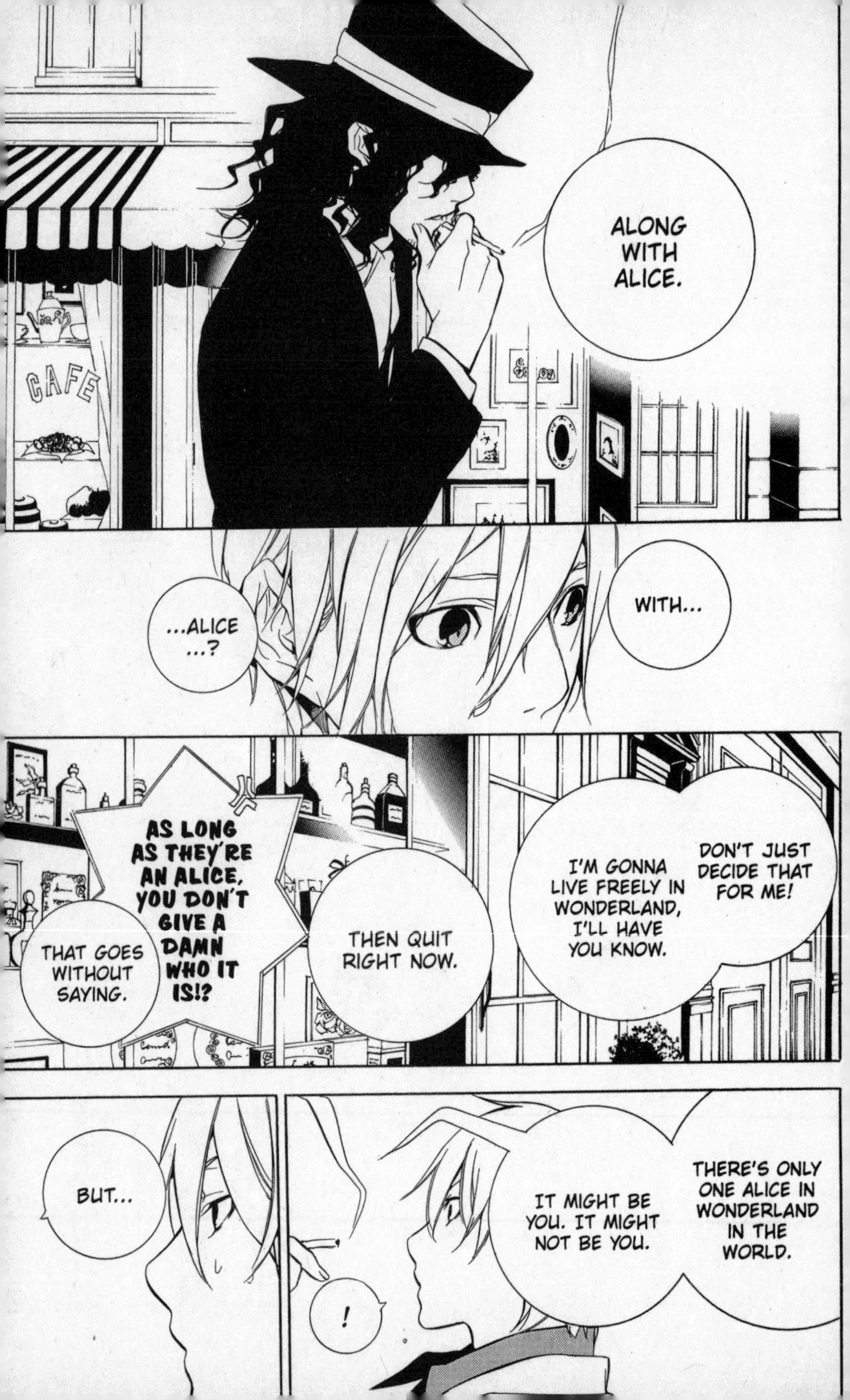

ALONG WITH ALICE.
WITH...
...ALICE ...?
DON'T JUST DECIDE THAT FOR ME!
I'M GONNA LIVE FREELY IN WONDERLAND, I'LL HAVE YOU KNOW.
THEN QUIT RIGHT NOW.
AS LONG AS THEY'RE AN ALICE, YOU DON'T GIVE A DAMN WHO IT IS!?
THAT GOES WITHOUT SAYING.
THERE'S ONLY ONE ALICE IN WONDERLAND IN THE WORLD.
IT MIGHT BE YOU. IT MIGHT NOT BE YOU.
!
BUT...

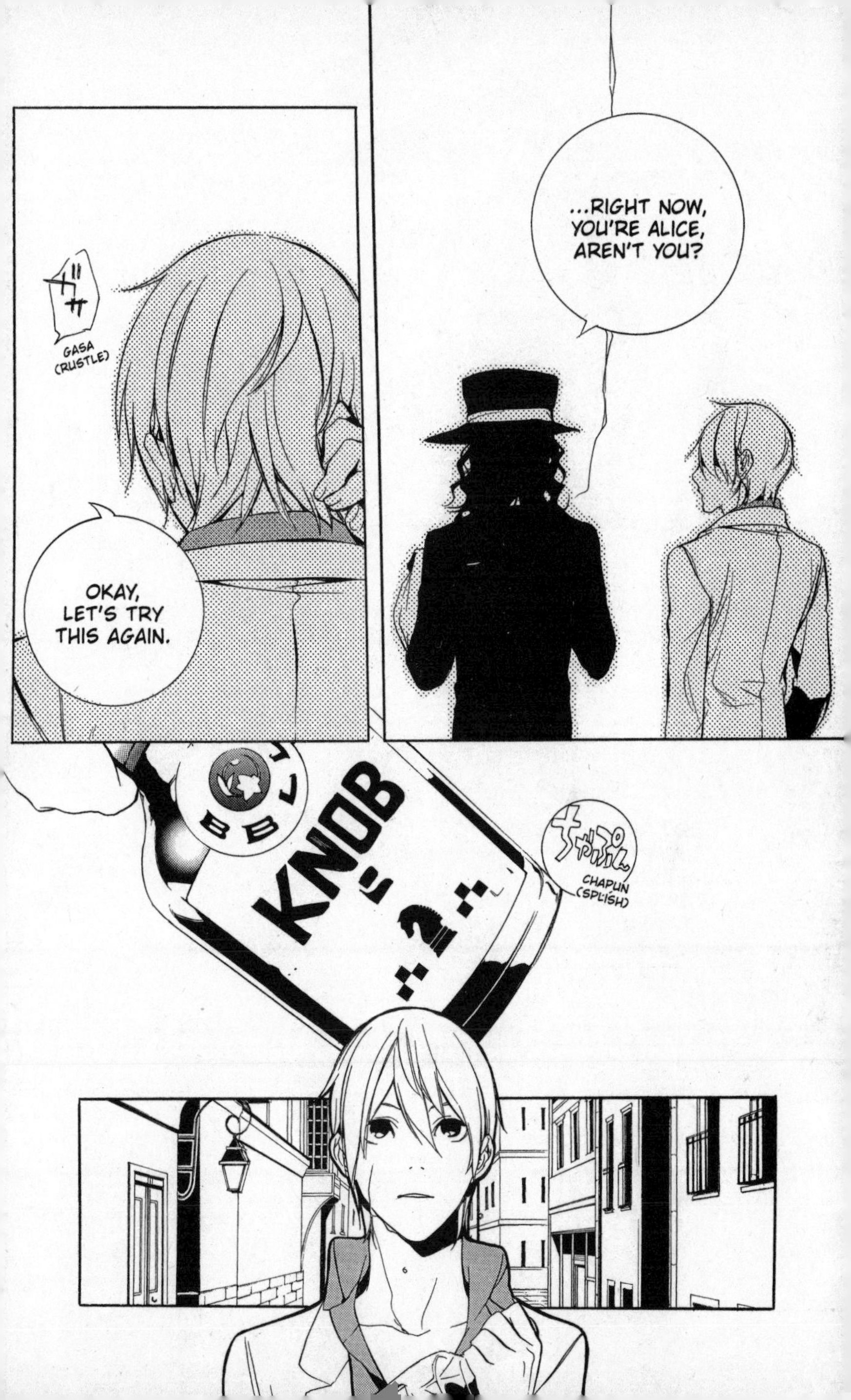
...RIGHT NOW, YOU'RE ALICE, AREN'T YOU?
ガサ
GASA (RUSTLE)
OKAY, LET'S TRY THIS AGAIN.
KNOB
ちゃぷん
CHAPUN (SPLISH)

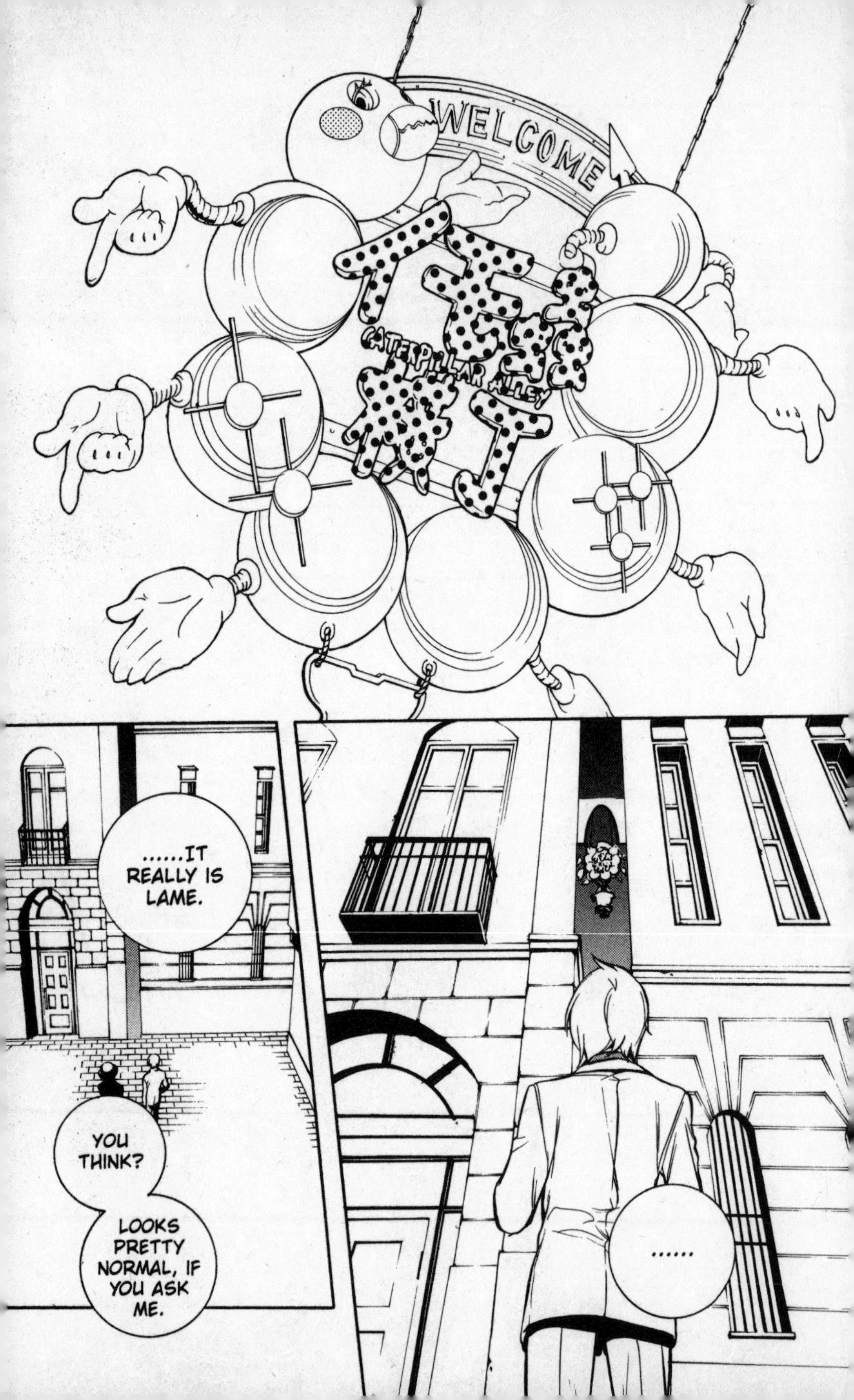
WELCOME
CATERPILLAR ALLEY
......
......IT REALLY IS LAME.
YOU THINK?
LOOKS PRETTY NORMAL, IF YOU ASK ME.

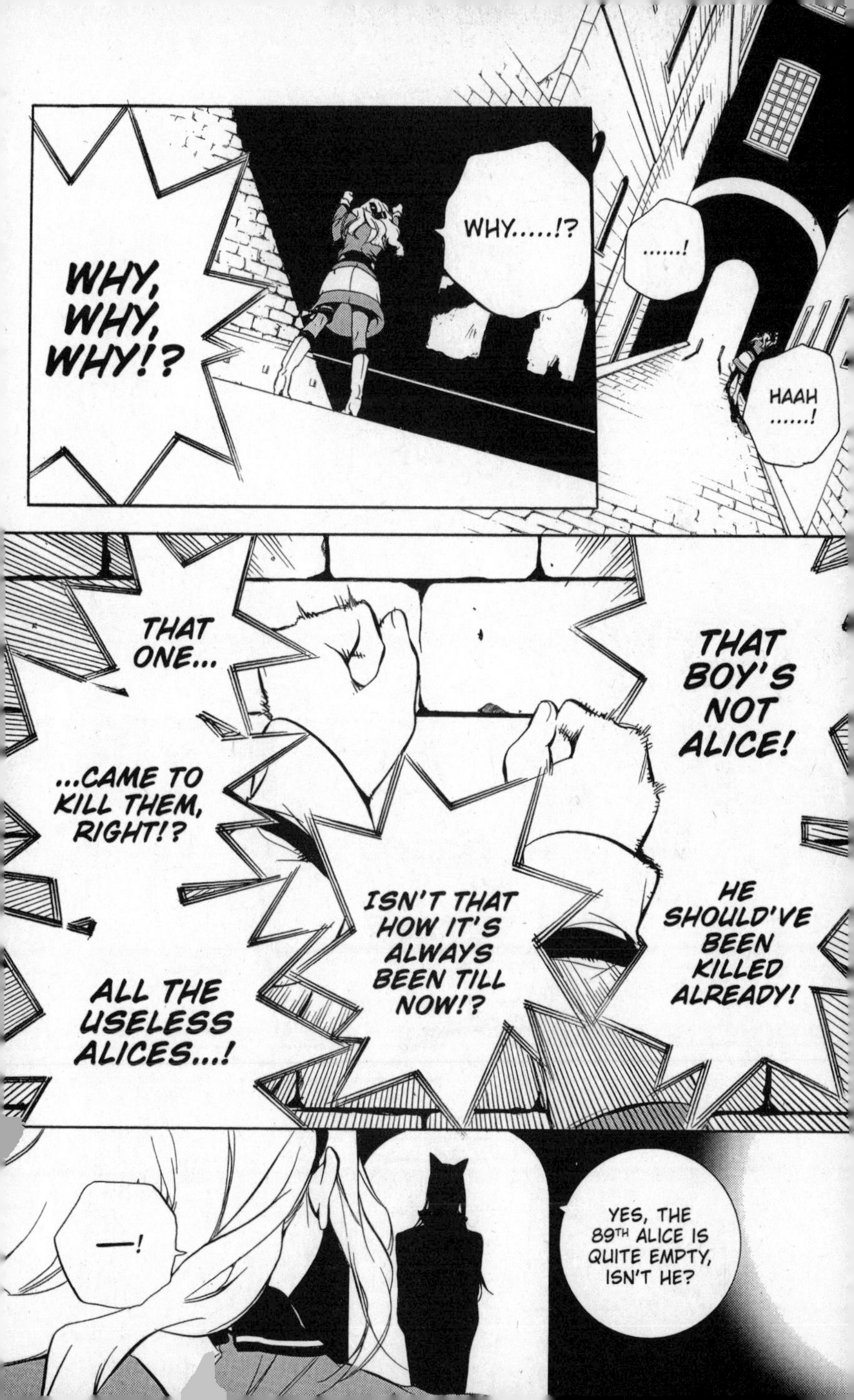
......!
HAAH ......!
WHY.....!?
WHY, WHY, WHY!?
THAT BOY'S NOT ALICE!
HE SHOULD'VE BEEN KILLED ALREADY!
ISN'T THAT HOW IT'S ALWAYS BEEN TILL NOW!?
THAT ONE...
...CAME TO KILL THEM, RIGHT!?
ALL THE USELESS ALICES...!
YES, THE 89TH ALICE IS QUITE EMPTY, ISN'T HE?
—!

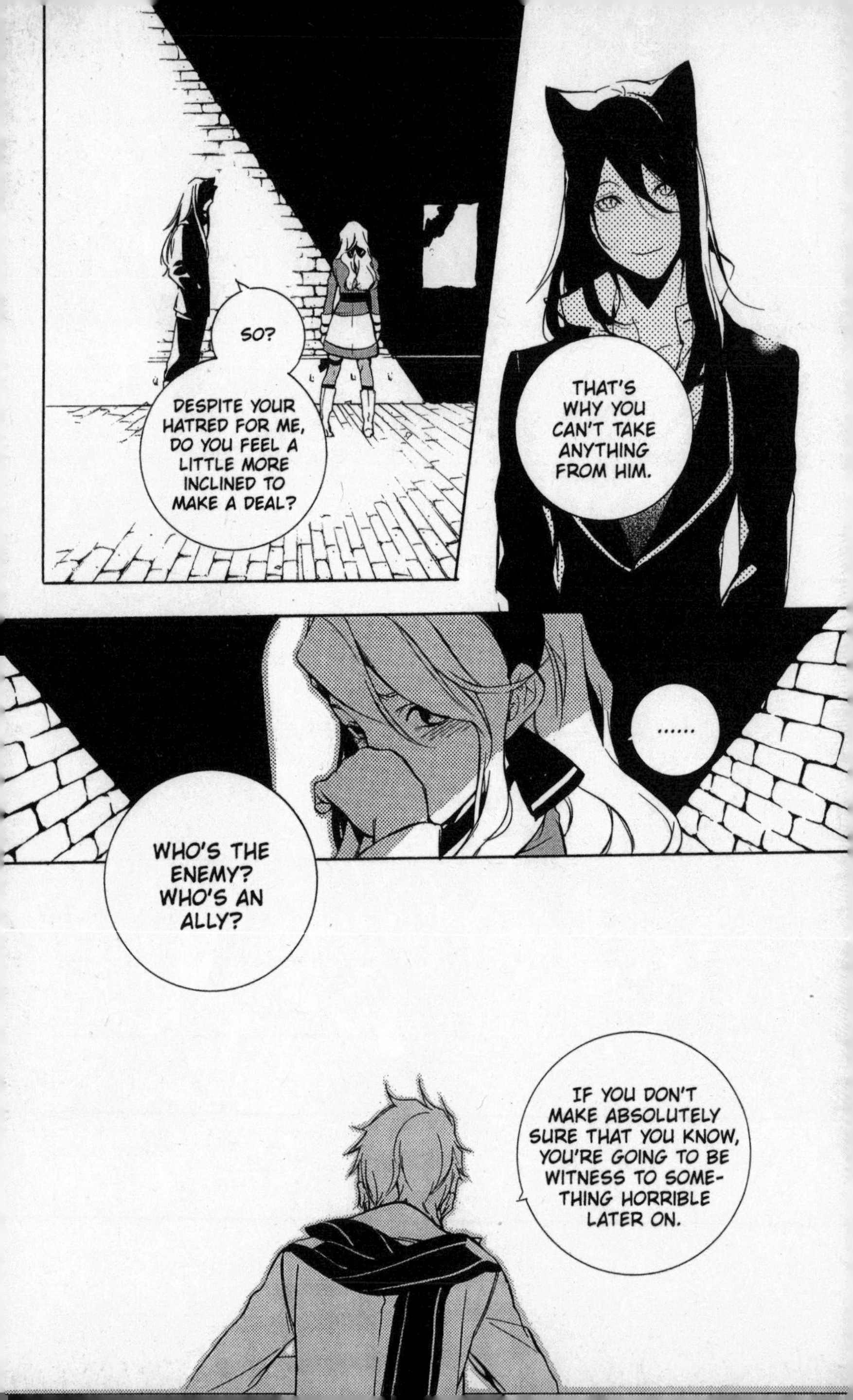
THAT'S WHY YOU CAN'T TAKE ANYTHING FROM HIM.
SO?
DESPITE YOUR HATRED FOR ME, DO YOU FEEL A LITTLE MORE INCLINED TO MAKE A DEAL?
......
WHO'S THE ENEMY? WHO'S AN ALLY?
IF YOU DON'T MAKE ABSOLUTELY SURE THAT YOU KNOW, YOU'RE GOING TO BE WITNESS TO SOME-THING HORRIBLE LATER ON.

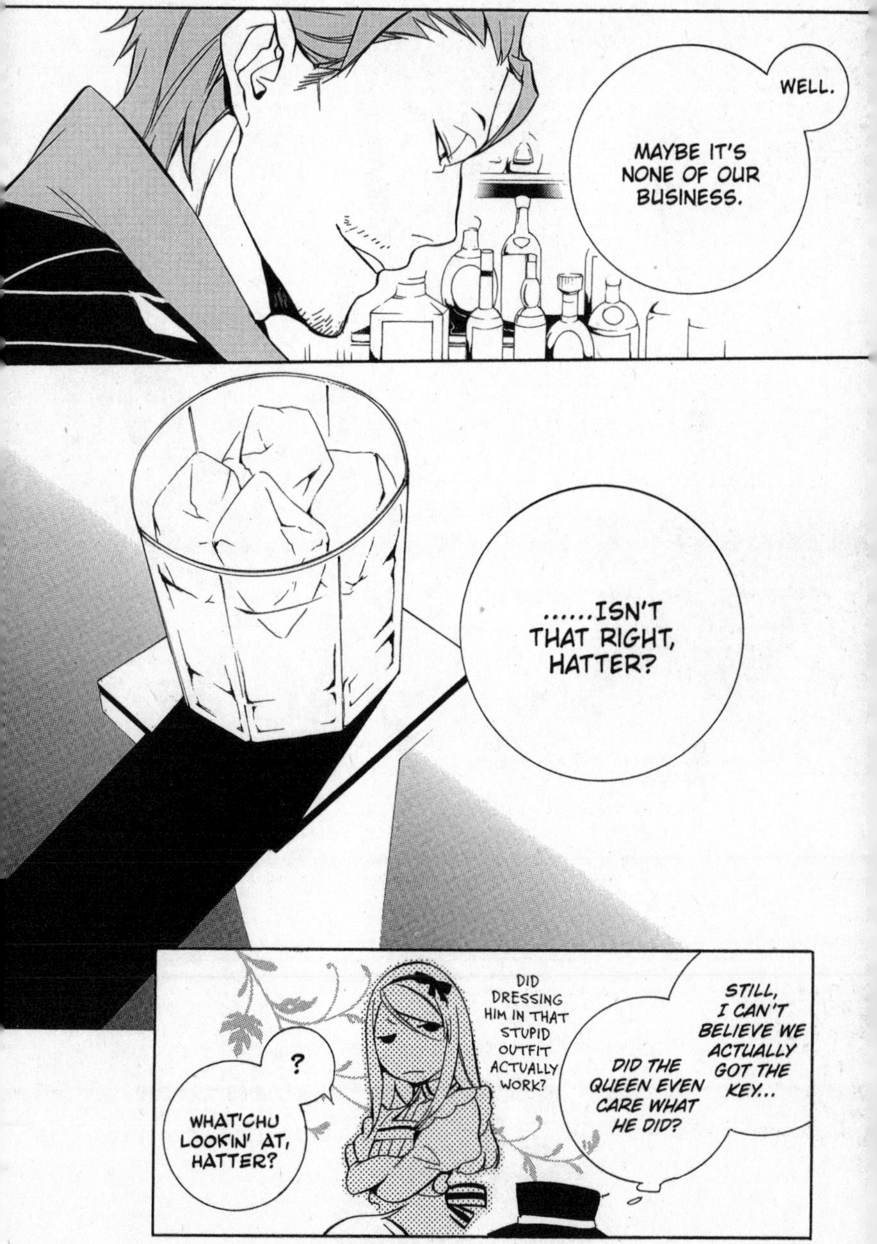
WELL.
MAYBE IT'S NONE OF OUR BUSINESS.
......ISN'T THAT RIGHT, HATTER?
STILL, I CAN'T BELIEVE WE ACTUALLY GOT THE KEY...
DID THE QUEEN EVEN CARE WHAT HE DID?
DID DRESSING HIM IN THAT STUPID OUTFIT ACTUALLY WORK?
?
WHAT'CHU LOOKIN' AT, HATTER?

Chapter 17

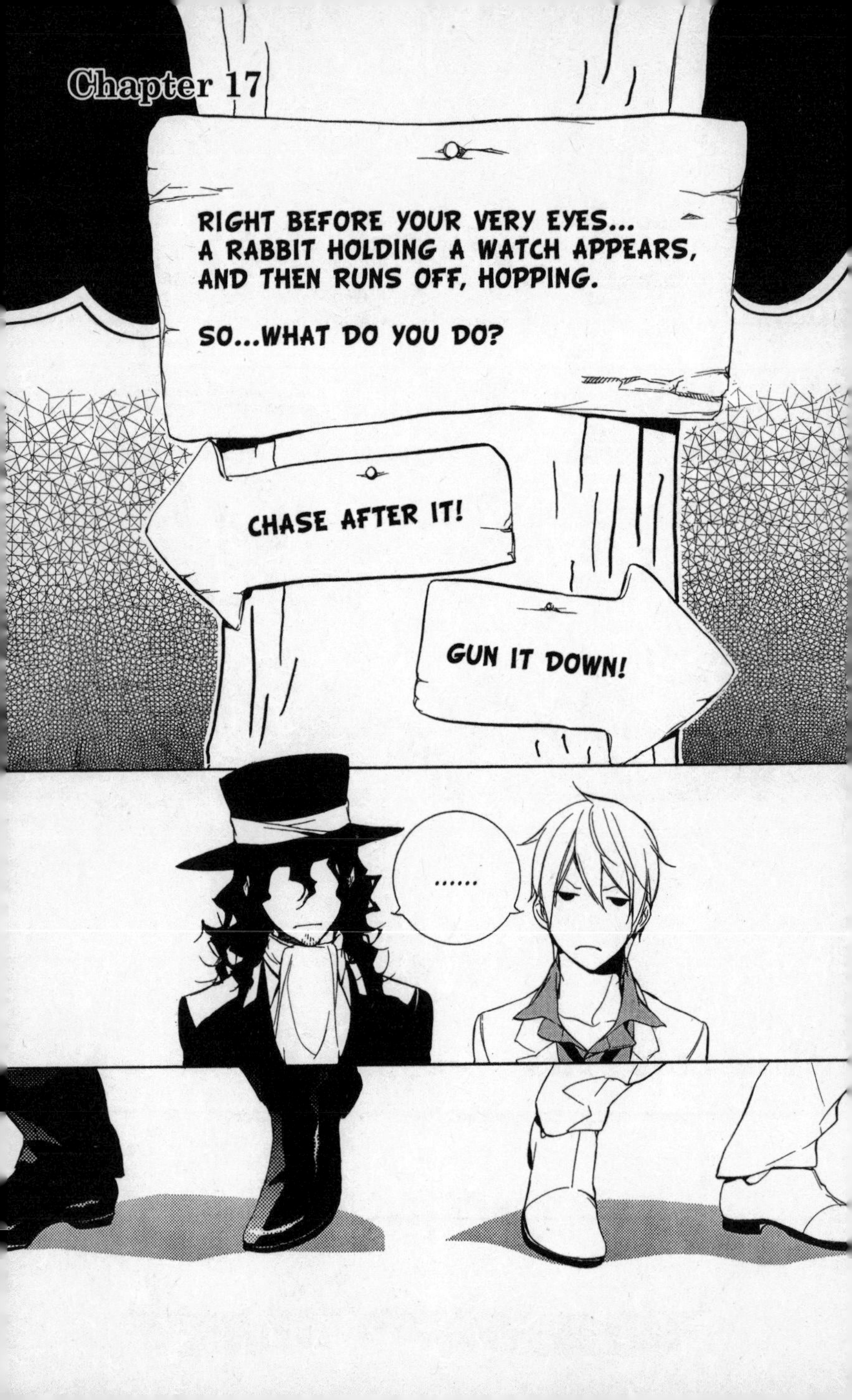
RIGHT BEFORE YOUR VERY EYES...
A RABBIT HOLDING A WATCH APPEARS,
AND THEN RUNS OFF, HOPPING.
SO...WHAT DO YOU DO?
CHASE AFTER IT!
GUN IT DOWN!
......

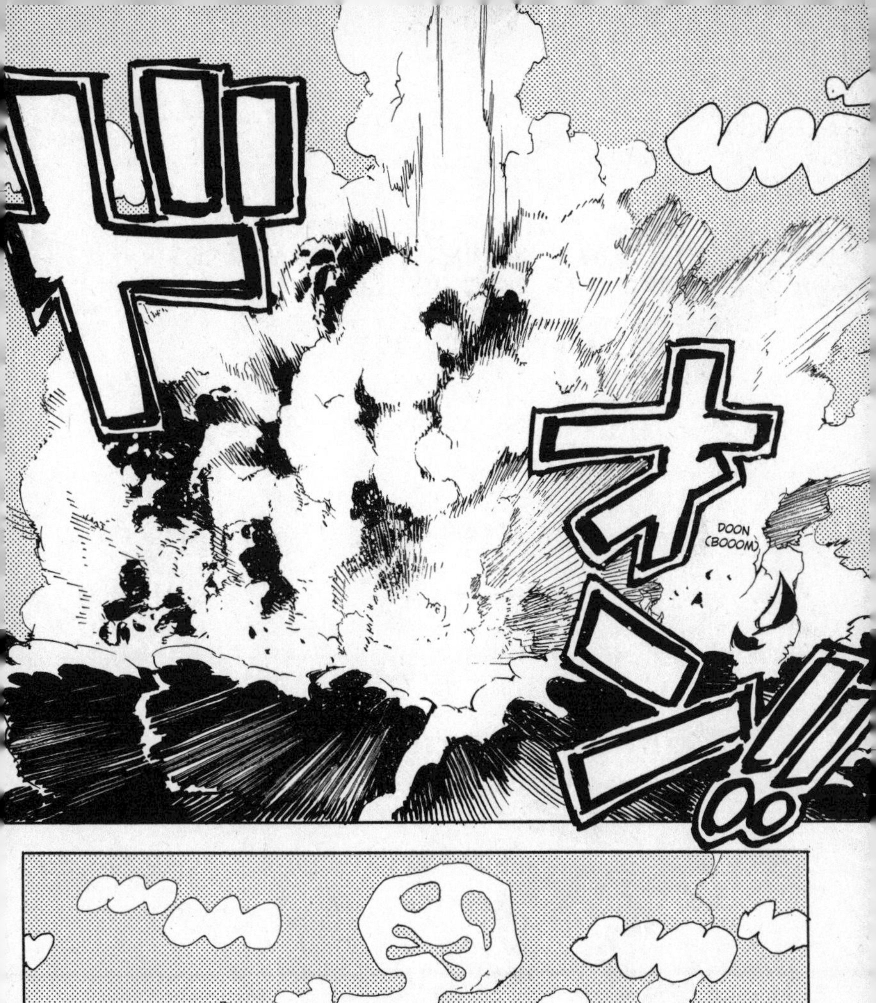
DOON
(BOOOM)
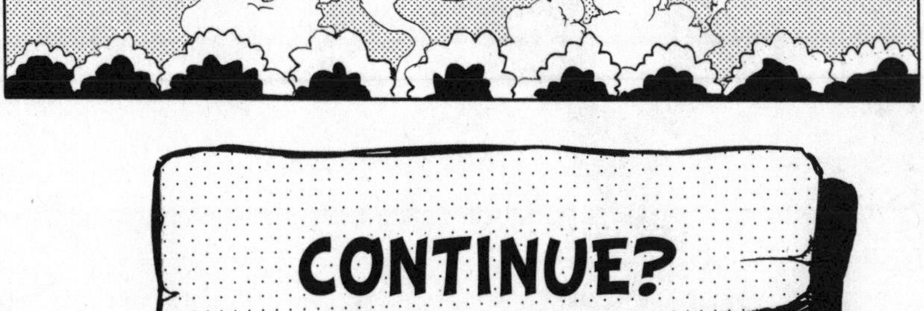

CONTINUE?

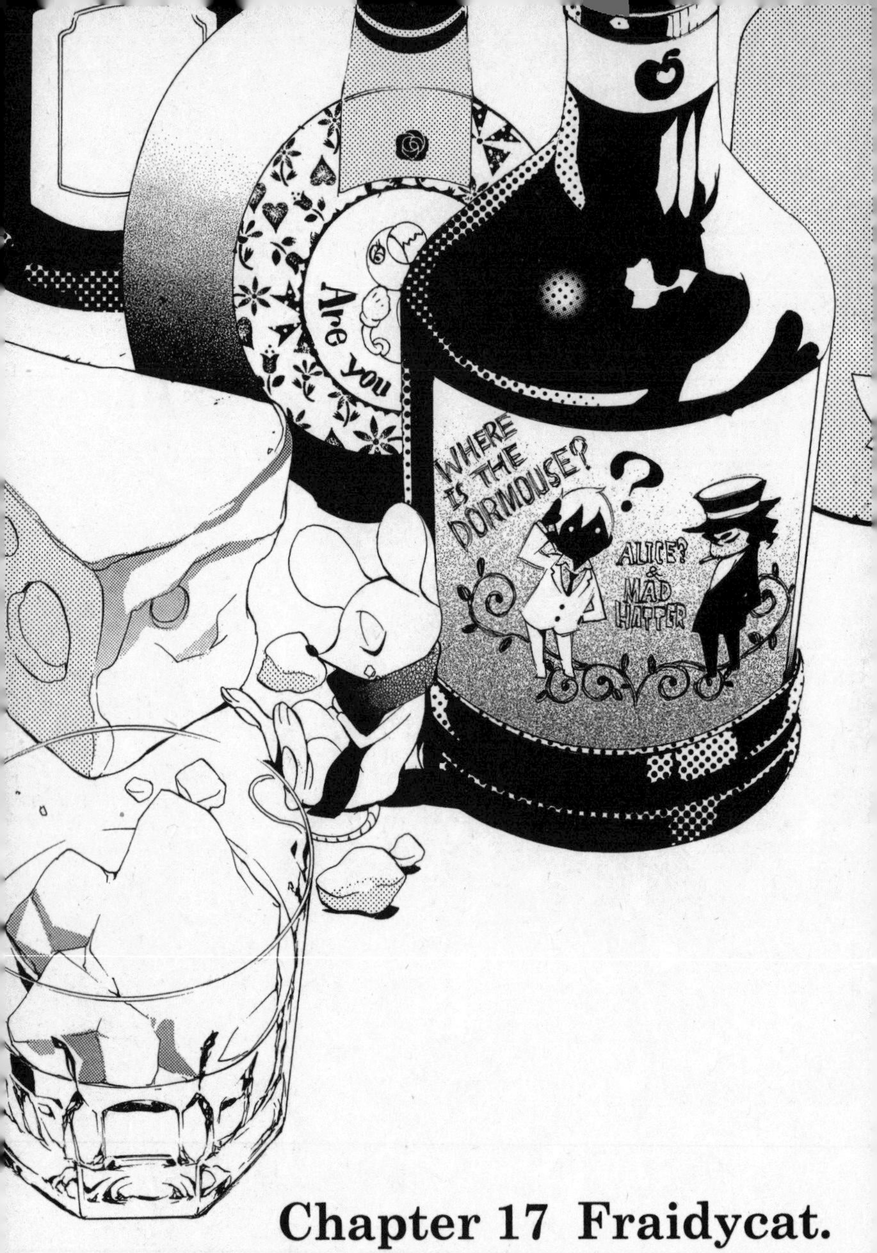
Are you
WHERE IS THE DORMOUSE?
?
ALICE? & MAD HATTER

Chapter 17 Fraidycat.

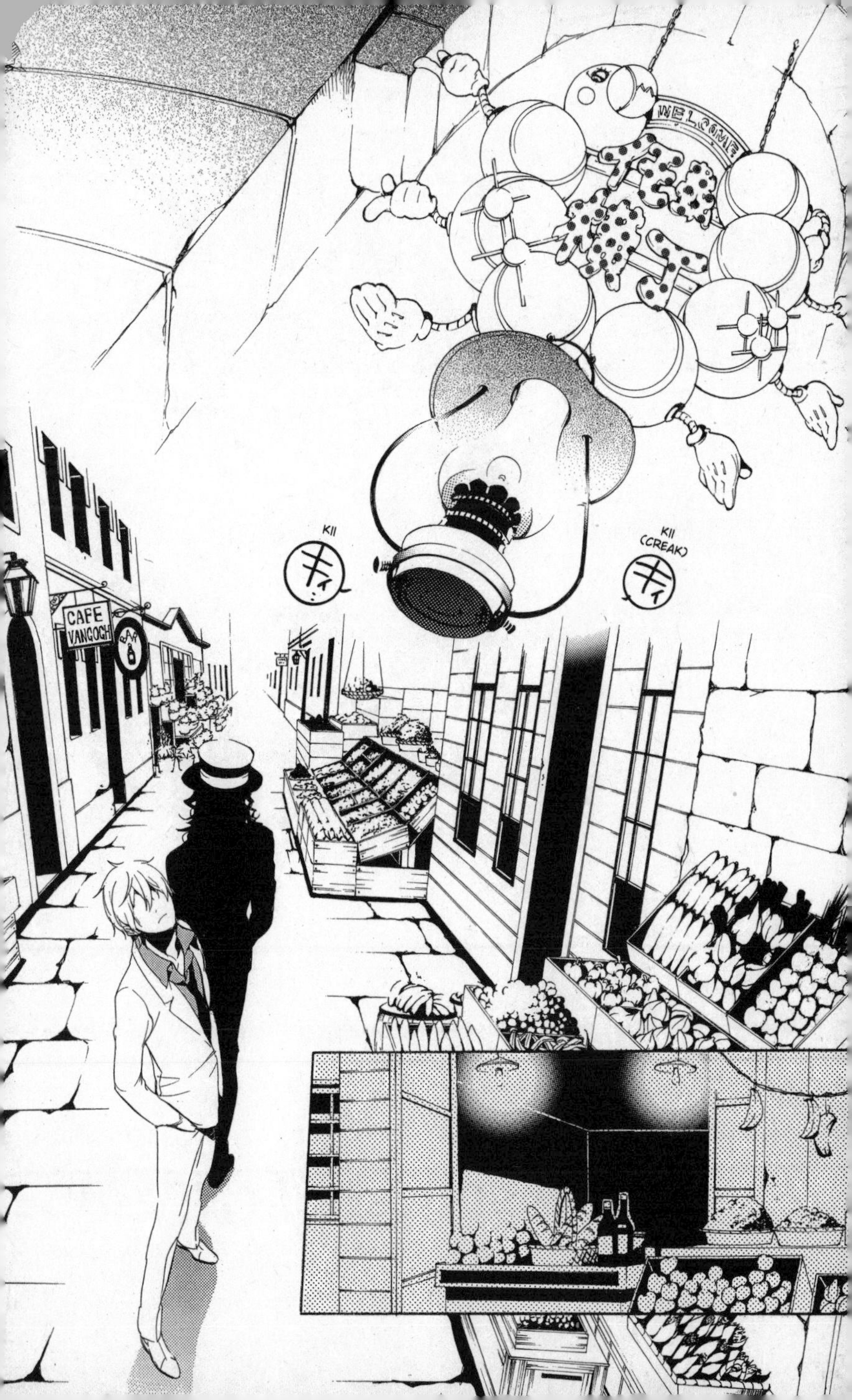
WELCOME
KII
(CREAK)
キィ
KII
キィ
CAFE VANGOGH
BAR

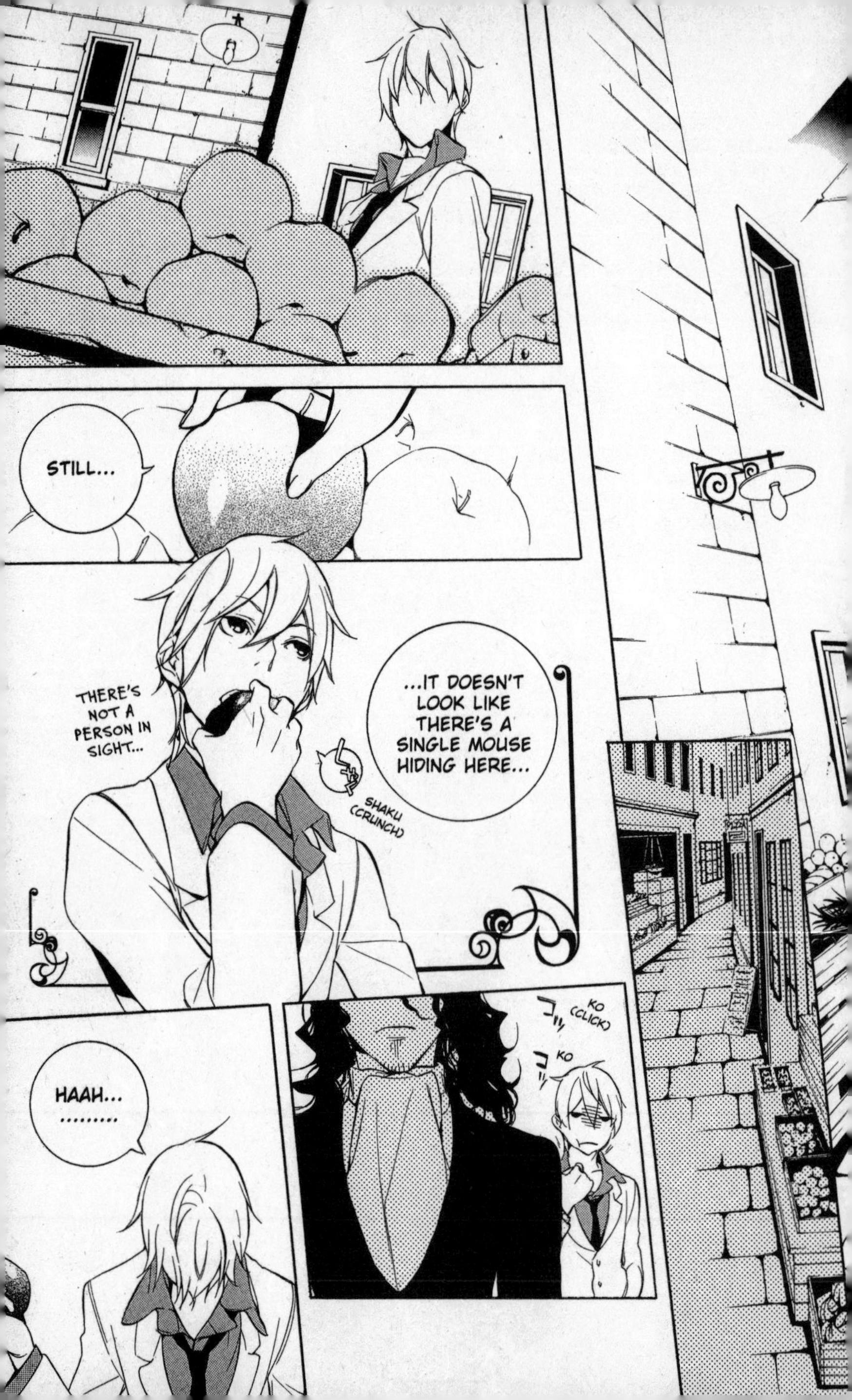
STILL...
...IT DOESN'T LOOK LIKE THERE'S A SINGLE MOUSE HIDING HERE...
SHAKU (CRUNCH)
THERE'S NOT A PERSON IN SIGHT...
KO (CLICK)
KO
HAAH... ....

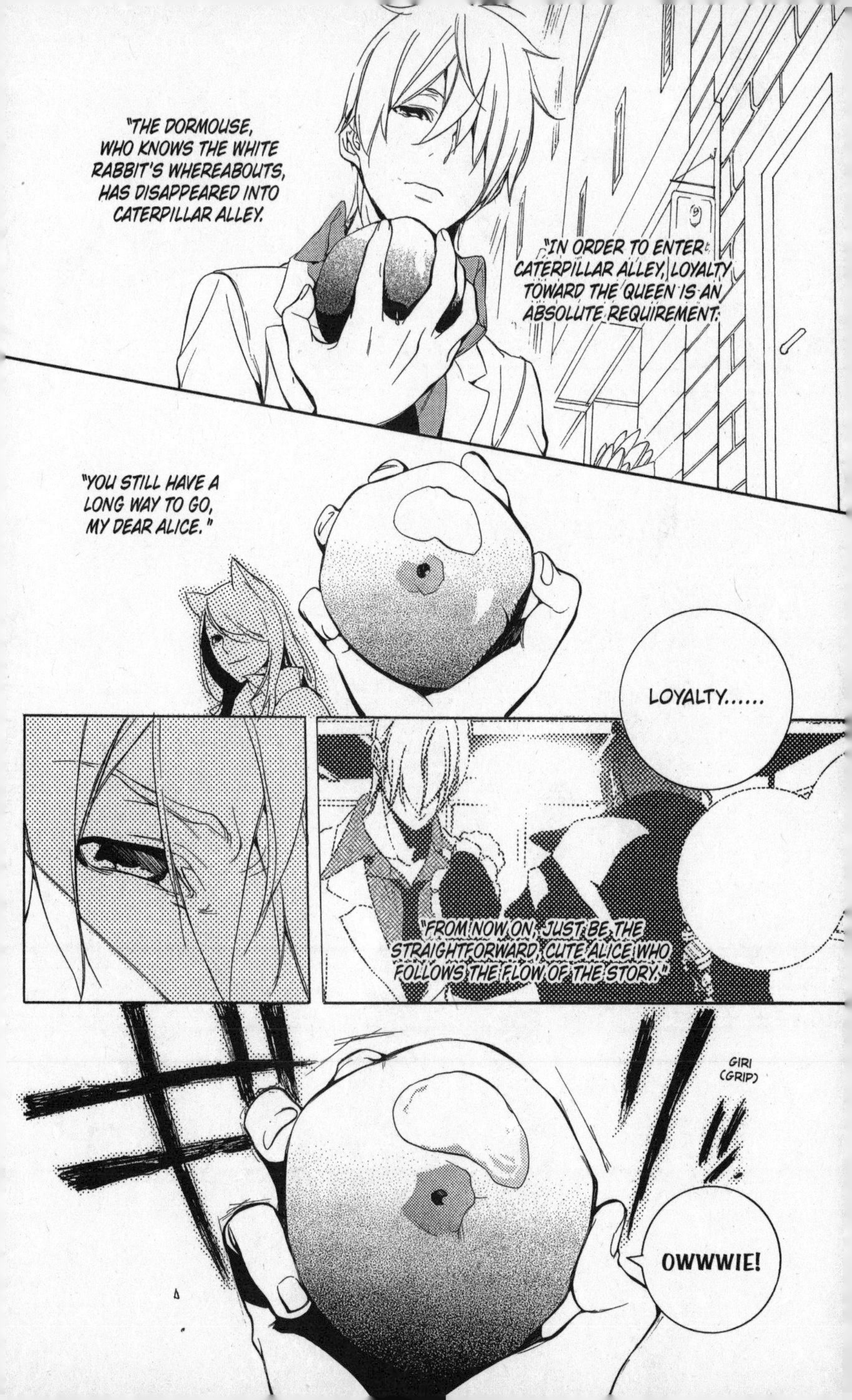
"THE DORMOUSE, WHO KNOWS THE WHITE RABBIT'S WHEREABOUTS, HAS DISAPPEARED INTO CATERPILLAR ALLEY.
"IN ORDER TO ENTER CATERPILLAR ALLEY, LOYALTY TOWARD THE QUEEN IS AN ABSOLUTE REQUIREMENT.
"YOU STILL HAVE A LONG WAY TO GO, MY DEAR ALICE."
LOYALTY......
"FROM NOW ON, JUST BE THE STRAIGHTFORWARD, CUTE ALICE WHO FOLLOWS THE FLOW OF THE STORY."
GIRI (GRIP)
OWWWIE!

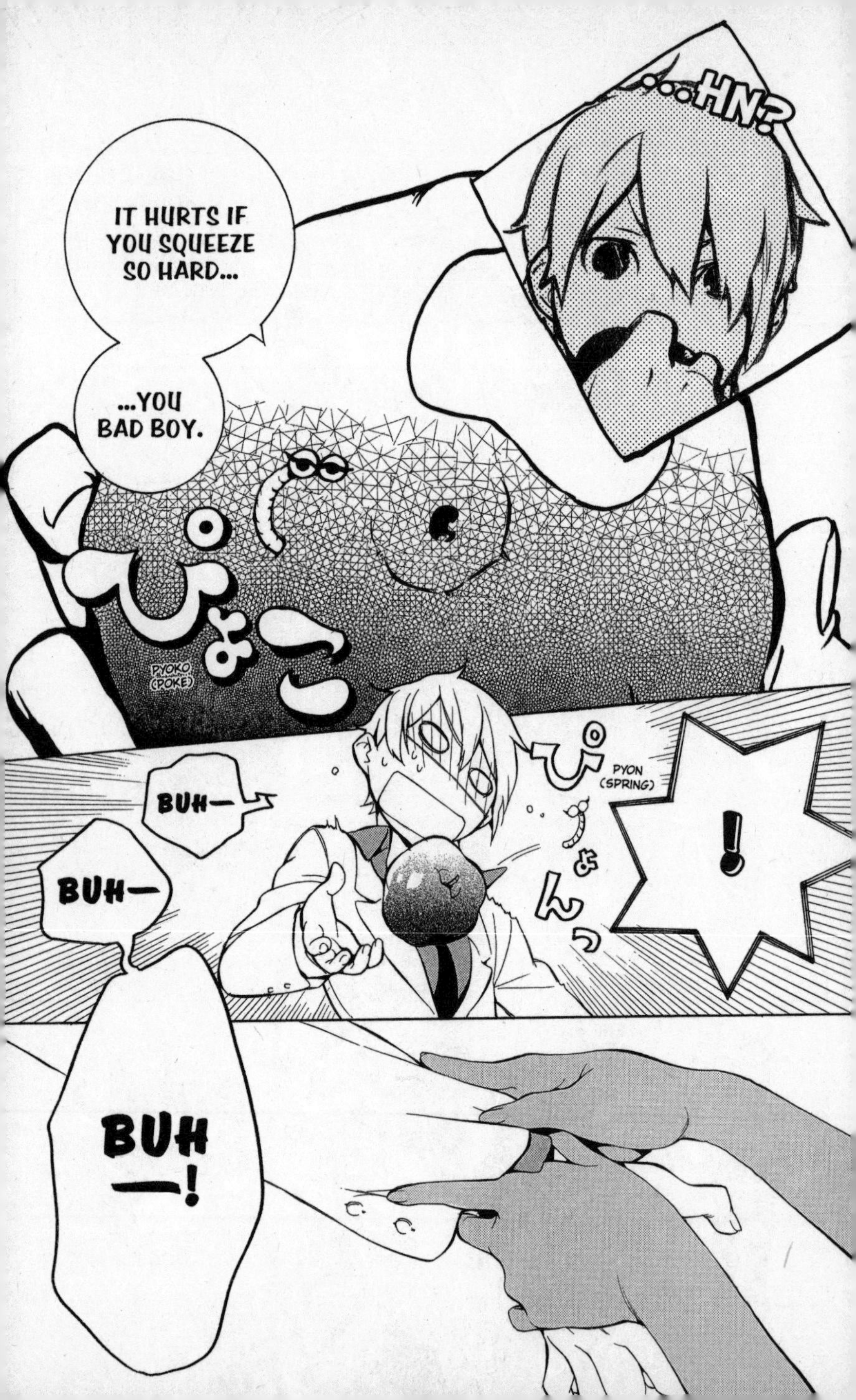
...HN?
IT HURTS IF YOU SQUEEZE SO HARD...
...YOU BAD BOY.
ぴょこ
PYOKO (POKE)
!
ぴょんっ
PYON (SPRING)
BUH—
BUH—
BUH—!

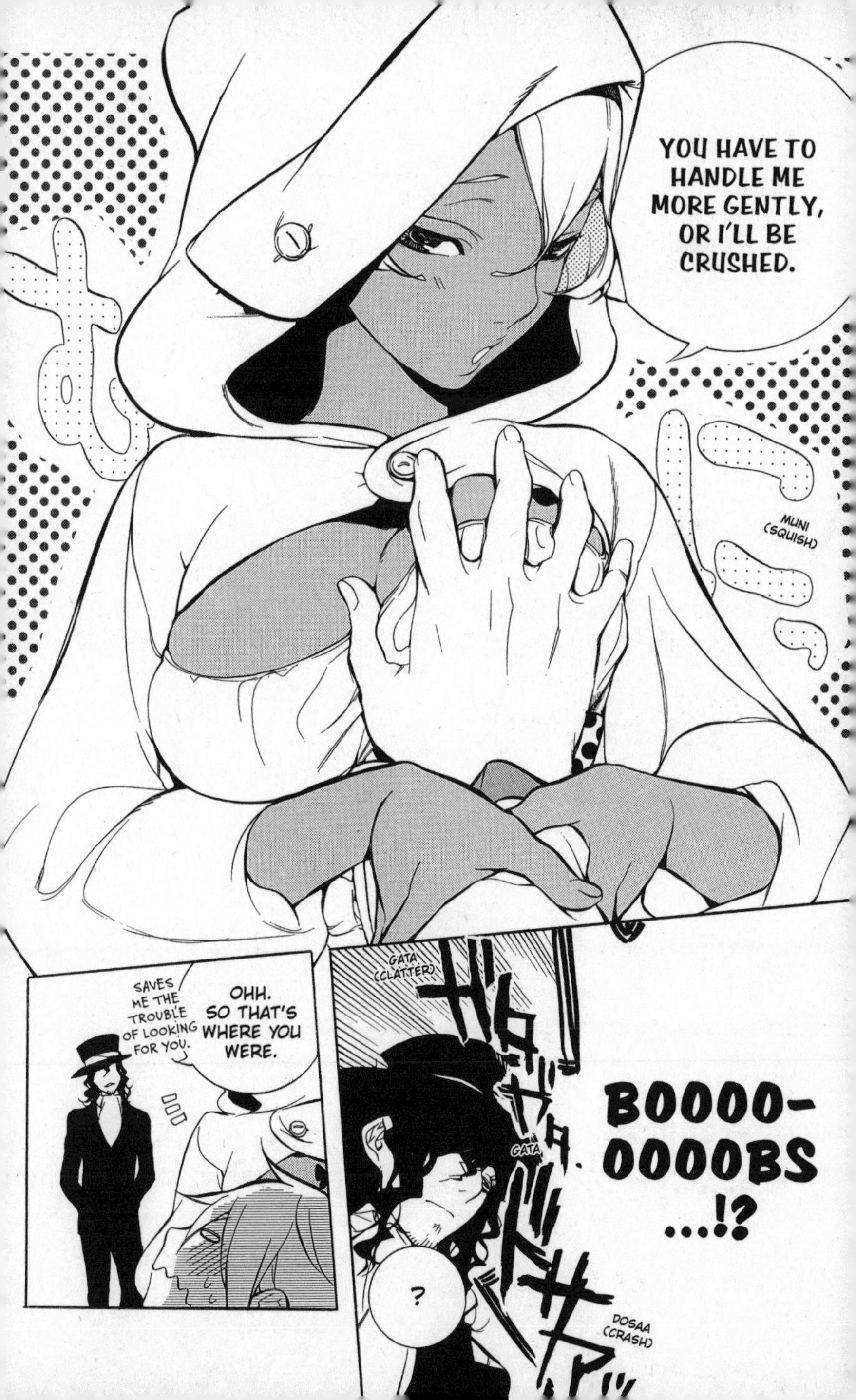
YOU HAVE TO HANDLE ME MORE GENTLY, OR I'LL BE CRUSHED.
MUNI (SQUISH)
GATA (CLATTER)
GATA
BOOOO-OOOOBS ...!?
?
DOSAA (CRASH)
OHH. SO THAT'S WHERE YOU WERE.
SAVES ME THE TROUBLE OF LOOKING FOR YOU.

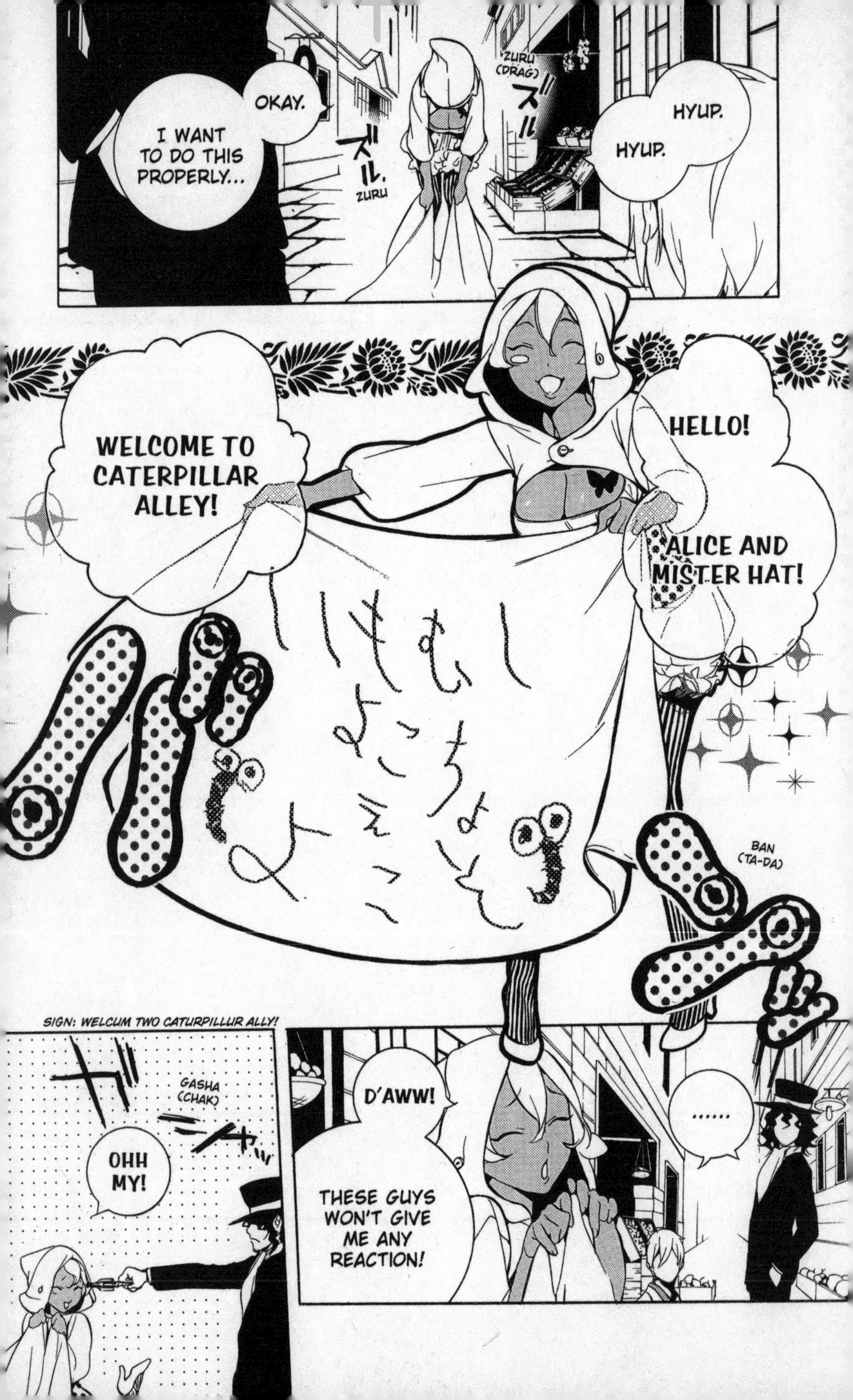
HYUP.
HYUP.
ZURU (DRAG)
ZURU
OKAY.
I WANT TO DO THIS PROPERLY...
HELLO!
ALICE AND MISTER HAT!
WELCOME TO CATERPILLAR ALLEY!
BAN (TA-DA)
SIGN: WELCUM TWO CATURPILLUR ALLY!
......
D'AWW!
THESE GUYS WON'T GIVE ME ANY REACTION!
GASHA (CHAK)
OHH MY!

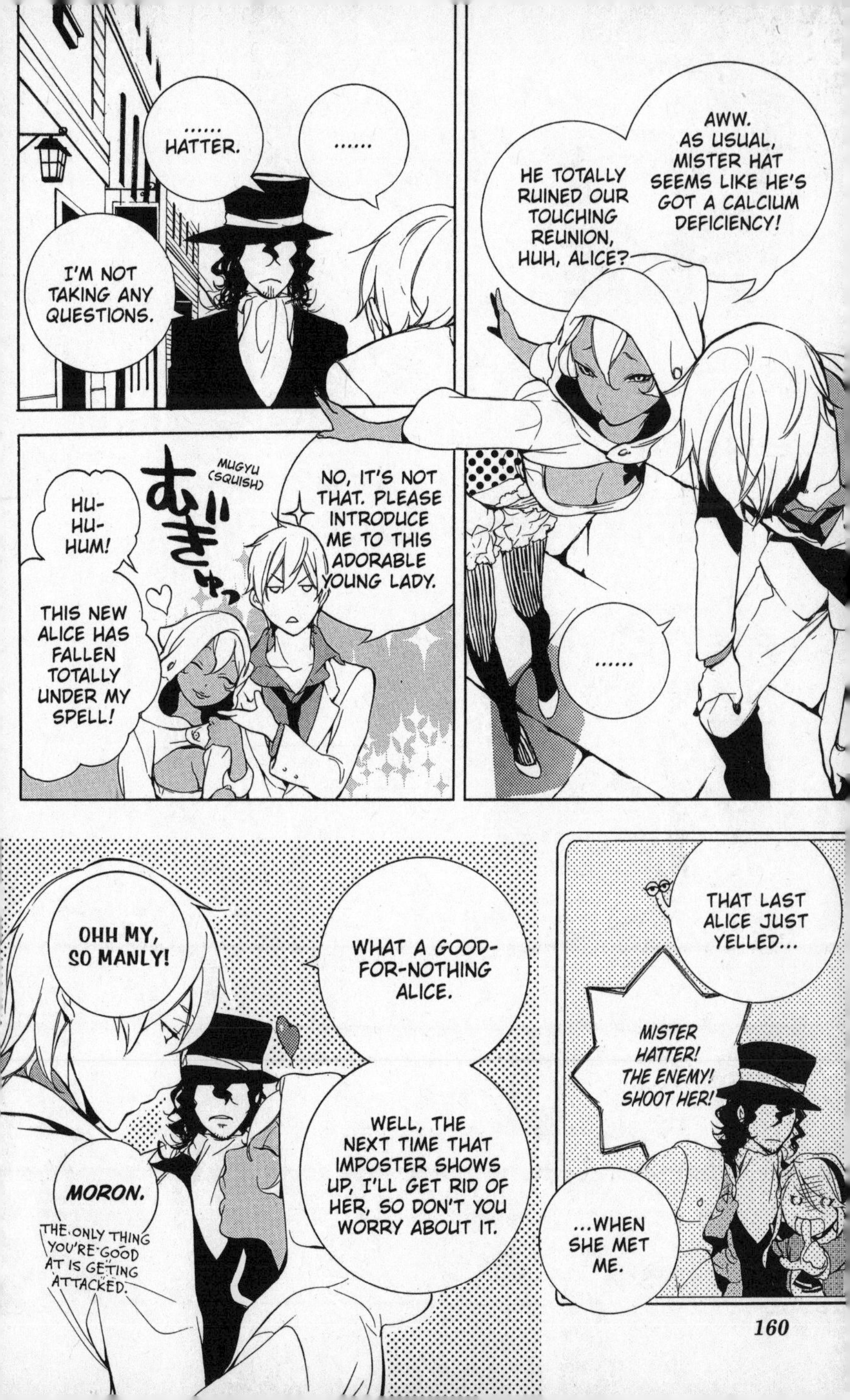
AWW. AS USUAL, MISTER HAT SEEMS LIKE HE'S GOT A CALCIUM DEFICIENCY!
HE TOTALLY RUINED OUR TOUCHING REUNION, HUH, ALICE?
...... HATTER.
......
I'M NOT TAKING ANY QUESTIONS.
......
NO, IT'S NOT THAT. PLEASE INTRODUCE ME TO THIS ADORABLE YOUNG LADY.
むぎゅっ
MUGYU (SQUISH)
HU-HU-HUM!
THIS NEW ALICE HAS FALLEN TOTALLY UNDER MY SPELL!
THAT LAST ALICE JUST YELLED...
MISTER HATTER! THE ENEMY! SHOOT HER!
...WHEN SHE MET ME.
WHAT A GOOD-FOR-NOTHING ALICE.
OHH MY, SO MANLY!
WELL, THE NEXT TIME THAT IMPOSTER SHOWS UP, I'LL GET RID OF HER, SO DON'T YOU WORRY ABOUT IT.
MORON.
THE ONLY THING YOU'RE GOOD AT IS GETING ATTACKED.

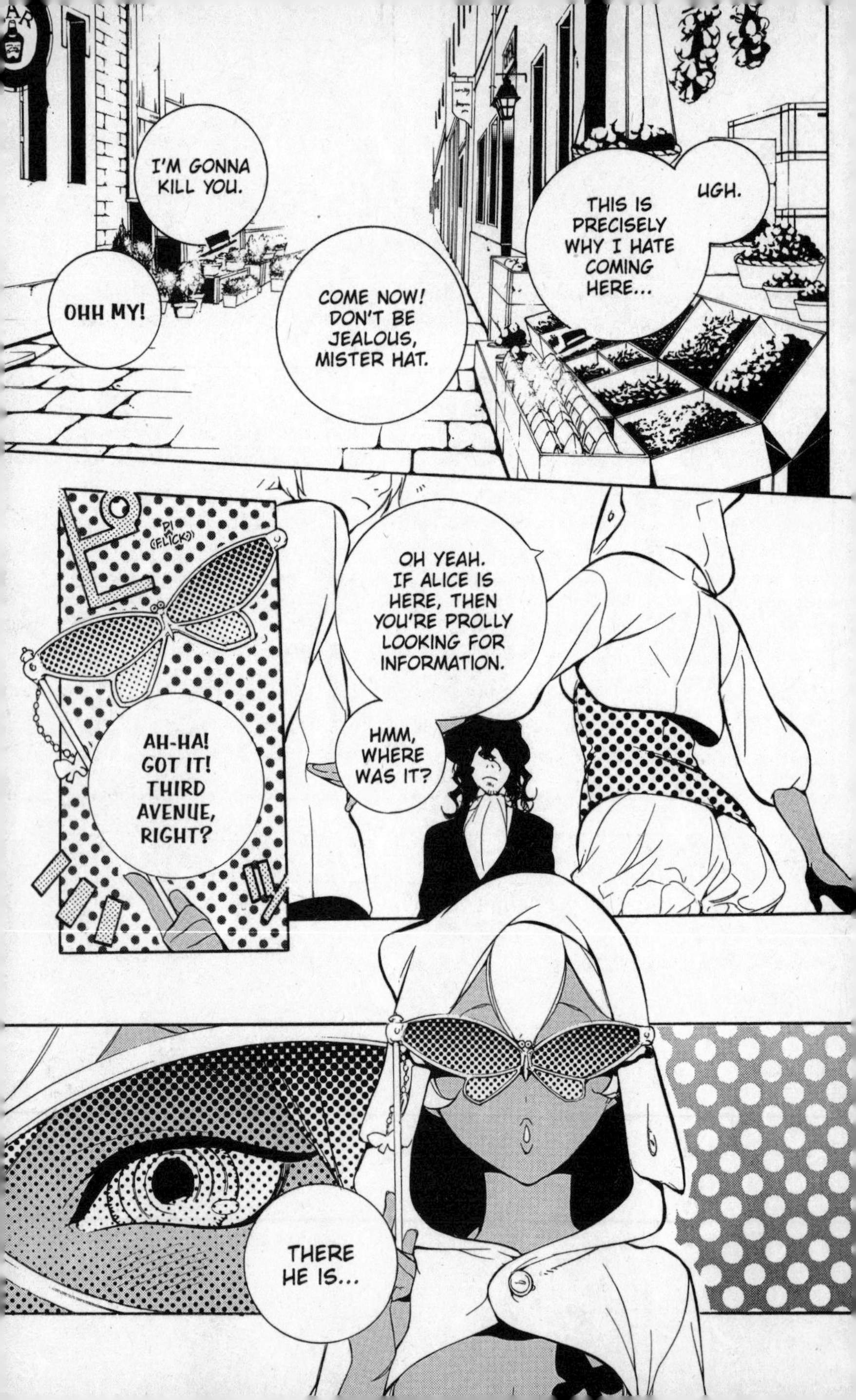
UGH.
THIS IS PRECISELY WHY I HATE COMING HERE...
COME NOW! DON'T BE JEALOUS, MISTER HAT.
I'M GONNA KILL YOU.
OHH MY!
OH YEAH. IF ALICE IS HERE, THEN YOU'RE PROLLY LOOKING FOR INFORMATION.
HMM, WHERE WAS IT?
(FLICK)
AH-HA! GOT IT! THIRD AVENUE, RIGHT?
THERE HE IS...

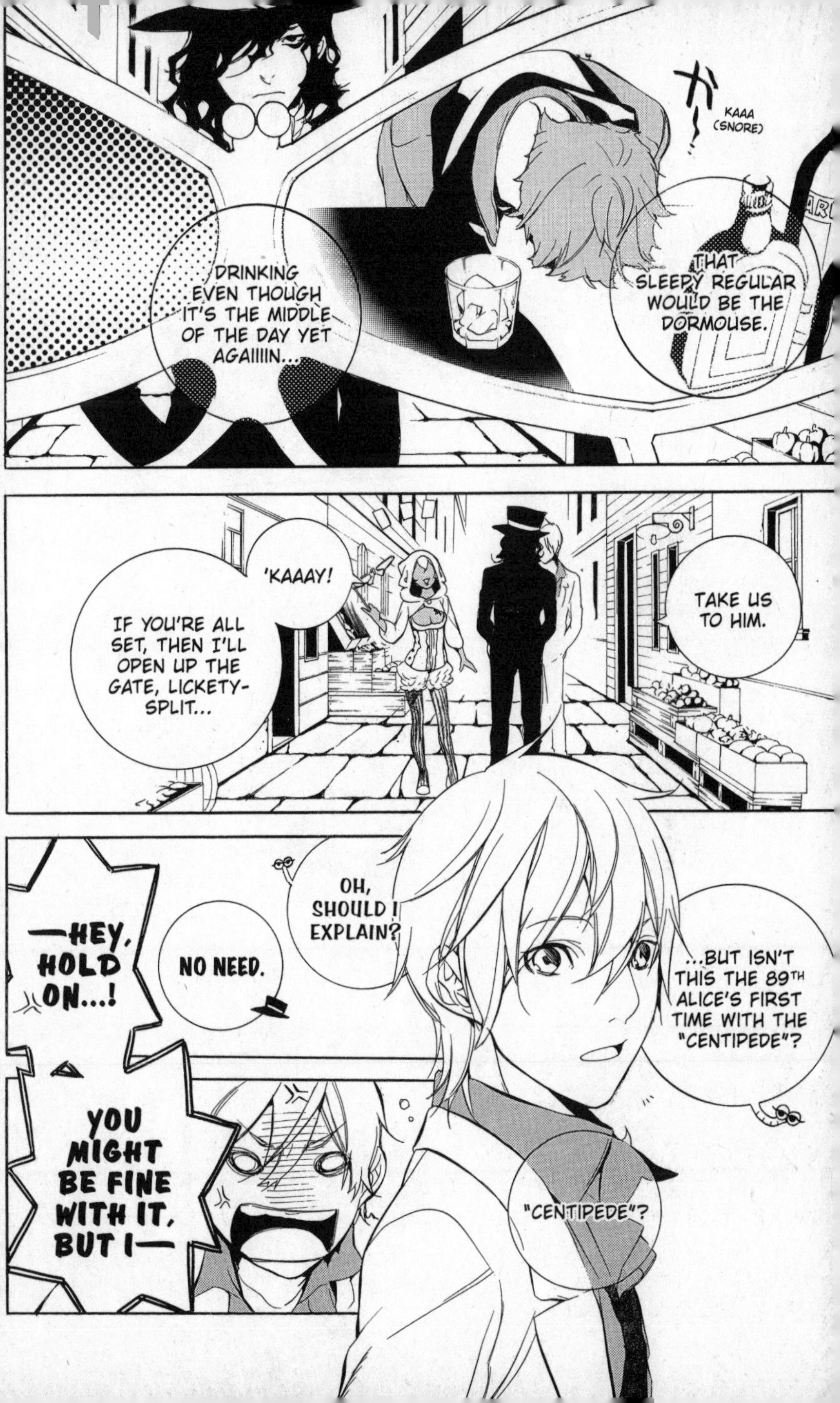
KAAA (SNORE)
THAT SLEEPY REGULAR WOULD BE THE DORMOUSE.
DRINKING EVEN THOUGH IT'S THE MIDDLE OF THE DAY YET AGAIIIIN...
TAKE US TO HIM.
'KAAAY!
IF YOU'RE ALL SET, THEN I'LL OPEN UP THE GATE, LICKETY-SPLIT...
...BUT ISN'T THIS THE 89TH ALICE'S FIRST TIME WITH THE "CENTIPEDE"?
OH, SHOULD I EXPLAIN?
NO NEED.
—HEY, HOLD ON...!
"CENTIPEDE"?
YOU MIGHT BE FINE WITH IT, BUT I—

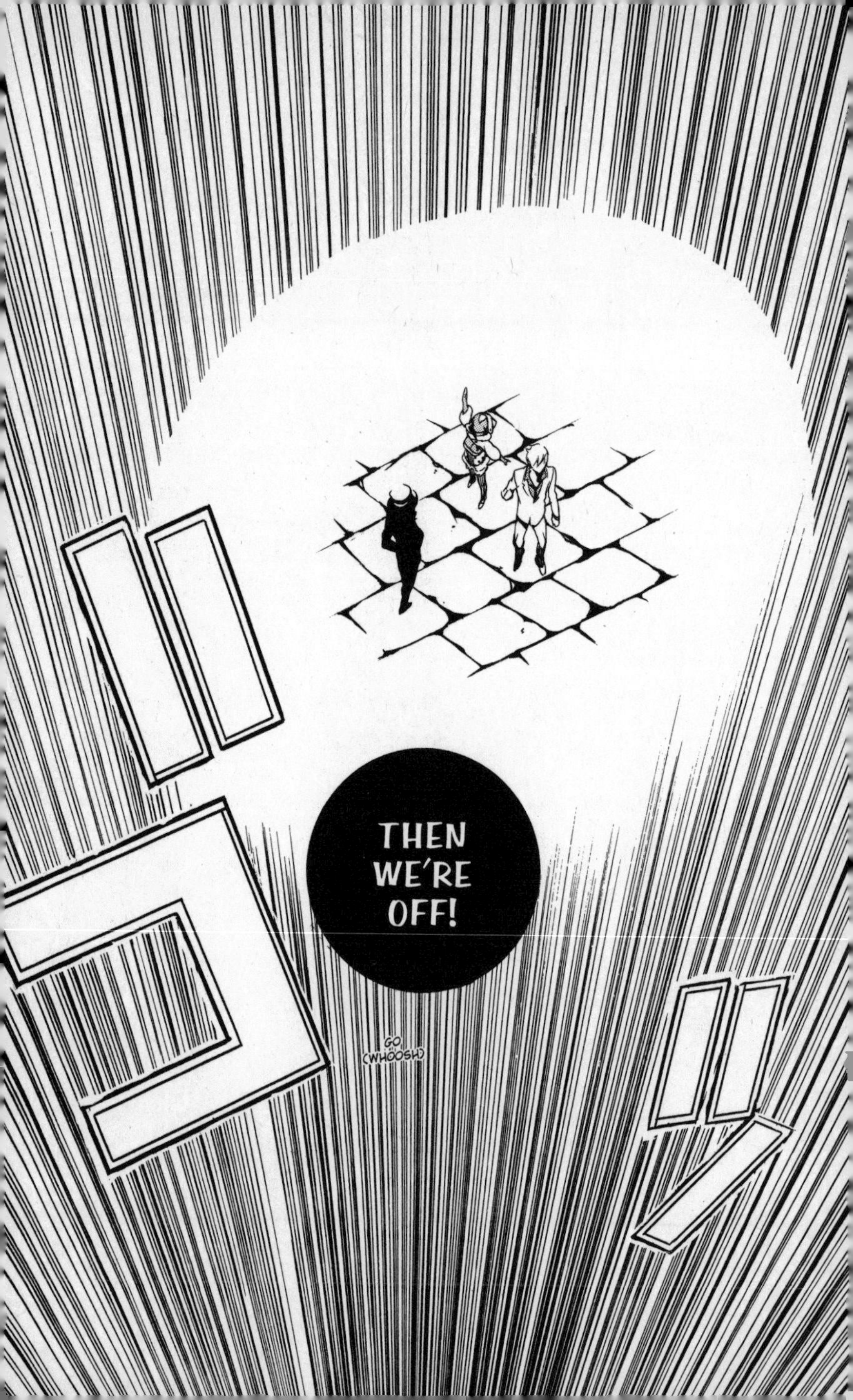
THEN WE'RE OFF!
GO (WHOOSH)

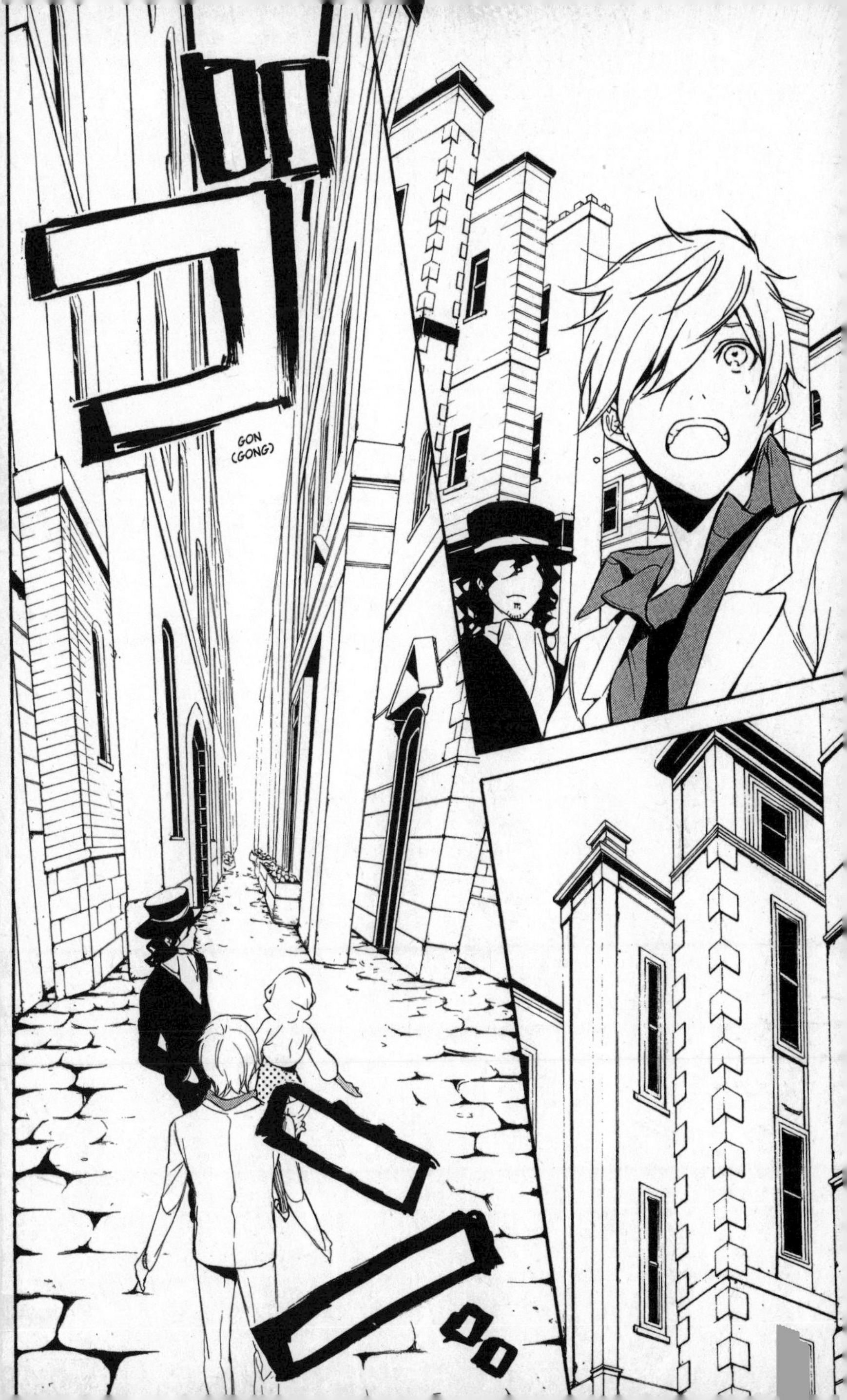
GON
(GONG)

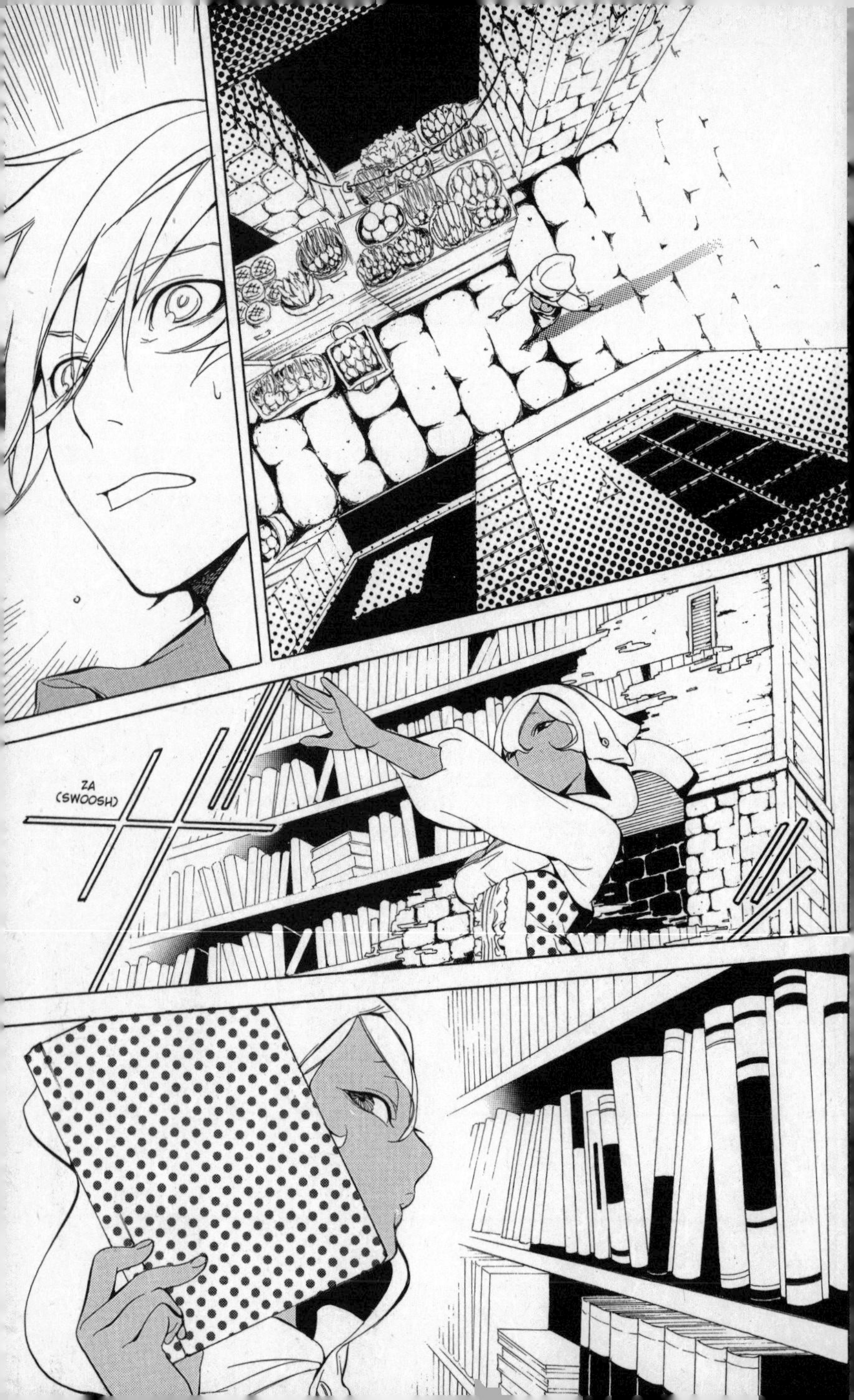
ZA
(SWOOSH)

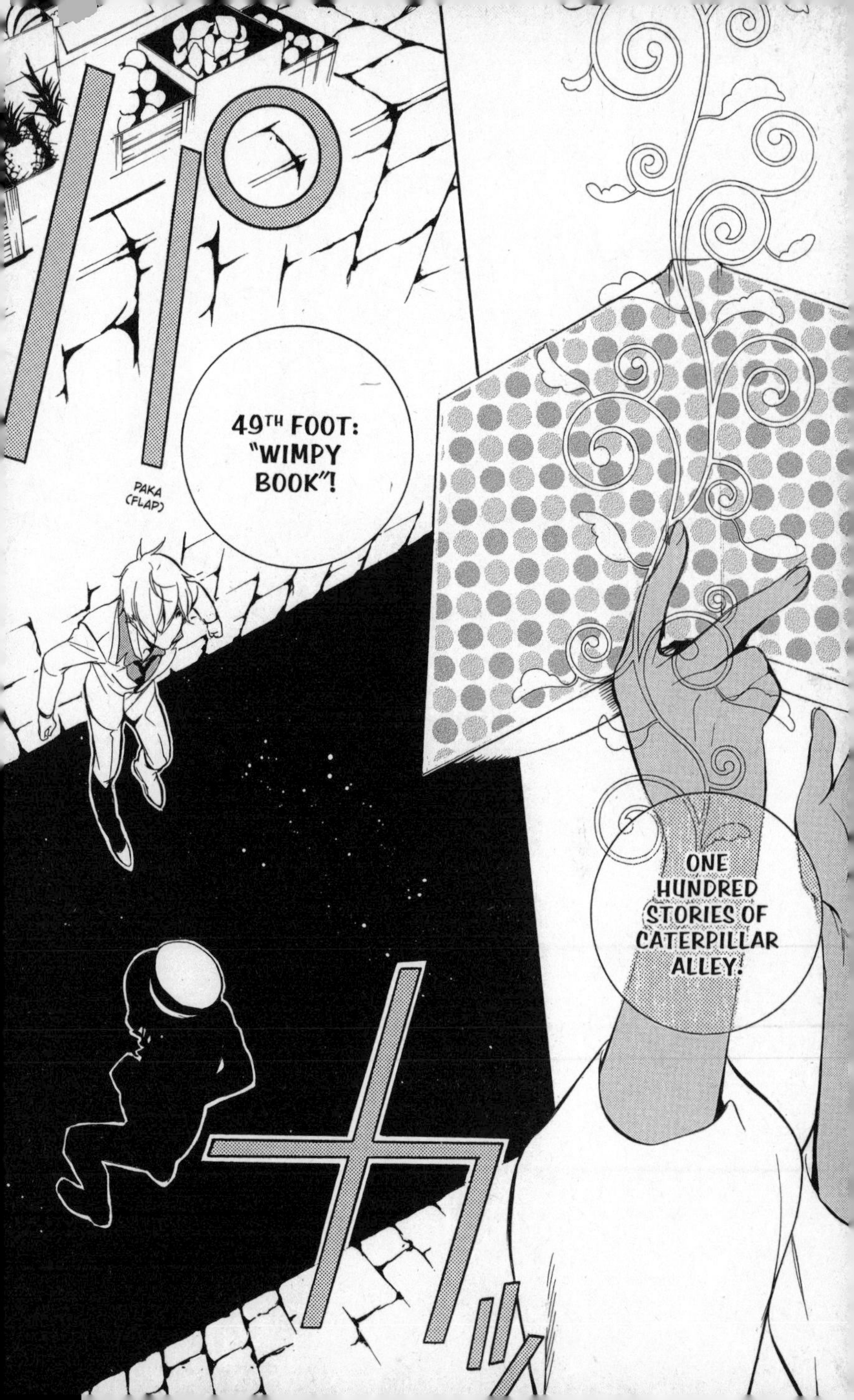
ONE HUNDRED STORIES OF CATERPILLAR ALLEY.
49TH FOOT: "WIMPY BOOK"!
PAKA (FLAP)

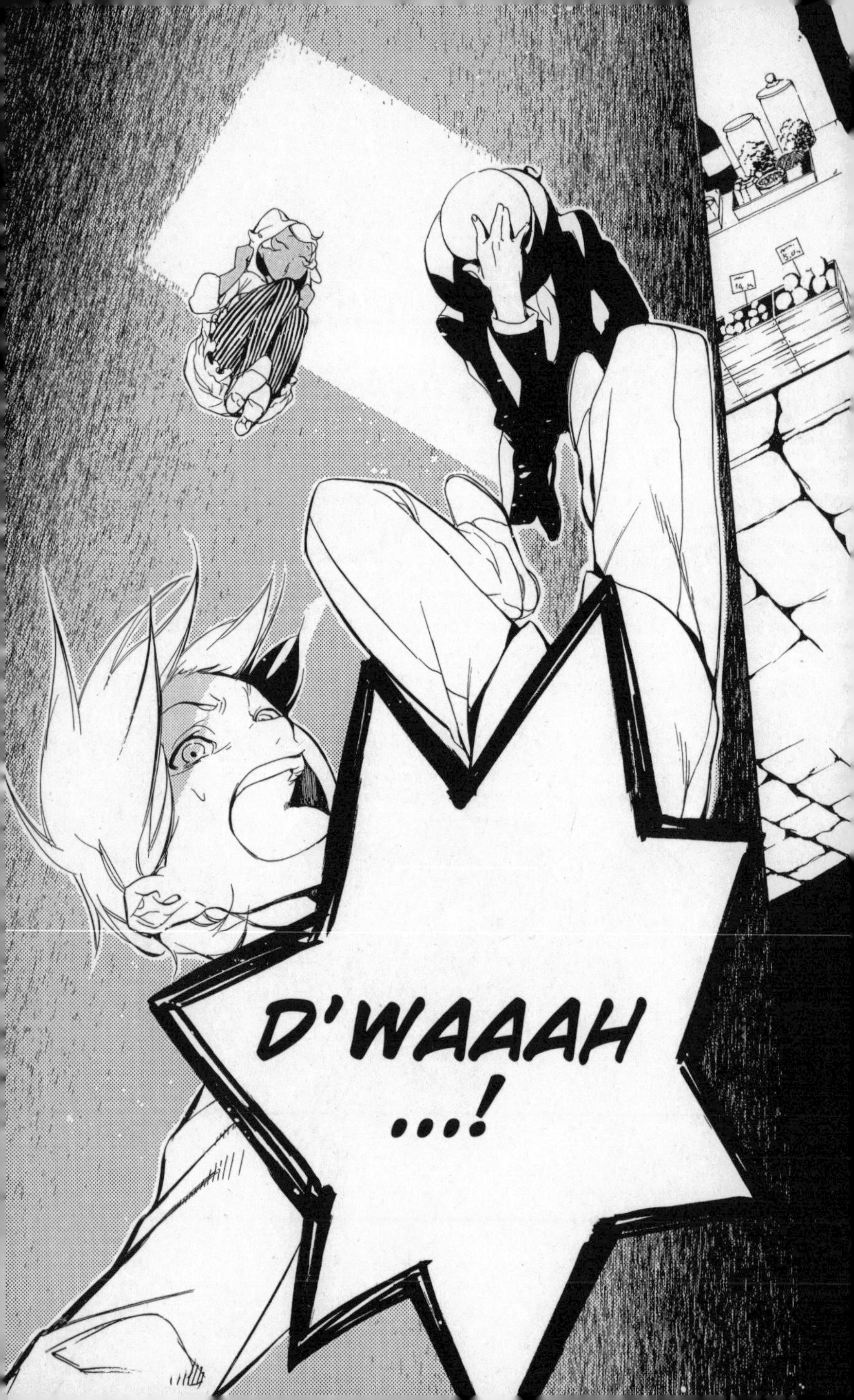
D'WAAAH ...!

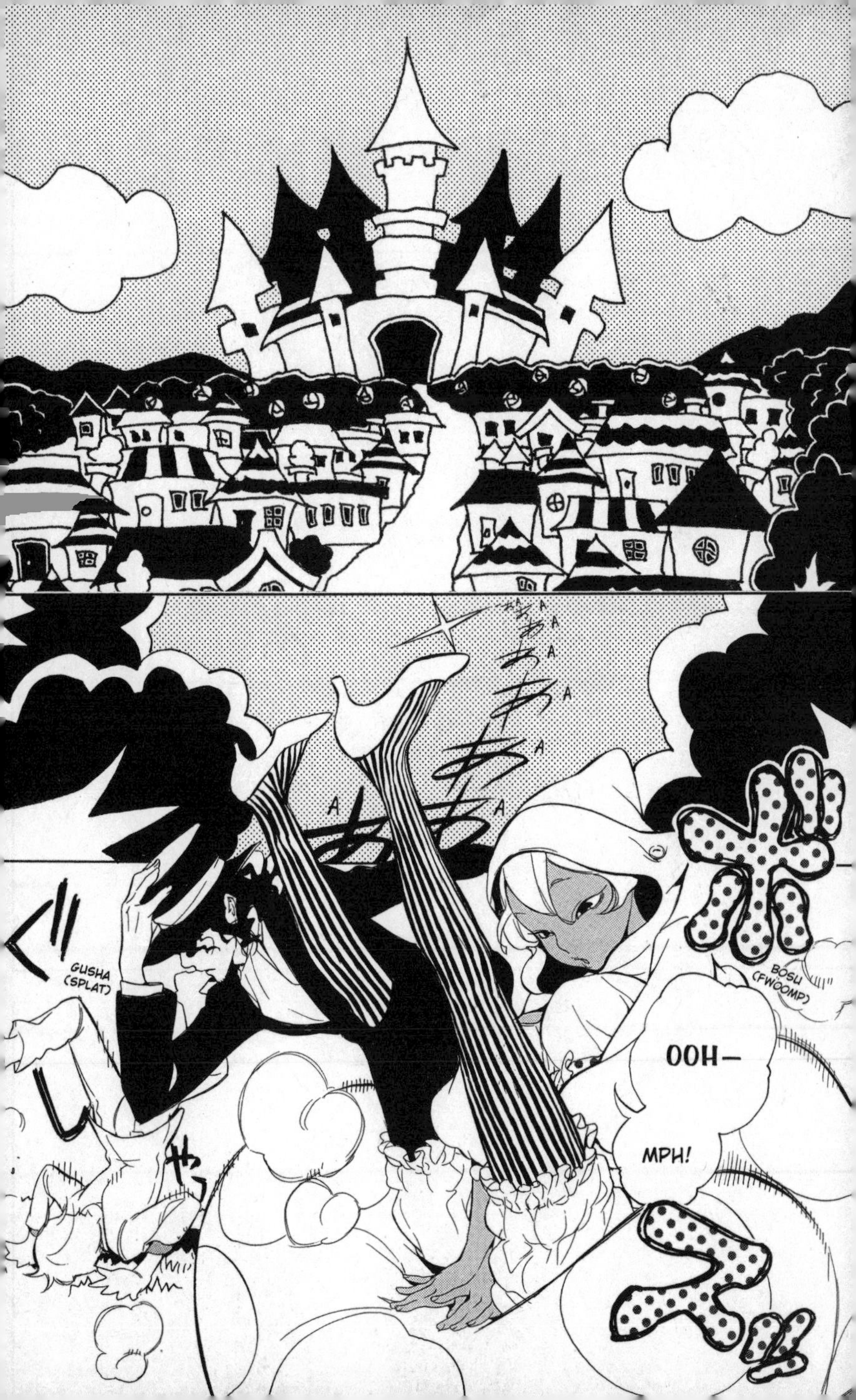
BOSU (FWOOMP)
OOH—
MPH!
GUSHA (SPLAT)

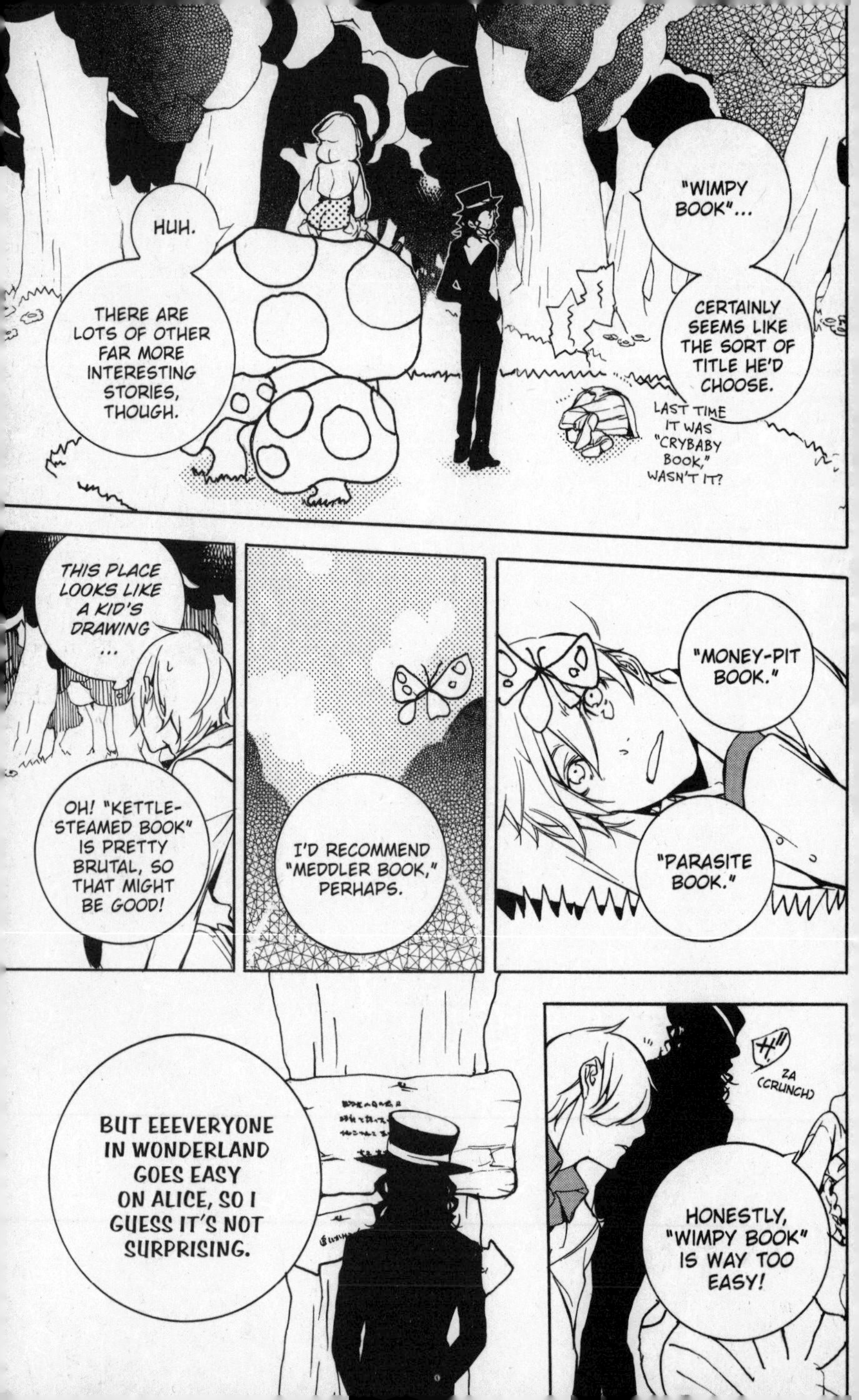
"WIMPY BOOK"...
CERTAINLY SEEMS LIKE THE SORT OF TITLE HE'D CHOOSE.
LAST TIME IT WAS "CRYBABY BOOK," WASN'T IT?
HUH.
THERE ARE LOTS OF OTHER FAR MORE INTERESTING STORIES, THOUGH.
"MONEY-PIT BOOK."
"PARASITE BOOK."
I'D RECOMMEND "MEDDLER BOOK," PERHAPS.
THIS PLACE LOOKS LIKE A KID'S DRAWING ...
OH! "KETTLE-STEAMED BOOK" IS PRETTY BRUTAL, SO THAT MIGHT BE GOOD!
ZA (CRUNCH)
HONESTLY, "WIMPY BOOK" IS WAY TOO EASY!
BUT EEEVERYONE IN WONDERLAND GOES EASY ON ALICE, SO I GUESS IT'S NOT SURPRISING.

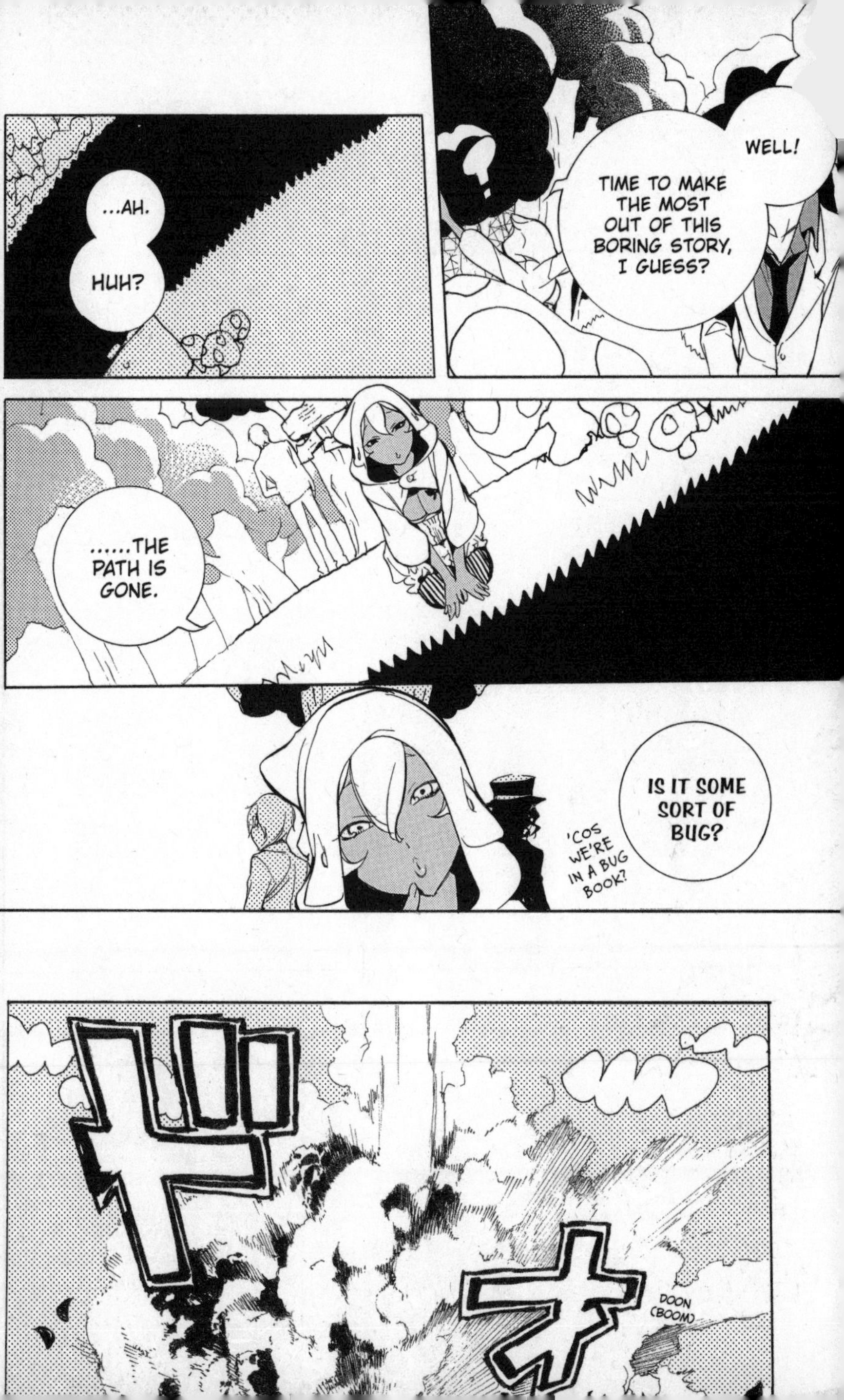
WELL!
TIME TO MAKE THE MOST OUT OF THIS BORING STORY, I GUESS?
...AH.
HUH?
......THE PATH IS GONE.
IS IT SOME SORT OF BUG?
'COS WE'RE IN A BUG BOOK?
DOON (BOOM)

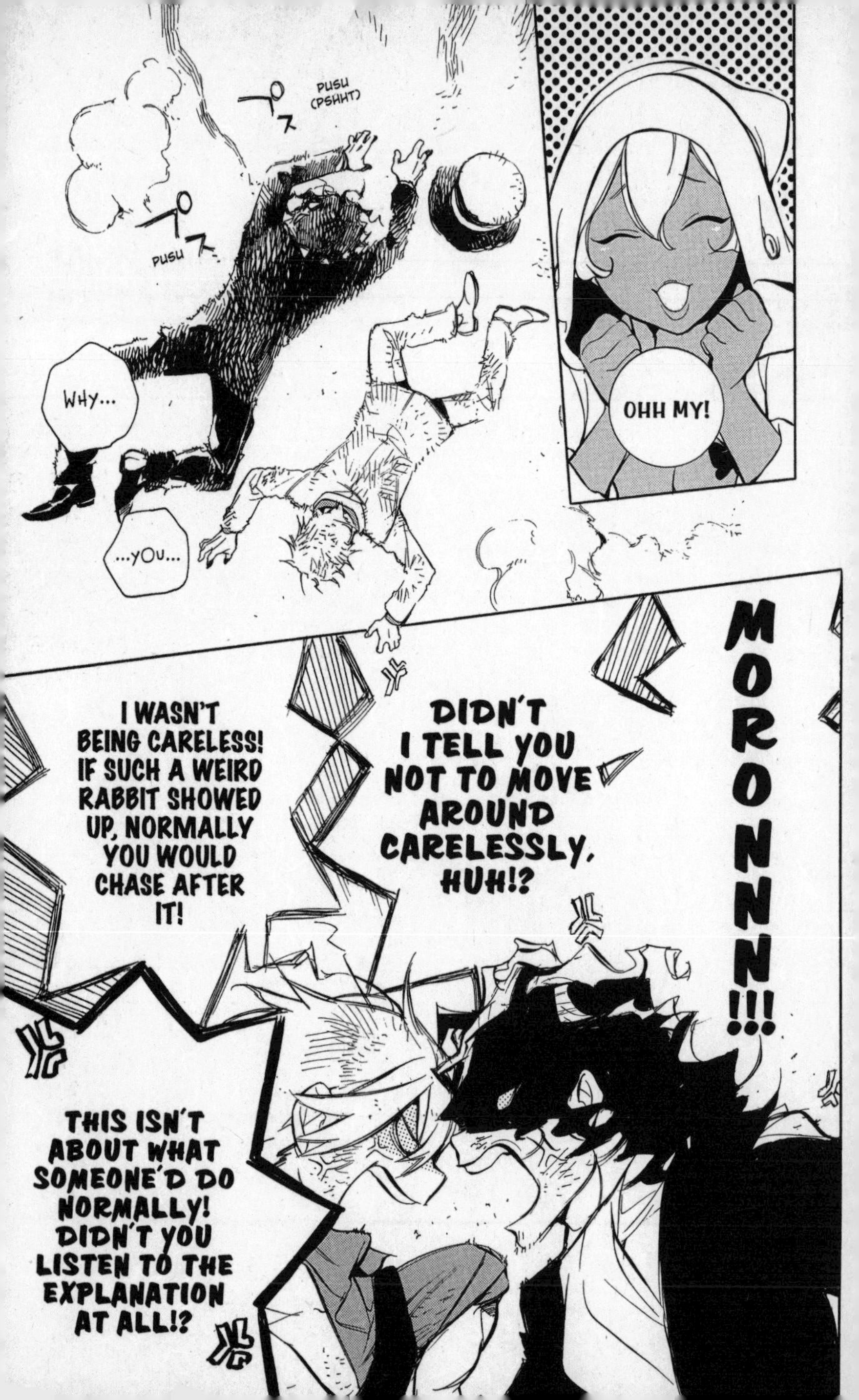
OHH MY!
PUSU (PSHHT)
PUSU
WHY...
...YOU...
MORONNN!!!
DIDN'T I TELL YOU NOT TO MOVE AROUND CARELESSLY, HUH!?
I WASN'T BEING CARELESS! IF SUCH A WEIRD RABBIT SHOWED UP, NORMALLY YOU WOULD CHASE AFTER IT!
THIS ISN'T ABOUT WHAT SOMEONE'D DO NORMALLY! DIDN'T YOU LISTEN TO THE EXPLANATION AT ALL!?

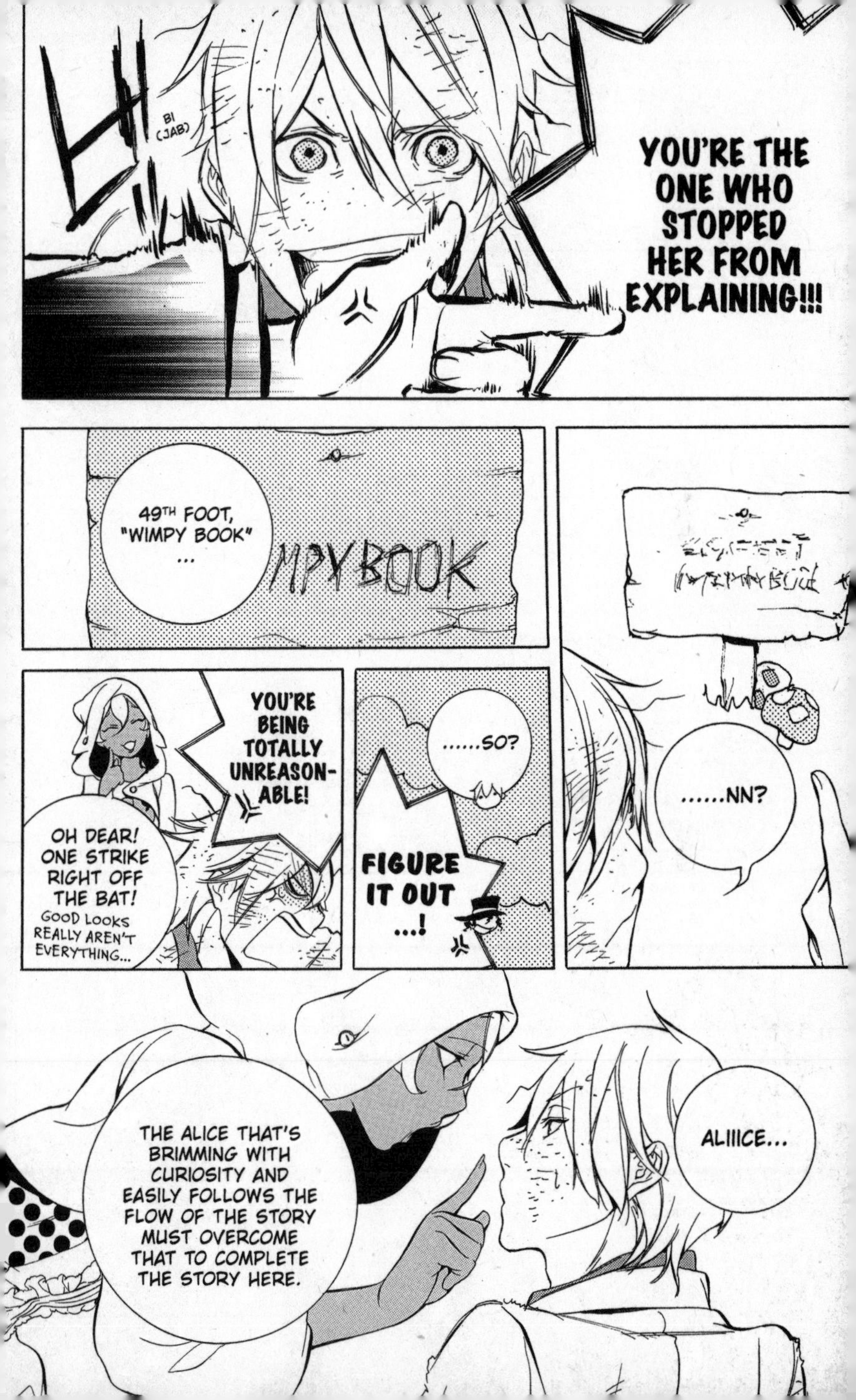
YOU'RE THE ONE WHO STOPPED HER FROM EXPLAINING!!!
BI (JAB)
......NN?
49TH FOOT, "WIMPY BOOK" ...
MPY BOOK
......SO?
FIGURE IT OUT ...!
YOU'RE BEING TOTALLY UNREASON-ABLE!
OH DEAR! ONE STRIKE RIGHT OFF THE BAT!
GOOD LOOKS REALLY AREN'T EVERYTHING...
ALIIICE...
THE ALICE THAT'S BRIMMING WITH CURIOSITY AND EASILY FOLLOWS THE FLOW OF THE STORY MUST OVERCOME THAT TO COMPLETE THE STORY HERE.

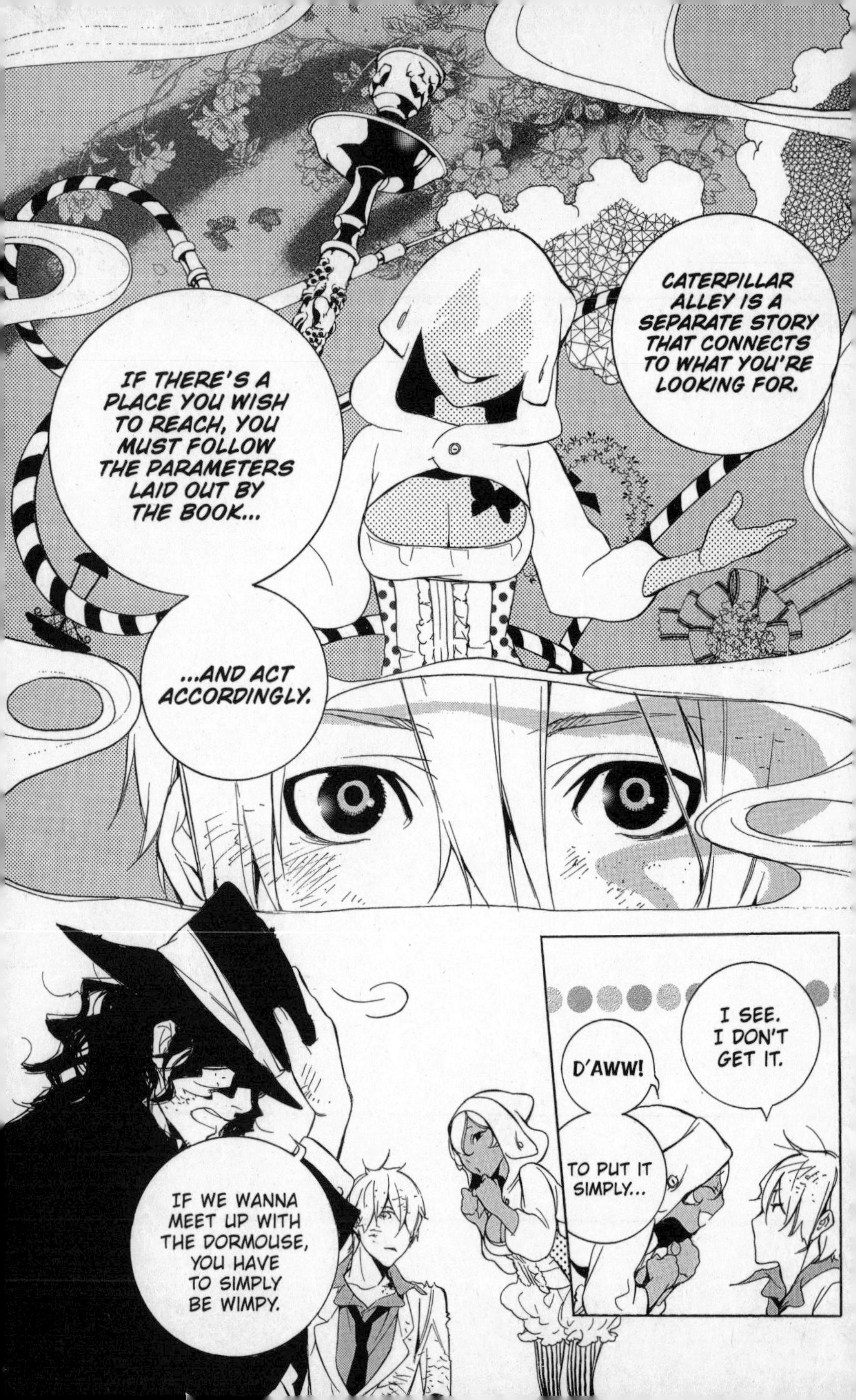
CATERPILLAR ALLEY IS A SEPARATE STORY THAT CONNECTS TO WHAT YOU'RE LOOKING FOR.
IF THERE'S A PLACE YOU WISH TO REACH, YOU MUST FOLLOW THE PARAMETERS LAID OUT BY THE BOOK...
...AND ACT ACCORDINGLY.
I SEE. I DON'T GET IT.
D'AWW!
TO PUT IT SIMPLY...
IF WE WANNA MEET UP WITH THE DORMOUSE, YOU HAVE TO SIMPLY BE WIMPY.

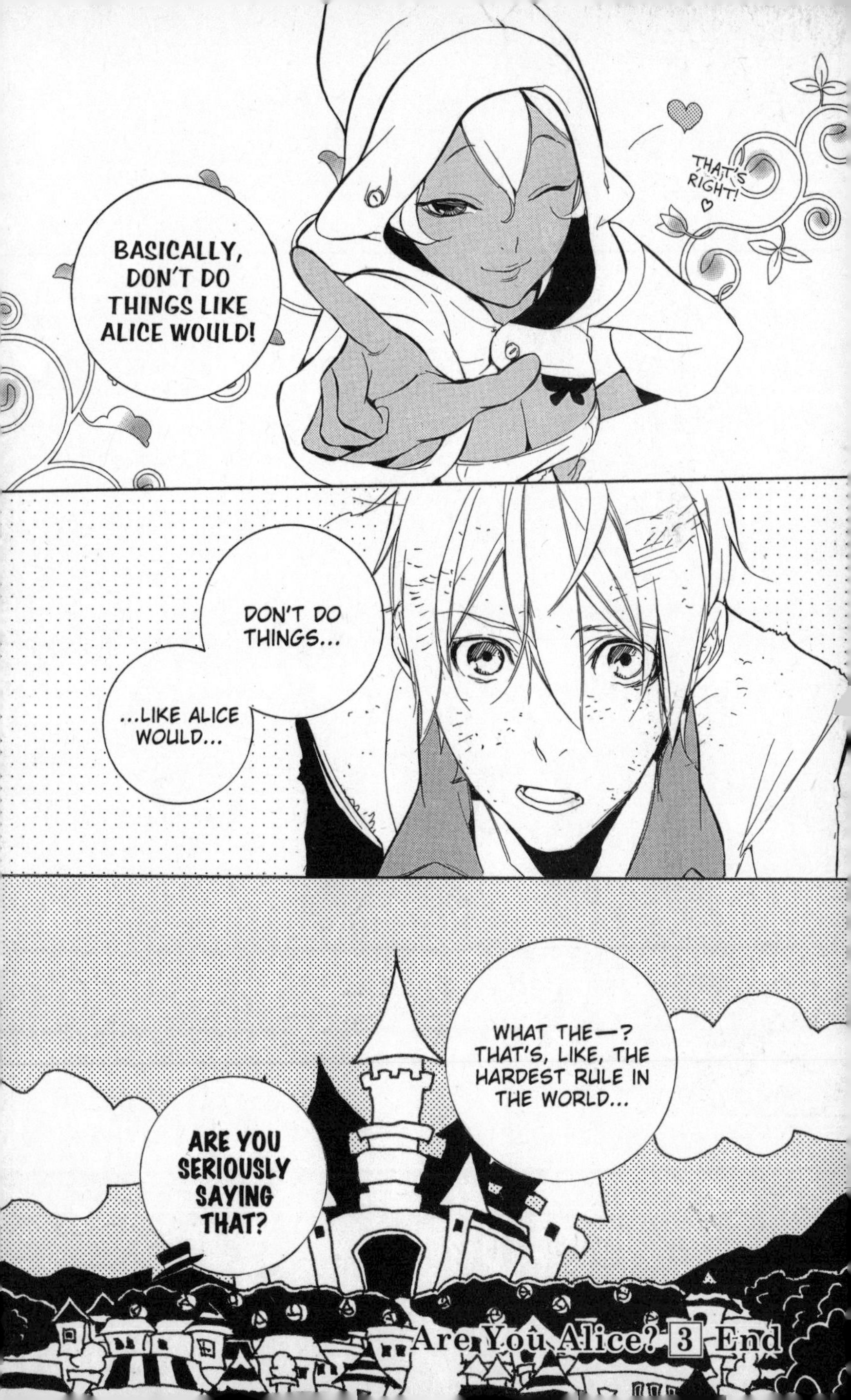
THAT'S RIGHT!
BASICALLY, DON'T DO THINGS LIKE ALICE WOULD!
DON'T DO THINGS...
...LIKE ALICE WOULD...
WHAT THE—? THAT'S, LIKE, THE HARDEST RULE IN THE WORLD...
ARE YOU SERIOUSLY SAYING THAT?
Are You Alice? 3 End

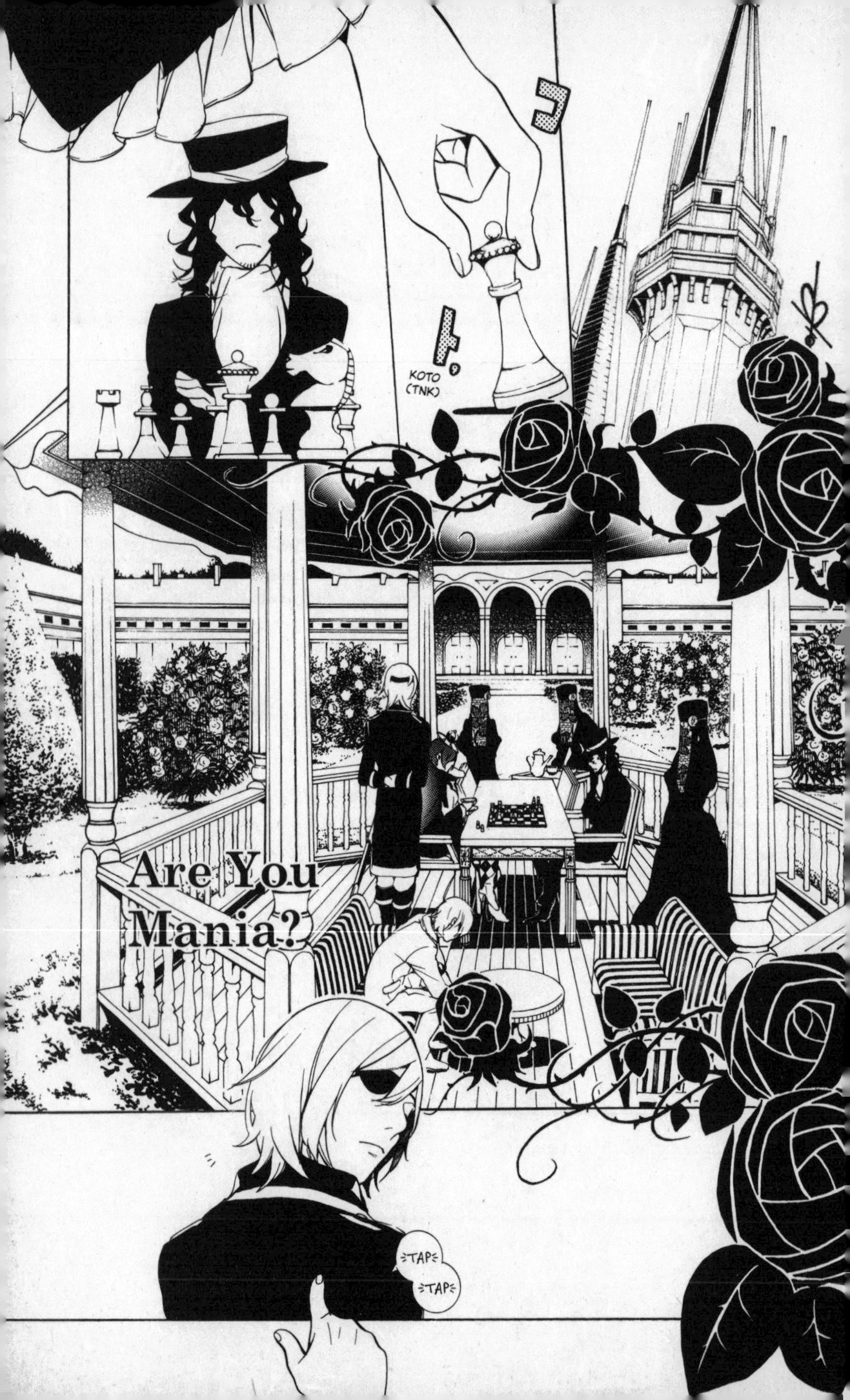
コト
KOTO (TNK)
Are You Mania?
TAP
TAP

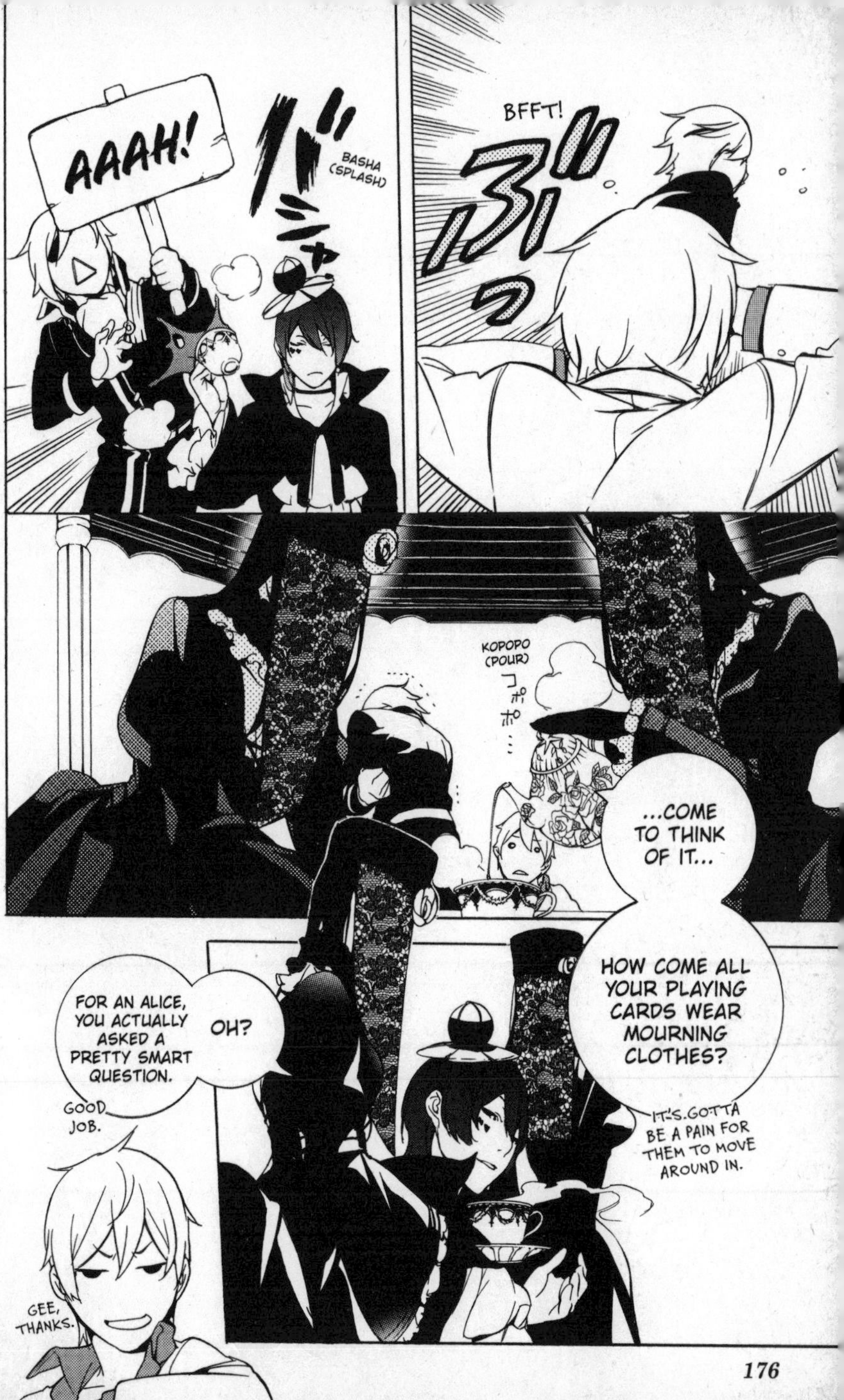
BFFT!
ぶっ
AAAH!
BASHA (SPLASH)
バシャ
KOPOPO (POUR)
コポポ…
...COME TO THINK OF IT...
HOW COME ALL YOUR PLAYING CARDS WEAR MOURNING CLOTHES?
IT'S GOTTA BE A PAIN FOR THEM TO MOVE AROUND IN.
OH?
FOR AN ALICE, YOU ACTUALLY ASKED A PRETTY SMART QUESTION.
GOOD JOB.
GEE, THANKS.

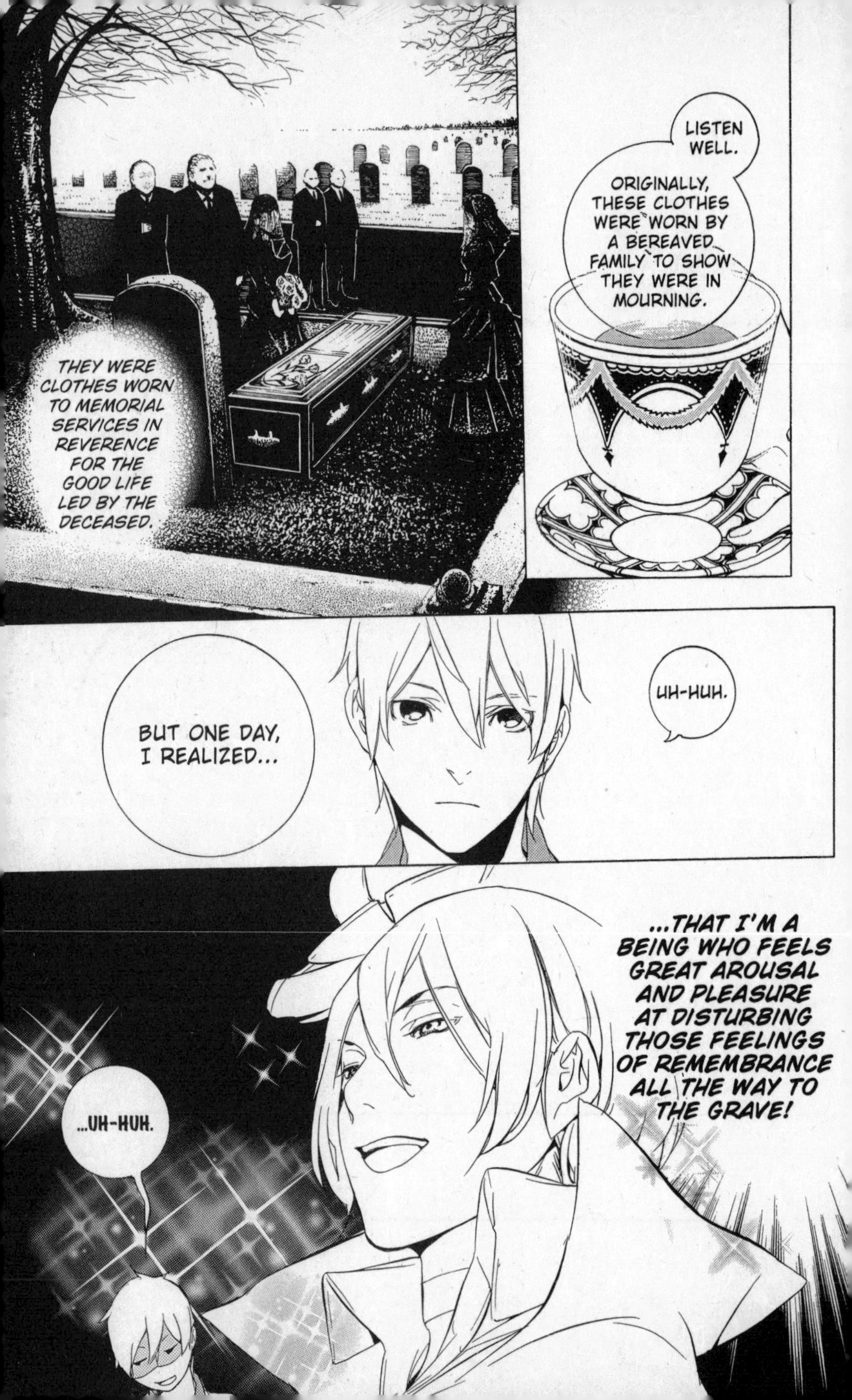
LISTEN WELL.
ORIGINALLY, THESE CLOTHES WERE WORN BY A BEREAVED FAMILY TO SHOW THEY WERE IN MOURNING.
THEY WERE CLOTHES WORN TO MEMORIAL SERVICES IN REVERENCE FOR THE GOOD LIFE LED BY THE DECEASED.
UH-HUH.
BUT ONE DAY, I REALIZED...
...THAT I'M A BEING WHO FEELS GREAT AROUSAL AND PLEASURE AT DISTURBING THOSE FEELINGS OF REMEMBRANCE ALL THE WAY TO THE GRAVE!
...UH-HUH.

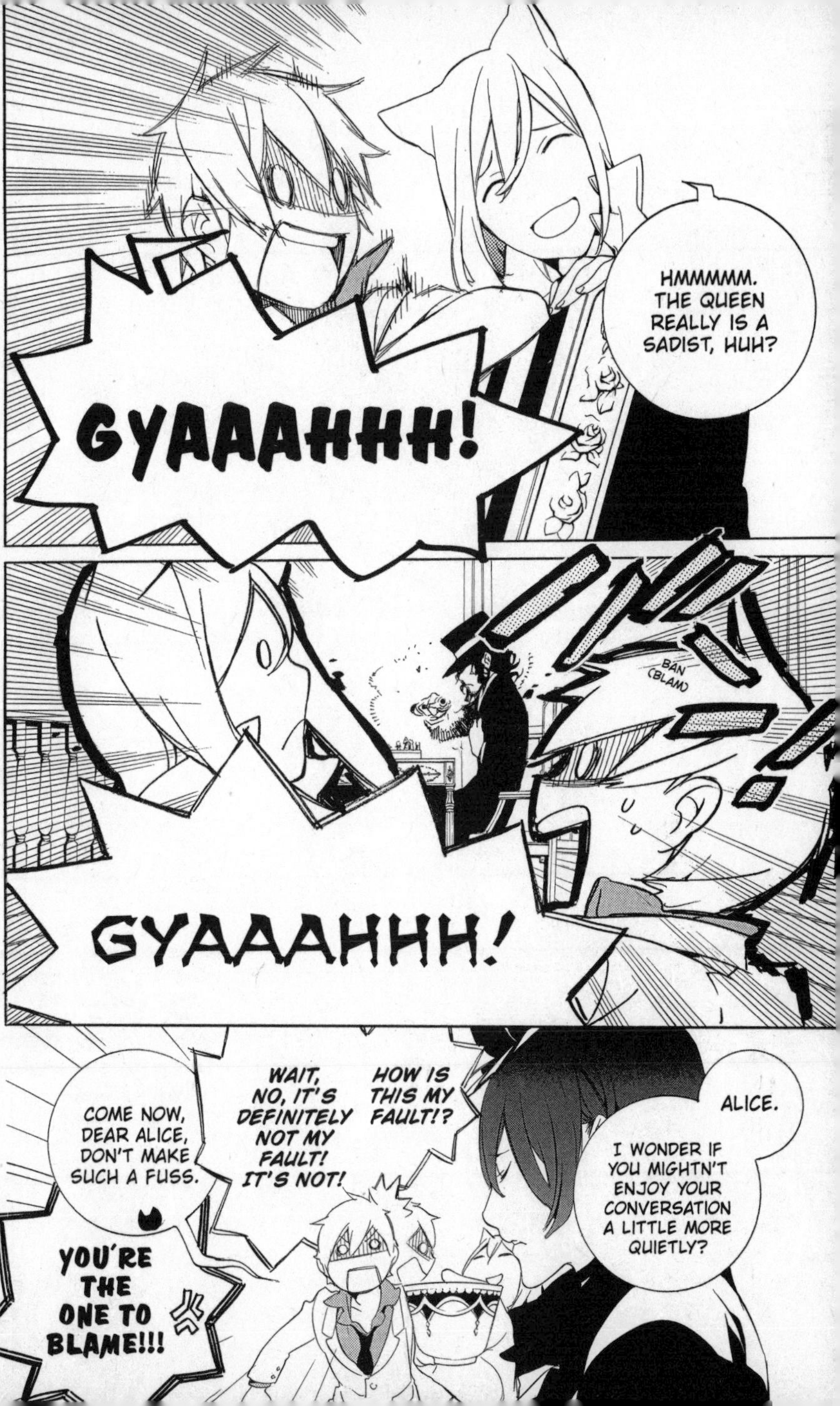
HMMMMM. THE QUEEN REALLY IS A SADIST, HUH?
GYAAAHHHH!
BAN (BLAM)
GYAAAHHH!
ALICE.
I WONDER IF YOU MIGHTN'T ENJOY YOUR CONVERSATION A LITTLE MORE QUIETLY?
HOW IS THIS MY FAULT!?
WAIT, NO, IT'S DEFINITELY NOT MY FAULT! IT'S NOT!
COME NOW, DEAR ALICE, DON'T MAKE SUCH A FUSS.
YOU'RE THE ONE TO BLAME!!!

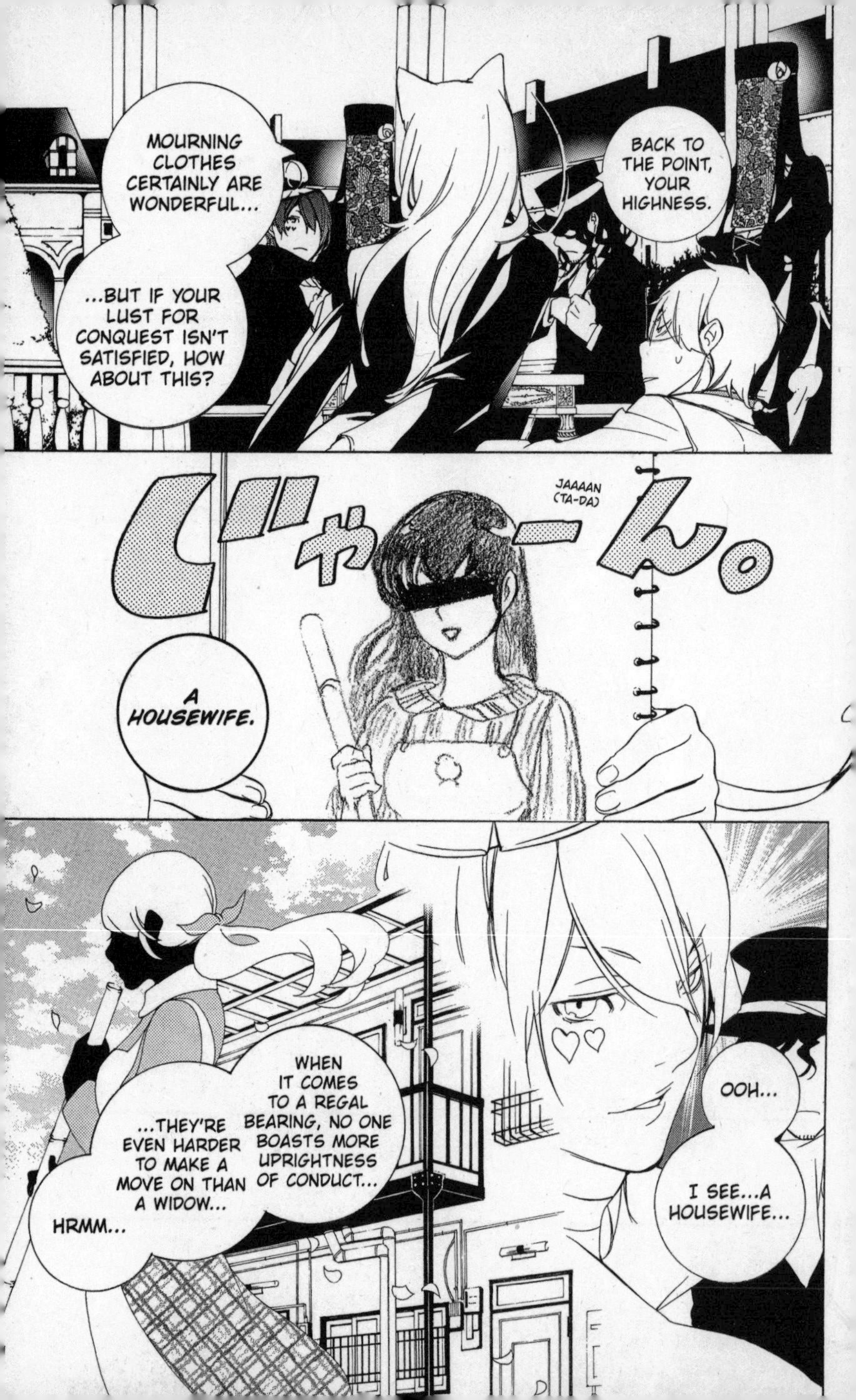
BACK TO THE POINT, YOUR HIGHNESS.
MOURNING CLOTHES CERTAINLY ARE WONDERFUL...
...BUT IF YOUR LUST FOR CONQUEST ISN'T SATISFIED, HOW ABOUT THIS?
じゃーん。
JAAAAN (TA-DA)
A HOUSEWIFE.
OOH...
I SEE...A HOUSEWIFE...
WHEN IT COMES TO A REGAL BEARING, NO ONE BOASTS MORE UPRIGHTNESS OF CONDUCT...
...THEY'RE EVEN HARDER TO MAKE A MOVE ON THAN A WIDOW...
HRMM...

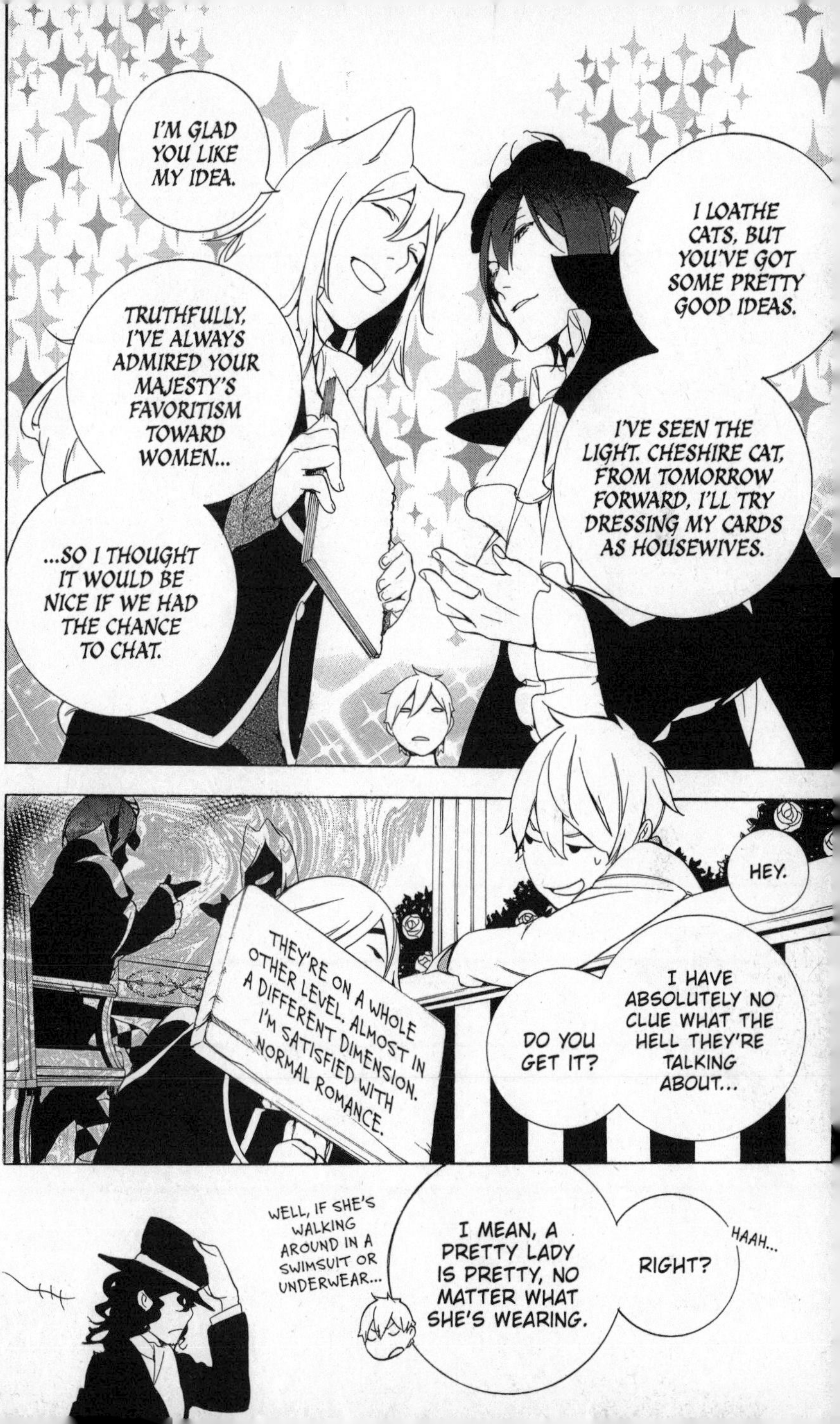
I LOATHE CATS, BUT YOU'VE GOT SOME PRETTY GOOD IDEAS.
I'M GLAD YOU LIKE MY IDEA.
TRUTHFULLY, I'VE ALWAYS ADMIRED YOUR MAJESTY'S FAVORITISM TOWARD WOMEN...
...SO I THOUGHT IT WOULD BE NICE IF WE HAD THE CHANCE TO CHAT.
I'VE SEEN THE LIGHT. CHESHIRE CAT, FROM TOMORROW FORWARD, I'LL TRY DRESSING MY CARDS AS HOUSEWIVES.
HEY.
I HAVE ABSOLUTELY NO CLUE WHAT THE HELL THEY'RE TALKING ABOUT...
DO YOU GET IT?
THEY'RE ON A WHOLE OTHER LEVEL. ALMOST IN A DIFFERENT DIMENSION. I'M SATISFIED WITH NORMAL ROMANCE.
HAAH...
RIGHT?
I MEAN, A PRETTY LADY IS PRETTY, NO MATTER WHAT SHE'S WEARING.
WELL, IF SHE'S WALKING AROUND IN A SWIMSUIT OR UNDERWEAR...

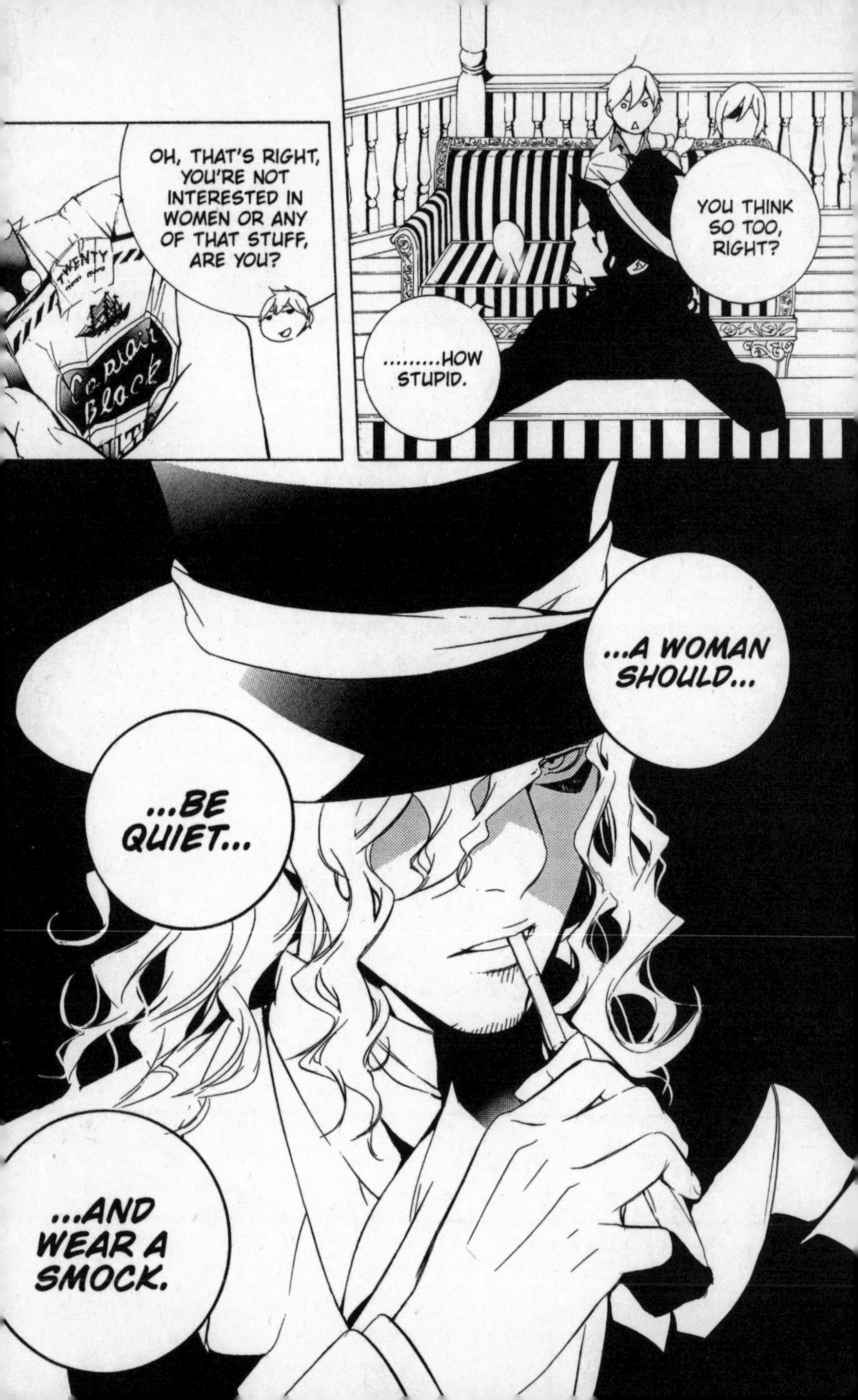
YOU THINK SO TOO, RIGHT?
.........HOW STUPID.
OH, THAT'S RIGHT, YOU'RE NOT INTERESTED IN WOMEN OR ANY OF THAT STUFF, ARE YOU?
...A WOMAN SHOULD...
...BE QUIET...
...AND WEAR A SMOCK.

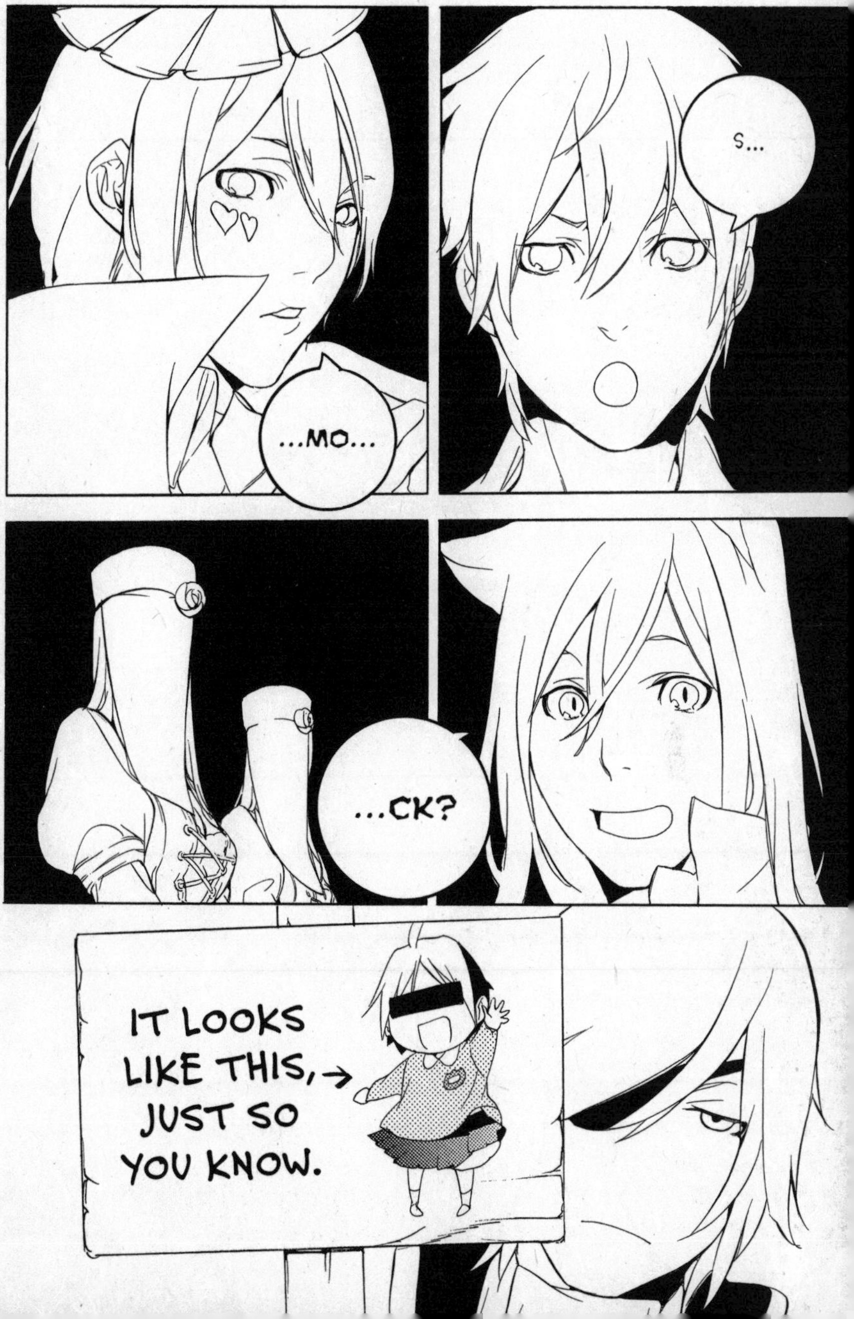
S...
...MO...
...CK?
IT LOOKS LIKE THIS, →
JUST SO YOU KNOW.

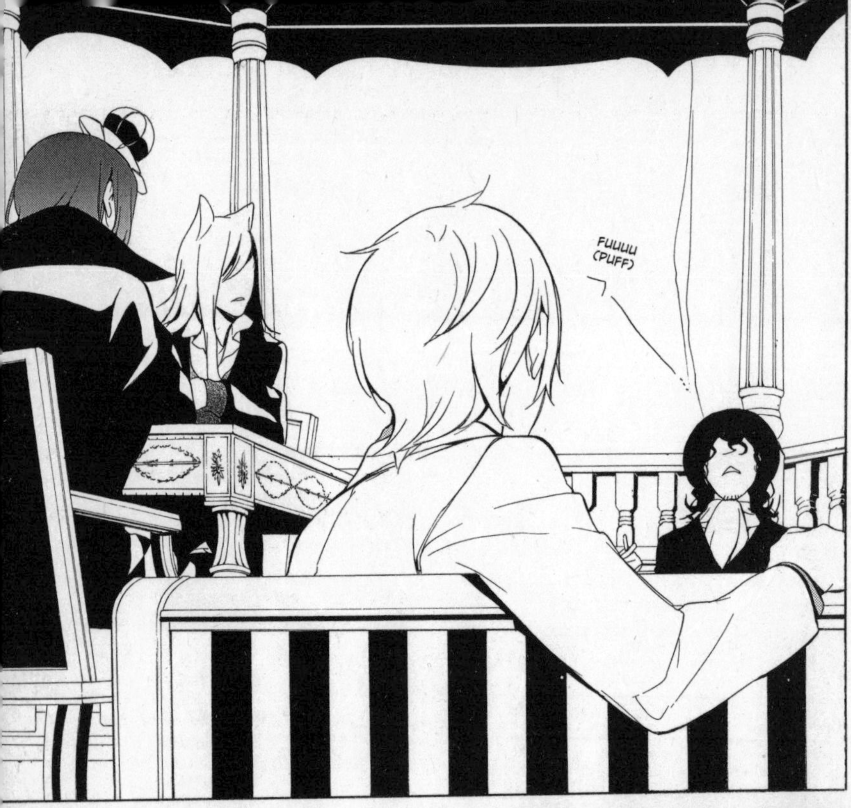
FUUUU (PUFF)

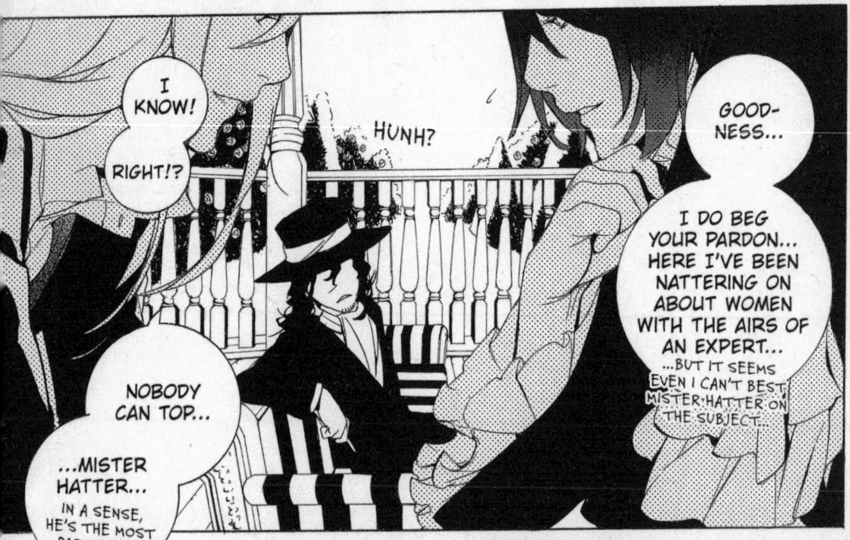
GOODNESS...
I DO BEG YOUR PARDON... HERE I'VE BEEN NATTERING ON ABOUT WOMEN WITH THE AIRS OF AN EXPERT...
...BUT IT SEEMS EVEN I CAN'T BEST MISTER HATTER ON THE SUBJECT...
HUNH?
I KNOW!
RIGHT!?
NOBODY CAN TOP...
...MISTER HATTER...
IN A SENSE, HE'S THE MOST PARTICULAR CONNOISSEUR...

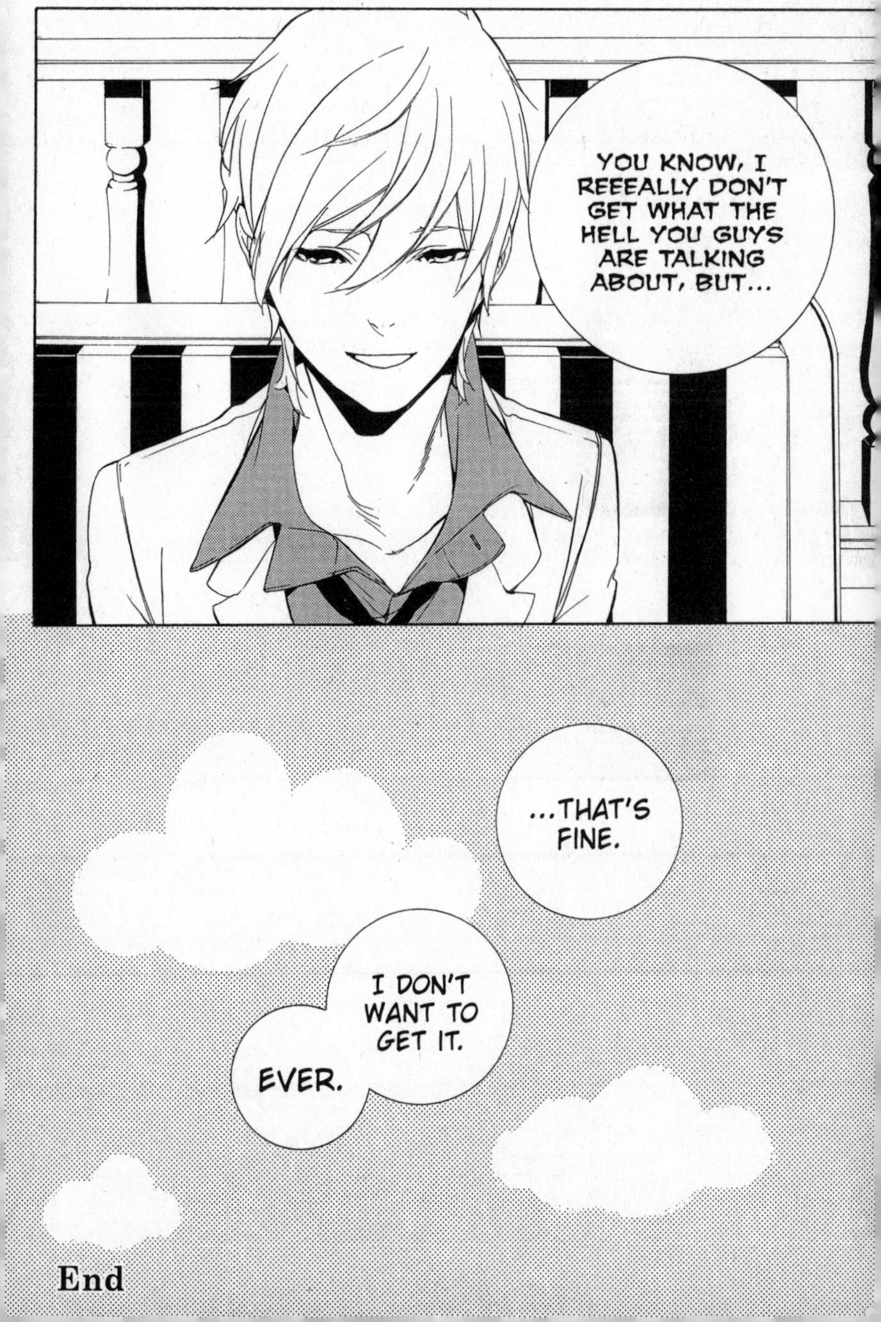
YOU KNOW, I REEEALLY DON'T GET WHAT THE HELL YOU GUYS ARE TALKING ABOUT, BUT...
...THAT'S FINE.
I DON'T WANT TO GET IT.
EVER.
End

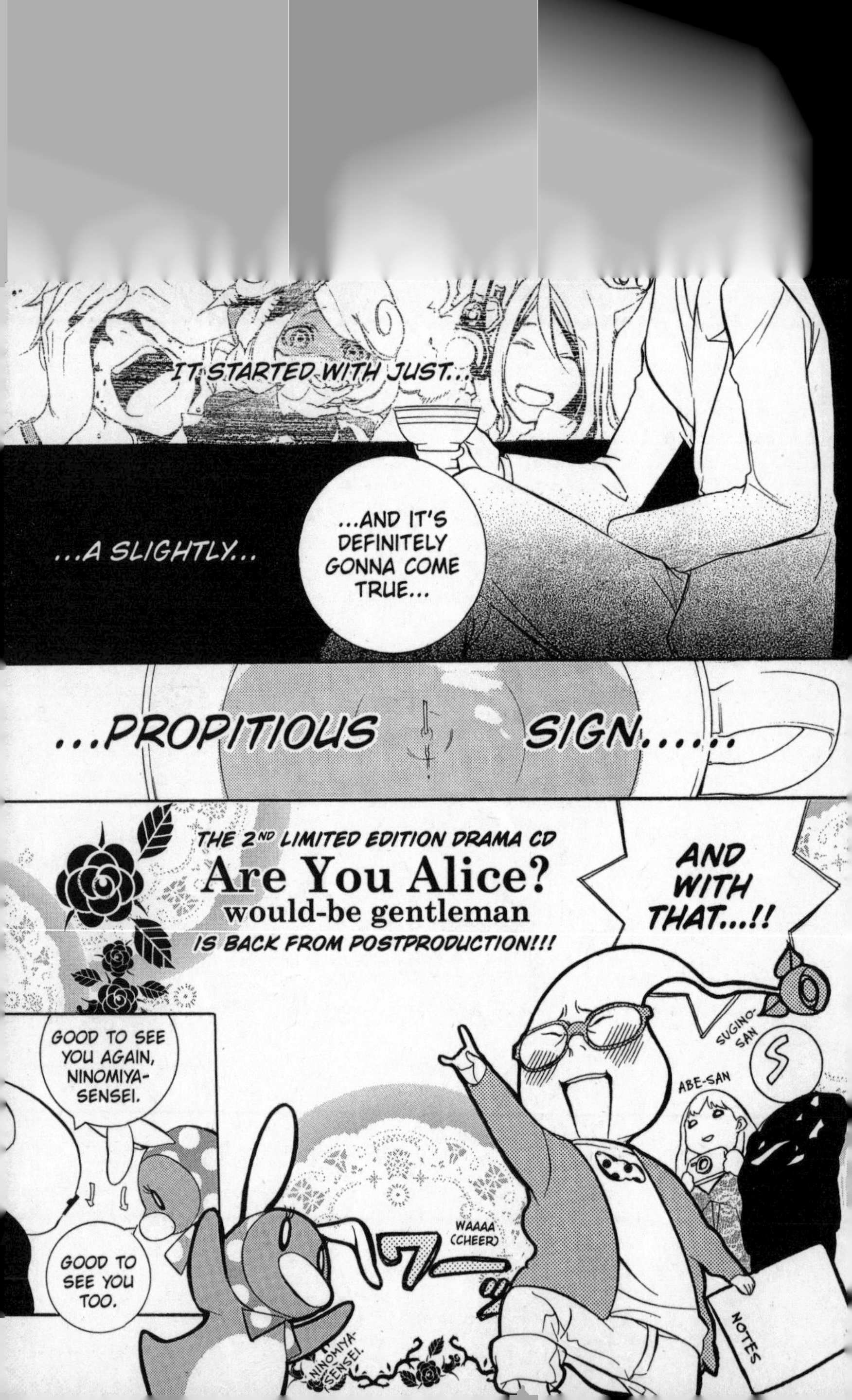
IT STARTED WITH JUST...
...AND IT'S DEFINITELY GONNA COME TRUE...
...A SLIGHTLY...
...PROPITIOUS SIGN......
AND WITH THAT...!!
THE 2ND LIMITED EDITION DRAMA CD
Are You Alice?
would-be gentleman
IS BACK FROM POSTPRODUCTION!!!
SUGINO-SAN
ABE-SAN
WAAAA (CHEER)
NOTES
NINOMIYA-SENSEI.
GOOD TO SEE YOU AGAIN, NINOMIYA-SENSEI.
GOOD TO SEE YOU TOO.

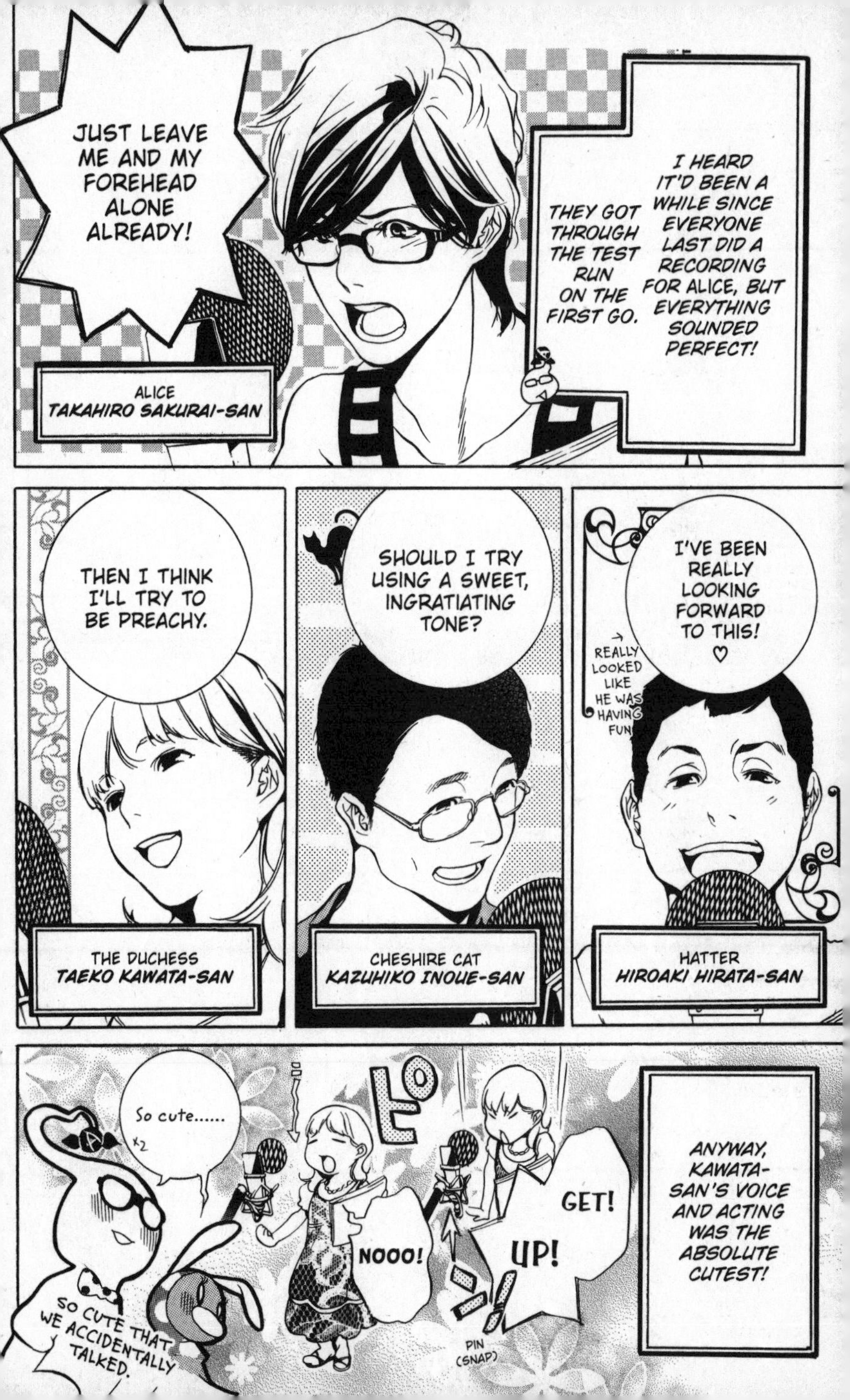
I HEARD IT'D BEEN A WHILE SINCE EVERYONE LAST DID A RECORDING FOR ALICE, BUT EVERYTHING SOUNDED PERFECT!
THEY GOT THROUGH THE TEST RUN ON THE FIRST GO.
JUST LEAVE ME AND MY FOREHEAD ALONE ALREADY!
ALICE TAKAHIRO SAKURAI-SAN
I'VE BEEN REALLY LOOKING FORWARD TO THIS! ♡
→ REALLY LOOKED LIKE HE WAS HAVING FUN
HATTER HIROAKI HIRATA-SAN
SHOULD I TRY USING A SWEET, INGRATIATING TONE?
CHESHIRE CAT KAZUHIKO INOUE-SAN
THEN I THINK I'LL TRY TO BE PREACHY.
THE DUCHESS TAEKO KAWATA-SAN
ANYWAY, KAWATA-SAN'S VOICE AND ACTING WAS THE ABSOLUTE CUTEST!
GET!
UP!
PIN (SNAP)
NOOO!
So cute...... ×2
SO CUTE THAT WE ACCIDENTALLY TALKED.

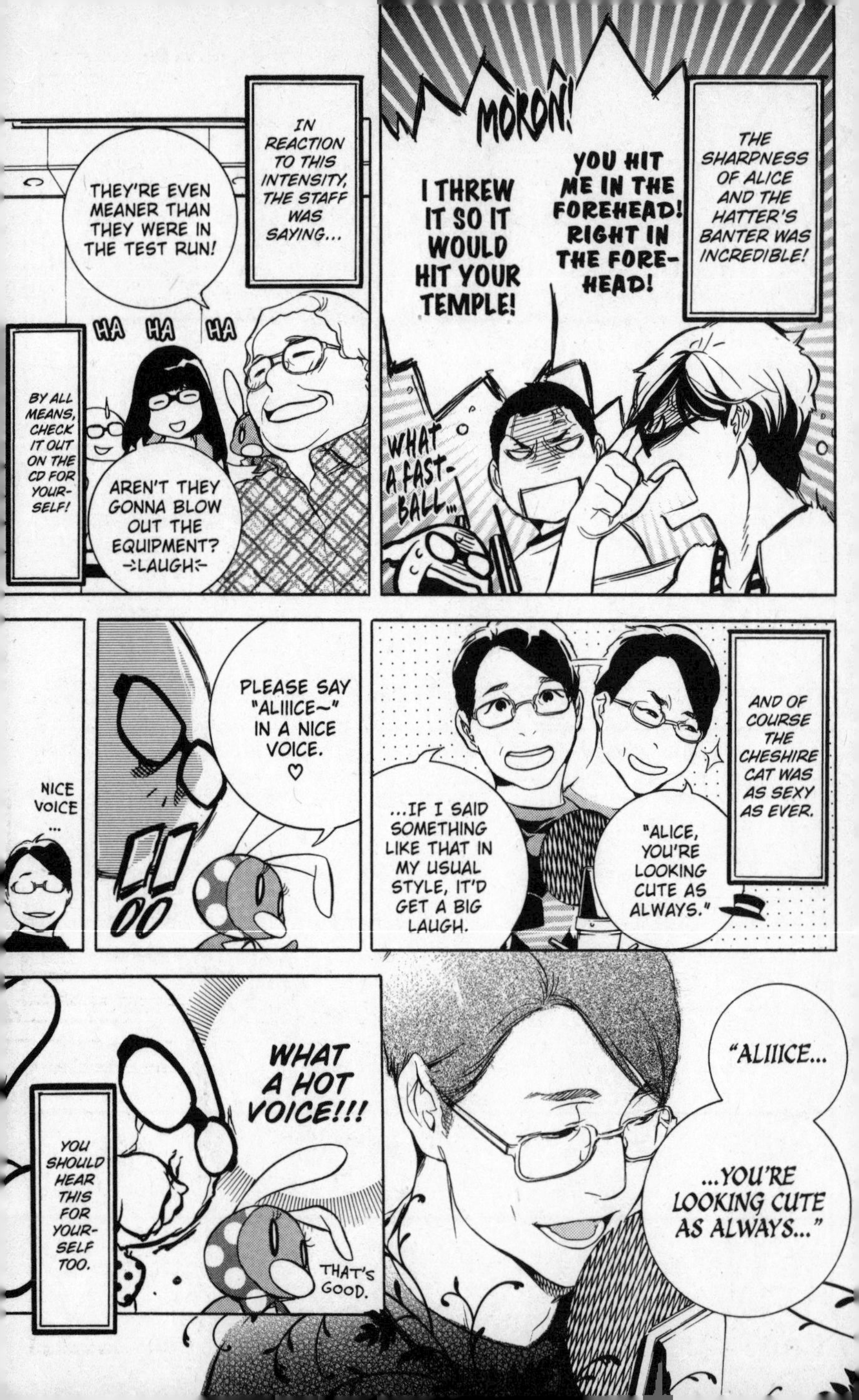
THE SHARPNESS OF ALICE AND THE HATTER'S BANTER WAS INCREDIBLE!
MORON!
YOU HIT ME IN THE FOREHEAD! RIGHT IN THE FOREHEAD!
I THREW IT SO IT WOULD HIT YOUR TEMPLE!
WHAT A FAST-BALL...
IN REACTION TO THIS INTENSITY, THE STAFF WAS SAYING...
THEY'RE EVEN MEANER THAN THEY WERE IN THE TEST RUN!
HA HA HA
AREN'T THEY GONNA BLOW OUT THE EQUIPMENT? -LAUGH-
BY ALL MEANS, CHECK IT OUT ON THE CD FOR YOURSELF!
AND OF COURSE THE CHESHIRE CAT WAS AS SEXY AS EVER.
"ALICE, YOU'RE LOOKING CUTE AS ALWAYS."
...IF I SAID SOMETHING LIKE THAT IN MY USUAL STYLE, IT'D GET A BIG LAUGH.
PLEASE SAY "ALIIICE~" IN A NICE VOICE. ♡
NICE VOICE ...
"ALIIICE...
...YOU'RE LOOKING CUTE AS ALWAYS..."
WHAT A HOT VOICE!!!
THAT'S GOOD.
YOU SHOULD HEAR THIS FOR YOURSELF TOO.

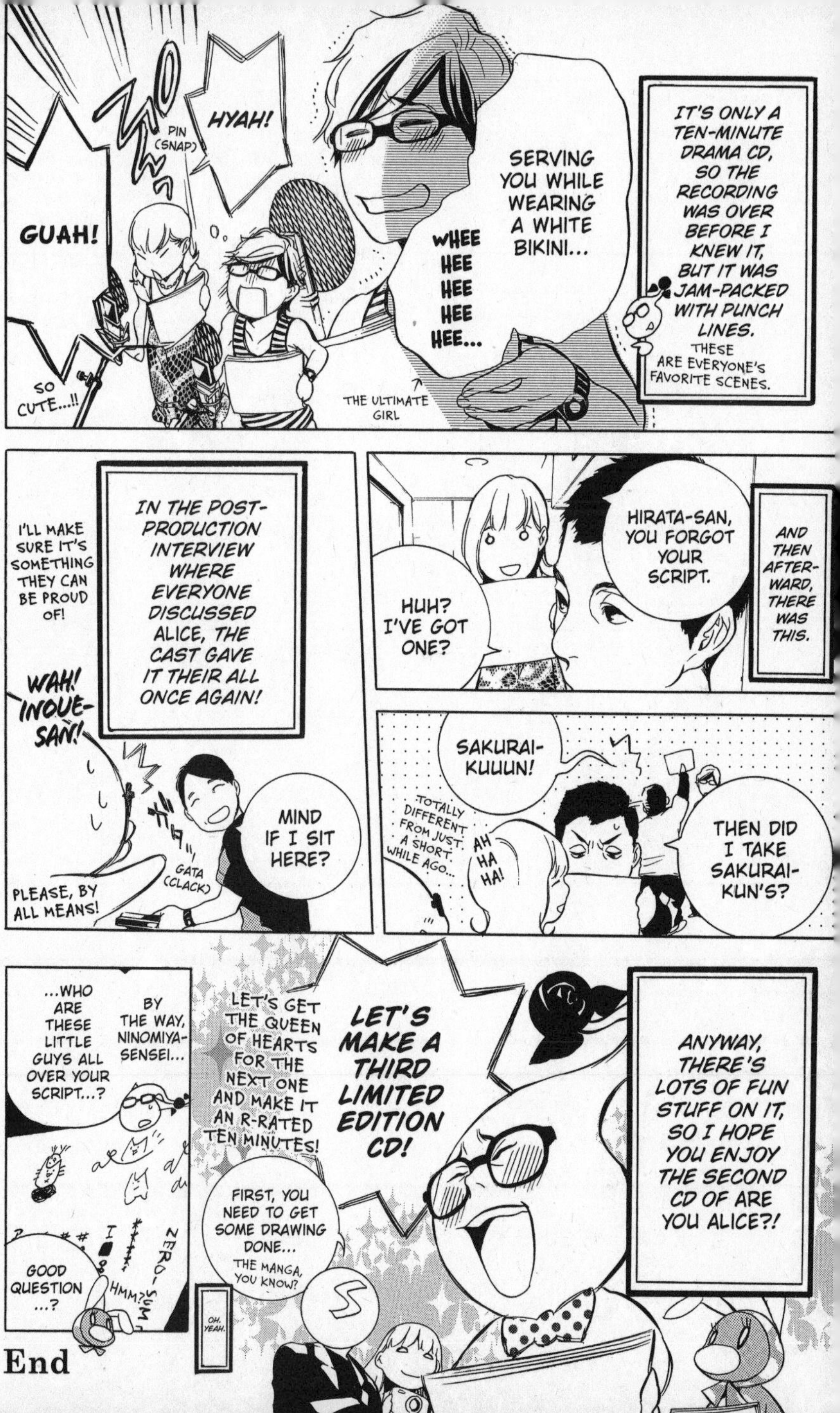
IT'S ONLY A TEN-MINUTE DRAMA CD, SO THE RECORDING WAS OVER BEFORE I KNEW IT, BUT IT WAS JAM-PACKED WITH PUNCH LINES.
THESE ARE EVERYONE'S FAVORITE SCENES.
SERVING YOU WHILE WEARING A WHITE BIKINI...
WHEE HEE HEE HEE HEE...
THE ULTIMATE GIRL
HYAH!
PIN (SNAP)
GUAH!
SO CUTE...!!
AND THEN AFTERWARD, THERE WAS THIS.
HIRATA-SAN, YOU FORGOT YOUR SCRIPT.
HUH? I'VE GOT ONE?
THEN DID I TAKE SAKURAI-KUN'S?
SAKURAI-KUUUN!
AH HA HA!
TOTALLY DIFFERENT FROM JUST A SHORT WHILE AGO...
IN THE POST-PRODUCTION INTERVIEW WHERE EVERYONE DISCUSSED ALICE, THE CAST GAVE IT THEIR ALL ONCE AGAIN!
I'LL MAKE SURE IT'S SOMETHING THEY CAN BE PROUD OF!
WAH! INOUE-SAN!
MIND IF I SIT HERE?
GATA (CLACK)
PLEASE, BY ALL MEANS!
ANYWAY, THERE'S LOTS OF FUN STUFF ON IT, SO I HOPE YOU ENJOY THE SECOND CD OF ARE YOU ALICE?!
LET'S MAKE A THIRD LIMITED EDITION CD!
LET'S GET THE QUEEN OF HEARTS FOR THE NEXT ONE AND MAKE IT AN R-RATED TEN MINUTES!
FIRST, YOU NEED TO GET SOME DRAWING DONE...
THE MANGA, YOU KNOW?
OH. YEAH.
BY THE WAY, NINOMIYA-SENSEI...
...WHO ARE THESE LITTLE GUYS ALL OVER YOUR SCRIPT...?
GOOD QUESTION ...?
HMM?
End

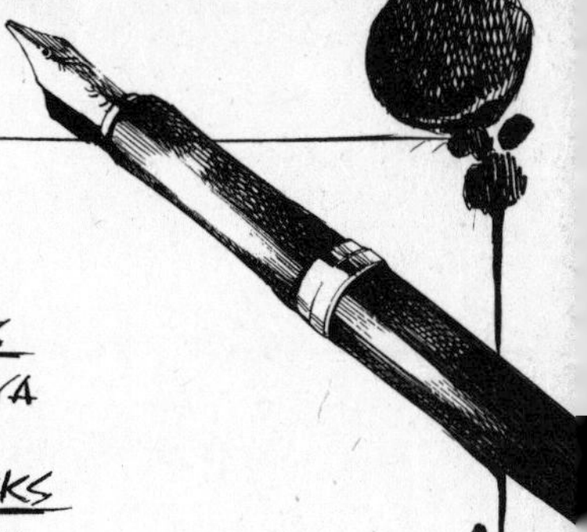

STAFF

ORIGINAL WORKS

AI NINOMIYA

ASSISTANT WORKS

MIZUKI SAKAMAKI
REIN OFUJI
DATENSI
IGACHAN

EDITOR

YOSUKE SUGINO

WHO WOULD YOU APPOINT TO ASSIST YOU IF YOU WERE THE QUEEN OF HEARTS? AND WHY!?

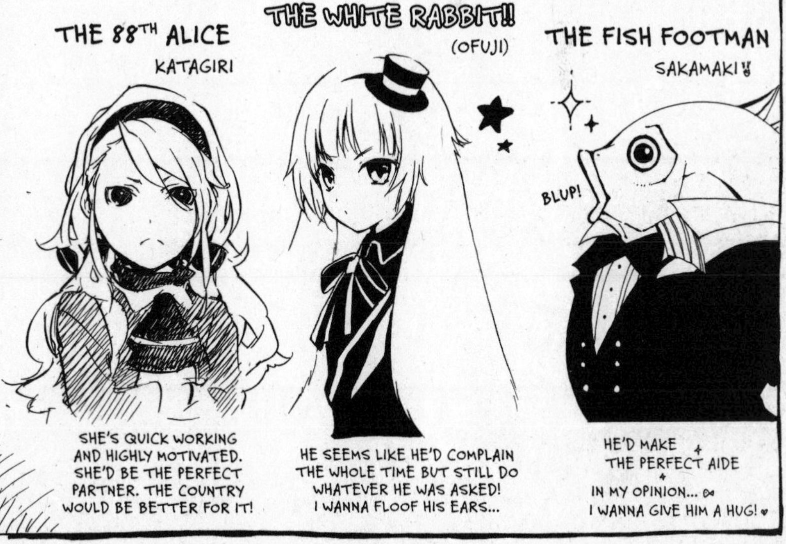
THE FISH FOOTMAN
SAKAMAKI
BLUP!
HE'D MAKE THE PERFECT AIDE IN MY OPINION...
I WANNA GIVE HIM A HUG!
THE WHITE RABBIT!!
(OFUJI)
HE SEEMS LIKE HE'D COMPLAIN THE WHOLE TIME BUT STILL DO WHATEVER HE WAS ASKED!
I WANNA FLOOF HIS EARS...
THE 88TH ALICE
KATAGIRI
SHE'S QUICK WORKING AND HIGHLY MOTIVATED. SHE'D BE THE PERFECT PARTNER. THE COUNTRY WOULD BE BETTER FOR IT!

A new storyline and new characters were introduced right at the height of Volume 3. But Wonderland is bound by a lot of constraints, so I can't just make up names as I please. The Queen of Hearts would chop off my head!

I gave the names Rodge, Bibi, and Coco to the children by looking at three characters that had some connection to the Duchess in *Alice in Wonderland* and playing off of them.

The Frog Footman → Frog → Rog → Rodge
The Baby → Baby → BB → Bibi
The Cook → Cook → CK → Coco

......Okay, I might've been forcing it a little (≧laugh≦) there, but hopefully you all enjoy these sorts of tiny details.

Well, see you in Volume 4!

Ai Ninomiya

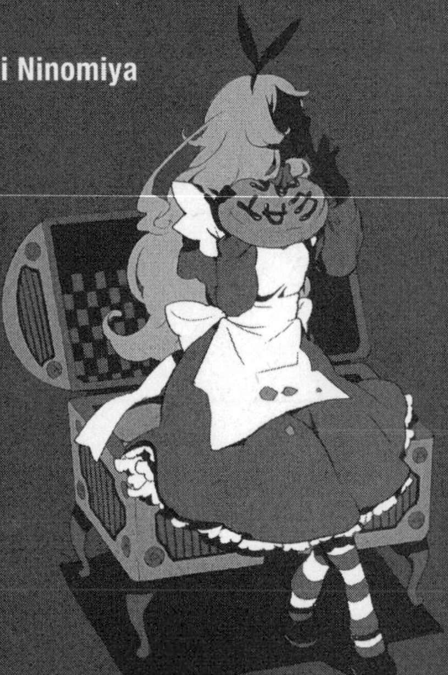

Translation Notes

Page 162
Centipede
The Japanese word for centipede also literally means "hundred feet."

Page 166
To go with *imomushi*, the Japanese word for "caterpillar," the names of the books all include the Japanese word for "bug" (*mushi*) in them. "Wimpy" is *yowamushi* (literally "weak bug").

Page 169
"Crybaby" is *nakimushi* (literally "cry bug").
"Money-pit" is *kanekuimushi* (literally "money-eating bug").
"Parasite" is *kiseichuu* (*chuu* is written with the same kanji as *mushi*).
"Meddler" is *ojamamushi* (literally "intruder bug").
"Kettle-steamed" is *dobinmushi* (any dish prepared by steaming in an earthenware teapot.)

Page 185
Propitious sign
A stalk floating upright in your tea is believed to be an auspicious sign in Japan.